TORNEL
AND
SANTA ANNA

Illustration of Tornel courtesy of the O'Gorman Collection and the Benson Latin American Collection. Used by permission of the University of Texas at Austin.

TORNEL
AND
SANTA ANNA

The Writer and the Caudillo, Mexico 1795–1853

Will Fowler

Contributions in Latin American Studies,
Number 14

GREENWOOD PRESS
Westport, Connecticut • London

Library of Congress Cataloging-in-Publication Data

Fowler, Will, 1966–
    Tornel and Santa Anna : the writer and the caudillo, Mexico
1795–1853 / by Will Fowler.
        p.   cm.—(Contributions in Latin American studies, ISSN
1054–6790 ; no. 14)
    Includes bibliographical references (p.   –   ) and index.
    ISBN 0–313–30914–0 (alk. paper)
    1. Tornel y Mendívil, José María, 1789–1853. 2. Santa Anna,
Antonio López de, 1794?–1876. 3. Mexico—Politics and
government—1821–1861. 4. Politicians—Mexico—Biography.
I. Title. II. Series.
F1232.T696F69 2000
972'.04'0922—dc21   99–43268
    [B]

British Library Cataloguing in Publication Data is available.

Library of Congress Catalog Card Number: 99–43268
ISBN: 0–313–30914–0
ISSN: 1054–6790

First published in 2000

Greenwood Press, 88 Post Road West, Westport, CT 06881
An imprint of Greenwood Publishing Group, Inc.
www.greenwood.com

Printed in the United States of America

∞

The paper used in this book complies with the
Permanent Paper Standard issued by the National
Information Standards Organization (Z39.48–1984).

10 9 8 7 6 5 4 3 2 1

Copyright Acknowledgments

Excerpted archival quotes courtesy of the Benson Latin American Collection, University of
Texas at Austin. Used by permission of the University of Texas at Austin.

For Anne Staples

Contents

Preface

José María Tornel y Mendívil (1795–1853) was one of Mexico's leading politicians and writers during the three decades that followed independence. Born in Orizaba, Veracruz, into a shopkeeper's family, he abandoned his studies in the capital to join the insurgent forces in 1813. Once the war was over, he moved permanently to Mexico City, where his involvement in the political life of the new republic was profoundly influential. To list the posts he held throughout his life, he was: Antonio López de Santa Anna's personal secretary (1821), Guadalupe Victoria's personal secretary (1824–1828), deputy for the federal district (1826–1828), governor of the Federal District (1826–1828, 1829, 1834, and 1847), deputy for Veracruz (1829), minister plenipotentiary in the United States (1830–1831), minister of war (1833, 1835–1837, 1838–1839, 1841–1844, 1846, and 1853), member of the Supreme Conservative Power (1839–1840), mayor of Mexico City (1841), and senator (1850–1852). In addition to his political posts, he was editor of the newspaper *El Amigo del Pueblo*, founder of the Instituto de Ciencias, Literatura y Artes, vice president and president of the Compañía Lancasteriana, and director of the Colegio Nacional de Minería. He was a compulsive writer whose articles and essays featured prominently in the press and was author of two historical volumes: *Tejas y los Estados Unidos de América en sus relaciones con la república mexicana* (1837) and *Breve reseña histórica de los acontecimientos más notables de la nación mexicana desde el año de 1821 hasta nuestros días* (1853), a play *La muerte de Cicerón* (1840), and three pieces of oratory written for the anniversaries of independence of 1827, 1840, and 1850.

Translator of French and English texts into Spanish (he was among the first translators into Spanish of Lord Byron), his cultural activities were matched by an equal dedication to the promotion of free education, and in a similar philanthropic capacity, he claimed that he was principally responsible for the abolition of slavery in 1829.

Associated with Santa Anna for most of his life, with the exception of their years of estrangement (1844–1847), Tornel was severely condemned and criticized by some of his contemporaries, such as José María Luis Mora and Lorenzo de Zavala, who accused him of being a turncoat and of having no political integrity. In spite of the fact that he was such an influential and controversial figure, he has, surprisingly, until very recently, attracted scant attention from biographers. This is in fact only the second published study concerning his contribution to independent Mexico (the first being María del Carmen Vázquez Mantecón's *La palabra del poder. Vida pública de José Maria Tornel, 1795–1853* [Mexico City: UNAM, 1997]), and the first that is published in English.

A study of the life of Tornel, Santa Anna's most dedicated adviser and intellectual friend, offers two new and particularly important insights into a period of Mexican history that continues to be among the least studied to date. Our understanding of the three decades that Josefina Zoraida Vázquez described as "the forgotten years" and that I called the "age of proposals" in my recent study on the factions and ideologies that emerged after independence (*Mexico in the Age of Proposals, 1821–1853* [Westport, CT: Greenwood Press, 1998]), is indeed made somewhat clearer through an analysis of Tornel's actions and writings. At one level this study illustrates the extent to which the Mexican political class developed during the early national period. In particular it highlights the evolution of the *santanistas*, as represented by Tornel, from their advocation of a radical liberal agenda in the 1820s to their defense of a diametrically opposed reactionary one in the 1850s. Paying particular attention to the changing circumstances to which Tornel found himself responding, as the hopes of the 1820s degenerated into the despair of the 1850s, this study proposes that the shifts in opinion that characterized the *santanistas'* political behavior (as well as that of the moderates, the radicals, and the traditionalists) were not simply due to their opportunism. The simplistic nature of such an interpretation is challenged as it becomes clear that Tornel and, to a certain extent, Santa Anna developed different agendas as time went by, following a particular logic in which their ideological thought changed and evolved as the many political proposals that surfaced one after another following independence each failed to establish a long-lasting constitutional framework in which modernity could be married to tradition, and where progress could be introduced without sacrificing the *hombres de bien*'s need for order and stability. It is also by concentrating on Tornel's relationship with Santa Anna, the way that he served the *caudillo* as his main informer in the capital, his leading propagandist, his master conspirator-intriguer, and the ideologue of the *santanistas*, that a fuller and more complex understanding of Santa Anna's own motivations and ideas can be attained. This study aims to offer, beyond an interpretation of Tornel's life, two new visions of the age of proposals: a vision in which the complexity of the politics of independent Mexico, and in particular that of the *santanistas*, is given its deserved attention bearing in mind the chronology and the impact this had on political thought, and a vision of Santa Anna's own political changes that goes beyond the simplistic and generally accepted view that he was a cynical opportunist.

This is a study that has been part of my life for ten years now. It started as a Ph.D. dissertation that began in 1989 and was completed in 1994. Coinciding with my move to the University of St. Andrews, my research had taken me away from Tornel and on to a more generalized study of the different ideologies that surfaced in Mexico between 1821 and 1853. It has only been over the past two years that, having completed my study on the views of Tornel's contemporaries on the main political issues of the period (*Mexico in the Age of Proposals*), I went back to relive his political and philosophical anxieties in what has represented a major rewrite and revision of the original study. I believe that my understanding of Tornel and Santa Anna has benefited greatly from having researched the ideologies and actions of their contemporaries in greater depth prior to writing this new version. This book would have had a number of important omissions had Vázquez Mantecón's study not been published before I got around to revising my thesis. I have been able to incorporate into *Tornel and Santa Anna* both the more comprehensive understanding of the period I acquired while researching *Mexico in the Age of Proposals* and the information that Vázquez Mantecón was able to provide for those years where my own research had proved limited.

Having researched the behavior of Mexico's political class in *Mexico in the Age of Proposals* and Tornel's own contribution to the period in this book, I am now left with the major task of trying to understand Santa Anna's own enigmatic position more fully, paying particular attention to his activities in Veracruz. It is for this reason that I find myself embarking on a research project that I hope will result in a new biography of Santa Anna.

Unless stated otherwise, translations of foreign-language passages are my own.

Acknowledgments

This study could not have been written without the support I have received over the years from a number of individuals and institutions. The British Academy and the University of Bristol provided financial support that enabled me to complete my Ph.D. dissertation on Tornel from 1989 to 1994. The University of St. Andrews and the Carnegie Trust for the Universities of Scotland provided further financial support that enabled me to return to Mexico and the United States in the summer of 1996. Moreover, the School of Modern Languages of the University of St. Andrews has consistently supported my research, allowing me to return to Mexico in 1997 and 1998. I am deeply indebted to the Spanish Department at the university. My colleagues Bernard Bentley, Nigel Dennis, Carmen García del Río, Louise Haywood, Virginia Lombraña de los Ríos, Alan Paterson, and Gustavo San Román supported and encouraged my research. I thank my SP3138 students Claudine Carpenter, Susanna Douglas, Lisa Griffith-Richards, William Fraser, Alicia Isasi Freire, Alison Heywood, Jamie MacFadyen, Mark McGivern, and Catriona Mills, who chose to take my course "Mexico in the Nineteenth Century" in the autumn of 1998 and whose enjoyment of the course was particularly encouraging. Similarly, I am grateful to my Ph.D. student, Cath Andrews, whose research into Anastasio Bustamante allowed me to talk about Independent Mexico (and Tornel) every Tuesday during the year in which I finally got around to writing this book.

Over the years a wide range of Mexicanists and historians have contributed through long formal and informal discussions in assisting me to form the interpretation of Tornel and Santa Anna presented in this study. To mention them all would take a long time, and I do not want to repeat here the detailed acknowledgments I included in *Mexico in the Age of Proposals*. The same people who are mentioned there were equally influential in molding the views espoused in this book. I am extremely grateful to the staff at the British Library, the Nettie Lee Benson Latin American Collection at the University of Texas at Austin, the Biblioteca Nacional de México, in particular at the Fondo Reservado, the Archivo General de la Nación, and the Archivo Histórico Militar.

Six individuals deserve a more concrete mention here. I thank Michael P. Costeloe, Josefina Zoraida Vázquez, and Anne Staples, all of whom supervised my Ph.D. dissertation at different points in time, whether it was in Bristol or Mexico City, and who have gone on to read and comment on my work even when there was no longer any institutional pressure for them to do so. I am equally grateful to Fernando Cervantes and John Fisher who examined me in 1994 and whose comments were particularly useful when it came to rewriting the dissertation for publication. Finally, I am particularly indebted to María del Carmen Vázquez Mantecón who has generously given up her time during my recent visits to Mexico, to discuss, in extraordinary depth, our parallel interpretations of Tornel.

I could not have completed this study without the encouragement, support, and affection of my family and friends. I thank, once more, Carlos Tenorio and his wonderful family for the many times they welcomed me to their home in Mexico City, and Wally and Marilyn Redmond, who also treated me as one of their own on the occasions I have gone to Austin, Texas. I thank my parents, W. S. Fowler and Rosa María Laffitte Figueras, and my in-laws, Peter and Susan Wilkes, for their continued support. Finally, my thanks go to my family—Caroline, Tom, Eddie, and Florence—who have shared, or at least tolerated, my "Tornel years."

It is only appropriate to dedicate this book to Anne Staples. When I first met her in the fall of 1990, she told me that I was gullible in the extreme and that Tornel was nothing but "a rat." Ever since, she has gone on reminding me that I should not believe everything the politicians say, even when, in the case of Tornel, he did so in such eloquent and persuasive terms. She has generously continued to supervise my work as the years have gone by, and time and again, I have had to readjust my interpretations according to her incisive comments. Her generosity knows no limits. She has gone out of her way to discuss my evolving understanding of Independent Mexico, while inviting me into the warmth of her home. In the same way that I owe much of my interpretation of the period to her numerous publications on Independent Mexico, I am equally indebted to the advice she has given me over the years. If the Tornel in this study is not as idealized as the Tornel of my Ph.D. dissertation, this is greatly due to her influence on me. I hope that this book reflects the time she has spent on guiding my research and that it is worthy of her work and vision, even if I never quite go as far as arguing that Tornel was a rodent.

1

The Formative Years (1795–1824)

FAMILY BACKGROUND AND CHILDHOOD

José María Tornel y Mendívil was born on 1 March 1795 in the town of Orizaba, in what was the *intendencia* of Veracruz,[1] in the mountainous foothills of the highest peak in Mexico, the volcano Citlaltépetl, also known as the peak of Orizaba.[2] The imposing scenery of his childhood was to remain in his memory throughout his life: "Oh Citlaltépetl! Proud mountain of my mother-country!"[3] By all accounts he was born into a relatively comfortable middle-class family. Although his father, Julián Tornel,[4] was a shopkeeper,[5] he was wealthy enough to donate over 2,000 pesos to the insurgents during the war of independence.[6] Moreover, according to the *Diario del Gobierno*, in what was perhaps a somewhat exaggerated statement, since the newspaper was defending Tornel from the accusations that had appeared in *El Cosmopolita*, in the fall of 1836, which claimed he was using the funds for the Texan war to purchase a suitably comfortable house: "Tornel is not a wealthy man today; however, he was born surrounded by opulence; and it is possible that what remains of his father's fortune is what has paid for his family's modest home."[7] At a time when higher education was largely a privilege of the aristocracy and prosperous Creole families, Tornel's extensive knowledge of the classics, his own literary use of rhetoric, and the ease with which he translated English and French texts into Spanish suggest that he must have come from a family that could at least afford the luxury of culture.[8] As Brian Hamnett rightly pointed out, shopkeepers in late colonial Mexico belonged to a profession that spanned several social classes, and although there were clearly those who were relatively poor, catering for the needs of the lower sector of the market, in the villages and the more rundown parts of the bigger towns and cities of New Spain, there were also those who belonged to a fairly prosperous middle class with close links to the main merchants of their region.[9] In other words, bearing in mind his generous donation to the insurgent forces and the confident and cultured prose his son would develop, Julián Tornel must have been an upmarket provincial shopkeeper, not a poor one.

Like so many of the other politicians of his generation who went on to hold important posts in government following independence, Tornel belonged to an archetypal Creole family. His father was a Spaniard from Murcia, and his mother, Manuela Jacinta Bernarda Mendívil Vidal, was a Creole, of Spanish parentage, from Cosamaloapan, Veracruz. He had an older brother, José Manuel, and a younger brother, José Julián, who in later years would also become important and influential in the political and economic context of the time; and he had a sister, Dolores Tornel, whose birth in 1805 cost his mother, Manuela Mendívil, her life.[10]

Although there is hardly any information available regarding his childhood, it is not difficult to reconstruct the provincial environment in which he spent his first fifteen years. Orizaba was a relatively small, prosperous town that had benefited, at least until the arrival of Viceroy José Iturrigaray in 1803, from the support of the businessmen of the capital, who believed that the all-important road (*camino carretero*) that would link the port of Veracruz to Mexico City should pass through Orizaba rather than Xalapa.[11] Its population was estimated at 8,485 inhabitants in 1762 and had probably grown to around 10,000 when José María Tornel was born.[12] It was located in one of the most fertile regions of New Spain. In fact, the land was so fertile and its produce so rich and plentiful that according to the traveler Alexander Von Humboldt, a laborer from the area did not have to work for more than two days a week to feed a whole family.[13] Just over a hundred years after Humboldt visited the foothills of the great Citaltépetl, another foreigner would note that "even a short stay in the delightful district of Orizaba cannot fail to impress the visitor with the great abundance and variety of Mexican fruit, nearly all of which he can see here growing wild or under cultivation."[14]

Surrounded by a profusion of orchids, gardenias, ferns, tree ferns, and tall palms, Orizaba lies on a slope between two rivers, in a richly watered and fertile valley.[15] The impact that nature had on the young Tornel would certainly stay with him throughout his life and feature in one of his most lyrical articles of the 1840s, "La Providencia en el Nuevo Mundo," in which he equated the existence of God with the breathtaking power and beauty of nature.[16] The valleys surrounding Orizaba were also among the most cultivated of New Spain. Vanilla, coffee, and bananas were grown and exported to the rest of the colony and Europe. In fact, according to Humboldt, "all the vanilla Mexico supplies to Europe comes from the two *intendencias* of Veracruz and Oaxaca."[17] As for the bananas of Orizaba, Humboldt could not help himself from praising their "extraordinary dimensions."[18] Moreover, the 1791 revolution in Santo Domingo (Haiti) and the subsequent collapse of the sugar market of the island had also resulted in the emergence of new and thriving sugar plantations (*haciendas de caña*) in Orizaba and neighboring Córdoba.[19]

Notwithstanding this, the most important product of Orizaba at the turn of the century was tobacco. Benefiting from José de Gálvez's 1764 imposition of a protectionist royal monopoly of tobacco (*estanco de tabaco*), which restricted the growth and processing of tobacco to Orizaba, Córdoba, and the *partidos* of Huatusco and Songolica (all in the *intendencia* of Veracruz), it would not be an exaggeration to say that everyday life in Tornel's home town was largely dominated by the tobacco industry. According to Humboldt's estimates the tobacco from Orizaba and Córdoba alone generated a yearly income of 38 million francs.[20] It comes as no surprise that in years to come, and once Tornel was actively involved in the political life of the republic, he represented and defended the interests of the tobacco growers of Orizaba on numerous occasions.[21]

Tornel's childhood must have been a relatively comfortable one, involving trips to his father's store and possible forays into the luxuriant countryside of Orizaba. No doubt the death of his mother when he was only ten years old must have been a fairly traumatic experience, and one can only assume that the economic and political tensions and problems that started to undermine the prosperity of New Spain in the early 1800s must have affected the financial well-being of the Tornel household, for otherwise it would be difficult to account for the way in which both he and his father were quick to support the insurgents in the area once the war of independence broke out.

THE MAKING OF AN INSURGENT

The young Tornel was no longer in Orizaba when Father Hidalgo's *grito de Dolores* unleashed the revolutionary whirlwind of the first years of the war of independence on 16 September 1810. In 1809, Tornel moved on from Orizaba, where he had been educated by a priest who was more concerned with condemning the philosophers of the enlightenment than teaching his pupils to read and write,[22] to study theology in the capital at the Colegio de San Ildefonso.[23] This was probably the most prestigious college of secondary and further education in New Spain at the time. Run by the church, its courses were divided into two levels, preparatory and professional. The preparatory courses lasted between three and five years, depending on the age of the pupils and their abilities at their time of enrolment in the Colegio; subjects such as Latin, elementary philosophy, logic, maths, physics, history, political economy, French language, and geography made up the main diet of their syllabus. Thereafter, and as long as the assessment requirements of the preparatory courses had been duly satisfied, the student had a choice of four fields in which he could then specialize, under the umbrella of professional studies: law, theology, medicine, or science.[24] Not only did Tornel and his brother José Julián study there, but also a constellation of alumni who would later go on to feature prominently in the political life of Independent Mexico—such notable politicians as José María Luis Mora (who went on to become the dean of San Ildefonso in the 1820s),[25] José María Bocanegra, Francisco Fagoaga, Melchor Múzquiz, Bernardo Couto, and Luis Gonzaga Cuevas.[26] In retrospect, Tornel's student days at San Ildefonso were not only important for educational reasons; they also introduced him to a significant proportion of those upper-class and upper-middle-class Creoles who would later work either with or against him in the corridors of power of early republican Mexico. According to one source, the intense mutual dislike Tornel and Mora felt for each other stemmed from their schoolboy rivalries at San Ildefonso.[27] In this sense, Tornel's education would become fairly representative of the average middle-class Creoles who would become *hombres de bien* in the 1830s. As Michael Costeloe notes in his sketch of the characteristics of a typical *hombre de bien*: "Born towards the end of the eighteenth century into a reasonably affluent family[,] he would have been educated at home in his early years and then have entered one of the colleges run by the Church, perhaps the highly respected Colegio de San Ildefonso, where . . . he would have acquired a thorough grounding in theology, civil and canon law, jurisprudence and possibly the French language."[28]

Tornel turned out to be a very applied student. Between 1809 and 1811 he obtained the highest grades in theology, ethics, logic, and general studies. Moreover, in 1811, he and Mora shared the prize for the best student *in recto* of his year.[29] Nevertheless, soon after the *grito de Dolores* was proclaimed on 16 September 1810, Tornel showed signs of wanting to abandon his studies to join the cause of the insurgents. Although there is no evidence of his having corresponded with the early insurgents, one later source would claim that he offered his services to the revolution soon after it erupted and that he was initially told to wait a while longer, since he was only fifteen years old, and that it would be a pity for him to abandon his studies, especially when he was doing so well. Whoever the insurgent he was in touch with was (probably a member of the underground organization of Creoles known as the Guadalupes, who served the revolution from Mexico City acting as "an intelligence network and a channel of arms, information and propaganda"),[30] the correspondent alleged that the revolutionaries believed that once he was a little older, "the mother-country could expect to profit more from his important services."[31]

Nevertheless, toward the end of 1812 Tornel's general outspokenness in his defense of independence while still a student in San Ildefonso became a matter of concern to his father. Don Julián was obviously worried about the possible consequences his son might suffer for speaking against the colonial regime. He ordered his son back home in order to get him out of trouble: "Tornel had to abandon his studies in the arts, summoned by his father to remove him from the risks he was taking in the school, declaring his undying love to the sacred cause of the mother-country."[32] Thus, in November 1812, Tornel escaped from San Ildefonso. According to the Marqués de Castañiza, dean of the Colegio de San Ildefonso, Tornel escaped "without [leaving] news of where he had gone."[33] It can be presumed that, obeying his father's orders, he fled back to Orizaba, which had been temporarily liberated by José María Morelos' insurgent army in the summer of 1812.

Inevitably a question that needs to be tackled is why Tornel was so keen to fight for the independence of Mexico. After all, with the notable exceptions of Nicolás Bravo, Guadalupe Victoria, and Carlos María de Bustamante and those twenty-odd Mexico City Creoles who formed the organization of the Guadalupes, the majority of the well-to-do Creole middle classes, however frustrated they may have been by the lack of opportunities with which the colonial status of New Spain provided them, did not support the first revolutionary outburst of the Bajío.[34] To quote John Lynch, "The majority of Mexico's one million Creoles opposed Hidalgo; his agrarian radicalism turned even anti-Spanish Creoles into supporters of the colonial government."[35] On one level, as proto-liberals or members of the educated classes, they mistrusted Hidalgo's messianic and even theocratic leadership of the insurgent forces, and on another, they feared the popular wrath of the impoverished and ignorant masses who went on to pillage and destroy the shops and properties of the accommodated classes, whether they belonged to *gachupines* (Spaniards) or Creoles, as they made their way from Dolores to Guadalajara in the fall of 1810. Moreover, with the advent of the 1812 Cadiz Constitution, a high proportion of Creole liberals, such as Lorenzo de Zavala and Miguel Ramos Arizpe, came to the conclusion that it was preferable to be governed by a liberal constitution, even though it was Spanish, than to support an independence movement that appeared to advocate reactionary tendencies, both in the way that it was led by a discontented sector of the clergy, disgruntled by the assault the church had suffered as a result of the enlightened Bourbon reforms of the latter half of the eighteenth century,[36] and in the way that Hidalgo went on to award himself the autocratic titles of *generalísimo* and *su alteza serenísima* (his serene highness) once he took over Guadalajara.[37]

Furthermore, Tornel's father was a Spanish shopkeeper. In other words, his father was not only a *gachupín* from Murcia, he belonged to the one profession that had brought about some of the worst popular grievances in the years building up to the revolution. The combined effects of an extraordinary increase in the population of New Spain in the latter half of the eighteenth century (between 1742 and 1793, demographic growth reached about 33 percent, and between 1790 and 1810 the population rose from 4.5 million to 6 million),[38] paired with a subsequent rise in unemployment and the disastrous drought of 1808–1810, had resulted in a situation where the lower sectors of society—in other words, the majority—had become the shopkeepers' dependent debtors. Suddenly there was not enough maize to go around, and money was difficult to come by.[39] It was the shopkeepers who, in response to the crisis and being the ones who provided their vicinities with what food was available, replaced the increasingly scarce copper coins with their own currency of blocks of wood or soap called *tlacos*, whose value they came to ascribe arbitrarily, depending on their own financial needs. According to Hamnett, "the behavior of the shopkeepers inspired hostility amongst the population and was a major source of social tension."[40] It is not surprising, as a result, that most of the violence that characterized Hidalgo's revolutionary movement in 1810 was directed at the shopkeepers and their shops. Therefore, it would have been fairly understandable for someone like Tornel to have mistrusted the early insurgent movement as the liberal he was to become and even to have defended the colony to safeguard his father's property and business.

In order to explain his insurgent impulses, it is important to bear in mind both the intellectual atmosphere he was immersed in at San Ildefonso and the situation in Orizaba at the time. As is evident in his later writings, in particular the pamphlets and speeches he wrote in the 1820s, Tornel, like Carlos María de Bustamante, became one of Mexico's most eloquent exponents of Creole patriotism.[41] Regarding Orizaba, and in fact, the *intendencia* of Veracruz in general, the local and regional grievances were markedly different from those that characterized the far more violent contexts of the north and southwest of the colony—the current states of Guanajuato, Jalisco, Michoacán, Morelos, Guerrero, Oaxaca, and Puebla. In fact, the violent outbursts that erupted between 1810 and 1821 in the present-day state of Veracruz were comparatively minor in comparison with those experienced elsewhere.

Whether the young Tornel had already been deeply influenced by the priest of Orizaba who had been responsible for his primary education is a matter of speculation. The fact that Tornel remembers that the priest in question spent his time criticizing the Enlightenment would certainly suggest that, like most of those members of the lower clergy who actively supported the 1810 insurrection, he was among those who had been in a position to witness the increasing suffering of his parishioners. After all, one of the reasons that it was the members of the lower clergy who led the revolution at the beginning was that they were the ones who, being "closest to the people, came to realize the desperate state of the *campesinos* and to appreciate the gross inequality of the agrarian structure."[42] Whether this generalized suffering had arisen as a result of a conflagration of issues, "population growth, migration, land shortages, growing social differences within communities, increasing labor demands from commercial agriculture, . . . and manufacturing, higher taxes,"[43] for many members of the lower clergy, the main culprit of Mexico's economic and moral decadence was the Spanish crown. The blame for all of the troubles of the early 1800s was placed on Bourbon absolutism and the enlightened views it had employed to limit the power of the clergy in society, while proceeding with "a generation-long assault against the inherited privileges and property of the church in America."[44] Inevitably Tornel must have been influenced in part by the teachings of his *cura*, especially since the reason he went to San Ildefonso was in order to become a priest himself.

Nevertheless, regardless of whether the priest from Orizaba had filled Tornel's head with anti-Bourbonist and proclerical ideals, what is clear is that he felt from very early on that sense of Creole pride, frustration, and resentment that would characterize the demands of the Creole officers who became involved in the 1809–1810 conspiracy of Querétaro that led to the *grito de Dolores*. In other words, he shared the beliefs of middle-class Creole revolutionaries like Ignacio Allende (whose father was also Spanish, wealthy, and a merchant), Juan de Aldama, and Miguel Domínguez, all of whom "were moved by hatred of *peninsulares*: . . . [and] wanted to depose the authorities, expel the Spaniards and establish a Creole ruling junta."[45] Like Carlos María de Bustamante, who believed that the three centuries of Spanish domination that had preceded the independence movement of 1810 had been nothing more than a parenthesis in Mexican history,[46] and that the Creoles who demanded independence were the descendants of the pre-Hispanic Anáhuac,[47] Tornel espoused the view that Christopher Columbus's discovery of the Americas had been more harmful than beneficial for the Continent: "Allow me, oh great God, that I may beg from you your celestial wrath: allow me to request you to cast your furious eyes on the man [Columbus] who destroyed the peace of my forebears, the evil astronomer who opened the gates [of our continent] to the usurpers, the Spanish tyrants."[48]

In the same way that in Spain the myth of the reconquest was developed in order to argue that after seven hundred years of Islamic rule, there had been such a thing as an oppressed Spanish nation that had fought for its independence, Bustamante and Tornel were to become among the first exponents of the great Mexican myth that the colony had interrupted Mexico's historical development with three hundred years of oppression and that the achievement of independence represented quite simply a reprise of that national historical narrative from where it had been interrupted the day the last Aztec emperor, Cuauhtemoc, was hanged.[49] In other words, the insurgents of the 1810s were picking up the historical narrative where they had left it in 1521, as if three hundred years had come and gone without leaving any significant trace of their existence, at least in terms of the Mexicans' identity, and they were intent on avenging the destruction the Spaniards had been responsible for during their occupation. To quote Tornel: "After three centuries of apathy . . . the sword of one Mexican [Hidalgo] severs the years that have separated us from our old selves, and a serene future is announced to all men. They recover their primitive dignity. Philosophy finds a refuge. Human kind wipes its tears."[50]

For Tornel there was nothing worth praising about the colony. Beyond the hyperbole—"three centuries of ignorance and barbarity,"[51] "the prolonged night of three centuries,"[52] and "three hundred years since our scream of despair has echoed throughout the region [*en todos los confines*],"[53]—Tornel, as a Creole patriot, supported the independence movement from the beginning for all the reasons that inspired the conspirators of Querétaro to plot what became the 1810 revolution of the Bajío. The financial relationship between New Spain and Spain was unjust: all trade between the colony and Madrid favored the latter with the continual exit of money to the metropolis; it was, in Tornel's words, a relationship in which "the interests of Spain were always opposed to the interests of America."[54] While this was a view that many Creoles had already voiced in the eighteenth century, the declaration of war with Britain on 12 December 1804 exacerbated the Creoles' resentment at the resulting marked rise in Spain's economic demands on the colonies. The taxes that ensued and the devastating impact the subsequent *consolidación de vales reales* had on the Creole population of New Spain cannot be overemphasized. Creoles like Tornel found themselves growing up in an environment in which they were forced to watch their country being spoliated in order to subsidize a foreign policy in which they had no interest. Although neutral trade was authorized in 1805, for the majority of Creoles it remained clear that "the monopolists of Cadiz would never concede a full free trade and the Crown would never grant one. Only independence could destroy monopoly."[55]

Tornel was also acutely aware of the difficulties he would have as a Creole in participating in the political life of the colony. As John Lynch noted, "Rivalry was greatest between first-generation Creoles [like Tornel] and new Spaniards, and it was from the former that many revolutionary leaders were recruited. The Creoles desperately needed office, and therefore they needed to control the government."[56] In other words, the simple fact that he had been born in the colony meant that he could not have any voice in the way that his *intendencia* or country was governed. Furthermore, it was equally aggravating to him that his country was ruled by a distant government that could not possibly understand the specific problems of the region and was not interested in attending to its particular needs. It was imperative that they separated from "a far-away government that never did, nor ever could, grant [Mexico] its deserved happiness."[57]

Since the people of Mexico had been dispossessed of all their social and political rights, the time had come "to allow the sword to do what three centuries of suffering had failed to achieve."[58]

It was also clear to Tornel that following the French occupation of the greater part of Spain in 1808, with the resulting imprisonment of King Ferdinand VII, the time had come for the people of the region to reclaim their sovereignty. Tornel was only thirteen when news of the Napoleonic invasion reached Mexico, and he had not yet packed his bags to go to study at San Ildefonso when the City Council of Mexico, "a bastion of Creole interest,"[59] urged Viceroy Iturrigaray to summon an independent junta to represent and govern the colony. Nevertheless, he must have been made aware, on his arrival in the capital in 1809, of the events that surrounded the 1808 coup (the first in modern Mexican history) in which Iturrigaray was forced to resign by the *peninsulares*-dominated bureaucracy and merchant guild of Mexico City.[60] The argument the Creoles adopted in 1808 was one that Tornel would use later: that "with the abdication of the legitimate monarch, Ferdinand VII, sovereignty returned to its original source, the people, with the corollary that the existing bureaucracy had lost its mandate."[61] New Spain, in other words, could no longer be governed by the king of Spain since he had been taken captive. They could not be expected to obey Napoleon's usurping brother Joseph, nor should they swear their allegiance to the self-elected rebel *juntas* of Seville and Asturias. The war in Spain meant that the time had come for the Creoles to start governing their own kingdom, at least until Ferdinand VII was returned to the throne. Tornel would not fail to note that the behavior of the *juntas* of Cadiz and Galicia toward New Spain at the time was contradictory. They sent "numerous armies to crush in America the very same cause they were fighting for against their [French] oppressors."[62]

Last but not least, although it is probably true that the 1810 revolution "responded first to interests, and interests invoked ideas,"[63] the importance of political thought and the influence it had should not be underestimated.[64] This becomes particularly clear when one delves into the motivations of an intellectual like Tornel. Most of the arguments he employed to justify and defend the 1810 revolution were based on political ideas. The need for liberty, justice, liberal and enlightened values, social (and even agrarian) reform, a constitutional order in which male universal suffrage could consolidate a truly representative government, free trade, and secular education were demands that featured prominently in his early writings. Tornel was not only a radical in the way he presented his defense of early Creole patriotism,[65] he was a radical liberal in the way he was deeply influenced by the political treatises of the Enlightenment and the French Revolution. Like Mora, Tornel became a great admirer of, and quoted frequently from, the works of Jean-Jacques Rousseau, Benjamin Constant, Alexis de Tocqueville, Montesquieu, and Destutt de Tracy.[66] For the young Tornel, independence was not the only goal of the revolution. The "nation need[ed] to be constituted," "adopting the social reforms that the century [of lights] demands," "attacking despotism in all of its manifestations."[67] For all of these reasons it is evident that the intellectual environment into which Tornel was thrown when he enrolled in San Ildefonso must have played a significant part in forming his political ideals. It was these ideas that inspired him to abandon the peace and tranquility of a privileged student life to join the insurgent forces in battle. Of course, his youth must have accounted to some extent for the readiness with which he supported the revolution. As a young idealist of the first half of the nineteenth century, Tornel was very much a romantic. It is no coincidence that, years later, he would be among the first Mexicans to translate some of Lord Byron's poems into Spanish.[68] Moreover, he was a student; in other words, his context was one of rarified intellectual and political discussion, and he had little to lose by taking up arms. Elena Poniatowska, albeit discussing the revolutionary zeal of the Mexican students of 1968, made the valid point that of all sectors of society, the students were those who could engage most easily in an open confrontation with the government because they did not have jobs, homes, and families to look after or worry about.[69] Both his age and his personal circumstances in 1812 lent themselves to revolutionary activity.

The majority of students in San Ildefonso did not become insurgents. Tornel's contemporary Mora despised Hidalgo's revolution. Similarly, other Creoles like Lucas Alamán, who witnessed Hidalgo's violent arrival in Guanajuato, were unable to ignore the threat the revolution posed to members of their social class.[70] Mora had, in fact, ended up in San Ildefonso precisely to escape from the revolution, after his father's fortune had been confiscated by Hidalgo's revolutionary forces during their occupation of Guanajuato.[71] However, in empirical terms, Tornel had not yet had firsthand experience of the terrifying threat of social dissolution that clearly traumatized the more affluent Creoles of the Bajío. While his revolutionary ideals gathered momentum, on an intellectual level, within the confines of San Ildefonso, everyday life in Orizaba was not shaken by any social, agrarian, or indigenous revolt. His father supported the insurgency because it, at least in Orizaba, had not resulted in the bloody assaults on property that had characterized the war in the Bajío. The arrival of Morelos's army in the area in the summer of 1812 had been relatively peaceful. Property was respected, and violence was controlled. The skirmishes that came with the occupation were strictly directed at the royalist forces in the region. The struggle was therefore a different one from the perspective of the *intendencia* of Veracruz. Tornel's view of the masses and his view that it was imperative that they were allowed to participate actively in the political life of the nation would change significantly after he had firsthand experience of their uncontrollable social and racial wrath during the Parián riot of 1828.

Finally, by the time Tornel joined the insurgency, Hidalgo had already been captured (21 March 1811) and executed (31 July 1811). The revolution he joined was now led by José María Morelos, who had gone on to capture Oaxaca in November 1812 and who had also, to quote Lynch, "tried to free the revolution of the encumbrance of the Hidalgo movement, whose anarchy and violence had presented the royalists with free propaganda."[72] This was a more organized revolutionary movement, one that could be deemed to be more appealing to those middle-class Creoles who believed the time had come to fight for independence and a new constitutional order, without risking being attacked by the lower sectors of society who formed the rank and file of the revolutionary army.

TORNEL AND THE INSURGENCY

Having escaped to Orizaba at the end of 1812, the young Tornel joined the insurgent army under the orders of Colonel Epitacio Sánchez in March 1813.[73] As he was boarding in the Colegio de San Ildefonso from 1809 to November 1812 and appears to have been married by the time he joined Sánchez in March 1813,[74] it can be presumed that he married María Agustina Díez Bonilla at some point between the date of his escape and that of his recruitment. We do not have the exact date of their marriage, nor do we know for how long they had known each other before they married.

María Agustina was the daughter of General Mariano Díez Bonilla, commander general of the insurgent forces in Puebla, and her family was relatively affluent. Tornel and his brothers-in-law, Miguel and Manuel Díez Bonilla, were to help each other from then on both financially and politically. According to Tornel, in a book he dedicated to his wife after she died in October 1843:

This good lady was opposed entirely to the Spanish party that ruled her mother country despotically. . . . Wherever she went, she could hear the cries of those unfortunate ones who were executed . . . , and she could see scaffolds being built to kill them by the dozens. . . . Her heart was full of bitterness, and she lived pained by a relentless agony; such was the tragic situation she lived in . . . that she spent all of her time crying, praying so that the fortunes of her mother-country would change for the better.[75]

This is Tornel's only existing portrayal of his wife,[76] and although the picture he offers of her suffering during the war of independence might appear to be an exaggeration, a year after they married, her father was arrested and sentenced to death by the Spanish authorities.[77]

Therefore, he was eighteen years old when he married and joined the insurgent army in 1813. Following the progress of Sánchez's forces, Tornel went from Orizaba, through the *intendencia* of Puebla, up to Cuautitlán, north of Mexico City and west of Teotihuacán, in the current state of Mexico, and from there on to Tlalpujahua, just north of Zitácuaro, in the Sierra de la Plata (Michoacán), on his way to join Morelos's army as it made its way northwest from Oaxaca toward Valladolid, now Morelia (Michoacán). He is reported to have acted heroically in the battles of Cuautitlán and Tlalpujahua. Showing "enthusiasm, resolution and honor" under the orders of Sánchez, he played an active part in the defeat of the Spanish commander Moreno in Cuautitlán. And shortly afterward, this time under the orders of brigadier Francisco Rayón, he showed equal determination and courage in the victory over the Spanish division at Tlalpujahua on 25 April 1813.

In September 1813 he became a sublieutenant under the orders of General Ramón Rayón y Navarrete. Within a month he rose to the rank of officer of the Ancient Patriots, and by December of that year, just as the insurgent regiments of Morelos, Nicolás Bravo, Mariano Matamoros y Orive, Hermenegildo Galeana, Vicente Guerrero, Guadalupe Victoria, and Ramón Rayón came together to initiate the offensive on Valladolid, the rebel government of Chilpancingo made him lieutenant colonel.[78] It would appear that Tornel's feats in the army were acknowledged and rewarded. It is worth noting that, some years later, on 22 August 1826, during one of the many anti-Tornel campaigns that would accompany his public life, a pamphlet, *Último golpe de paz al ciudadano Tornel*, actually questioned, with a good dose of irony, the speed with which Tornel was promoted: "It is certainly amazing: the military career must have been like the trepidating horse-races of San Juan. Even then the horses could not have been as fast in passing the finishing-line! At this rate, had Tornel stayed on in the American army for another six months, he would have been proclaimed Absolute Emperor!"[79] Some of Tornel's critics went so far as to claim that he never fought for the insurgents and that in fact he was a royalist until the Plan of Iguala was proclaimed. Nevertheless, the sheer number of documents that exist in the Archivo Histórico Militar of the Mexican Ministry of Defense concerning his insurgent years would appear to prove that he did fight against the colony and that he did rise to the rank of lieutenant colonel in a short period of time.

Among the various recorded accounts of Tornel's feats in the insurgent army, one was to become particularly important in later years. During the battle of Puruarán (5 January 1814), Tornel saved Colonel Guadalupe Victoria's life.[80] At the time, this did not have any major significance. The battle marked a definite turn in the war of independence. The royalist forces under the command of Colonel Agustín de Iturbide and Colonel Llano succeeded in crushing the insurgent forces in the hacienda of Puruarán, on the outskirts of Valladolid, as Morelos retreated to the hacienda of Santa Lucía, leaving Matamoros and Rayón in command of the rebel army. Over six hundred insurgents were killed, and seven hundred were taken prisoner.[81] While Matamoros's regiment was caught on the wrong side of the river and was subsequently either gunned down or captured as it desperately tried to cross it, fleeing from the intense onslaught of the royalist artillery and cavalry, Rayón's division, to which Tornel belonged, was fortunate enough to be positioned on the other side. It was a military disaster. To quote Carlos María de Bustamante, Puruarán became famous "for the battle in which all of our misfortunes were consummated."[82] The Spanish forces made great progress, and the rebel forces had no alternative but to retreat. However, while in all senses nothing good had come out of the battle, Tornel had inadvertently made a very fortunate move to further his career. Guadalupe Victoria was to become, in October 1824, the first elected president of Mexico. According to Tornel, Victoria asked him to accompany him as his personal secretary to Oaxaca to quell the León brothers' revolt, in August 1824, because he had saved the future president's life at the battle of Puruarán.[83] Tornel went on to be the president's personal secretary and counsellor from 1824 to 1828.

Although Tornel was fortunate enough to escape alive from the defeat of Puruarán, his heroic feats in the insurgent army came to an abrupt end in March 1814. Finding himself in Ixtapan del Oro, in the current state of Mexico, during Rayón's retreat to the south, he received a letter from Rafael Rayón, who was in the hacienda of La Petaca at the time, inviting him to command the infantry battalion of San Miguel. After being given permission to leave, accompanied by one Captain Jiménez and five soldiers, Tornel set off back north to Tlalpujahua (Michoacán). On arrival they were informed that there was a large royalist division in nearby Angangueo. Moreover, the royalist Maravatío division was heading toward the hacienda of La Petaca. Ignacio Arévalo, the priest of Tlalpujahua, told Tornel to go into hiding. Tornel and his men went to Real del Oro and stayed there for a few days hoping they would not be found. Unfortunately, some of Colonel Manuel de la Concha's men discovered their hiding place and took them by surprise while they were asleep. Tornel was almost executed on the spot. However, a Spaniard, one José Juárez, convinced his fellow soldiers that it was not up to them to decide whether he should be killed. Consequently, he was taken prisoner to the hacienda of La Jordana, where Concha had camped.[84] Concha, seeing his military distinctions and various pro-independence documents he had with him, sentenced him to death.[85]

He was locked up that night in the barn of the hacienda and the following day was marched with other prisoners to Ixtlahuaca (in the current state of Mexico). There he was given the last rites. According to his own account of the events, he spent two days "in such a bitter situation."[86] Fortunately for him, a Spaniard, Diego Rubín de Celis, a colonel in the royalist army, recognized him as Don Julián's son. He asked Concha to spare his life for the sake of gentlemen's etiquette and because Don Julián was an old acquaintance of his: "Concha decided to have him shot and would have done so without difficulty, had I not used all the efforts and resolution I was capable of to change his mind . . . until I succeeded in the end, in my purpose of freeing him, as I did, from the grip of death."[87]

The two days Tornel spent waiting to be shot served Celis's purposes. With the aid of Ignacio Arévalo, he succeeded in dissuading Concha from carrying out the order to have Tornel executed. Concha gave way to his pleas and accepted the alternative of sending Tornel as a prisoner to Mexico City, where Viceroy Calleja would decide whether he deserved to be shot.[88] Tornel was to remember Celis's help. The Spaniard had saved his life. Fourteen years later, in June 1828, when Tornel was asked to account for the exemption he had granted Celis from the 1827 law that expelled Spanish residents from Mexico, he answered that he owed his life to him.[89]

Concha ordered him to go to the capital. He was to make his own way there, unescorted. If he did not get there within the next eight days, he would be shot on the spot.[90] To ensure that Tornel obeyed, one José María Rosas accepted the responsibility of accompanying him to the capital and making sure that he arrived in the time accorded. Tornel did not actually meet Rosas until a couple of days later in San Felipe del Obrage (in the current state of Mexico). Hoping that Rosas would not be hard on him, he pretended to be a Spaniard as well as Andrés Mendívil's nephew. Rosas did not believe him.[91] According to one later account, Tornel, on his way to Mexico City, arrived in Lerma "naked, and in the greatest poverty."[92]

As noted by Ernesto de la Torre, after Puruarán, a high proportion of insurgents opted to surrender and accept the *indulto* (pardon) Viceroy Calleja decided to offer to all of those rebels who gave up the armed struggle against the colony. They did this either because they had become disheartened or because they realized that it made sense to turn themselves in temporarily. In either case, it remains probably true that most of them hoped that they would continue the struggle at a later date, when the political situation changed, resulting in one that was more favorable to fighting the colony with some success.[93] According to María del Carmen Vázquez Mantecón, it was José María Rosas, the ex-secretary of the Inquisition, who met up with Tornel in San Felipe, who persuaded him to accept the *indulto*.[94] Thus, Tornel presented himself before Calleja in March 1814 and repented for his past actions in the hope that the viceroy would grant him the *indulto*. Tornel was pardoned on 27 April after Calleja sentenced him to confinement in the Colegio de San Ildefonso, where he had studied theology only two years before.

There are two possible explanations for Calleja's leniency. One, which was to appear years later in the press as part of an attempt to prevent Tornel from rising further in the political hierarchy, was that he gave names and places of the insurgent movement to obtain Calleja's forgiveness. Although there is no conclusive proof, it could easily have happened. In Tornel's own words, "The papers I signed at the time were signed as a result of the well-founded fear that I could lose my life."[95] What is certain is that he obtained the official pardon, the *indulto*, by swearing that he repented of having fought against the colony. He argued in 1826 that except for Victoria and Guerrero, all the other national heroes had done exactly the same as him.[96]

The other explanation is that he succeeded in deceiving Calleja by convincing him that he sincerely regretted having joined the insurgent movement. Evidence might be found in a letter Calleja addressed to the marqués de Castañiza on 14 May 1814. In it Calleja stated that he expected Castañiza to act "with the greatest responsibility over Don José María Tornel in order that he does not join the rebels again." He recommended that he should be placed far from the street where "it is much easier for him to be distracted" and where he was less likely to be in touch with "the inconsiderate youths that almost certainly perverted him." Calleja concluded the letter by reaffirming that he was "firmly convinced that his repentance is sincere and effective."[97] Whether Tornel succeeded in deceiving Calleja, appearing sincerely ashamed of his conduct, or whether his "sincerity" is what Calleja euphemistically called the information Tornel had given him in exchange for a pleasant imprisonment, must be left an open question.

Tornel spent two months as a prisoner in the Colegio de San Ildefonso, from the end of March to the end of May 1814. Castañiza locked him up in the library at the beginning, then in the infirmary "for greater security."[98] By all accounts, it appears that Castañiza did not like Tornel and was not at all happy having to contend with him again in his college. On 24 April, after Tornel had been confined in the school for one month, Castañiza had started a letter addressed to Calleja about his previous behavior and how he had left the school to join the insurgents. His remarks boiled down to the following: "I truly believe that it is a great inconvenience that such an individual should stay in this school. The school's honor is being seriously harmed."[99] The letter ended with him "begging" Calleja "to please find a way so that the aforementioned Don José Ma[ría] Tornel leaves this school as soon as possible on the terms your excellency may consider the most just and convenient."[100]

Tornel was not happy either. Furthermore, he claims he was scared that Calleja eventually would realize that he had deceived him. Therefore, "not satisfied with these harangues and afraid that the viceroy would eventually discover the truth and have me executed, I escaped."[101] Tornel claims that he took his jailer by surprise and ran to hide in the house of one Juan Villarello. However, his escape did not go according to plan. Villarello gave him away to the authorities. He was taken prisoner again that night and marched through the dark streets of Mexico City.[102] The order was given

that he be taken from the Colegio de San Ildefonso to the Colegio Seminario Palafoxiano of Puebla. He was escorted by the Spanish cavalry past
the volcanoes Popocatepetl and Iztaccíhuatl to Puebla, where he was confined for a further year.

The year Tornel spent in the seminary does not appear to have been too
testing. He was no longer confined to a single room and had the chance of
conversing with others there. In fact, "his behavior in the school not only
showed how brilliant he was in literature and how remarkable was his
honesty, but it won him much admiration, particularly because of the way
he imprudently manifested his patriotism in those difficult circumstances
under the vigilance of a Spanish dean."[103]

Even though there was a Spanish dean, it does not seem as if his punishments were that severe. He had the chance of converting other students to
the cause of independence. He was able to continue his studies in theology,
having access to the exceptional college library. Instead of pursuing an
understanding of Christian doctrines, he even used the volumes of the library to justify with historical facts his written portrayal of the "distribution of the Indians" and the "injustice of the conquest."[104] There is no
record of his having been reprimanded. Instead, as the year went by, he
became more and more outspoken. Not only did his texts and his outspoken defense of independence start influencing the other students, but he
even helped one Juan Nepomuceno Pérez escape from the seminary to Tehuacán.[105] In approximately May 1815, José María Tenorio, dean of the
seminary, expelled him.[106] The fact that he was expelled suggests that his
confinement was only relative. Free once more, he was able to return to
his family in Orizaba.

By all accounts, he spent the rest of 1815, all of 1816, and most of 1817
in his home town. It seems plausible that it was at this time that his wife,
María Agustina, gave birth to at least one of their six children. A later
account states that Tornel, "in Orizaba maintained his old position and his
attachment [to the cause] but with greater care."[107] It is reasonable to de-
duce that he had a family of his own to worry about now and was consequently more restrained in his public defense of independence. Moreover,
the insurgent movement was beginning to falter. Hidalgo and Allende had
been killed in 1811, although their heads could still be seen rotting in the
main square of Guanajuato. Morelos was to die on 22 December 1815.
Although Victoria and Guerrero continued fighting, the war of independence had deteriorated into separate and individual skirmishes and minor
outbreaks of defianse. While, to quote Ernesto de la Torre, "1811 to 1815
[had been] the most dynamic period of the war of independence,"[108]
thereafter the insurgency lost both its strength and its momentum. From a
total of forty thousand insurgent militias at the height of Morelos's leadership of the revolution, armed with a respectable number of guns and cannons, by 1816, there were no more than eight thousand poorly armed

insurgents remaining in the field, and these were divided and scattered over the vast territories of the south and center of the country.[109] Although Francisco Javier Mina's 1817 revolutionary expedition gave the revolution some respite, he was taken prisoner after a few months of fighting and was executed on 11 November that year.

Nevertheless, Tornel continued to be active: "he continued to work, wherever it was possible, supporting the efforts of the Hidalgos and the Morelos, of Iturbide and of all those who fought in the name of freedom."[110] The means by which he continued to help the struggle for independence are confirmed in subsequent accounts by Colonel Bernardo María de Pérez y Argüelles and General Francisco Miranda. In the words of the former, he supplied rifles, munitions, and clothes to the rebel army throughout 1816 and the first three months of 1817. Moreover, he states that he maintained "with the afore-mentioned Tornel, a daily correspondence on the importance of providing the best service for the nation."[111]

According to Miranda, "he aided me with weapons he could obtain and which he kept in his house, sending them to me via my sergeant, Major don Manuel Cabrera."[112] Miranda also confirms that he held long conversations with Tornel, portraying him as an ideologue and a strategist who throughout his stay in Orizaba gave constant advice to the insurgent forces in the area. At one point during these years, according to Pérez y Argüelles, Tornel became dissatisfied with his efforts to further the cause of independence. Finding that supplying weapons to the insurgents in the area was not enough, he considered joining the rebel army once more. However, Pérez y Argüelles prevented him from doing so because "the state of the revolution is not good, after the defeat at Cerro Colorado . . . our self-esteem and enthusiasm have suffered more than could ever have been expected."[113] Whether his contributions to aid the war of independence during his stay in Orizaba were considerable cannot be known.

The fact remains, however, that his various rendezvous with the active insurgents of the area aroused the Spanish authorities' suspicions. Toward the end of 1817, Colonel Hevia, the "sanguinary" Spanish commander of Orizaba,[114] sent his men to arrest him for having renewed his contacts with the rebel forces. This time, he heard of the arrest order and escaped, probably with his wife and children. Forced from Orizaba, he fled to Puebla, where he went into hiding for the following two to three years.

Very little is known about Tornel's stay in Puebla. According to one later account, he "cooperated effectively in aiding the forces of freedom, and propagated the system of emancipation"[115] from the moment of his arrival there. However, there is no indication as to how he "cooperated effectively" or indeed "propagated" the cause of independence. With the Díez Bonillas living in Puebla, it can be presumed that they found somewhere where he could hide in relative comfort. At least this time the Spanish authorities did not capture him.

THE GIFTED WRITER AND THE INCIPIENT *CAUDILLO*

What is not clear is whether Tornel returned to Orizaba in 1820. One has to assume that he must have gone back to the *intendencia* of Veracruz at some point before February 1821, for he was serving as Antonio López de Santa Anna's captain of grenadiers and aide by the time Iturbide proclaimed the Plan of Iguala (24 February 1821). In other words, by the end of 1820, it is clear that he had made two important decisions: to make a career in the army, giving up his initial intention of becoming a priest, and to do so in the royalist army rather than in the insurgent one. Clearly, the first decision must have been one he had already taken in 1812, when he gave up his studies to join the insurgency. However, the second decision requires some explanation, even if it is mainly speculative, since we have so little information about his activities between 1817 and 1821. It could be argued that there were at least two good reasons for this change in direction. First, by 1820, there was no longer an insurgent army worth speaking of, except for Vicente Guerrero's guerrilla force in the south. By then, Guadalupe Victoria had disappeared into the jungle of Veracruz and was no longer directing any military operations in the area. Second, the political context of New Spain had changed considerably since the beginning of the war of independence.

On one level, the war had resulted in a significant politicization of the army and a parallel militarization of politics. Whether it was the need to mount an effective counterinsurgency war or the fact that high-ranking royalist officers were able to use the war as an excuse to expand their increasingly broad powers over the regions in which they were garrisoned, the fact remains that, as was the case with Brigadier José de la Cruz, commander general of Guadalajara for the duration of the conflict, the army quickly established their supremacy over the different civilian administrations. To quote Christon Archer, "wartime conditions forced army commanders to exercise precedence over the civil administrations."[116] While a considerable number of high-ranking Creole officers started to resent the fact that their expanding power was nevertheless subordinated to a higher command made up of *peninsulares*, events in Spain in 1820 pushed them into seriously considering rebelling against the colony. In other words, the fact that the majority of Creoles who had fought against the insurgents for the better part of ten years started to consider fighting for independence "came not from the Mexican insurgents who in 1820 lacked the conventional military power to confront the royalist military at the battlefield but rather from the Riego Rebellion in Spain and the restored Spanish Constitution."[117]

On 1 January 1820 General Rafael Riego staged a *pronunciamiento* in the south of Spain that led to the reestablishment of the 1812 Cadiz constitution (9 March 1820). On 27 May 1821, Viceroy Juan Ruiz de Apodaca proclaimed the constitution in the colony, and Mexican deputies went on to be elected to attend the Cortes in Spain in September that year. As is noted by Lynch, "The new Spanish regime, in a kind of death wish, proceeded to subvert the very empire that it proclaimed."[118] The new radical Cortes in a series of decrees issued in August and September 1820 attacked the church's properties and privileges like no other previous Spanish ruler had done before, alienating even the higher clergy of Mexico. Furthermore, on 29 September 1820, a law was passed that abolished the colonial militia's privilege of trial by military courts in nonmilitary cases. The army was thus assaulted on two fronts: "under the constitution, the military temporarily lost the dominance that for years permitted soldiers to control Mexican politics";[119] and the army's most sacrosanct privilege, the *fuero militar*, that made its institution immune to civil law, was attacked and fully abolished in June 1821. In other words, the army Tornel joined in 1820, albeit royalist, was beginning to consider embracing the cause of independence, all at a time when even the more reactionary elements of society, including the higher clergy, were becoming persuaded that the colony's ties to Spain were becoming untenable. Evidently Iturbide's motivations and those of the more reactionary royalist officers who turned against the colony in 1821 were very different from those that had inspired the early insurgents like Allende and, for that matter, Tornel. Nevertheless, it remains true that by the time Tornel became a royalist officer, the Creoles in the royalist army were warming toward the ideal of independence. In brief, although there was a certain degree of pragmatism in Tornel's actions (however much he supported the insurgent cause, the prospects of leading a successful military career by joining Guerrero's troops were bleak and thus not worth pursuing), the fact that he joined the royalist army in late 1820 was not in itself such a contradictory action, since the high-ranking Creole officers within it were considering challenging Madrid. Evidence of this is the remarkable suddenness of the collapse of New Spain after the proclamation of the Plan of Iguala. By September 1821 there was not a Creole within the royalist forces who had not already joined Iturbide's rebel Army of the Three Guarantees. His plan succeeded in converting the majority of the eighty-five thousand men who made up the royalist army in Mexico, and the opposition to independence quickly disappeared.[120]

At some point in late 1820, whether it was during his stay in Puebla or, almost certainly, after having returned to his home province as a new recruit in the royalist army, Tornel became acquainted with Santa Anna. All that can be said is that they must have established a rapport from the moment they met. They were both in their twenties (Tornel was twenty-five; Santa Anna was twenty-six). They were both Creoles. Both belonged to relatively wealthy families with links to the commercial sectors of the province. Both were ambitious. The two of them were from Veracruz (Santa Anna was from the rival mountain town of Xalapa). They were both military men. They were both compulsive schemers. They both liked women (in years to come, the two of them would have notorious extramarital relationships). They both enjoyed a good night out (Tornel preferred the theater; Santa Anna favored cockfights). Their friendship was to last from then until Tornel's death. The only significant difference between them at the time, and it was not a minor one, was that Santa Anna had fought for the Spaniards.

Santa Anna (born on 21 February 1794) had joined the army in 1810 as a cadet in the Fijo de Veracruz infantry regiment when he was sixteen years old, resisting parental pressure to follow a commercial career. Although he joined the royalist army just before the war of independence broke out (9 June 1810), he did not participate in any counterinsurgency operations until 1816. Between 1810 and 1816 he spent most of his time fighting nomadic Indian tribes in the north, first in Nuevo Santander (current state of Tamaulipas) (March to May 1811) and later in Texas (July to August 1813), rising to the rank of lieutenant and officer by 1813. Moreover, since the *intendencia* of Veracruz was hardly affected by revolutionary activity, he did not engage in any fighting in the two years that followed his return to Veracruz, on 14 March 1814, where he became Governor José García Dávila's personal aide. In other words, Santa Anna was not involved in any of the key campaigns of the war of independence. This fact might have accounted in part for the way in which Tornel and Santa Anna were able to overlook their recent past as they consolidated their long-lasting friendship in the winter of 1820–1821. They had not actually fought against each other during the first half of the war.

It was only after October 1816 (after Morelos had been captured and executed) that Santa Anna, at the age of twenty-two, became involved in counterinsurgency duties forming part of the new militia, the Realistas del Camino Real, that replaced the Spanish Expeditionary Infantry Regiment of Barcelona, once the high-ranking officers of the latter realized that they "could not cope with the climate and the rough backcountry of Veracruz."[121] By all accounts Santa Anna was excellent at his job; "he knew the country intimately, understood the population and could appeal to the insurgents in a variety of ways";[122] and in 1818, after he had participated in the pursuit that brought an end to Mina's 1817 revolutionary expedition in Soto de la Marina, he was made commander of the Realistas de Extramuros Veracruz y Pueblo de la Boca del Rio. He was not just effective but also ruthless in his actions. Going against the orders of the senior military authorities of the area, he ordered a number of executions and was accused of insubordination. Nevertheless, Viceroy Apodaca forgave him after he went to Mexico City that year to defend himself. In 1819, his star now ascending, Santa Anna led a series of reckless search missions to root out guerrilla bands in the area, and although he did not succeed in finding the elusive Victoria, he nevertheless caught three guerrilla leaders—Manuel Salvador, Félix González, and Mariano Cenobio—who together with a priest and 230 armed men surrendered to him, begging for amnesty.[123] By the time Tornel met him, Santa Anna had received the Shield of Honor and Certificate of the Royal and Distinguished Order of Isabella the Catholic for his services to Spain.[124] He had also played a significant role, between 1819 and 1820, in overseeing the creation and construction of eight villages (Medellín, Jamapa, San Diego, El Tamarindo, Huehuistla, Paso de Ovejas, La Antigua, and Santa Fe), ensuring that the former insurgent communities who moved into them became grateful and loyal followers of the colonial administration.[125] As he was to record in his memoirs, he had been spoiled or pampered (*mimado*) by the vice-regal government, and his gratitude had no limits.[126]

Although Tornel's acceptance of the Plan of Iguala (news of Iturbide and Guerrero's alliance reached Veracruz on 5 March) was clearly understandable since he had believed in an independent Mexico since 1810, the conversion from royalist to insurgent for Santa Anna, even if it was in Iturbide's Army of the Three Guarantees, was a far less easy step to make. He had been a dedicated and loyal defender of the colony, something that had been duly recognized by the vice-regal high command. In March 1821, less than a month before he defected to the insurgent cause, the viceroy promoted him to the rank of lieutenant colonel.[127] He had also developed a close relationship with the Spanish general José García Dávila. According to Enrique González Pedrero, they had become like father and son.[128] To change sides represented a major betrayal, and a personal one at that—one that, according to Lynch, the Spaniards never forgave him for. When he besieged Veracruz later that year, now at the head of the rebel forces, the royalists garrisoned in the port issued a statement in which they said that they would not surrender to a traitor. Iturbide promptly had to replace Santa Anna "by a commander more acceptable to the royalists and Veracruz surrendered."[129] Nevertheless, Santa Anna, like the rest of the Creoles in the royalist army, converted to the cause of independence not long after the Plan of Iguala was proclaimed. One wonders whether Tornel played a part in persuading him. After all, as Wilfrid Hardy Callcott notes, "it is hard to see how such a reasoned decision [changing sides, on 26 April 1821, after he had successfully taken Orizaba from the rebels and fortified himself in the Carmen Convent] could have been reached during those few hours between the successful sortie in the morning and 2 P.M—hours when he would normally have been very busy caring for the details of his victory."[130] One source suggests that Tornel was already writing speeches in support of the Plan of Iguala by the end of March,[131] a month before Santa Anna and he actually defected openly to the rebel cause. In other words, Tornel could well have been trying to persuade Santa Anna to change sides for at least a month before he actually did so.

The Plan of Iguala was, at least on paper, an incredibly seductive proposal. In the words of Archer, Iturbide's "message offered soldiers and civilians, royalists and insurgents, an escape from chaos and expectations of a return to prosperity."[132] With the promise of three guarantees—religion, independence, and union—and an end to eleven debilitating years of war, the Plan of Iguala had something to offer everybody with the promise of independence from Spain. It pleased the church by guaranteeing the defense of Catholicism as the sole religion of the new nation. It pleased the old insurgents who by then knew that they could not win the war on their own, and the new, who were beset by financial crises and the impact of the 1812 Constitution. And it appeased the Spanish population in Mexico by guaranteeing their peaceful permanence in the country as integral members of that union. In Santa Anna's own words, having recognized that he had been pampered by the colony, "the Plan of Iguala appeared, proclaimed by Colonel Don Agustín de Iturbide on 24 February 1821, and I hastened to support it, because I wanted to contribute my grain of sand to the great work of our political regeneration."[133] Three factors must have influenced him. The first, although there is no evidence to sustain this point, was Tornel's influence. Finding themselves in Tornel's home town, it would be hard to believe that he would not have tried to talk him out of attacking a community that was supporting independence once more, just as it had done when Morelos's army liberated it in 1812, and from where he had personally supported the guerrilla bands in the area after he had been *indultado* (1815–1817). The second was José Joaquín de Herrera's influence. On 26 April, Herrera met with Santa Anna in order to persuade him to join the rebellion. According to González Pedrero, Herrera explained to Santa Anna, in exhaustive detail, what was contained in the Plan of Iguala and the benefits that lay in store for the country if the nation as a whole supported it.[134] The third was that Santa Anna's defection would be rewarded with a further promotion, this time to the rank of colonel.

Therefore, although the exact date of their first encounter is unknown, by April 1821, they were defecting to the rebel cause together. When Santa Anna was promoted to colonel, he named Tornel his personal secretary and made him treasurer as well as chief postmaster of the province. When Tornel wrote to Iturbide later that year, asking to be promoted to the position of colonel, he produced, as a letter of recommendation, a note from Santa Anna in which the incipient *caudillo* stated that "my secretary, the captain of grenadiers—Don José María Tornel has been throughout the revolutions a good friend of the mother country. I am aware of his good services and that he deserves the post he is requesting for his good will and patriotism."[135] Tornel went on to say that Santa Anna had given him the position of captain of grenadiers and made him secretary to the military commander of Veracruz "with other proof of his trust."[136] Their close relationship—that of the impetuous *caudillo* and the gifted writer—was in the making.

As Santa Anna's secretary, Tornel spent the following six months travel-
ing around the *intendencias* of Veracruz and Puebla, composing Santa
Anna's speeches and proclamations in favor of independence together with
those of other rebel generals. While Santa Anna set about liberating Alvarado, Perote, and eventually the port of Veracruz, Tornel put his velvet
prose to good use.

In his July pamphlet, *Valor y constancia es nuestra divisa*, he could not
decide whether Santa Anna could be equated with Julius Caesar because
of his military prowess or because he wrote so well. Tornel wrote Santa
Anna's speeches, and in between lines he was indirectly celebrating his own
literary contribution to the conflict. At the age of twenty-six, Tornel, with
no sense of modesty whatsoever, was more than convinced that he was a
gifted writer. And he used his Caesarean prose to confirm that: "The burning war of Dolores, of September 1810, in spite of the tragic end of its
propagators, and of its successors, is kept alive by Guerrero, Ascencio,
Izquierdo; and the love of freedom remained, always, albeit hidden, alight
in everybody's heart. The time came for it to manifest itself openly the
moment Iturbide, the hero, placed himself at the head of the liberators of
the mother-country." He wondered how the reactionary cities of Mexico,
Puebla, and Veracruz could continue to support the tyrants. Nevertheless,
he remained persuaded that the people of Veracruz (to whom this pamphlet
was addressed) would listen to him and turn against their oppressors: "To
die or to win: that is our motto. I can see the patriotic fire alight in your
faces, and I see you run to take up arms, to defend your homes, to avenge
the insults, and destroy the shackles your tyrannical masters placed on the
blessed earth of Anáhuac." The time had come for the Veracruzans to rebel
against their royalist authorities: "Mexicans, Carthage did not offend Rome
as much as Veracruz offends Mexico. Be Romans!"[137]

In his August pamphlet, *El grito de la patria*, he went on to harangue
the population of Puebla. Once more the choice was the same: "Death or
freedom." In Iguala, "the immortal Iturbide" had proclaimed the cry of
salvation or death. Nothing could oppose their moral strength: "*Poblanos!*
You are free and blessed: a step back would lead to the grave: the tyrants
of three centuries do not forgive: there is no middle ground between Independence and the ruin of our future descendants; you saw the hero, you
admire his virtues, the cause is sacred, show that you are worthy of the
mother-country, of the century, of yourselves."[138]

In his September pamphlet, *Manifiesto del origen, causas, progresos y
estado de la revolución del imperio mexicano con relación a la antigua
España*, he continued to stress the belief that their choice was a simple,
albeit drastic one: "salvation or death." Moreover, unlike Mora and Alamán, who condemned the 1810 revolution but celebrated the 1821 movement, or Carlos María de Bustamante, who believed in Hidalgo and
Morelos but despised Iturbide, Tornel saw the Plan of Iguala as a continua-

tion, or a reprise, of the *grito de Dolores*. Hidalgo had been the first national hero. Iturbide was his more successful follower. And "the tree of freedom, born in the midst of cadavers, watered with the blood of so many victims, stretches its glorious branches up to the sky throughout the Mexican Empire." Furthermore, in the wake of the Treaties of Córdoba (24 August 1821), Tornel showed for the first time a belief in reconciliation. If Spain was ready to accept their independence, then it only made sense that Spain should become "the first of Mexico's allied nations." With the Cadiz Constitution back in place, Spain was now governed by liberal principles that "had been welcomed by us with enthusiasm, solemnly sworn in all of the villages, applauded and engraved in all of our hearts."[139]

Tornel was in fact present at the signing of the Treaties of Córdoba,[140] in which the newly arrived Spanish viceroy, Juan O'Donojú, legitimized the insurgent movement and authorized the surrender of the Spanish troops in the capital. On 27 September 1821, with Iturbide, O'Donojú and Guerrero riding at the head of the Army of the Three Guarantees, they marched into Mexico City, ending the eleven-year war. A month later, on 27 October, Tornel printed in Mexico City his *La aurora de México* celebrating the nation's new freedom, dedicating all his praise to Iturbide: "Immortal ITURBIDE! You are Pompeii, Brutus, Washington, you are the redeemer of the mother-country."[141]

TORNEL, *ITURBIDISTA*

After that 27 September, Tornel was to become a dedicated supporter of Iturbide. On 16 October, either in response to his letter asking for promotion or as a means of rewarding him for the praise inherent in his various pamphlets, Iturbide promoted him to the rank of colonel.[142] Of course, Tornel's admiration for Iturbide was fairly characteristic, both of the way the majority of the Creole political elite at the time responded to his rise to power (Carlos María de Bustamante, Servando Teresa de Mier, Vicente Rocafuerte, Guadalupe Victoria, and Anastasio Zerecero being the notable exceptions)[143] and of the way those politicians who would eventually become *santanistas* in the 1830s welcomed his leadership of the new nation.[144] After all, as confirmed by Timothy Anna, the vast majority of the population celebrated Iturbide's rise to power and saw him as the natural leader of the new nation since it had been he who had succeeded in liberating Mexico from Spain.[145] For Tornel, Iturbide had been chosen by destiny in the same way that Moses had been: to free his people from slavery. Among his many qualities, Tornel praised his courage, energetic disposition, and extraordinary foresight. It was his profound understanding of the political situation of the country and its most urgent needs that enabled him to conceive of a plan that not only brought about independence in a comparatively peaceful fashion and in a remarkably short period of time, but also united the most disparate of elements. With a certain dose of nostalgia, following the debacle of the Mexican-American War (1846–1848), Tornel would lament, in 1850, that the Mexican people had forgotten those magical words, *religion, union* and *independence*, with which Iturbide had forged a nation out of the chaos. "With reason," he wrote, "the Mexican people applauded [him]."[146] It would be only in retrospect that Tornel lamented Iturbide's flaws and mistakes.

Thus Tornel came to argue in 1852 that Iturbide had lacked the authority that can hold a country together: "The prestige of one man can at times be the best foundation for a society, and history offers us several examples of its importance during extreme conflicts. What would have become of France had Napoleon not held the reins of the state with such a firm hand?"[147] He also thought that Iturbide had been too eager to change the main pillars of the colony's society, carrying out too many reforms in too short a period of time: "The natural disquiet [that could be seen amongst the nation's population] . . . could have been cured with the hope of improvement, which needed no other sacrifice than that of allowing a little more time."[148] Therefore, he criticized him for reforming the country's political system in a rush and for naming a congress "that could be no such thing except in fiction, since he named it, it received its mission from him and the people had no say in the matter."[149] Moreover, he condemned Iturbide and Congress's mismanagement of the economy: they "destroyed everything they touched and dealt the first blows to that monument to three centuries of wisdom; blows which have since continued to be dealt, thus bringing the whole edifice to the ground. It will always cause amazement, this policy of simultaneously increasing the expenditure whilst crushing all the adequate means of paying for it."[150] As he stated in 1841, "The Empire fell because the immortal Iturbide was not able to pay the expenses of the soldiers he had just led to victory, and because he indebted his ministry by asking for unheard of contributions from the people."[151]

Nevertheless, having said this, Tornel was an ardent *iturbidista* in 1821–1822, and he went on to write a number of tributes to Iturbide in the 1830s, 1840s, and 1850s, the most famous of which was the poem he wrote for the commemoration of his birthday on 27 September 1838, which can be seen to this day engraved on the urn in which the emperors's ashes were placed to rest:

> Agustín de Iturbide.
> Author of the Independence of Mexico.
> Patriot, cry for him.
> Traveller, admire him.
> This monument holds the ashes of a hero.
> His soul rests in God's arms.[152]

Like other subsequent *santanistas*, such as José María Bocanegra, Tornel not only openly celebrated Iturbide's initial regency but also went on to defend the empire proposed on 18 May 1822. Tornel's support for the coronation of Iturbide was characteristic of the way the majority of the political class at the time saw fit to place the liberator on the Mexican throne. As noted by Anna, there are no indications that there was any significant opposition to the creation of a Mexican empire with Iturbide at its head.[153] If we are to believe Bocanegra, republicanism had not yet become a generalized creed in 1822. The issue as to whether Mexico should be a monarchy or a republic was not on the agenda. Mexico was to become a monarchy. The issue was, rather, whether a member of the Bourbon dynasty should be placed on the Mexican throne, as had been recommended in the Treaties of Córdoba, or whether it was preferable to start a new monarchy by crowning a Mexican-born hero.[154] Given that Ferdinand VII had firmly refused to recognize Mexico's independence and was pressing for the reconquest of Spain's former American colonies, it was evident for someone like Tornel, who had fought for independence, that the crowning of Iturbide was a necessary step to consolidate independence: "On the 18th of May we solved the great problem that tormented us day and night . . . remaining united against the schemes of the Spanish government."[155] Bearing in mind the influence the liberal ideas of the 1812 Constitution of Cadiz had had on Tornel's generation, the monarchy that was created on 19 May was a strictly constitutional one in which the emperor swore to obey the "constitution, laws, orders and decrees formulated by Congress, the representative of the nation."[156] Evidently Santa Anna, like Tornel and Bocanegra, was a passionate *iturbidista* as well. In fact, the *caudillo*'s *iturbidismo* was such that he even attempted to marry the emperor's sister, the sexagenarian Doña Nicolasa.[157]

On 15 September 1822, as a demonstration of his support for the emperor and an attack on any Bourbonist plots to overthrow him, Tornel printed his *Derechos de Fernando VII al trono del imperio mexicano*. In this pamphlet he clearly stated his admiration for Iturbide: it was the liberator's hands that had drafted "that political and ingenious masterpiece that united the will of the people under one common banner."[158] The Mexican people needed to rally behind him and maintain a united front against the very real threat of a pro-Spanish Bourbonist conspiracy. He emphatically demanded unity as a response to the crisis the country had been in since the summer. The increasing tensions that surfaced between Congress and the emperor had led to Iturbide's arrest of sixty-six alleged conspirators on 26 August 1822, nineteen of whom were deputies.[159] Tornel dreaded the possible consequences of civil war. If the Mexicans fought each other, they would be divided, and the opportunity for the defenders of the colony to strike back would be all the greater: "We are independent. Let us preserve this gift from God."[160]

Nevertheless, once Iturbide dissolved Congress (31 October 1822), Tornel, Bocanegra, and Santa Anna started to distance themselves from the imperial proposal. It is worth noting that although Bocanegra accused Iturbide of allowing himself to be ruled by his despotic tendencies, Tornel argued that, on the contrary, the emperor had made the fatal mistake of delegating too much power, which meant that he became too dependent on a hostile Congress. Nevertheless, Tornel was to join Bocanegra in stressing that Iturbide made a fundamental mistake by closing down Congress because, having made a mockery of their national representation, "the redeemer of the mother-country was transformed, as if by magic, into a despot and an oppressor."[161]

However, while Santa Anna launched his *impulso de Veracruz* (2 December 1822), Bocanegra continued to serve in Iturbide's new Junta Instituyente (with which the emperor replaced the dissolved Congress), and Tornel, fearing the debilitating consequences of a major civil war at the same time of a threat of a Spanish invasion, went to the extreme of writing publicly to Santa Anna to ask him not to persevere with his revolt. He claimed that it was his duty, as Santa Anna's most dedicated friend, to save him from falling into the abyss he was heading toward. He knew that Santa Anna would listen to him: "There does not exist in the entire world a person you trust more than myself. Neither is there one who has shown as many proofs as myself of the constant interest that has characterized my endeavors to achieve your happiness."[162] He was both surprised and disturbed that Santa Anna could have fallen into the trap of his enemies and that he could have thought that by rebelling against Iturbide, he was not in fact assisting the Spaniards' ambitions. He conceded that a republican form of government (like that which Santa Anna had proposed in his *Proclama a los habitantes de Veracruz*, 2 December 1822) was a worthy cause to uphold, but stressed that now was not the time to impose such a major change in their form of government by force, when there were still Spanish troops garrisoned in the island San Juan de Ulúa, just outside Veracruz. Tornel argued that a rebellion against Iturbide would indirectly, if not directly, lead Mexico into a chaotic civil war that could only help the Spaniards to regain power: "[The Spaniards'] intention is to agitate us, to destroy all the ties that unite us, to then dominate and conquer us."[163]

The outcome of the conflict, with the subsequent Plan of Casa Mata (1 February 1823) and the eventual abdication of Iturbide (19 March 1823), would be enough to persuade Tornel that his fears regarding the Spanish threat had been unfounded and that Santa Anna had been right in persevering with his revolt, ignoring his advice in the process. The failure of the *iturbidista* proposal resulted in a generalized defense of republican values among the majority of the political class. Therefore, as Bocanegra noted, while in 1822 republicanism was supported by a rather hesitant minority, by April 1823, following the fall of Iturbide, the newly convened Congress "openly manifested from the beginning a particularly pronounced republican spirit."[164] Both Bocanegra and Tornel became outspoken republicans, and it was not long before they also joined those factions that demanded the adoption of a federalist constitutional system.[165] Nevertheless, Tornel would look back in 1852 and wonder whether the first national decades would have been altogether different had the two men he most admired come to an understanding:

If Iturbide and Santa Anna, the only two Mexicans who have been blessed from above with the sacred fire of genius, had studied each other and had understood each other, the two, together, would have merited the admiration of the mother-country, providing it with a free and stable government for over half a century. . . . United by their ideas of freedom and justice, Mexico would not be what it is today: the mockery and the jibe of the universe.[166]

A MAN WITH "AN OUTSTANDING TALENT"

Although Tornel's pamphlets and later works offered an interesting commentary and interpretation of the events that brought about the rise and fall of Iturbide, unlike his friends Santa Anna and Bocanegra, he did not actually play a significant role on the political stage of the First Empire. While Santa Anna became involved as the commanding general of Veracruz in the personal feud with Iturbide that led to his revolt of 2 December 1822 and went on to lead another rebellion, this time in San Luis Potosí, demanding the creation of a federal republic (5 June 1823), and Bocanegra served as a deputy in both the empire's Congress and its Junta Instituyente, Tornel's public life was limited to serving as a clerk in the Ministry of War in Mexico City.

Immediately after independence was achieved, Tornel and his family moved to the capital; he remained a *capitalino* for the rest of his life. Even though his brothers remained in Orizaba and he went to visit them on a number of occasions thereafter, his home town became Mexico City. Being an ambitious man, this is not surprising. Mexico City was, as it still is, the epicenter of power in Mexico. As Anna has noted recently, "The city and the state of Mexico together accounted for nearly 20 percent of the country's entire population of roughly 6.2 million people in the 1820s. The capital city by itself had a larger population than eight of the original nineteen states."[167] Moreover, unlike his friend Santa Anna, who preferred to live in his hacienda in Veracruz, whether it was Manga de Clavo first or later El Encero, Tornel came to adore Mexico City, stating that it was in "one of the most beautiful valleys of the universe."[168] As would be verified in so many contemporary accounts, by Mexicans and foreigners, Mexico City at the time was one of the most extraordinary cities of the world. To quote Henry George Ward, the first British minister plenipotentiary who was posted to Mexico in 1823: "Among the many capitals of Europe few compare favorably with Mexico City."[169] Waddy Thompson, the U.S. minister plenipotentiary, describing the city as it was in 1843, was equally complementary: it was "the finest built city on the American Continent."[170] Its captivating beauty was to be found in its wide and spacious avenues and majestic buildings; the cathedral, the National Palace, and the College of Mines all deserved a mention, as did its numerous splendid churches and convents, such as La Profesa and San Francisco. Its breathtaking squares and gardens, the Plaza Mayor (currently known as the Zócalo), and the Plaza de Santo Domingo, with parks such as the Alameda, were all considered captivating. And the crystal clear air of the capital allowed one to enjoy, from most streets, the view of the surrounding valley, with the panorama of the ever-impressive volcanoes in the southwest, Popocatepetl and Iztaccihuatl. Mexico City was, in the words of a nineteenth-century Mexican poet, a city of wonders that appeared to be "swimming in an ocean of light, under the splendid canopy of the sky, showing off its ostentatious blazing colors, as its lakes reflect[ed], in their mirrors, the graceful and fleeting clouds."[171]

The time had now come for Tornel to exploit all of the possibilities that had come with independence to further his political career. There is no record of where he and his family moved to in the capital. However, it is almost certain that he bought at least one of the many properties he would eventually own near the central Plaza Mayor. During October 1821, as he settled in the capital, he continued to work as Santa Anna's personal secretary, promulgating Santa Anna's proclamations such as his *Proclama del Sr. Coronel Santa Anna a los habitantes de Veracruz* and his *Manifesto* on the murder of Colonel Manuel de la Concha.[172] As will be seen in the following chapters, Tornel would play a key role in furthering Santa Anna's political career in three different yet interrelated ways: he acted as Santa Anna's main and most active propagandist; served as Santa Anna's main informer, keeping the *caudillo* abreast of the latest developments in the capital whenever Santa Anna retired to his hacienda in Veracruz; and became one of Santa Anna's shrewdest organizers of conspiracies, plotting and planning almost all of the revolts or *pronunciamientos* by which Santa Anna came back to power after 1833. It is therefore interesting to note that as early as 1821, only a year after having met Santa Anna, Tornel was ensuring that his virtues were publicized in the capital. In the introduction he inserted in the pamphlet containing Santa Anna's *Proclama*, he stated in unequivocal terms that Santa Anna was "a young immortal" who was both "brave and moderate, who does not fear death, yet fears despotism." Claiming that he had been a personal "witness of [Santa Anna's] glories," a "companion of his fatigues," and one who "had been honored by this hero with his friendship," it was his "duty to remind the Mother-Country of how much it owes [to this great man] and of what he was capable of offering [the nation] at the tender age of twenty-five [*sic*]."[173]

Moreover, he persevered as Santa Anna's main propagandist in the capital, regardless of the fact that Santa Anna ignored his advice in 1822 and went on to play a key role in provoking the circumstances that led to Iturbide's abdication. When Santa Anna was taken to court on 18 August 1823 for his federalist revolt of San Luis Potosí (5 June 1823), Tornel attended the trial and defended his friend on the basis that his actions during the assault of the Spanish garrison in Veracruz (7 July 1821) made him a national hero, something that could not be overlooked or forgotten. He protested that "generals Don Miguel Barragán, Don Luis Cortázar, Don Antonio León and others had preceded General Santa Anna with revolutionary proclamations that had not been seen as scandalous and had not merited even the smallest of punishments."[174] It would be unjust to condemn Santa Anna to imprisonment when other generals, less worthy than the *caudillo jarocho*, had not even been subjected to the humiliation of a trial. Santa Anna was eventually pardoned on 22 March 1824[175] and subsequently was posted to Yucatán as the new commander general of the province (18 May 1824–30 April 1825).

In addition to the pamphlets he published in praise of Santa Anna and the role he played in defending him during the trial, after he settled in the capital, Tornel displayed his belief in ensuring that the *caudillo*'s image was not tainted or used in vain again in January 1824, when he went in person to the convent of Belemitas where General José María Lobato's rebels were entrenched and struck Santa Anna's name of Lobato's Plan of 23 January. Lobato, at the head of the Mexico City guard, demanded the removal of the alleged Spanish sympathizers Miguel Domínguez and José Mariano Michelena from the supreme executive power (which replaced Iturbide with a triumvirate at the head of the nation, while the Constituent Congress prepared what would become the 1824 Constitution [1823–1824]), and the removal of all European Spaniards from public office, stating that Santa Anna supported his mutiny. According to Tornel, Lobato had the cheek not only to lie about Santa Anna's intentions in order to give his *pronunciamiento* more prestige, but also went as far as forging Santa Anna's signature. Thus, following Santa Anna's orders, Tornel did the proper thing and forcefully disassociated Santa Anna from the revolt.[176] To quote Anna, "The mutiny almost immediately began to buckle when on the following day Antonio López de Santa Anna issued a flurry of public statements insisting that, although he had been listed as one of the mutineers, he was loyal to the Congress."[177]

In brief, apart from becoming Santa Anna's propagandist in Mexico City, Tornel spent the first years of Independent Mexico (1821–1824)—the years in which Iturbide rose to and fell from power and those in which the emperor was replaced by a triumvirate that supervised the Constituent Congress in its major task of drafting the 1824 Constitution—working as a bureaucrat in the Ministry of War.[178] In November 1821, after surviving an assault in which his life was threatened with a knife,[179] he became a clerk in the Ministry of War, a post he retained until 20 December 1825.[180]

There is little information on what Tornel actually did as a clerk in the Ministry of War. However, the accounts that exist of the role he played as *oficial segundo-primero* give the impression that he worked hard, was respected by the people who worked with him, and was actively involved in the composition of the *Memorias de Guerra*, or annual ministerial reports that were presented by the various ministers of war during the four years in which he served as a government official.

Antonio de Medina y Miranda, minister of war in 1821 and 1822, stated on 22 June 1822, "Tornel has executed everything I have asked him to do, to my satisfaction; he has worked under my immediate orders on the annual ministerial reports of the Ministry of War and Marine, and in other delicate matters, working even on days when the ordinances did not compel him to do so."[181] José Cacho, Medina y Miranda's successor, went on to confirm on 30 July 1823 that "the knowledge of his enlightened ideas encouraged his leaders to trust him with many difficult and interesting affairs, and his hard work demonstrated that he possessed moderation, reserve and was gifted with an excellent talent [for such tasks]."[182] José Joaquín de Herrera y Ricardos, minister of war in 1824, appears to have been equally pleased with Tornel's work. On 16 December he wrote:

All the time he was under my orders in the Ministry of War and Marine, he executed his work to my satisfaction, his desk was one of the ones which was always in order and up to date, due to his zeal and efficiency, and similarly, all of the tasks which he was requested to carry out were done with alacrity. Equally satisfied with his aptitude and his talent, I trusted him with the preparation of the annual ministerial report that was presented to the sovereign congress.[183]

Manuel de Mier y Terán, minister of war in 1825, expressed the same views as his predecessors on 22 August:

Every day he proved to be more worthy of the tasks which were assigned to his section, whether they concerned weapons, engines and artillery, or the extraordinary affairs which, being strictly confidential, were assigned to him because of the circumspection and delicacy I observed in him at all times; as a result of this and because of his outstanding talent and the constant work he dedicates to sustaining it, he merited not only my gratitude and admiration but also that of the Supremo Poder Ejecutivo, among whose members I noticed a great respect towards Tornel for his services and that he was thought of in the most honorific of terms.[184]

The image of Tornel provided in these accounts is one that will be looked into in detail further on. Basically, it would appear that he took his first job very seriously. He is described as having worked after hours and as having been efficient and talented. Everything would appear to indicate that he succeeded in earning himself the trust of each of the ministers who dealt with him. Proof lies in the statements that he was assigned tasks of great delicacy, as well as the important duty of preparing the *Memorias de Guerra*, which contained the essence of the ministry's policies regarding the state of the Mexican army.

In many ways, these four years as a clerk in the Ministry of War were to serve as his apprenticeship. It can be presumed that they acted as an ideal induction for later years—that he learned the inside mechanisms and methods of the Ministry of War and developed a passion for the ministry he was to hold on six different occasions during his life. To a certain extent more significant, these four years also provided him with the chance to make himself known, as well as get to know those influential figures in Mexican politics that in years to come were to determine, at least partially, the course of history. By the summer of 1824 he was ready to take on a far more important post as the president's personal secretary and adviser. By 1826 he would be considered as a potential candidate for the presidency, when the next presidential elections took place in 1828.

NOTES

1. Archivo de la Parroquia de San Miguel, Orizaba, Veracruz (henceforth referred to as APSM): *Libro de bautismos de españoles* (1795); María del Carmen Vázquez Mantecón, *La palabra del poder. Vida pública de José María Tornel (1795–1853)* (Mexico City: UNAM, 1997), p. 29.

2. The peak of Orizaba, the Hill of the Star, is the highest in Mexico. Alexander von Humboldt calculated its height at 5,295 meters during his notorious journey of 1803–1804. See Alexandre de Humboldt, *Essai politique sur le Royaume de la Nouvelle-Espagne*, vol. 1 (Paris: Imp. de J. H. Stone, 1811), p. 38. Its actual height is 5,747 meters; see Peter Bakewell, *A History of Latin America. Empires and Sequels 1450–1930* (Malden and Oxford: Blackwell Publishers, 1997), p. 3. Its striking view from the coast features in almost all of the travelogues that were written in the nineteenth century. For examples of descriptions of the volcano, see: Henry George Ward, *México en 1827* (Mexico City: Fondo de Cultura Económica, 1995), p. 426; Madame Calderón de la Barca, *Life in Mexico* (London: Century, 1987), p. 37. One of the most lyrical descriptions belongs to Waddy Thompson, *Recollections of Mexico* (New York: Wiley and Putnam, 1847), pp. 1–2: "Few sights can be more grand and imposing than the mountain of Orizaba, as seen from the sea. . . . The first view which I had of it was literally a glimpse, for it was difficult to distinguish the mountain from the clouds which surrounded it. I can conceive of nothing which combines more of the sublime and beautiful than this lofty mountain, 'with its diadem of snow', seen from on board a ship of war; a union of all the grandeur and sublimity of a lofty mountain with the vastness and the power of the ocean, and the symmetry and beauty of one of the noblest structures of man."

3. J. M. Tornel y Mendívil, *Oración pronunciada por el Coronel José María Tornel, diputado al congreso de la unión, vice-presidente de la compañía lancaster-*

iana de México, socio de número de la academia de legislación y economía de la misma ciudad, y corresponsal de la de amigos del país de Zacatecas, en la plaza mayor de la capital de la federación, el día 16 de septiembre de 1827, por acuerdo de la junta de ciudadanos que promovió la mayor solemnidad del aniversario de nuestra gloriosa independencia (Mexico City: Imp. del Águila, 1827), p. 10.

4. His full name was Patricio Julián José Tornel Ramos.

5. Years later, in 1833, Pedro Lemus, in a particularly vitriolic attack on Tornel, had a dig at him for belonging to a shopkeeper's family and, by default, for being a pretentious nouveau-riche: "Ignoro por qué habrá empezado Tornel trayendo a colación el TIEMPO SANTO DEL CÓLERA MORBUS, si ha sido esto por el solo gusto de escribir con CH o si no es más que alguna de las AGUDEZAS con que solía divertir a sus marchantes, cuando vendía aceite de pavos y colectaba el fondo de bulas de Naolinco." *La Columna*, 28 September 1833. Naolinco is a small town 32 kilometers away from Xalapa, in the state of Veracruz.

6. Archivo Histórico Militar (henceforth referred to as AHM), Exp. XI/III/I-93, José Joaquín de Herrera to Tornel, 10 January 1823.

7. *Diario del Gobierno*, 10 November 1836.

8. The French traveler Mathieu de Fossey stated, rather surprisingly, in his 1857 travelogue *Le Mexique* (Paris: Plon, 1857), that Tornel was of French origins (accounting for the ease with which he could read and understand the French language) and that his original surname was Tournelle. This assertion is repeated in Hubert Howe Bancroft, *History of Mexico*, vol. 5 (San Francisco: A. L. Bancroft & Co., 1885), and again in Nancy Nicholas Barker, *The French Experience in Mexico, 1821–1861: A History of Constant Misunderstanding* (Chapel Hill: University of North Carolina Press, 1979), where she notes on p. 53: "The new minister of war, General José María Tornel, despite the French origin of his family, was notoriously ill-disposed to French commerce." However, neither María del Carmen Vázquez Mantecón nor I have found any evidence to support this view. See Vázquez Mantecón, *La palabra del poder*, pp. 30–31.

9. Brian R. Hamnett, *Raíces de la insurgencia en México. Historia regional, 1750–1824* (Mexico City: Fondo de Cultura Económica, 1990), p. 37.

10. APSM: "Acta de Bodas," Francisco Cantero and Dolores Tornel, 30 May 1819.

11. It was the same businessmen who had succeeded in financing the road from Mexico City to Toluca at the end of the eighteenth century and beginning of the nineteenth who were hoping to build a modern road along the Nopaluca, San Andrés, Orizaba, Córdoba, Cotastla route from Puebla to Veracruz. However, in 1804, the influential businessmen of Veracruz who had country houses in Xalapa, where they spent the months in which there were yellow fever (*vómito negro*) epidemics in the port, succeeded in influencing Iturrigaray's new Real Tribunal del Consulado so that the road was built following the Xalapa route. At the time of Humboldt's visit, construction of the road was already under way under the direction of the engineer M. García Conde (no doubt a relative of the García Conde brothers, who would join the political class of Independent Mexico in later years). Humboldt, *Essai politique*, vol. 2, pp. 685–688. Both *Xalapa* and *Jalapa* are acceptable ways of spelling the city's name. For reasons of consistency and in line with the spelling favored by *xalapeños* today, I have chosen to write *Xalapa* with an *X* throughout this book.

12. Francisco de Ajofrín, "Diario del viaje que por orden de la sagrada Congregación de Propaganda Fide hice a la América Septentrional en compañía de fray Fermín de Olite, religioso lego y de mi provincia de Castilla," in Ana Laura Delgado (ed.), *Cien viajeros en Veracruz. Crónicas y relatos, vol. 2: 1755–1816* (Veracruz: Gobierno del Estado de Veracruz, 1992), p. 58.

13. Ibid., p. 367.

14. Hans Gadow, *Through Southern Mexico* (London: Witherby and Co., 1908), p. 28.

15. Humboldt provides a vivid description of the flora of the area, noting the abundance of sweet gum trees, satin walnuts, American gooseberries, arbutes, strawberry trees, bastard plantains, banana trees, black bryonies, mandrakes, rough bindweed, prickly ivy, greenbriers, sarsaparillas, and jalap plants. Humboldt, *Essai politique*, vol. 1, pp. lxxix–lxxx, 271; vol. 2, pp. 362, 442–443.

16. José María Tornel, "La Providencia en el Nuevo Mundo," *El Mosaico Mexicano* 5 (1841). The opening paragraph of the article, on p. 529, exemplifies his vision of nature and the way the environment in which he grew up in, on the foothills of the Peak of Orizaba, was a strong influence in his writing: "Yo me remonto a las cumbres del Chimborazo, del Pinchincha, del magnífico Cotopaxi, del Orizava (sic) y del erguido Popocatepetl, y cercano ya a tu excelso trono, oigo mugir las tempestades, veo brillar los relámpagos, y que se lanza el rayo bajo mis pies. Allí observo sin telescopio el curso luminoso de los astros, respiro un aire sereno y puro, noto a lo lejos mares dilatados y que corren grandes ríos, como hilos de plata, en campos de esmeralda. ¿Dónde están los hombres? Son sus ciudades puntos imperceptibles, leves manchas en la extensa superficie de la tierra. ¿Y ellos? Átomos inteligentes, valiosos en la presencia de los seres, nada delante de Dios."

17. Humboldt, *Essai politique*, vol. 2, p. 438.

18. Ibid., vol. 1, p. 271.

19. Ibid., vol. 2, pp. 426, 431.

20. Ibid., pp. 444–445.

21. For examples, see in particular: José María Tornel, *Manifestación presentada a la cámara de senadores por el General José María Tornel, apoderado de las diputaciones de cosecheros de tabaco de las ciudades de Jalapa y Orizaba, pidiendo la reprobación del acuerdo sobre amortización de la moneda de cobre, por medio del estanco de aquel ramo* (Mexico City: Imp. de I. Cumplido, 1841), and *Vindicación del General José María Tornel, administrador de la renta del tabaco del departamento de Veracruz, por la ligereza con que se le ha acusado de omisión en el cumplimiento de sus deberes, ante la dirección general de la renta* (Orizaba: Imp. de Mendarte, 1842).

22. Vázquez Mantecón, *La palabra del poder*, p. 31.

23. AHM: Exp. XI/III/I-93, Report by J. Velázquez de León, "Campañas y acciones de guerra donde se ha hallado," Mexico City, 1839.

24. Ruth R. Olivera and Liliane Crété, *Life in Mexico under Santa Anna, 1822–1855* (Norman: University of Oklahoma Press, 1991), pp. 224–225.

25. Dorothy Tanck Estrada, *La educación ilustrada, 1786–1836* (Mexico City: El Colegio de México, 1984), p. 34.

26. Charles A. Hale, *El liberalismo mexicano en la época de Mora, 1821–1853* (Mexico City: Siglo XXI, 1987), p. 301.

27. *El Mexicano*, 1 June 1839.

28. Michael P. Costeloe, *The Central Republic in Mexico, 1835–1846*: Hombres de Bien *in the Age of Santa Anna* (Cambridge: Cambridge University Press, 1993), p. 19.

29. Vázquez Mantecón, *La palabra del poder*, p. 33.

30. John Lynch, *The Spanish American Revolutions, 1808–1826* (New York: Norton, 1973), p. 309. For the *Guadalupes*, see Ernesto de la Torre Villar (ed.), *Los Guadalupes y la independencia* (Mexico City: Porrúa, 1985), and Virginia Guedea, *En busca de un gobierno alterno: Los Guadalupes de México* (Mexico City: UNAM, 1992).

31. AHM: Exp. XI/III/I-93, letter by Manuel Arguelles, Jalapa, 31 August 1826.

32. Ibid.

33. Centro de Estudios Sobre la Universidad (henceforth referred to as CESU), Hemeroteca Nacional de México, Fondo Antiguo del Colegio de San Ildefonso, Caja 101, Exp. 77, Correspondencia Rectoría, draft of letter, by Castañiza to Viceroy Calleja, 24 April 1814.

34. Having said this, as Juan Ortiz Escamilla has shown in his recent article, "Las élites de las capitales novohispanas ante la guerra civil de 1810," *Historia Mexicana* 46: 2 (1996): 325–357, a surprisingly high proportion of Creoles who belonged to the more important urban elites of New Spain did in fact support the insurgency during the first five months of the war of independence.

35. Lynch, *The Spanish American Revolutions*, p. 311.

36. For an in-depth study of the impact the Bourbon reforms had on the Mexican church and, in particular, in Hidalgo's diocese, see: David Brading, *Church and State in Bourbon Mexico: The Diocese of Michoacán 1749–1810* (Cambridge: Cambridge University Press, 1994). Also see William B. Taylor, *Magistrates of the Sacred. Priests and Parishioners in Eighteenth-Century Mexico* (Stanford: Stanford University Press, 1996).

37. For Hidalgo, see: Rafael Moreno M., "La teologia ilustrada de Hidalgo," Luis Villoro, "Hidalgo: violencia y libertad," and Manuel Carrera Stampa, "Hidalgo y su plan de operaciones," in Virginia Guedea (ed.), *La revolución de independencia* (Mexico City: El Colegio de México, 1995), pp. 40–55, 56–72, 73–87, respectively. Also see Luis Castillo Ledón, *Hidalgo, la vida del héroe*, 2 vols. (Mexico City: INEHRM, 1985), and Hugh M. Hamill, Jr., *The Hidalgo Revolt: Prelude to Mexican Independence* (Westport, CT: Greenwood Press, 1970).

38. Lynch, *The Spanish American Revolutions*, p. 297.

39. For a compelling study of the impact that the maize shortages had on the 1810 revolutionary movement, see: Enrique Florescano, *Precios del maiz y crisis agrícolas en México, 1708–1810* (Mexico City: El Colegio de México, 1969).

40. Hamnett, *Raíces de la insurgencia*, p. 43.

41. For Creole patriotism, see David Brading, *The Origins of Mexican Nationalism* (Cambridge: CLAS, 1985).

42. Lynch, *The Spanish American Revolutions*, p. 297.

43. Taylor, *Magistrates of the Sacred*, p. 449.

44. Brading, *Church and State*, p. 63.

45. Lynch, *The Spanish American Revolutions*, p. 306.

46. An example of this historical interpretation can be found in the speech

Bustamante wrote for the inauguration of the Congress of Chilpancingo: "¡Genios de Moctezuma, de Cacamitzin, de Cuauhtimotzin, de Xicotencatl y de Catzonzi, celebrad, como celebrasteis el mitote en que fuisteis acometidos por la pérfida espada de Alvarado, este dichoso instante en que vuestros hijos se han reunido para vengar vuestros desafueros y ultrajes y librarse de las garras de la tiranía y fanatismo, que los iba a sorber para siempre! Al 12 de agosto de 1521 sucedió el 14 de septiembre de 1813." Quoted in Victoriano Salado Álvarez, *La vida azarosa y romántica de Carlos María de Bustamante* (Mexico City: Editorial Jus, 1968), p. 157.

47. Bustamante's glorification of pre-Hispanic Mexico can be found in the following exemplary texts: *Galería de antiguos príncipes mexicanos* (Puebla: Oficina del Gobierno Imperial, 1821); *Juguetillo Nono. Antiguedades mexicanas. Historia del primer monarca conocido en el reyno Tulteco* (Veracruz: Imp. Constitucional, 1821); *Manifiesto histórico a las naciones y pueblos del Anáhuac* (Mexico City: Imp. de Valdés, 1823); and *Para inmortalizar el valor heroico de los indios cascanes por causa de su libertad de la tiranía española* (Mexico City: Imp. del Águila, 1827).

48. Tornel, *Oración pronunciada . . . el día 16 de septiembre de 1827*, p. 8.

49. Brading, *The Origins of Mexican Nationalism*, pp. 81–88.

50. Tornel, *Oración pronunciada . . . el día 16 de septiembre de 1827*, p. 4.

51. José María Tornel, *Manifiesto del origen, causas, progresos y estado de la revolución del imperio mexicano, con relación a la antigua España* (Puebla and Mexico City: Imp. de Ontiveros, 1821), p. 3.

52. José María Tornel, *La aurora de México* (Mexico City: Imp. de Celestino de la Torre, 1821), p. 1.

53. José María Tornel, *El grito de la patria* (Puebla: Imp. de Pedro de la Rosa, 1821), p. 1.

54. Tornel, *Manifiesto del origen, causas, progresos*, p. 4.

55. John Lynch (ed.), *Latin American Revolutions, 1808–1826: Old and New World Origins* (Norman: University of Oklahoma Press, 1994), p. 11.

56. Lynch, *The Spanish American Revolutions*, p. 300.

57. Tornel, *Manifiesto del origen, causas, progresos*, p. 10.

58. Ibid.

59. David A. Brading, *Prophecy and Myth in Mexican History* (Cambridge: CLAS, 1984), p. 38.

60. For the 1808 coup, see: Virginia Guedea, "El golpe de estado de 1808," *Universidad de México* 48 (September 1991): 21–24.

61. Brading, *Prophecy and Myth*, p. 38.

62. Tornel, *Manifiesto del origen, causas, progresos*, p. 5.

63. Lynch (ed.), *Latin American Revolutions*, p. 27.

64. For the impact of ideas; see: Luis Villoro, *El proceso ideológico de la revolución de la independencia* (Mexico City: UNAM, 1967), and François-Xavier Guerra, *Modernidad e independencias. Ensayos sobre las revoluciones hispánicas* (Mexico City: Fondo de Cultura Económica, 1993).

65. See María del Carmen Vázquez Mantecón, "La patria y la nación en el discurso de José María Tornel, 1821–1852," *Tiempos de América* 1 (1997): 131–140.

66. For the influence the *philosophes* had on Mora's thought, see: Hale, *El liberalismo mexicano*, pp. 42–73.

67. Tornel, *La aurora de México*, pp. 1–2.

68. "El Lord Byron a los napolitanos en 1823. Estancias," trans. and with an introduction by José María Tornel, *El Mosaico Mexicano* 6 (1841): 73–76.

69. Elena Poniatowska, *Fuerte es el silencio* (Mexico City: Ediciones Era, 1989), p. 45.

70. See his account of the attack on Guanajuato in Lucas Alamán, *Historia de México*, vol. 1 (Mexico City: Fondo de Cultura Económica, 1985), pp. 425–444. The impact that the violence of insurgency had on Alamán is perfectly expressed in the following lines: " 'Viva la Virgen de Guadalupe y mueran los gachupines'. Reunión monstruosa de la religión con el asesinato y el saqueo: grito de muerte y de desolación, que habiéndolo oído mil y mil veces en los primeros días de mi juventud, después de tantos años resuena todavía en mis oídos con un eco pavoroso" (p. 379).

71. Hale, *El liberalismo mexicano*, pp. 25–28.

72. Lynch, *The Spanish American Revolutions*, p. 313.

73. AHM: Exp. XI/III/I-93, Velázquez de León, "Campañas y acciones de guerra."

74. In the introduction to his *Fastos militares de iniquidad, barbarie y despotismo del gobierno español, ejecutados en las villas de Orizaba y Córdoba en la guerra de once años, por causa de la independencia y libertad de la nación mexicana, hasta que se consumió la primera por los Tratados de Córdoba, celebrados por d. Agustin de Iturbide y d. Juan de O'Donojú. Dálos a luz como documentos que apoyan las relaciones del cuadro histórico de la revolución y a sus espensas D. José María Tornel* (Mexico City: Imp. de Ignacio Cumplido, 1843), p. iv, Tornel states that while his wife suffered the torments of witnessing the cruelty of the Spanish division in Orizaba, "su esposo se hallaba en las filas de los patriotas." In other words, they must have been married before he joined the insurgents.

75. Ibid.

76. She is also mentioned in a poem about independence by Juan Rodríguez Cuahutli, *A la señora doña Agustina Bonilla esposa del Sr. D. José María Tornel*, which carries the following dedication: "Hoy señora que tu esposo/Y mi siempre caro amigo/Es objeto de la intriga/Del más infame partido:/Y que tú también das pruebas/De un heroico patriotismo/Afectuoso te dedica/Mi musa, el siguiente himno." The poem is a loose paper, dated in Mexico City, 14 September 1828, held in the Colección Lafragua, Biblioteca Nacional de México.

77. Tornel, *Fastos militares*, p. iv.

78. The details regarding his military activities are taken from: AHM: Exp. XI/III/I–93, Velázques de León, "Campañas y acciones de guerra."

79. El Amigo de la Libertad, *Último golpe de paz al ciudadano Tornel* (Mexico City: n.p., 1826), p. 23.

80. José María Tornel, *Breve reseña histórica de los acontecimientos más notables de la nación mexicana desde el año de 1821 hasta nuestros dias* (Mexico City: INEHRM, 1985), p. 23. Tornel's presence at the battle of Puruarán is further confirmed in a report certified by General Ramón Rayón on 11 June 1824 inserted in José María Tornel, "Esplicación de los documentos con que se quiere manchar el honor del Coronel José María Tornel y se prueban con otros sus servicios y padecimientos en obsequio de la Patria." *El Aguila Mexicana*, Supplement, 2 September 1826, p. 4.

81. For detailed accounts of the battle of Puruarán, see: Lucas Alamán, *Historia de México*, vol. 4, pp. 10–13; and Carlos María de Bustamante, *Cuadro histórico de la revolución mexicana*, vol. 2 (Mexico City: Fondo de Cultura Económica, 1985), pp. 419–422.

82. Bustamante, *Cuadro histórico*, vol. 2, p. 419.

83. Tornel, *Breve reseña histórica*, p. 23.

84. José María Tornel, "Esplicación de los documentos con que se quiere manchar el honor del Coronel José María Tornel y se prueban con otros sus servicios y padecimientos en obsequio de la Patria," *El Aguila Mexicana*, Supplement, 2 September 1826, pp. 1–2.

85. AHM: Exp. XI/III/I-93, report by Colonel Diego Rubín de Celis, Mexico City, 25 October 1821.

86. Tornel, "Esplicación," p. 2.

87. AHM: Exp. XI/III/I-93, report by Colonel Diego Rubín de Celis.

88. Tornel, "Esplicación," p. 2.

89. *Correo de la Federación Mexicana*, 23 June 1828.

90. Tornel, "Esplicación," p. 2.

91. Ibid.

92. AHM: Exp. XI/III/I-93, report by José Ignacio Inclán, 24 July 1823.

93. Ernesto de la Torre, *La independencia de México* (Madrid: Editorial Mapfre, 1992), p. 99.

94. Vázquez Mantecón, *La palabra del poder*, p. 32.

95. Tornel, "Esplicación," p. 2.

96. Ibid., p. 1.

97. CESU: Fondo Antiguo del Colegio de San Ildefonso, Caja 101, Exp. 77, Correspondencia Rectoría, letter by the Viceroy Calleja to the Marqués de Castañiza, 14 May 1814.

98. Tornel, "Esplicación," p. 2.

99. CESU: Fondo Antiguo del Colegio de San Ildefonso, Caja 101, Exp. 77, Correspondencia Rectoría, letter by the Marqués de Castañiza to Viceroy Calleja, 24 April 1814.

100. Ibid.

101. Tornel, "Esplicación," p. 2.

102. Ibid.

103. AHM: Exp. XI/III/I-93, report by Manuel de Ordaz Bonilla, Puebla, 22 September 1826.

104. Ibid.

105. AHM: Exp. XI/III/I-93, report by Juan Nepomuceno Pérez, 23 September 1826.

106. AHM: Exp. XI/III/I-93, report by Manuel de Ordaz Bonilla, Puebla, 22 September 1826.

107. AHM: Exp. XI/III/I-93, report by Manuel Arguelles, Jalapa, 31 August 1826.

108. De la Torre, *La independencia de México*, p. 99.

109. Ibid.

110. AHM: Exp. XI/III/I-93, report by Manuel Arguelles, Jalapa, 31 August 1826.

111. AHM: Exp. XI/III/I-93, report by Colonel Bernardo María de Pérez y Ar-guelles, 18 August 1826.

112. AHM: Exp. XI/III/I-93, report by General Francisco Miranda, 13 September 1826.

113. AHM: Exp. XI/III/I-93, report by Colonel Bernardo María de Pérez y Ar-guelles, 18 August 1826.

114. Tornel's *Fastos militares* contains a detailed account of Colonel Hevia's bloody deeds in Orizaba. It was also Hevia, who captured and sentenced María Agustina's father to death in 1814.

115. AHM: Exp. XI/III/I-93, Velázquez de León, "Campañas y acciones de guerra."

116. Christon I. Archer, "Politicization of the Army of New Spain during the War of Independence, 1810–1821," in Jaime E. Rodríguez O. (ed.), *The Evolution of the Mexican Political System* (Wilmington, DE: Scholarly Resources, 1993), p. 34. Archer's article is reprinted in Jaime E. Rodriguez O. (ed.), *The Origins of Mexican National Politics, 1808–1847* (Wilmington, DE: Scholarly Resources, 1997), pp. 11–38.

117. Ibid., p. 42.

118. Lynch, *The Spanish American Revolutions*, p. 318.

119. Archer, "Politicization of the Army," p. 42.

120. Josefina Zoraida Vázquez, "Iglesia, Ejército y Centralismo," *Historia Mexicana* 39:1 (1989): 211.

121. Christon I. Archer, "The Young Antonio López de Santa Anna: Veracruz Counterinsurgent and Incipient Caudillo," in Judith Ewell and William H. Beezley (eds.), *The Human Tradition in Latin America: The Nineteenth Century* (Wilmington, DE: Scholarly Resources, 1992), p. 9.

122. Ibid.

123. Ibid., pp. 11–13.

124. Wilfrid Hardy Callcott, *Santa Anna. The Story of an Enigma Who Once Was Mexico* (Hamden, CT: Archon Books, 1964), p. 19.

125. Enrique González Pedrero, *País de un solo hombre: el México de Santa Anna*, vol. 1 (Mexico City: Fondo de Cultura Económica, 1993), pp. 55–56.

126. Antonio López de Santa Anna, *Mi historia militar y politica. 1810–1874. Memorias inéditas*, in Genaro García (ed.), *Documentos inéditos o muy raros para la historia de México*, vol. 59 (Mexico City: Porrúa, 1974), p. 6.

127. Callcott, *Santa Anna*, p. 20.

128. González Pedrero, *País de un solo hombre*, p. 65.

129. John Lynch, *Caudillos in Spanish America, 1800–1850* (Oxford: Clarendon Press, 1992), p. 316.

130. Callcott, *Santa Anna*, p. 20.

131. AHM: Exp. XI/III/I-93, report by General Francisco Miranda, 13 September 1826.

132. Archer, "Politicization of the Army," p. 43.

133. Santa Anna, *Mi historia militar y politica*, p. 6.

134. González Pedrero, *País de un solo hombre*, p. 66.

135. AHM: Exp. XI/III/I-93, Antonio López de Santa Anna to Agustín de Itur-bide, Orizaba, 26 February 1821(?!). The date of this letter is surprising since Santa Anna did not join Iturbide's Army of the Three Guarantees until April 1821.

136. AHM: Exp. XI/III/I-93, José María Tornel to Agustín de Iturbide, Orizaba, n.d.

137. José María Tornel, *Valor y constancia es nuestra divisa* (Puebla: Imp. de Pedro de la Rosa, 1821), pp. 1–3.

138. Tornel, *El grito de la patria*, p. 1.

139. Tornel, *Manifiesto del origen, causas, progresos*, pp. 1, 9, 11.

140. Vázquez Mantecón, *La palabra del poder*, p. 34.

141. Tornel, *La aurora de México*, p. 2.

142. AHM: Exp. XI/III/I-93, Agustín de Iturbide to Tornel, Mexico City, 12 October 1822.

143. Timothy E. Anna, *El imperio de Iturbide* (Mexico City: Alianza Editorial, 1991), p. 27.

144. See Will Fowler, "El pensamiento político de los santanistas, 1821–1855," in Luis Jáuregui and José Antonio Serrano Ortega (eds.), *Historia y nación, vol. 2: Política y diplomacia en el siglo XIX mexicano* (Mexico City: El Colegio de México, 1998), pp. 186–187.

145. Anna, *El imperio de Iturbide*, pp. 39–47.

146. José María Tornel, *Discurso pronunciado en la alameda de la ciudad de México en el día 27 de septiembre de 1850* (Mexico City: Imp. de Ignacio Cumplido, 1850), pp. 6–7, 12.

147. Tornel, *Breve reseña histórica*, pp. 6–7.

148. Ibid., p. 7.

149. Ibid., p. 6.

150. Ibid., p. 9.

151. Tornel, *Manifestación presentada a la cámara de senadores por el Gral. José María Tornel apoderado de las diputaciones de cosecheros de tabaco*, p. 6.

152. Niceto de Zamacois, *Historia de Méjico, desde sus tiempos más remotos hasta nuestros días*, vol. 12 (Barcelona: J. F. Parres y Cía, 1879), p. 145. A photo of the engraved poem is included in Vázquez Mantecón, *La palabra del poder*, just after p. 118.

153. Anna, *El imperio de Iturbide*, p. 86.

154. José María Bocanegra, *Memorias para la historia de México independiente, 1822–1846*, vol. 1 (Mexico City: Fondo de Cultura Económica, 1987), p. 62.

155. José María Tornel, *Derechos de Fernando VII al trono del imperio mexicano* (Mexico City: n.p., 1822), p. 12.

156. Bocanegra, *Memorias*, vol. 1, p. 63.

157. Will Fowler, *Mexico in the Age of Proposals, 1821–1853* (Westport, CT: Greenwood Press, 1998), p. 221.

158. Tornel, *Derechos de Fernando VII al trono del imperio mexicano*, p. 7.

159. Anna, *El imperio de Iturbide*, pp. 113–115.

160. Tornel, *Derechos de Fernando VII al trono del imperio mexicano*, p. 12.

161. Tornel, *Breve reseña histórica*, p. 9.

162. *Gaceta del gobierno imperial de México*, 21 December 1822.

163. Ibid.

164. Bocanegra, *Memorias*, vol. 1, p. 207.

165. Fowler, *Mexico in the Age of Proposals*, pp. 221–222.

166. Tornel, *Breve reseña histórica*, p. 12.

167. Timothy E. Anna, *Forging Mexico, 1821–1835* (Lincoln: University of Nebraska Press, 1998), p. 101.

168. José María Tornel, *Discurso pronunciado . . . el día 27 de septiembre de 1850*, p. 11.

169. Ward, *México en 1827*, p. 442.

170. Thompson, *Recollections of Mexico*, p. 37.

171. Marcos Arróniz, *Manual del viajero en México* (Mexico City: Instituto Mora, 1991), p. 221.

172. Antonio López de Santa Anna, *Manifiesto que hace público el teniente coronel D. A. López de Santa Anna, comandante general de la provincia de Veracruz, sobre lo ocurrido con la persona del coronel D. Manuel de la Concha, asesinado al amanecer del día 5 del corriente en los extramuros de la villa de Jalapa, camino de Veracruz* (Puebla: Imp. Pedro de la Rosa, 1821), and Antonio López de Santa Anna, *Proclama del sr. coronel D. Antonio López de Santa Anna a los habitantes de Veracruz en ocupación de aquella plaza* (Mexico City: Imp. de Mariano Ontíveros, 1821).

173. Santa Anna, *Proclama*, p. 1.

174. Tornel, *Breve reseña histórica*, p. 74.

175. González Pedrero, *País de un solo hombre*, p. 266.

176. Tornel, *Breve reseña histórica*, pp. 74–75.

177. Anna, *Forging Mexico*, p. 197.

178. For an excellent study on bureaucrats at the time, see Linda Arnold, *Burocracia y burócratas en México, 1742–1835* (Mexico City: Grijalbo, 1991).

179. Tornel, "Esplicación," p. 3.

180. *El Aguila Mexicana*, 26 December 1825.

181. Ibid.

182. Ibid.

183. Ibid.

184. Ibid.

2

From Hope to Disenchantment: The Emergence of the Professional Politician (1824–1829)

A TIME OF HOPE

The Constituent Congress of 1823–1824 was characterized by the intensity of debate. The main tensions that surfaced among its representatives arose over the extent to which Mexico would become a federal as opposed to a central republic. Moreover, while the aggressive discussions of the Constituent Congress started to favor the claims of the federalists, the triumvirate was actively involved in quelling federalist revolts and *pronunciamientos* throughout the country, with marked military resolution. The end result was, in fact, a compromise in which the federalism of the constitution paradoxically granted considerable power to the central government in Mexico City. The conflict between federalists and centralists, which would polarize the politics of their opposed advocates in subsequent decades, would clearly stem from the ambiguous compromises that were made in the spring of 1824.[1]

Nevertheless, the presidential elections that were organized in the summer of 1824, once the constitution had been completed and accepted, were carried out with a generalized sense of goodwill, hope, and optimism. The progressive nature of the constitution needs to be highlighted. Not even in the United States was there universal male suffrage. The electoral victory of General Guadalupe Victoria was celebrated by radicals and traditionalists alike. The conservative Lucas Alamán would look back at the end of the 1840s and say that "President Victoria found himself . . . in the most prosperous of circumstances: the Republic was enjoying a pe-

riod of peace, the factions had been repressed, and the hope of a happy future burned in everybody's hearts [*lisonjeaba los ánimos de todos*]."[2] The
radical Lorenzo de Zavala stated, in his 1831 history of the first national
decade, that

a Mexican cannot remember this period without experiencing a deep affection born
from the happy circumstances in which the Republic found itself. It seemed as if a
long-lasting government had been established: the parties had gone quiet and the
legislatures proceeded peacefully with the great act of naming the supreme magistrates of the Republic. . . . Who did not foresee then days of glory, prosperity and
liberty? Who did not forecast a glorious and blissful future?[3]

Tornel and Bocanegra shared the hopes and expectations that became
generalized with the adoption of the 1824 Constitution and the electoral
victory of Victoria. An example can be found in Bocanegra's speech of 1
January 1827 when he was acting as president of the Chamber of Deputies:

Let us congratulate ourselves, citizens, for having been able to see amongst us demonstrated that a popular federal representative government is not a dream but a
completed organization, and a perfect system, capable in itself of elevating our men
in their associations of rank, power and notoriety to ones comparable with . . . the
most powerful peoples of the world. . . . In our circumstances the political state of
the republic could not be more promising . . . ; in the states the greatest of harmony
prevails, and under the shadow of peace, abundance grows.[4]

Thus, like the great majority of the political class at the time, Tornel
became a dedicated republican following the fall of Iturbide. Moreover,
unlike those traditionalists who would become monarchists as the hopes
of the 1820s degenerated into the despair of the 1840s, Tornel remained a
republican for the rest of his life. When José María Gutiérrez Estrada published his notorious and extremely controversial 1840 pamphlet in which
he proposed imposing a constitutional monarchy in Mexico with a European prince on the throne,[5] it was Tornel who wrote, in the words of
Bocanegra, the most "exhaustive challenge" to Gutiérrez Estrada's monarchist proposal, analyzing it point by point in the "most logical and impartial way."[6] Apart from questioning Gutiérrez Estrada's sanity in the
particularly vitriolic and witty preface to his "A. D. José María Gutiérrez
Estrada. O sean Algunas observaciones al folleto en que ha proclamado la
destrucción de la república, y el llamamiento al trono mexicano de un
príncipe estrangero," Tornel argued, in a curiously Hegelian fashion, that
republicanism represented the next natural step, following the stage of
monarchism, in political evolution from an age of slavery to one of liberty.
Republicanism was therefore synonymous with progress: "The absolutist
monarchies of Europe collapse before the spirit of our era and become
constitutional [monarchies]; and those that are moderate or constitutional,

invariably become republics."[7] He claimed that much had been achieved since independence, in spite of all the revolts and conflicts that had characterized the first two national decades. Mexican society favored progress. It was thus anachronistic and tortuously reactionary to try to turn the clock back in time, proposing the reestablishment of a monarchy. Moreover, by 1840, the political customs and traditions of the Mexican people had become deeply republican. It would be tyrannical to go against the will of the people. As a high-ranking officer, Tornel could comfortably say that the army was a profoundly republican institution and that he had no doubt that so was the church. He also found a way of excusing the shift that took place among the majority of Mexico's political class (and which he himself effected) in 1823, from defending the monarchy of Iturbide to supporting a republican system, arguing that the imperial experiment had been a necessary, albeit pragmatic, requirement: "There was no contradiction because the conservation of independence was the all-important aim, and the context of the time dictated that we closed our eyes to the means by which the end was achieved."[8] The bottom line was that "the most dignified government, the only one that in terms of universal thought is capable of responding to the need of society to be governed, is the republican one."[9] How else could one account for that universal impulse that throughout history had shown the people to be adamant in their will to correct the incorrigible abuses monarchs were prone to committing, by seeking in republicanism the necessary guarantees for their freedom and happiness? It was absurd to claim, as Gutiérrez Estrada had done, that republicanism could be equated with chaos and degeneration. The United States was a good enough example of how political perfection had been achieved with a republican system.[10] Even in 1852, when Tornel started to enter into negotiations with Alamán's Conservative party over the possibility of forging an alliance that could bring about the return of Santa Anna to power from his exile in Colombia, Tornel continued to portray republicanism as the best form of government: "A republic is the only possible government, because admitting the essential principles of free government, it calls society to order and represses the excesses of violence."[11]

Thus, formerly a supporter of Iturbide and his empire, Tornel moved on with the times, and defined his republicanism further by defending the need for a federalist system on 23 and 24 November 1823 in the "Contestación" he inserted in the newspaper *El Sol*.[12] The key arguments Tornel used to support the creation of a federal political system are the same as those that Timothy E. Anna has developed in his recent study on federalism and the First Federal Republic: that "the Mexican nation was created by the actions of its constituent parts; the states created the nation, not the other way around."[13] Tornel stated that it was absurd to pretend that the army had been exclusively responsible for the achievement of independence. The provincial deputations played a fundamental part in the establishment of their public liberties. Moreover, there was nothing new about federalism. Their political system was already a federalist one in all but name. Therefore, the creation of a federal system did not imply a drastic change, but rather a natural step in political evolution. As an example he noted that the man known as "governor of the State of Jalisco was known before as the *jefe superior político*, and he is even the same person."[14] It was that peaceful a progression. There was nothing brutally destabilizing about it. Moreover, federalism was at the heart of Mexico's bid for independence. After all, one of the main complaints of those Mexican deputies who assisted the Cortes in Madrid in 1820–1821 was that Spain was not prepared to grant deputations to all of its provinces.[15]

Displaying an early belief in representative government, Tornel went on to stress that since it appeared to be obvious that the majority of deputations, town halls, high-ranking officers, and writers were proposing a federalist model, it would be despotic to create a centralist republic that ignored their will. In fact, to ignore the federalists' demands could only lead to conflict. Therefore, it was essential that they had a federal system, because it would bring an end to the tensions that existed between the states and the national power.[16] While Anna has argued that "federalism remains not only the fundamental cement of Mexican nationhood but the instrument by which that nationhood was forged" and that the federalists' "object was to forge a Mexican nation, one based on union, not uniformity"[17] Tornel stated that "unity will be established with a federalist constitution" and went on to claim, quoting Benjamin Constant to substantiate his views, that an edifice could not be built by destroying the components that serve to make it.[18] In 1852, having changed considerably in his political stance and become a staunch defender of centralism, he claimed that the reason for his federalist years was a straightforward reaction against the triumvirate that replaced Iturbide: "The dictatorship of the Mexican Triumvirate became unbearable, and as a last resort, with despair, the federal system was sought; a system everybody was talking about, but which nobody actually understood."[19] Nevertheless, Tornel was writing with a very specific political agenda in 1852, and his retrospective interpretation of certain past events reflected more what he was hoping to achieve in the early 1850s than what he had actually thought in the early 1820s. The young Tornel had become by 1823 both a republican and a federalist. In other words, Tornel sustained, discussed, and explained what Santa Anna proposed through action: the creation of a republic (Plan of Veracruz, 6 December 1822) and the creation of a federal republic (Plan of San Luis Potosí, 5 June 1823).

THE PRESIDENT'S SECRETARY

It was as a republican, a federalist and an *escocés* (a member of the Scottish Rite of Masons)[20] that Tornel started to play a prominent part in

Mexican politics when, in August 1824, General Guadalupe Victoria, one of the presidential candidates, asked Tornel to accompany him, as his personal secretary, in his expedition to quell the revolt in Oaxaca led by Colonel Antonio León and his brother Manuel, who were demanding the expulsion of all Spaniards. According to Alamán, the traditionalist faction represented by Nicolás Bravo knew that it had lost the elections the moment Victoria agreed to go and end the uprising.[21] In contrast, according to Tornel, it was Alamán's and Mier y Terán's decision to send Victoria to Oaxaca because "whatever violent action and side he adopted to end the revolt, it would always be damaging to him, and it would prevent him from assuming the supreme command of the republic."[22] Whether it was Alamán's or Victoria's decision, Victoria left the capital on 8 August with Tornel and his troops and set off to Tehuacán. They succeeded in quelling the revolt without any bloodshed. It was a decisive factor in the victory in the forthcoming election.

The fact that Guadalupe Victoria asked Tornel to accompany him as his personal secretary highlights two important aspects of Victoria's subsequent presidency in terms of his past as an insurgent and his affinities with the state of Veracruz and, by default, Santa Anna and Tornel. Whether Tornel actually saved his life at Puruarán is, in the end, less significant than the fact that they had both fought together with the so-called ancient patriots (those insurgents who fought for independence prior to the Plan of Iguala). One of the repercussions of the fall of Iturbide was that it acted as a deterrent to any ex-royalists who might have considered standing as presidential candidates in 1824. With the resulting temporary marginalization of ex-royalists, the only candidates who were deemed to be eligible for the presidency were old insurgents: Victoria, Nicolás Bravo, and Vicente Guerrero. No doubt the fact that the constitution guaranteed universal male suffrage gave these popular heroes of the war of independence a greater chance of winning than any ex-royalist. Of course, Victoria's advantage was that, unlike Bravo, who gave himself up and accepted the *indulto*, and Guerrero, who, in a way, betrayed the old insurgents by joining forces with Iturbide in 1821, Victoria remained the one insurgent who had neither surrendered to the Spanish authorities nor compromised his original belief in independence by supporting those royalists who had opportunely changed sides in 1821. Tornel was therefore a man he could trust, since he had been close to him during the war of independence and had continued to support the insurgency in Veracruz, where Victoria was at the head of the guerrilla forces in the area, after he had been *indultado*. Moreover, although Victoria was originally from Durango, he became an adopted son of Veracruz after his experience in the war of independence and settled there (with the exception of the four years he served as president).

Santa Anna and the *santanistas* would have two major and deeply influential strongholds of support after 1833: the regular army and the people of Veracruz. These Veracruzan affinities between Victoria and Santa Anna were already present in December 1822 when Victoria joined Santa Anna's Veracruzan revolt against Iturbide. Furthermore, they remained present during his presidency. According to Ruth Solís Vicarte, Victoria was the "strong male" (*varón fuerte*) of the Xalapa-based Masonic society known as the Black Eagle (Gran Legión del Aguila Negra), which had as one of its main goals to bring about the independence of Cuba from Spain.[23] The fact that in 1825, as commander general of Yucatán, the *xalapeño* Santa Anna proposed to lead an expedition to free Cuba from Spain and that Victoria defended Santa Anna's proposal in spite of the fact that the entire political class in the capital (with the notable exception of Tornel) thought it was a completely preposterous idea, suggests that there were clear, albeit hidden, ties among Victoria, Tornel and Santa Anna.

On 4 October 1824 Victoria became the first elected president of the First Federal Republic of Mexico.[24] Tornel became his personal secretary and played this role from August 1824 to October 1828, promulgating the president's decrees, writing his speeches,[25] and playing an active part as one of his main advisers. One question that inevitably arises is to what extent Tornel's advice influenced Victoria's decisions. Was he merely a servant of the president, or was he in a position of power? In the summer of 1828, a pamphlet attributed to Justo Simplicio el Tapado, *Preguntas al Payo del Rosario*, asked this same question: "Are the rogues right in saying that Victoria is Charles the Fourth and that Tornel is Manuelito Godoy? When Señor Victoria has stated that the man of merit he has as his advisor is Tornel, can it be assumed that he said this as a joke or was he being serious? In your view, is the President a wise man?"[26]

Tornel, in his *Breve reseña histórica*, does not offer any indisputable facts as to how he might have influenced Victoria. Nevertheless, there is some evidence of his secret services as well as of the recommendations he made to the president. He claims, for instance, that Victoria "confidentially used his private secretary, Colonel Tornel,"[27] in the various attempts that were made to negotiate an unbiased treaty of commerce with Lionel Harvey, Henry Ward, and James J. Morier who were acting as representatives of the British government toward the beginning of 1825. He claims that Victoria offered Manuel Gómez Pedraza "a part in his administration, advised by his secretary Tornel."[28] Tornel also states that he was the one to convince Victoria of the need to include Miguel Ramos Arizpe in their cabinet. He says that, having belonged to the Scottish Rite of Masons, he tried to persuade Victoria not to allow the regularization of the Rite of York, because "such associations, even when they proclaim their loyalty to the government, soon start to disturb its actions and end up judging it."[29] He failed, however, to convince Victoria, who believed in "middle of the road policies."[30] There is no proof that he was responsible for Victoria's decisions. Nevertheless, he was in frequent, if not daily, consultation with the president, and he must have known what Victoria's motivations were and what he intended. Carlos María de Bustamante, who called Tornel the "palace intriguer," believed that he was deeply influential in Victoria's decisions and was responsible, as an example, for the eviction of Servando Teresa de Mier from his rooms in the National Palace.[31]

If we are to believe Tornel, Victoria was "a man akin to Plutarch's famous republicans. Ambition, that leads to the fall of some of the greatest of men, and is the obsession of the smallest of them, was never a characteristic of his; the deeds of his long and notable career were invariably carried out to serve the public cause."[32] In other words, according to Tornel, Victoria was straight and honest, and responsible for his own actions and decisions. As he stated in 1833 regarding Victoria, "Never did I discover the smallest cause for those suspicions that could only have been conceived out of malice and to satisfy the hunger of treachery."[33] It is, of course, possible that these words were intended to cover up any illicit profits that may have come Tornel's way as the president's secretary, in which case, Victoria might not have been as virtuous as Tornel gave us to understand, and was possibly influenced more often than not by his personal secretary, as Justo Simplicio el Tapado implied in 1828.

An example of the kind of incident that could easily be interpreted as clear evidence of Simplicio el Tapado's suspicions is the wrangle that arose in mid-1826 over Tornel's rooms in the National Palace. Apparently his palace rooms on the first floor were better furnished than anybody else's, displaying the kind of luxury that could not be obtained on a government official's wage:

When I said that Tornel had magnificent rooms in the palace, I did not state that he could not decorate them as he pleased with all the comfort and luxury he could afford with his own money. What I repeat and what is scandalous is that he enjoys them without paying any rent. The National Palace is meant to serve the public interest. It should not be turned into a cosy neighborhood [casa de vecindad] for the worst kind of flatterers.[34]

The attack on his lifestyle did not go undefended, and it became an issue during the 1826 electoral campaign. After all, once Tornel became the president's secretary, it was not long before he became fully involved in what Anna has described as "the descent into politics"[35] that soon soured the sense of goodwill that had flourished with the advent of the 1824 Constitution.

TORNEL, *YORKINO*

In what remains the most complete political history of the First Federal Republic,[36] Michael Costeloe notes that "the formation of the Rite of York in the fall of 1825 stimulated the re-emergence of the political divisions and disputes that had characterized the years that came immediately after the achievement of independence."[37] Only a year after Victoria came to power, the political stage of the republic had become fraught with the partisan and factional power struggles that eventually were to lead to the collapse of representative government in 1828. While the centralists, although loosely united, remained in the heterogeneous Scottish Rite of Masons, the federalists and the more radical members of the emergent political class used the arrival of the American minister plenipotentiary, Joel Poinsett, to consolidate a more cohesive faction that could challenge the *escoceses*, along party lines, with the regularization of the Rite of York on 29 September 1825.[38]

Tornel duly abandoned the Scottish Rite and joined the newly regularized Rite of York, becoming the master of one of the *yorkino* lodges in Mexico City: la India Azteca (the Aztec Indian). In a way preparing the ground for his change, Tornel, as early as February 1825, had moved from the more traditionalist paper *El Sol* to writing for the more radical *El Aguila Mexicana*. The Rite of York was a success from the first moment of its official existence in Mexico. It presented itself as a vibrant populist liberal federalist sect of masons that could successfully oppose the more traditionalist centralist and elitist liberalism represented by the *escoceses*. In the words of Tornel:

Generals renowned for their past services, members of the military from all ranks, not a small number of ecclesiastics, deputies, senators, employees of different categories, innumerable citizens; they all enrolled under a flag that was said to be that of independence, of the federation and of the government. Several Scottish lodges and many individuals from other areas left to join the ranks of the new Masonic sect, which benefited from the popularity that emerges when the powers that be openly protect a new enterprise.[39]

Nevertheless, although Tornel was a liberal republican federalist at the time and it made sense for him to join the Rite of York, especially since, as a politician in the making, he needed to be part of one of the dominant parties, there does exist another possible explanation for his affiliation to the Rite of York. To quote Costeloe, since Victoria was unable to prevent the emergence of the *yorkinos*,

he decided to infiltrate the lodges with his intimate friends and allies, in the hope that he could exert some control and influence through them. . . . It is significant that his friends and advisors, Esteva, Tornel and Guerrero, were all founding members of the society. There is no doubt that not only did they keep him well informed, but that they transmitted his wishes to the lodges and perhaps even ensured that these were carried out accordingly.[40]

In short, he joined the Rite of York because it was the forum where radical federalists like himself met to discuss the political situation of the republic and to influence its decisions on Victoria's behalf.

Whether it was as a dedicated *yorkino* or as Victoria's spy within the Rite of York, the fact remains that by the summer of 1826, as the congressional elections got under way, Tornel was perceived to be, together with José Ignacio Esteva, minister of the exchequer and grand master of the Rite of York, one of the most promising politicians within the *yorkino* faction. Evidence can be found in the way that the Scottish Rite press, represented by *El Sol*, attacked both Esteva and Tornel throughout the summer of 1826, considering them to be the politicians most likely to be nominated as presidential candidates by the *yorkinos* in the 1828 general elections. In other words, the two men believed by the *escoceses* to pose the greatest threat to them, and whose reputations therefore needed to be sullied among the general public, were Esteva and Tornel. While Esteva, as minister of the exchequer, was accused by *El Sol* of stealing government funds for his own purposes,[41] Tornel was accused of being a power-mongerer and of having changed sides whenever he had thought it necessary in order to further his career.[42]

DEPUTY IN CONGRESS, 1826–1828

The unpleasantness of the 1826 electoral campaign certainly undermined any sense of goodwill that may have lingered from the 1824 presidential elections. In fact, from 1826 to 1828 the prevalent freedom of the press, guaranteed in the constitution, was consistently abused with a proliferation of acrimonious and libelous articles. The increasingly combative and vitriolic nature of the press became one of the key sources of discontent that led to the collapse of representative government in 1828.[43] Evidently the formation of a second faction/society/party, which could challenge the *escoceses* and take away from them all those jobs in public office that they had enjoyed since the triumvirate, led to a particularly violent campaign in 1826. As Zavala himself confessed in 1831, the one thing that united the *yorkinos* was their goal to oust the *escoceses* and the Spaniards from their positions in the public administration and create a constellation of jobs that would satisfy the ambitions and the financial needs of their members.[44] José María Luis Mora presented in his own historical account of the period a strikingly similar version of what the *yorkinos* were all about: they were not concerned with promoting a political agenda; all they were after were jobs for their members.[45] In brief, there was more than ideology at stake in the 1826 congressional elections. There was the extremely important and material issue that a large number of politicians could either remain unemployed or could suddenly find themselves unemployed, depending on the outcome of the elections. As it happened, the *yorkinos* enjoyed a landslide victory at both the national and state levels. They gained control of the Chamber of Deputies in Congress and of the majority of state legislatures, with the notable exceptions of Puebla and Veracruz, where the *escoceses* succeeded in retaining their posts.

Therefore, it was as a prominent *yorkino* and as the president's secretary that Tornel was elected deputy for the Federal District (Mexico City) in September 1826. He proved to be very active as a deputy. From the beginning of 1827 through February 1828, the press almost daily reported his proposals, speeches, and votes in the column entitled *Cámara de Diputados*. A close analysis of these interventions offers an interesting insight into his political beliefs in the mid- to late 1820s and shows that Tornel was remarkably consistent as a defender of that particular brand of early Mexican liberalism that the *yorkinos* came to represent. His political actions were dictated by five major concerns (excluding the expulsion of Spaniards, which will be looked at in the following section): (1) the nature of Mexico's representative government and its federal constitution (he systematically defended federalism and the liberties guaranteed in the 1824 Constitution); (2) the abolition of slavery, focusing Congress's attention, in passing, on issues such as the oppression of the Indians; (3) the improvement of the army (he adopted at the times, the federalist banner that favored the strengthening of the civic militias rather than the regular army); (4) the preservation of law and order in the Federal District as well as in Mexico as a whole; and (5) an evident interest in the country's legislation regarding its commerce, trade, and economy (advocating free market economics).

Tornel received 267 votes on 3 September 1826 and was able to move into the next round of the elections for Congress. On 4 October it was announced that he had been elected deputy for the Federal District alongside Isidro Gondra.[46] On the very day on which this was confirmed, he stated that as the population of the capital had increased considerably since the last census had been carried out in 1816, the Federal District needed three, rather than two, deputies.[47] He believed that for a country to be truly democratic, the number of people's representatives in Congress had to reflect the size of the population for which they were acting as deputies. In his mind, it was wrong for one state to have the same number of deputies as another if its population was half the size of the other. He returned to this point in the session of 13 January 1827, when he proposed a date for the creation of a junta that would provide the Federal District with a third deputy.[48]

He had precise ideas on what he considered to be the nature of representative government. On the third day of the Junta Preparatoria, he gave a long speech in answer to the complaints and accusations made by the Scottish Rite faction that the elections had been fixed. He celebrated Mexico's progress toward civilization, claiming that the controversies over the elections illustrated the maturity of the Mexican people, for they were now able to contest and discuss the elections without necessarily resorting to violence. He claimed that had his party lost, they would have been voicing the same kind of protests the *escoceses* were making. This was, according to Tornel, the nature of party politics. Nevertheless, the results had to be accepted whatever they were; such was the nature of democracy. He also stated that it was only right to investigate the opposition's claims and listen to their criticisms, for it was always possible that they were right. He was obviously saying this from a position of power, knowing, as did his faction, that nothing of the sort would be done. It was certainly part of his effective rhetoric—giving the impression that he was impartial and that his first priority was what was best for Mexico rather than his own career or his party. However, it was also a reaffirmation of the virtues of the 1824 Constitution; "Article 35 in the Constitution says that *Each chamber will assess the elections of its respective members, and will solve any doubts that may emerge about them.* The Constitution is not only concerned with the personal qualities of the deputies: it subjects the elections themselves to the inspection of the chambers."[49]

His pose, if that is what it was, as a believer in representative government was certainly convincing. He claimed that if a junta was needed to investigate the results of the elections, there should be one. It was wrong of the *yorkinos*, he said, to disapprove of such an investigation: "I do not share Sr. Enríquez's fear that the decision this junta arrives at, whatever it be, will alter the public peace."[50] His confidence was indisputable. His speech ended with hope and an emotional reaffirmation of optimism. Whatever the outcome of the investigations into the election results, Mexico had reached an admirable stage in its democratic process:

I sense symptoms of life and youth in the state of Mexico. Those illustrious children of hers who have done so much for the existence and grandeur of the mother-country are still alive. Mexicans enjoy those esteemed rights they have acquired with so many heroic sacrifices in the warmth of a young and free nation. After the clashes freedom will settle forever on its foundations.[51]

Although, in the context of the third day of the Junta Preparatoria, these words had the definite purpose of challenging the *escoceses'* accusations of electoral corruption, the notion that the animated confrontation of two parties was an inherent aspect of a healthy political system was something that Tornel expressed on several occasions. In the first issue of *El Amigo del Pueblo*, he praised an electoral process that allowed two opposing parties and factions to coexist. He compared the *yorkinos* and the *escoceses* to the Tories and Whigs in England, illustrating how radically opposed parties contributed constructively to the progress of a civilized and democratic country:

England, which rests on eternal foundations; England, which offers us the most admirable example of stability that a country governed constitutionally could dream of, owes its ever increasing happiness to the Tories and the Whigs, to its radicals, to the wise and patriotic opposition of one ministry against another, for whom the people's opinion invariably serves as an oracle.[52]

He praised even the extreme articles of the press as a preferable alternative to violent demonstrations. Extreme words and remonstrances were all part of a healthy political life. Revolutions and conspiracies were not.

On 17 January, he gave a speech in which he analyzed Mexico's legislative system in relation to the "popular will" or the "will of the people," defending the right to amend the constitution if it were deemed necessary, as was stated within its articles. He defined what he considered to be the "sovereignty of the people" and expressed his confidence in the system, convinced that it was suited to such noble and democratic aims. For him, Hobbes's concept of reducing the sovereignty of the people to the will of either one person, such as a king, or that of a limited group of people, such as the aristocracy, was completely despicable. In the same speech, he also criticized Rousseau, "who allowed himself to be dragged away by his wonderful and splendid imagination, more so than by any sense of reality,"[53] for trusting the sovereignty of the people to nobody in particular and everybody at the same time. He thought that a belief in the statement, "The sovereignty of the people should neither be suppressed nor delegated," could only plunge a nation into a complete state of anarchy.[54] He balanced the pros and the cons of these two views and arrived at the conclusion that a synthesis of the two models was the best system for a civilized country. In other words, "The people cannot enjoy sovereignty unless it is by using the vote that expresses their will. . . . The laws that establish the right to vote are fundamental laws in a democratic system. Thus . . . the people of . . . Mexico are sovereigns when they vote; in other words, when they express their will."[55]

Working from this premise, the decree that had been proposed in Congress demanding an end to elections was not only anticonstitutional, but also destroyed, according to Tornel, the so-called people's sovereignty "because it destroys the faculty of the people to choose."[56] He defended the right to propose amendments within the constitutional framework. Nevertheless, if amendments involved issues of such fundamental importance as the right to vote, it was against the law even to suggest its abolition. In brief, his speech of 17 January 1827 illustrates the extent to which Tornel was opposed at that time to any form of dictatorship. He was showing his republican beliefs by mocking Hobbes's monarchic theories, and he was also exhibiting his radicalism by criticizing a political system that placed the reins of government in the hands of an aristocracy, and supporting, in contrast, a constitutional framework that guaranteed universal male suffrage. His defense of the political participation of the masses would falter after the experience of the Parián riot of 1828.

His vow to crush all military coups and revolts, whatever they stood for, in his speech of 21 March 1827 can be interpreted to stem from the early constitutionalist ideology he upheld in the 1820s, which included the notion that all revolts should be quelled and the participants punished, regardless of their political motivations. In other words, he solemnly appeared to defend the constitution and, with it, the process of elections as the only acceptable means of changing a government. The revolt he was specifically referring to was one that had taken place in Durango. One officer, González, reacting to the increasing anti-Spanish outbursts of fighting that were becoming widespread in 1827, had taken over Durango by force, locking up the governor, Vaca Ortiz, who was acclaimed for having fought bravely for Mexico's independence and for being an outspoken federalist. González had stated that his revolt was an act of justice because Vaca Ortiz was an "enemy of the people's freedom" and an "enemy of Durango." Moreover, the deputy for Durango, Francisco Landa, stated that González should not be stopped, as the events in Durango were an expression of "the will of the people." To this Tornel replied:

Sr. Landa has told us something else which needs correcting. "That it is the will of the people." The people should not have a will that can overrule the law. It is well known how the people are stirred; those unfortunate people are always the victims of the intriguing, aspiring enemies of order and of our institutions. How can that funereal and always dangerous right of insurrection be sanctioned from the national tribune; a right that can bring along with its abuse, the ruin of the mother-country?[57]

He protested that after three years in which Mexico had achieved a state of permanent peace, during which a representative government seemed to be consolidated, and in which the world was beginning to recognize its independence and its maturity, it was ridiculous, if not potentially tragic, to let such revolts take place and accept the right of insurrection as if it were a clause within the constitution. He demanded immediate action. Any revolt, whatever its factional interests, had to be suppressed the moment it started. Any *caudillo* who took the law into his hands and used physical force in an attempt to disrupt the present system should be punished on the spot:

I will be quick to propose to the chamber that all of the *caudillos* of disorder be declared outlaws, as long as they do not put down their weapons on receiving the first warning from the government. We must remember, gentlemen, that energy and the inexorable strength of the legislative power saved the republic from the horrors of anarchy on a previous occasion. The symptoms of a widespread conflagration can be felt everywhere. We need to be firm, gentlemen, and embracing the book in which our sacred pact was written we will defend it without any hesitation for the good and conservation of our dear mother country.[58]

The revolt in Durango represented the views of the *escoceses*. There was nothing necessarily outstanding about Tornel's demand to have it quelled. Nevertheless, in later accounts, Alamán was to argue that the government did little to crack down on any revolts at the time because it was then able to justify the drastic laws that were approved on 10 May and later on 20 December that year, expelling Spanish citizens from Mexico. In other words, he argued that they allowed the anti-Spanish revolts to proliferate so that they could claim that the laws they passed responded to this angry expression of "the will of the people" and allowed the *escocés* revolts to take place so that they could claim that the threat of a pro-Bourbonist counterrevolution was significant enough for the adoption of the drastic measures they eventually took.[59] It is bearing Alamán's assertions in mind that Tornel's speech could be seen to represent a strong defense of constitutionalism, one, in fact, that the *yorkinos* as a whole were not adopting, as they allowed the revolts to spread, waiting for the best moment to propose the outright expulsion of Spaniards. Tornel would continue to be a passionate constitutionalist until the late 1840s, when infected by the politics of despair that overwhelmed the Mexican political class in the wake of the 1846–1848 war, he came to the conclusion that only a dictatorship could save Mexico from disappearing as a sovereign and independent nation.

His defense of the constitution and his condemnation of all violent attempts to overthrow the elected government did not falter, regardless of whether it was an *escocés* or a *yorkino* revolt he was hoping to crush at the time. Evidence of the consistency of his beliefs is that he would eventually criticize, with Alamán, the apparent passivity with which the government responded to the numerous outbreaks of violence that started to afflict the republic in 1827, whether they were led by *escoceses* or *yorkinos*: "It was observed that the ministry, even when the agents it chose . . . went on betraying it, continued to name individuals who had similar backgrounds; . . . the revolution spread like a fire in a field in summer, and the public forces were not fully employed either to contain or quell it."[60]

Another issue inevitably related to his concept of government at the time was the much debated freedom of the press. On 3 September 1827, Tornel strongly opposed the Senate's proposal to limit this freedom. He claimed that a polemical press was one of the main components of a healthy political system.[61] It must not be forgotten that he was editor, at the time, of *El Amigo del Pueblo*. His own ties with the press must have influenced, to a certain extent, his rejection of the Senate's proposal. However, his opposition to censorship was consistent with his argument that for a country to be truly civilized, it needed to have two radically opposed parties, and the press was one of the obvious places where they could voice their opinions.

Although he was to abandon this belief in a running debate, his defense of freedom of the press and a healthy constructive confrontation of government and opposition parties in 1827 would appear to indicate that his views on Mexico's form of government were as enlightened as those of his more progressive contemporaries. After all, to quote Costeloe, freedom of the press became "a sacred cow for *hombres de progreso* and was seen by them to be an essential feature of an independent, civilized society."[62]

It is also evident that his faith in the federal system had not yet begun to falter. On 10 September 1827, he passionately defended the differences that existed between the state legislatures.[63] Each state had its own separate needs and problems. He opposed uniformity and any suggestion of centralizing the laws, making them the same for everybody. It was important to delegate power, to cater to the different local and regional needs that differentiated one state from another. Centralization would mean weakening the 1824 Constitution and thus, by default, the Federal Republic, which the people had fought for and voted for and accepted. It would essentially mean a return to the way things were before 1821. In 1827, he was still convinced that Mexico's federal system was "the form of government . . . the only one that is based on the material rights of man."[64] In his article "Federación," which took up ten columns and two issues of *El Correo*, he painstakingly went to great lengths to demonstrate this.

The abolition of slavery and his attempt to focus Congress's attention on the oppression of the Indians were two other of the major concerns to which he gave priority in his early interventions as deputy for the Federal District. On 4 January 1827, he delivered his proposal to abolish slavery: *Queda abolida para siempre la esclavitud en los Estados Unidos Mexicanos.* It is a good example of his use of rhetoric:

They are our brothers because they are men and they do not cease to be so because of their flat noses, their frizzy hair and their beautiful white teeth. How can a nation which is obliged to sustain the rights of man by its constitution with its just and benevolent laws, have tolerated for so long such a scandalous violation of them? Scandalous I have said, and I will repeat it, because it is not conceivable that a free Republic should subject some of its children to slavery. Let us leave such contradictions to the United States of North America.[65]

He was also anxious to defend the ethnic communities of Mexico in the light of their oppression. On 26 February 1827, he demanded that preference be given to the initiative that requested "the naturals known as Indians . . . be freed of all unjust tributes within the Federal District."[66] However, his proposal was postponed indefinitely.

Although this proposal, unlike that to abolish slavery, was not followed up with any concrete legislation, he expressed his concern for the indigenous populations of Mexico at least in writing on several occasions throughout his life. Nevertheless, he never seriously embraced the cause of the Indians. He allegedly wrote about the "distribution of the Indians" and the "injustice of the conquest" during his confinement in the Colegio Seminario Palafoxiano of Puebla. In his *Oración* of 16 September 1827, his *indigenista* portrayal of the lifestyle of the Indians before the conquest idealized Mexico's ancient cultures. In 1841, *El Mosaico Mexicano* printed several articles he wrote that focused on different aspects of Indian culture. His *"Noticias sobre las poesías aztecas,"* for instance, were homage to the literature of "his" Mexican ancestors. In *"Bosquejo de la administración de los incas en el Perú,"* he praised the forgotten civilizations of the New World, generally neglected in favor of the better-known ancient Greek and Roman civilizations.[67] As was the case with Carlos María de Bustamante, Tornel's *indigenismo* contained the essential contradiction that it was capable of praising the indigenous culture of pre-Cortesian Mexico while simultaneously despising the Indians of nineteenth-century Mexico.[68]

Tornel's third major concern during his years as deputy, as during most of the rest of his life, was the army. A high percentage of his interventions in Congress from 1827 to 1828 were concerned with ways of improving it. On 9 January 1827, for example, he argued for and then voted in favor of providing more mules. Three days later, he proposed the creation of a committee made up of a treasury committee and war committee that could work out the right pay for soldiers. Two days later, he argued that the government should grant unlimited licenses and pensions to retired officers of the permanent militia. On 25 January, he voted in favor of their chamber having the faculties to grant the army whatever might be needed to obtain the adequate number of mules. On 31 January, he proposed awarding generous sums of money to the soldiers who had finally defeated the last Spanish stronghold in Mexico—the so-called victors of San Juan de Ulúa. On 6 February, he proposed a series of laws that limited the sale of guns to the general public and attempted to keep them within military jurisdiction. On 8 February, he stated that they had to decide whether the *Estado Mayor del Ejército* should be improved or dissolved. Six days later, adopting a particularly radical stance, he criticized the *Estado Mayor* for having too much power. On 27 February, he defended the officers' widows' rights to a pension. Clearly Tornel was determined to improve the army on several fronts, while curtailing the power of the high command of the regular army.[69]

Three of his proposals merit particular attention: the creation of a new corps of engineers, his defense of local militias, and his law on deserters. On 22 February 1827, together with Antonio Manuel Cañedo and José Joaquín Herrera, he tabled twenty-one articles sanctioned by the president that created a new engineers' corps. It is interesting to note that every time he became minister of war, the engineer corps was to feature prominently in his annual ministerial report as an element of the army that repeatedly needed improvements. As he stated, "In every nation the engineers' corps is recognized as one of the elements of a perfectly organized army."[70] It was, according to Tornel, Cañedo, and Herrera, of fundamental importance to have a regular army that was not numerically large but was organized and disciplined and could offer the nation, besides military support, civil services such as bridge building and other construction work that only an engineers' corps could create. Two of his main objectives were the modernization of the army and ensuring that the military could also make valid contributions to civilian society. In time, and coinciding with his change to centralism, Tornel ceased to defend the civic and provincial militias and instead came to advocate the creation of a large national regular army.

On 23 February, he also intervened in the long debate on whether the local militias should be dissolved. On this occasion he defended their existence. After the discovery of the Arenas conspiracy on 19 January 1827, the threat of a Spanish attack, which would in fact become a reality in the Barradas expedition of 27 July 1829, was good reason to have the people of Mexico readily armed, trained, and prepared to fight. He also argued that civilians under threat had more incentive to fight than professional soldiers; they had their families and homes to protect. On 24 February, with the Chamber of Deputies dominated by federalist *yorkinos*, forty deputies voted in favor of the militia and ten against it.[71]

Having said this, in October 1827, he reached the conclusion that although he was in favor of the existence of the local militias, they were in need of some major reforms. In his proposal *Proyecto de ley para el arreglo de la milicia*, he outlined the flaws and problems of the existing militias and the discontent they were causing among the population. The officially proposed numbers of recruits had been inflexible and had not taken into account either population distribution or the needs of the population in the different areas of Mexico. As a result, there was major discontent among the working population, who were, in some areas, all obliged to become soldiers, as the recommendations for numbers of recruits applied in the same way to the underpopulated settlements of Sonora as they did to the densely populated Federal District of Mexico City: "The force that exists in terms of the active militia is badly distributed throughout the states of the Republic, and their inhabitants suffer a burden that has terrible effects on their interests, because not only do they have to supply men to this force but to the regular army as officially stated in the law of recruitment."[72]

He criticized the current lottery system (*sorteo*) for its arbitrariness in recruiting men without taking into consideration the provenance of the recruits, their marital status, or profession; in some parts of the country, whole families were fleeing from one state to another to avoid their military obligations:"People abandon their homes and whole families are ruined for they abandon their region, their land and their belongings and thus our industry and agriculture are undoubtedly harmed and the original aim [of

our military service] is not achieved."[73] However, it was absolutely necessary, in his view, to continue to have an active militia to protect Mexico
from the ever-present threat of a Spanish invasion. Nevertheless, it was
equally important to eradicate those aspects of the militia that were unfair
and, most important, unpopular. Therefore, his reforms were based around
three issues: the number of soldiers the nation needed in general, the way
men were recruited, and a system of recruitment that took into account
Mexico's population distribution. He radically proposed that the existing
twenty battalions of the militia be reduced to fourteen.

With the threat of a counterrevolution becoming more likely in the fall
of 1827, Tornel's proposal was intended to have several immediate effects
on the current troubled situation. With the spate of armed revolts greatly
increased by the large numbers of fully equipped bandits (men forcibly
recruited who had subsequently deserted) whom the militias had indirectly
dressed and armed, it was fundamental to reduce the number of battalions.
By reducing their number, Tornel was disarming a potentially rebellious
army that could easily side with the Scottish Rite faction if there was any
discontent among their ranks over the way they had been recruited in the
first place. In many ways a continuation of the *Proyecto de ley para el
arreglo de la milicia*, his *Dictamen* on deserters of 20 November 1827
sought to reform those unpopular features of the army that were causing
all the desertions, while at the same time attempting to limit, as far as
possible, the probable repercussions of a situation in which armies of deserters could join the Scottish Rite rebels and wage war on the government.
In an attempt to remove the motives for desertion, he advocated decreasing
the length of service from nine years to not more than six years. However,
if promises of improvement were not sufficiently persuasive, he also made
it clear that there was a long list of punishments for those who deserted.
His criteria followed the belief that "the more liberal the laws of a nation
are, the harder they must be in the army."[74] The first time an individual
deserted he would lose all the time he had served in the army previously,
together with all his ranks and official positions, and during peacetime he
was to carry out construction work for the army for four months. Those
who deserted a second time would be sentenced to six years' imprisonment.
In times of war, deserters would be executed. At the time, anybody could
claim Mexico was still at war with Spain. In other words, he was suggesting
that the generals in command could, if they thought it was appropriate,
execute any deserters they caught. Watering down the severity of his proposal, and, once more, in an attempt to make a popular impact, he also
proposed *indultos* to all of those deserters who had been serving their sen-
tences in prison for the past six years. The benefits of such a proposal were
twofold: it would appease the general discontent of a large sector of the
population whose lives were affected by the demands of the militia and

lighten the burden placed on the national economy of guarding all of those deserters in prison since 1821.

His concern to improve the army and ensure that the troops remained loyal to the government was paralleled by his concern to preserve law and order in the Federal District as well as in the country as a whole. On 12 February 1827, for instance, he proposed a series of drastic reforms to be carried out in the Federal District involving the police, who, in his words, were a "a disgrace to all Mexicans," as well as demanding more power for the governor of the Federal District.[75] Tornel spent a great deal of time organizing the policing of the capital.

His concern to preserve law and order in Mexico at the time was not limited to ensuring an effective police force. On 21 February 1827, together with Isidro Gondra, José Joaquín Herrera, Antonio Manuel Cañedo, and Sabas Domínguez, he proposed the creation of a committee that would look into the state of the capital's prisons and act quickly to improve their atrocious conditions.[76] On 4 March 1828, acting as governor, he wrote to Juan José Espinosa de los Monteros to reiterate his concern over the appalling conditions of Mexico's prisons:

Just at first sight it is obvious that the unfortunate offenders are condemned to moan in our prisons for many years. If our government does not adopt extraordinary measures to remedy this evil, its perpetuation will be the dishonor of the republic. . . . Humanity will suffer acutely and neither our prisons nor our trials will differ from those in Constantinople.[77]

He was advocating the liberal principle that a prison should serve not only as a place of punishment but also as a place of rehabilitation. This was why he was completely astounded to find "offenders of both sexes who are very young and of a tender age, imprisoned generally because of minor offences, locked in the same cells as other criminals whose age and long history of crimes have made incorrigible."[78] There is evidence that this interest in improving the condition of prisons and transforming them gradually into institutions where their inmates' faults could be corrected was one of his lifelong concerns.

His concern with law and order was not exclusively based on philanthropic ideals aimed at improving society. He was also actively involved in several campaigns against corruption, of which the case of Vicente Rocafuerte[79] became quite notorious at the time. On 1 March 1827, together with Antonio Escudero and José Matías Quintana, he proposed an investigation into Rocafuerte's transactions with Colombia.[80] On 2 March it was proved that Rocafuerte had, on his own account and without proceeding through the correct channels, donated £63,000 to the government of Colombia. Tornel became the champion of the government's funds: "Señor

Rocafuerte did not post the wretched sixty three thousand pounds to the Colombian minister with the government's authorization. It is well known that this citizen abused the trust he was awarded in his post, however much it may be said that *so much wrong was done for our good*. The bird is in the hand, are we to let it fly away?"[81]

Tornel proposed the immediate arrest of Rocafuerte, and the press praised him for doing so.[82] The Rocafuerte crisis revealed him in an increasingly popular light. Although the money would never be recovered, he argued that the case cried out for justice: Rocafuerte must be imprisoned. However, it was not until 24 April 1827 that the Chamber of Deputies got around to voting on Rocafuerte's fate. By this time, Rocafuerte was on a ship in the middle of the Atlantic, sailing toward London, far from Mexican justice. The government's delayed reactions to the discovery of Rocafuerte's transactions gave Tornel the perfect platform from which to attack their incompetence and the way the chamber had wasted so much time; in contrast, he appeared as a hero of the taxpayers, foiled by the slow reaction of Congress: "Yesterday the chamber of deputies approved in the form of a decree the agreement that the government should demand from Don Vicente Rocafuerte the 63,000 pounds he lent to Colombia without any authorization whatsoever. . . . However, Rocafuerte has already departed to London."[83] In fact, his criticism of everybody in the Chamber of Deputies was so severe that he could not help concluding his speech of 24 April by admitting that having said what he had said, he had probably lost most of his friends: "My enemies will have increased in number."[84]

His speech of 21 March concerning the revolt in Durango was also related to his belief that law and order must be preserved at all costs. It could be argued that he wanted to see all revolts crushed, regardless of which party was promoting them, because of his own pronounced belief that law and order must be maintained above all other possible ideals. Many of his reforms as governor of the Federal District would appear to suggest that he was obsessed with maintaining law and order—as if discipline and peace were ideals in themselves, with as much weight and importance as any more overtly political notion. It is not surprising that in the portrait painted of him in his later years (now hanging in the Museum of the Army in Mexico City), his hand is resting by a volume entitled *El poder de la ley* (The Power of the Law).

The fifth major issue evident in his interventions as deputy was his interest in the country's trade, commerce, and economy. Examples of this interest include proposals such as the one he put forward together with Isidro Gondra, on 21 March 1827, asking that 100,000 pesos out of the total sum of the reserves of the Federal District be spent on the capital's administration and its various departments.[85] Not surprisingly, his interest in the economy was on more than one occasion closely related to his own interest in demanding funds for those institutions or people with whom he was involved in one capacity or another. He asked for 3,000 pesos for the Instituto de Ciencias, Literatura y Artes he had founded in 1825,[86] opposed the laws that prevented the tobacco plantations from having credits,[87] and pleaded for economic help to reduce the deficit of the guild of plantation owners and growers of his home town, Orizaba.[88]

What becomes immediately clear from his interventions as deputy is that he was not only trying to aid those people who were closest to his own interests, but was also acting as a leading *yorkino*, promoting the liberal economic philosophy of *laissez-faire, laissez-passer*. For example, during the debates that took place between 7 April and 9 May concerning the economy, Tornel advocated the free entry of timber from the United States, as well as the free entry of wool and cotton into the Federal District and opposed the proposal that they should be taxed.[89] It was for the same reason that he advocated allowing the free import of foreign maize in Yucatán.[90]

Tornel appeared to have definite beliefs as to the policies he expected the government to follow in order to establish Mexico as a country of liberal ideals and progress. He was a federalist and a constitutionalist who believed in representative government, and thought that parliamentary debate and party opposition were all part—indeed a vital part—of a healthy political system with popular elections. As a man of progress, he advocated freedom of the press, condemned slavery and the mistreatment of Indians, and favored free-market economics. At the same time, as a colonel, he was equally concerned with improving and modernizing the army, and in preserving law and order at all costs. Nevertheless, he was keen to curtail the power of the regular army and favored the improvement of the provincial militias. If anything started to shake his confidence as a well-established *yorkino* politician and publicist, it was the laws that brought about the expulsion of Spaniards in 1827.

THE EXPULSION OF SPANIARDS

On 19 January 1827, Tornel was asked, along with Francisco Molinos del Campo, Ignacio de la Garza Falcón, Joaquín Muñoz, and Francisco Ruíz Fernández, to be a witness and observer of the dismantling of a Spanish conspiracy. At four o'clock in the morning, they were summoned to a house in the suburb of San Cosme, where they hid in rooms adjacent to the one where Father Joaquín Arenas had arranged to meet Ignacio Mora.

Father Arenas, a Spaniard who belonged to the reformed Instituto de San Pedro de Alcántara, had already held a meeting with Mora in which he had told him that a Comisionado Regio[91] had been sent from Spain and was organizing a Spanish conspiracy to reconquer Mexico under the orders of Ferdinand VII. Arenas was hoping that Mora, who had been an "old supporter of the King" and was considered a "man of honor," would join the plan. However, Mora told Arenas that he needed time to think about it, and arranged to meet Arenas again on 19 January. For Mora it was fundamental to have witnesses who could verify the existence of a Spanish conspiracy before the government set about finding the means of ending it. To ensure the impartiality of the witnesses, Molinos del Campo was chosen to attend the exposure of the conspirators because he was "well esteemed by the *escoceses*." Tornel was chosen because he was a "very outspoken *yorkino*." They all hid and listened intently to the conspiratorial conversation that developed between Mora and Arenas. Arenas asked Mora if he had made up his mind. Mora answered that he needed to know more about the conspiracy before he could commit himself to supporting it. Arenas then fell into the trap and explained that the plan had been drafted in Madrid; the king had named a *comisionado regio* who was already in Mexico, and several generals and priests, among others, had promised to support the cause. However, he refused to continue talking unless Mora promised to commit himself to the struggle. Mora argued that it was a major decision for him to make and that he needed to know more in detail what the conspiracy entailed. Arenas started to list, with an expression that "denoted a profound conviction and an unperturbed serenity . . . the errors we had committed since the year of 1821." His speech went on and on, the criticisms never ceasing, and Molinos del Campo lost his patience, abandoned his hiding place and started swearing violently at the priest. Arenas defiantly stated that he was proud to become a Spanish martyr.[92]

News of the Arenas conspiracy spread like fire, along with the fear of an imminent Spanish counterrevolution. Tornel would look back in 1852 and lament the far-reaching consequences of the exposure of the conspiracy. In his mind, the tragedy was that what was essentially an insignificant gathering of Spanish reactionaries, who would probably never have succeeded in organizing a counterrevolution, sparked off a disproportionately violent reaction on the part of the press and the population at large: "The conspiracy of Father Arenas, insignificant because of the number and circumstances of its accomplices, was not a grave threat to the nation in itself; however, it was dangerous in that the parties . . . found plausible pretexts to inflame their fatal disputes; to contaminate the masses with the venom of their passions; to divide the country in opposite directions."[93] The news of the conspiracy was cynically used by the political factions, who started a process of accusations and paranoia that led to the expulsion laws of 20 December 1827, the Plan of Montaño (23 December 1827), and Bravo's subsequent revolt, the battle of Tulancigo (7 January 1828), the consequent witch-hunt of Spanish citizens, the revolution that placed Guerrero in the presidential seat (September–December 1828), and the counterrevolution of Xalapa (December 1829) that overthrew him: these "are all events that resulted from the plans of an ill-fated friar, who without imagining or understanding it, placed himself at the forefront of a period plagued with disasters."[94]

As a professional politician and a leading *yorkino*, Tornel did not at the time judge the actions he took in response to the Arenas conspiracy to be anything other than a justified response to the threat the Spaniards posed to Mexico's independence. On 23 February 1827, Tornel, Bocanegra, Andrés Quintana Roo, and Antonio Escudero took the first step toward the laws of 20 December. It was a moderate proposal in that it did not arbitrarily condemn or affect a large proportion of the population purely on the basis of nationality or origin, but rather took into consideration individuals' actions and beliefs. Rather than pointing directly at the Spaniards, it concerned anybody who openly and overtly attempted to bring down the Mexican republic. The first article stated, "Foreigners who belong to nations that are at war with the Mexican Republic, may be expelled by the government, always provided that there is evidence to suspect that their conduct is contrary to independence or the present form of government."[95]

Considering the anger the Arenas conspiracy aroused (Arenas was eventually executed), Tornel's proposal was reasonable and, comparatively modest in its attempt to appease the popular call for an outright expulsion and deter nostalgic Bourbonists from plotting the downfall of the republic. He said that foreigners, not Spaniards, *could be*, not *would be*, expelled, and only if there were proof of their involvement in a conspiracy. It was a compromise, aimed in theory at appeasing the wave of hatred toward all Spaniards provoked by the threat of an imminent Spanish counterrevolution. It also aimed to avoid creating a situation whereby xenophobia could become prevalent, with the systematic condemnation of innocent people who, regardless of their Spanish origins, might have made an important contribution to Mexico's independence. Had Tornel's father been alive (he died toward the end of the war of independence), he would have certainly fit this description. What remains clear is that, at least initially, Tornel's intention was to end the hostility through appeasement, adopting measures that were not entirely arbitrary. In 1852, with the benefit of hindsight, he admitted that this policy of appeasement did not work: "The Mexican representatives who flattered themselves with the belief that this would be the last law of this kind and that the revolutionaries would deem themselves satisfied, did not know that popular demands increase with concessions, in the same way that an individual suffering from dropsy wants more water the more water he is offered."[96]

However, Tornel found himself speaking in favor of and voting for the initial laws of 10 May 1827 that stated that "no Spaniard, whatever rights he may have acquired as a result of the plans the nation adopted on becoming emancipated, may be asked to exercise or fulfill any form of employment in the republic."[97] And, by December, he was backing laws that stated that all Spaniards were to be expelled from Mexico. Nevertheless, it is worth noting that the speeches he made to justify the laws of 10 May, and later for those of 20 December, were never as extreme or xenophobic as those of many of his contemporaries. The wording was on both occasions moderate and precise, never abusive. His speech of 9 May opened, for instance, with the following lines: "After having struggled for a long time with myself, I have reached a peace of mind that is difficult to arrive at when the interests of the nation are opposed to the interests of individuals who are, after all, members of the great Mexican family."[98] Even when he eventually arrived at the conclusion that no Spaniard could continue to work in public office in Mexico, his words expressed the doubts that he felt about such as decision, as well as an awareness of the pain it would cause. The Spaniards who lived in Mexico were, after all, members of the great Mexican family. Essentially the reason for his support of the laws of 10 May was, in his own words, circumstantial: "The events have precipitated themselves; things have reached a state where upon we cannot retreat."[99]

In his speech of 6 December, the same principle applied. He insisted that although he was not condemning the Spaniards for the previous centuries of tyranny or their conduct in the eleven-year war, they had, tragically, abused the generous rights they had been granted in the Plan of Iguala: "The day will come when our republic will be well established on solid foundations, and then, Spaniards, Greeks and Turks, people born all over the globe will be able to live peacefully among us. In the meantime to satisfy the will of the people who believe their existence and their freedom to be in danger, the discussed measures are a necessity."[100] In the end, he argued that the main reason for his support of the expulsion was a question of pleasing the people who had elected him as their representative in Congress. They believed that their existence and their rights were in danger. It was his obligation as their deputy to represent their anxieties and their beliefs.

Nevertheless, despite his moderate words, he supported the laws. After the Arenas conspiracy had been exposed and it was common knowledge that the Spaniards were preparing a counterrevolution, the general anger of the majority of the population was such that it was obvious to him that he had to support such laws to remain a popular politician. At this point, some more principled men, such as Lorenzo de Zavala and Carlos Maria de Bustamante, did oppose the laws. Tornel, instead, to ensure the continued support of the *yorkinos*, deemed it right to promote not only the anti-Spanish laws but a hatred of the Spaniards. In his *indigenista* speech of 16 September during the annual celebrations of independence, he went as far as to condemn everything that Columbus had stood for, praising, in contrast, the indigenous cultures of Mexico. Moreover, in 1828, as Harold Sims's research has shown, he was to become one of the most relentless persecutors of the Spanish communities in Mexico.[101]

By May 1827, the increasing anger of the people meant that there was no middle position. It was a question of either supporting or rejecting the move toward expelling all Spaniards from Mexico. Rejecting it was essentially seen as a defense of the Spaniards and, indirectly, as an acceptance of the conspirators and their aims. Tornel chose not to risk being thought of as a sympathizer of the conspirators. To be seen protecting the enemies of the republic would be political suicide, even if the laws that were voted on were extreme and arbitrary.

His speech of 9 May 1827 illustrates the extent to which Tornel had become a versatile politician, portraying himself as a man struggling with himself, finding it hard to say what the majority wanted to hear, and having to convince himself methodically that such brutal laws as those that would be passed on the following day were essentially justifiable within the context of the period. Tornel was as much a gifted political writer in 1827 as he had been in 1821. He stated that if he had believed the laws they were discussing were wrong, he would have opposed them with all the courage that such a stance would have required: "I confess, gentlemen, that had my opinions been contrary to the strong measures we are discussing today, . . . I would have addressed the chamber of representatives [on the Spaniards' behalf] because I tend to favor the weak and take pleasure in drying the tears of the afflicted."[102] Slowly and methodically he explained to the Chamber of Deputies why the measures had to be passed. He claimed it was a natural aim to protect and conserve one's country, whatever the cost; although the laws were extreme, the current situation demanded them. There was no doubt that the Spanish monarchy and its sympathizers in Mexico were plotting a counterrevolution. To expel them was necessary to protect Mexico's integrity and independence. Moreover, he argued that it was in the nature of Spaniards never to forget the mother country; they were likely to betray Mexico and join an organized revolution against the republic to bring back Spanish rule. It was simply a legislative decision brought about by the will of the people—the people who had voted for them and expected to be listened to; the people who were rebelling and resorting to violence because the Chamber of Deputies previously had ignored their demands. Although he still respected Iturbide, it was ridiculous to abide by laws a man had passed in a specific historical context—laws that were no longer applicable because the times had changed and the needs of the nation had changed. The Mexicans had always been kind to the Spaniards. As a result of the Plan of Iguala, they had been allowed to go on living in Mexico, with equal opportunities to prosper. There had never been any reason for them to complain or rebel. Therefore, by conspiring to overthrow the Federal Republic, they were abusing Mexico's benevolence, and as they had gone so far in attempting to regain Mexico for Spain, the least they could expect was the treatment they were going to get. In other words, the expulsion of the Spaniards was a natural and direct result of their own actions. He concluded his speech by quoting Horace: "You thought of hurting us; you have hurt yourselves."[103] He was claiming by the end of his speech that the deputies who would pass the laws the next day were not responsible for the outcome of the events. The Spaniards were solely to blame for their own fate. Garnished with the rationale of common sense, his speech was the more convincing. He gave the reasoned impression that there was no alternative.

Although Tornel's political career benefited from his pronounced *yorkin-ismo* and the position he adopted toward the expulsion laws (he was rewarded with the post of governor of the Federal District on 14 February 1828),[104] he would look back at the expulsion years in his *Breve reseña histórica* and emphatically regret the extremist stance he adopted during this period. In 1852 he claimed that he seriously lamented the outcome of the laws and that the "exaggeration of the period" caused in him "a veritable martyrdom,"[105] as he felt he was forced by circumstances to support such arbitrary and drastic measures:

It is well known that Sr. Tornel has anxiously hoped and looked for a solemn occasion to confess that he committed a terrible mistake, that he repented many years ago of his submissiveness, that he bitterly cries because of the harm that was done to justice and humanity, and that he prays to heaven so that his noble and distinguished nation never reproduces events that history would silence if it were possible to rule the memory of men.[106]

The fact that he attempted to dissuade Lobato from persevering with the January 1824 revolt that demanded the expulsion of all Spaniards, and that he went with Victoria to quell the León brothers' Oaxaca revolt of August 1824 that reiterated these demands, may give his assertions of repentance some credibility. Nevertheless, there was good reason for Tornel to regret the outcome of the expulsion laws. It became obvious to him that as the Spaniards left the country, so did all their money: "One of the most fatal consequences, apart from the loss of an industrious people, was the loss of Spanish capital, an amount that rose to the enormous sum of twelve million pesetas [*sic*]."[107] Ironically, although Colonel Santiago García recommended that all expelled Spaniards should leave with only a third of their possessions (all money having to remain, objects being negotiable), his proposal was dismissed on 24 November,[108] in part thanks to Tornel's exertions, who would look back with pride that they had had the decency to allow those Spaniards who were expelled to take their wealth and belongings with them.[109]

The fact remains that, repentant or not, Tornel supported the expulsion of Spaniards in 1827, and again in 1828 and 1829. Moreover, consistent with his own personal mistrust and dislike of the Spanish community in Mexico (let us not forget that he fought against the colony), his aversion for all things Spanish was apparent throughout his life. In 1841, as an example, a group of Spaniards felt so strongly about some of Tornel's writings that they printed a lengthy *Réplica de varios expañoles al Sr. Tornel*, in which they criticized him for portraying the colonial years "with the foul breath of his partisanship; palpitating with old resentment and offended pride."[110]

EL AMIGO DEL PUEBLO AND EL CARDILLO

In the mid- to late 1820s, Tornel was a radical federalist *yorkino* who supported the expulsion laws of 1827. Evidence of this can be found in the editorials he composed with his friend Bocanegra, as editor of two radical newspapers that were first published in 1827: *El Amigo del Pueblo* and *El Cardillo*. The title of the first and better known of these two newspapers was in itself an indication of how he had decided to embrace the extreme and radical spirit of the increasingly aggressive *yorkinos*. The name of the newspaper was taken from Marat's revolutionary paper *L'Ami du peuple*, published during the years of Robespierre's so-called Reign of Terror. To quote Sims, "The deputies José María Tornel and José María Bocanegra published *El Amigo del Pueblo*, a newspaper that appeared for the first time on the 1st of August and had the support of the radical federalists and was of anti-Spanish tendencies."[111] It was through the editorials of *El Amigo del Pueblo* that Tornel and Bocanegra projected an ideology that stressed the importance of education in Mexico's path to progress, the need to guarantee freedom of thought, that federalism was the "favorite object" of their "endeavors," and that it was fundamental to defend Mexico's popular representative federal system against the threat of monarchism, centralism, and a Spanish offensive.[112] Bearing this in mind, it is not that surprising that Carlos María de Bustamante went on to note in his diary that Tornel had become a "Parisian terrorist."[113]

Although *El Amigo del Pueblo* was of radical tendencies, it nevertheless retained a certain composure in its editorials. After all, the newspaper's motto was "Truth and impartiality."[114] Although it soon became evident that such a claim was preposterous given the nature of the newspaper's articles, there was nevertheless a clear attempt on the part of the editors to disguise their radicalism with the consistent use of a literary style that embellished their more strident views with a moderate vocabulary that was not abusive, extreme, or vitriolic. Also, the way the news was presented tended to take into account the views of the *escocés* opposition (*El Sol* was quoted regularly), thus creating a false sense of objectivity that allowed the paper to appear less radical than it actually was.

It was in order to provide a forum for the more savage and libelous articles Tornel wanted to write, which openly attack the Spaniards and the *escoceses*, that he started up a more dogmatic, popular, and less literary paper, *El Cardillo*, at the end of 1827. In *El Cardillo* Tornel protected himself by publishing anonymous articles that, to quote one upset *escocés* who, under the pseudonym Defensor del Honor, appealed to the president to put a stop to the increasingly violent nature of the press, were "cruel, filthy, ugly and indecent, unlike any that may have been published in the most barbarous of nations."[115]

REVOLT OF MONTAÑO

While Tornel had become an outspoken radical *yorkino* immersed in the increasingly conflict-ridden political stage of Mexico City, his friend Santa Anna had kept a strikingly low profile in his home province of Veracruz. Having been the commander general of Yucatán (May 1824–April 1825), where his proposal to lead an expeditionary force to liberate Cuba from Spanish control had been mocked and then ignored, he had bought in August 1825 what would become his favorite hacienda, Manga de Clavo (between Veracruz and Xalapa) and had married the fourteen-year-old María Inés García, the daughter of wealthy Spanish parents. To quote Josefina Zoraida Vázquez, "He returned to Veracruz and stayed [out of the way] in the shade for a while. He always had that peculiar habit of acting and then retiring, and it was perhaps this formula that accounted for his extraordinary success."[116]

Considering the role he was to assume in September 1828 as the first general to rebel against the electoral victory of Manuel Gómez Pedraza, there is little doubt that his politics had evolved in step with those of his friend Tornel. Nevertheless, although he kept his distance from the *escoceses* in Veracruz, he did not join the *yorkinos*. There were two reasons. One was personal. The other had to do with that fundamental distinction, which still needs to be researched more fully, between national and regional politics. In other words, Santa Anna sympathized with the cause of the *yorkinos* at a national level but despised them in Veracruz. Veracruz, together with Puebla, was one of the two states of the republic where the *escoceses* had remained in power in the 1826 state elections. Since Veracruz was a stronghold of Spanish interests, with a significantly high population of Spanish merchants and businessmen, the leading politicians of the province were opposed to the expulsion laws and were wary of the power the *yorkinos* had acquired at a national level. There were fundamental economic reasons to justify their apprehension since most of them were linked in one way or another to the threatened Spanish community of the area.

Santa Anna was no exception, especially since his marriage to Doña María Inés. However, although there is evidence that he actively exempted a high percentage of Spaniards from the expulsion laws in 1828, he did not, unlike his brother Manuel, join the Veracruzan *escoceses* when they supported the revolt of Manuel Montaño (23 December 1827). Although his personal, economic, and family interests were represented, to a certain extent by the Plan of Montaño, at a national level, and in terms of ideology, he supported Victoria and the *yorkinos*. Nevertheless, he could not bring himself to join the *yorkinos* in Veracruz since their leading politicians were the Rincón brothers: José Antonio, Manuel, and Joaquín. This was due to two reasons. First, there existed a long-term rivalry between the López de Santa Annas and the Rincones, two of the more dominant families of Xalapa, which dated back to the colonial period. Second, the animosity Santa Anna felt toward Manuel Rincón, in particular, stemmed from the fact that it was Manuel who was named by Iturbide to liberate Veracruz when the port refused to surrender to a traitor like him.[117]

The Plan of Montaño was a clear expression of the extent to which the political atmosphere of the republic had become profoundly violent and unstable by the end of 1827. Instigated by the *escoceses* and the *novenarios* (a breakaway Masonic society formed in 1827, made up of disillusioned *escoceses* and moderate liberals such as José María Luis Mora who had become afraid of the excessive power the *yorkinos* had come to enjoy),[118] the Plan of Montaño proposed to abolish all Masonic organizations, especially the Rite of York, since they were considered detrimental to the well-being of the republic; to change the members of the cabinet, so that it was less radical; to expel Poinsett from Mexico, since he was considered to be one of the founding members of the Rite of York; and to ensure that the federal constitution was abided by in full (*exacta y religiosamente*), stressing that this was not a centralist revolt and that it was not the intention of the rebels to overthrow the existing political system.[119]

On 1 January 1828, acting as president of the Chamber of Deputies, Tornel made the welcoming speech for Victoria after the president had reopened Congress. As was to be expected, he advocated the end of the revolt and the end of anarchy. Moreover, he stated that the laws of 10 May and 20 December had considerably reduced the threat of a conspiracy and a revolt of far greater proportions than the one that was taking place in Otumba: "The laws of 10 May and 20 December completely eradicated the plans of those who have dared to attempt to bring about the ruin of our most cherished freedom."[120] Nevertheless, he took advantage of this opportunity to accuse the *escoceses* of fighting for Spain's interests. Although there was no reference to the expulsion laws in Montaño's *pronunciamiento*, Tornel claimed that "the treacherous enemies of the Republic, skilful after three hundred years in insidious arts, agitate our passions and hope to dissolve the state because they cannot dominate it. Gentlemen, let us chain the monster of anarchy!"[121]

Although Montaño had made the mistake of starting the revolt only three days after the expulsion laws of 20 December had come into force, Tornel used the sequence of events to draw the inevitable conclusion that the revolt was a pro-Spanish reaction to Congress's deliberations. Furthermore, he concluded his speech with a patriotic and passionate call to arms to halt those foreign ambitions that were the driving force behind a revolt that was threatening Mexico's independence and constitution: "He who dares to stop the nation in its glorious march towards the summit of prosperity will suffer! The general Congress of the United States of Mexico . . . will force the agents of unrest to listen to its omnipotent voice. Representatives of the people, Mexicans, the constitution, our oaths or death."[122]

Indicative of the extent to which he had become a skillful politician was the fact that Tornel, like Victoria, knew perfectly well that it was not a pro-Spanish revolt. General Nicolás Bravo, vice president of the republic, who went on to assume the leadership of Montaño's revolt, was a friend of both Victoria and Tornel. Throughout the month prior to the revolt, in fact, both had attempted to persuade him to abandon his revolutionary plans: "Sr. Victoria, with great affliction, heard of the affiliations of his friend and companion Sr. Bravo, and he commissioned individuals he trusted to dissuade him from his intentions without success."[123] Obviously, once the conspiracy came out into the open in the form of a violent revolt, the government was then forced to take action. Nevertheless, it is significant that action was not taken before, and that even when it became known, "the time that [Bravo] was leaving and the direction he was heading for, [Victoria] refused to authorize his imprisonment as was being recommended by his hard working minister of war [Gómez Pedraza]. 'In order that we can justify', he said, 'any government action against Sr. Bravo, it is essential that he gives evidence of his conduct before the eyes of the nation.' "[124]

On 5 January it became public knowledge that Bravo was leading the allegedly pro-Spanish revolt. He took the town of Tulancingo, northeast of Mexico City, and waited with six hundred men for other generals to join the revolt and come to his aid. The support he expected never came. Santa Anna, who was suspected of originally favoring the Plan of Montaño, since his brother was involved and the town hall of Xalapa had followed in Miguel Barragán's (governor of Veracruz) steps in proclaiming their allegiance to the Plan of Montaño,[125] wrote to Gómez Pedraza on 2 January offering his allegiance to the government. By the time Guerrero reached Tulancingo, he had three thousand men under his command. On 7 January, he attacked. Bravo's troops were defeated and forced to surrender almost immediately after the attack was launched. Only eight soldiers died in battle. All the instigators of the revolution were taken prisoner, and on 10 January 1828, Bravo and his followers were locked up in the convent of Carmelitas of San Joaquín de Tacuba. Now the *yorkinos* finally had the chance to consolidate their absolute control over Mexico's government.

Following the defeat of General Nicolás Bravo at the hands of the government troops led by Guerrero, at the battle of Tulancingo (7 January 1828), the chances of the *escoceses'* acquiring power at government level seemed doomed. The unfortunate timing of Montaño, three days after the anti-Spanish expulsion laws were approved by Congress on 20 December 1827, together with the subsequent treatment that the *pronunciamiento* received in the press, which associated the cause of the *escoceses* with that of the Spaniards, meant that the Plan of Montaño was condemned to failure almost from the outset.[126] Nevertheless, although the *escoceses* were excluded from the corridors of power as a result, the *yorkinos* were unable to consolidate their hold on government. In fact, the divisions that soon evolved within the ranks of the *yorkinos*, and that Tornel came to embody as governor of the Federal District, were so virulent that when General Manuel Gómez Pedraza was elected president in 1828, a violent revolt ended the dream of Mexico's having a constitutional representative government.

GOVERNOR OF THE FEDERAL DISTRICT, 1828

On 14 February 1828, the Senate asked Tornel to replace Esteva as governor of the Federal District. Benefiting from a situation in which the *yorkinos* appeared to be in full control of the country's politics, he was naturally pleased to oblige. The news that he had been chosen to act as governor and had accepted was celebrated in all of the *yorkino* papers. On 15 February the *Correo* stated that "the inhabitants of the Federal District should expect a lot from the activity and zeal of this citizen, who, serving as representative of this very district has not ceased to promote everything he has considered fit to improve its happiness and grandeur."[127] On the 16 February, the *Correo* repeated how much "these nominations cause so much pleasure among the Mexicans!" and on 17 February, it emphasized the extent to which the Federal District would benefit from his "patriotism and activity of immense good."[128] A few days later, it printed a poem praising him:

> Who is that youth, the Cyprian exclaims,
> With such robust and gentle gallantry?
> Who is that literary figure whose fame,
> Receives a thousand respects every day?
> Who is that soldier who is proclaimed
> Governor with unanimous celebration?
> It is Tornel, the great youth has replied,
> The resolute enemy of *Escocia*.[129]

The year 1828 could not have started better regarding Tornel's career as a politician. On 4 January, he had been elected vice-president of the Compañía Lancasteriana, and along with the position of governor, he also became the president of the Junta de Caridad del Hospicio de Pobres. On 25

February he gave a speech to the members of the philanthropic Junta de Caridad, which was praised the next day in the *Correo* as "an eloquent piece of oratory."[130]

It is immediately evident that he had the full support of the *yorkinos*. According to the *yorkino* press, he was incapable of doing anything wrong. It was not only the *yorkinos* who thought he was a successful governor. In 1833, José María Luis Mora, who passionately hated him, was prepared to say, when he again became responsible for organizing the policing of the capital under the Gómez Farías administration, that "as for that odious but necessary job of enforcing police measures . . . Don José de Tornel . . . takes pleasure in such things and possesses, in this case, an admirable disposition."[131]

A brief study of his actions as governor shows that he was extremely active in his new position. Apart from devoting a lot of time and effort to enforcing the expulsion laws in the Federal District, he concentrated on such issues as the eradication of crime and the maintenance of law and order. It was, to a great extent, his determination to clean up the capital that gained him the respect of certain members of the opposition as well as that of his own party. His endeavors to protect the property of the privileged classes and ensure that the streets were safe and peaceful were as much in the interests of the *escoceses* as they were of the *yorkinos*. It comes as no surprise that in Manuel Payno's extraordinary nineteenth-century novel *Los bandidos de Río Frío* (1891), he has one of his characters lament that crime is on the increase since Tornel is not in power anymore: "You only kill a viper if you stamp on its head, not on its tail, as the great Tornel would say. Unfortunately he is not in power at the moment."[132]

His *Bando* of 26 February had no purpose other than to ensure that the expulsion was carried out to the letter of the law in the Federal District. From that date on, he stated, no Spaniard could leave the Federal District without first giving notice in the town hall; any Spaniard without a passport or documents must be taken to the *secretaría* of the Federal District, where an investigation would be carried out into his destination and the whereabouts of his home; all Spaniards resident in the Federal District had thirty days to appear in the town hall to pick up their passport and documents for departure. Tornel's men were out in the streets looking for them to ensure the expulsions were carried out.[133]

On 28 February, the new governor's severity toward the Spaniards made the news. The readers of the *Correo* were offered the case of a Spaniard who refused to leave, one José Armero Ruiz. Apparently Ruiz walked into the *secretaría* of the Federal District and refused to swear to abide by the laws of expulsion. Tornel gave him two days to reconsider his rebellion and to return to swear the oath. He did not come back. Tornel went out to look for him personally, and in the space of three days, José Manuel Cadena, one of Tornel's men, discovered that Ruiz had moved to five different houses in his attempt to escape being expelled. On 27 February, Lozano was proud to send the documents of the chase and expulsion of Ruiz to the *Correo*.[134] Examples of his endeavors to see the expulsion laws obeyed are abundant. On 26 March, for instance, he made sure that all Spaniards who were demanding exemptions for reasons of ill health passed through his office in the palace. He wanted to see every Spaniard in the Federal District who claimed that his or her illness was too serious to allow travel, and decide himself whether the allegations were true.[135]

One of the theories behind the fact that he took such a personal interest in supervising the expulsion is that he was making a small fortune at the Spaniards' expense. According to Carlos María de Bustamante, Tornel accepted bribes *not* to issue passports to any Spaniards who were prepared to pay.[136] He went as far as claiming that Tornel succeeded in acquiring the rather substantial sum of 70,000 pesos by exempting Spaniards from expulsion.[137] The editors of the *Redactor de Nueva York* also accused him of accepting bribes and estimated Tornel's illicit fortune at 10,000 pesos.[138] Although there is no definite evidence, the following two letters seem to imply that Bustamante's allegations were not far from the truth. On 19 March, concerning the fate of one Miguel Badillo, Tornel wrote:

I enclose for your Excellency the documented papers of Don Miguel Badillo, Commander of a squadron, who requests from the Supreme Government an exemption from the expulsion law for the reasons detailed below. The government of the Federal District cannot support this application as the individual in question manifested his opposition to Independence after the *grito* of Iguala, serving in the *Secretaría* of the Viceroy.... His talents, knowledge and relations are all fairly suspicious, which is why we recommend you do not grant him the exemption and that he is forced to leave the Republic.[139]

On 19 July, however, Tornel wrote about the very same Miguel Badillo: "Taking into consideration the services he paid to the cause of Independence, his peaceful conduct and the fact that he has a Mexican family, Don Miguel Badillo is to be exempted from the expulsion."[140] Taking Bustamante's words into account, Tornel's change of attitude regarding Badillo appears to indicate that something happened between the writing of one letter and the other. The possibility of a bribe does not appear to be completely out of place, even when Tornel reiterated in 1833 that it was absurd to suggest that "the compassionate actions of my heart had any other gratification than the reward of carrying out a good deed."[141]

There is certainly evidence that he exempted a high proportion of Spaniards (between 21 February and 7 March he exempted ninety-seven)[142] and that he was not totally unbiased in his granting of exemptions. In June 1828, he exempted Diego Rubín de Celis on the grounds that the Spaniard had saved his life in 1814.[143] It was also for personal reasons that he exempted all the Spaniards who made up the main theater company of Mexico City. His well-known love of the theater was strong enough to overrule the guidelines to the expulsion laws as generally practiced with everyone else. His justification for their exemption was that it was important "as a gift to the interested public . . . that the theater is well served."[144]

The fact that he had a certain amount of leeway as governor and he was to a certain extent responsible for his own actions and decisions concerning the exemption or expulsion of Spanish citizens in the Federal District has significant implications. It was he who decided to allow actors such as Diego María Garay or commanders such as Miguel Badillo to stay. It was he who decided who did not qualify for exemption. In other words, it is difficult to believe that all he was doing was obeying orders and sacrificed, to put it in his own words, "what a citizen esteems most: his opinions."[145]

According to his own version of the events, he was completely impartial in the way he granted exemptions: "In the granting of exemptions I proceeded with absolute impartiality." He was, in his mind, the victim of his faithful adherence to his moderate beliefs. "It was a scandal for some that I applied exceptional laws; and for others it was the cause of murmurs that I softened their impact." The fact that he did not embrace the views of one extreme or the other meant that he was criticized by both sides: by the Spaniards for their persecution and by the radical *yorkinos* for not being severe enough.[146] Certainly the notion that he applied the expulsion laws halfheartedly, or without the extreme vigor that might have been expected from a radical *yorkino*, is also questionable. If he regretted supporting the laws of 10 May and 20 December, it becomes even more difficult to understand why he supported the laws of 20 March 1829.

The laws of 20 March were even more extreme than those of 20 December 1827. Again, he was prepared to admit that he had suffered moral torment as a result of supporting such inhumane measures. He was to state that he was at all times aware of the "voice of humanity." However, in the same way as he had justified his support of the previous anti-Spanish laws, so he now returned to his claim that the integrity of the nation was his main priority: "The mother country, and only the mother country presented itself before my anguished imagination during those turbulent and dangerous days." The other interpretation is that after Guerrero's successful rise to power, with the radical faction of the Rite of York taking over most of the influential positions in government, it appeared to be right to support any radical laws again, and the current tide of belief, the views of the victors and the strongest party, and to enjoy the fruits of his political professionalism, which allowed him to be rewarded for cheering the winning side. Nevertheless, he claimed years later that he did all that was in his power to soften the laws of 20 March.[147]

As soon as he assumed his new position on 16 February 1828, since it was fundamental that he was seen to ensure the expulsion of as many

Spaniards as possible, he proved to be highly efficient in issuing passports, and it was not long before he had earned himself the reputation of being extremely industrious. In what was left of February, he found time to write twenty-two letters of recommendation for exemption and issued twenty-three passports for Spaniards to leave the republic.[148] He did this in addition to having to receive in his palace rooms between eight in the morning and six in the evening all those people who might have had *negocios pendientes* with the *secretaría* of the Federal District—for example, merchants in debt, shopkeepers, and bartenders.[149]

The fact that he was seen to be determined to supervise the expulsion efficiently was certainly applauded by the *yorkinos*. The fact that he was seen to be hard working had a more general appeal. It was his personal involvement in the policing of the capital that he was more significantly appreciated by both *yorkinos* and *escoceses*. On 6 March, for instance, he broke into a house where he suspected there were criminals forging money and succeeded in arresting them all: "In the afternoon—the governor, with a force of this corps, personally discovered an office full of equipment to produce false money in the house of Falcón in the neighborhood of Santa María. The criminals were caught in flagranti and a considerable number of false silver, bronze and copper coins, as well as the tools that are needed for such a complete operation, were all confiscated."[150]

The first major issue he had to tackle in an attempt to ensure that the streets were safe and peaceful was the sale of *pulque*. *Pulque* was, in the words of Fanny Calderón de la Barca, "the most wholesome drink in the world, and remarkably agreeable when one has overcome the first shock occasioned by its rancid odour." She did not fail to point out that "primitive Aztecs may have become as intoxicated on their favourite *octli*, as they called it, as the modern Mexicans do on their beloved pulque."[151] On 25 February, the *Correo* printed a letter by Spes in Livo addressed to Tornel, hoping that, as governor, he would do something soon about the abominable sale of *pulque*. The poorer members of society, who were inevitably the majority, seemed, he claimed, to waste their days drinking this evil beverage, getting more and more drunk and becoming a serious threat to the honorable, wealthy citizens of the capital. Tornel decided to prohibit the sale of *pulque* in response to the letter.[152]

The *pulquerías* in the capital fiercely complained about the injustice of the prohibition since their livelihoods were being suddenly eradicated, and hundreds of consumers took to the streets in angry protest. The decision caused chaos. Moreover, some of the wealthier families of the Federal District were affected too. Calderón de la Barca stated in 1841 that the "consumption of pulque being enormous, . . . the richest families in the capital owe their fortune entirely to the produce of the magueys."[153] It is not surprising that the prohibition provoked such a reaction. More significant, it is not surprising that by the end of February, Tornel was forced to publish in the *Correo* an apology for the brutality with which his men had dealt with the protesters and the *pulquerías* and that he had changed his law so that the sale of *pulque* was allowed after all, even if it was at limited and specific times of the day.[154] In an attempt to amend the damage caused by his mistaken evaluation of the response the prohibition would have, he went so far as to suspend various of the soldiers of the 2nd Battalion who had violently made sure that some of the *pulquerías* would never open again.[155]

Tornel's intent in forbidding the sale of *pulque* was quite clearly to please those privileged sectors of society who considered themselves threatened by the effects *pulque* had on the more riotous and impoverished citizens of the republic. However, he had not taken into account the fact that certain members of Mexico's elite benefited from the sale of *pulque*. It is evident that he did not believe in limiting the sources of wealth of his own circle of friends. Having made a mistake, he immediately rectified it. Therefore, the problem that had inspired the prohibition of *pulque* in the first place remained. In other words, the capital's streets were still littered with drunken beggars and thieves who posed a threat to the families of the *hombres de bien*. On 7 March 1828, he created thirteen laws that were intended to solve this dilemma—the very controversial *Ley de vagos y maleantes*.[156] He showed no concern over the reasons behind the existence of beggars and thieves, and the causes of their social situation were not considered. What was important was that their existence should be terminated as quickly as possible, thus ending the distress such street scenes obviously caused the wealthier members of society.

His laws stated that an increase in policemen was necessary; that it was equally important that "*pulquerías*, stalls, cellars, billiard rooms and other game-houses" were subjected to strict observation; a 25 peso fine was to be imposed on anybody who begged in or in front of churches, squares, theaters, *alamedas*, and other streets, restaurants, bars, and public places; squatters could be made to pay a fine of 100 pesos, and any foreign *vagos* were to be arrested and locked up.[157]

Tornel was praised in the *Correo* on 11 March for his dedication to his job. They called him the "infatigable governor." There is no doubt that he was working hard, and this time his laws did not harm the economy of the *hombres de bien*. Nevertheless, a large proportion of the population, consisting of the unemployed and desperate members of the lower echelons of society, resorted to violent riots. The support he obtained was from the property owners, who saw the beggars in the street in the same terms as Calderón de la Barca defined them in 1840. The streets were full of

lounging *léperos*, moving bundles of rags, coming to the windows and begging with a most piteous but false sounding whine, or lying under the arches and lazily in-haling the air and the sunshine, or sitting at the door for hours basking in the sun or under the shadow of the wall: . . . At midday the beggars begin to be particularly importunate, and their cries, and prayers, and long recitations form a running accompaniment to the other noises.[158]

Furthermore, the churches were crowded,

especially with *léperos* counting their beads, and suddenly in the midst of an "Ave María Purísima," flinging themselves and their rags in our path with a "Por el amor de la Santísima Vírgen" and if this does not serve their purpose, they appeal to your domestic sympathies. For men they entreat relief "By the life of the Señorita." For women, "By the life of the little child." From children it is "By the life of your mother." And a mixture of piety and superstitious feeling makes most people, women at least, draw out their purses.[159]

By 12 March, regardless of the support of the elite, the riots had become so violent that he found himself having to defend his laws publicly in a letter printed in the *Correo* on 16 March: "Protests have appeared everywhere against the alleged abuses that were carried out against the citizens (of Mexico City) the day I ordered the requisition of beggars." He claimed the riots were not a consequence of his laws but a coincidence. Moreover, the kind of scenes the people of Mexico City had witnessed proved that it was of fundamental importance to enforce his laws vigorously and to clean the city of that very rabble that was creating havoc among the respectable and honorable citizens of the capital. To prove that his laws were reasonable, he quoted eight different documents and letters in which his *alcaldes* and *regidores* applauded the justice of his laws and condemned the iniquity of the beggars who had rioted:

The precautions [Tornel] asked the mayors and the aldermen to take during the arrest of beggars were most reasonable; [Tornel] strongly recommended that under no circumstances were we to harass the Indians, and that we were only to arrest legitimate beggars that the priests knew about, and that we were to avoid any disturbance, to the extent that were one of the beggars to run away, he would be allowed to escape rather than be shot and cause a scandal.[160]

Whether Tornel really insisted that there should be no racial discrimination in the persecution of the beggars and that his men should let them go if they ran away must be left an open question. The fact is that his local troops did nothing of the sort. The same men who had taken the prohibition of *pulque* to mean the destruction of all *pulquerías*, interpreted the *ley de vagos* in a similar fashion. The concept of "legitimate/legal beggars" was so subjective and vague that it enabled the troops to decide for themselves whether the poverty-stricken Indians were begging or whether they needed beating. These troops also found themselves deciding whether the beggars had their backs turned to them because they had not seen them or because they were running away, thus breaking the law by resisting arrest. That summer, a pamphlet entitled *Victoriosa defensa del esclarecido patriota, gobernador del distrito, ciudadano José María Tornel*, stated that "if certain excesses were carried out, these were not recommended in the strict precautions that the governor outlined [to the men]. This was testified by the deputy Sr. Gondra, the trustee *Licenciado* Don Manuel Lozano, and also by the mayor Sr. Cadena."[161]

All the same, whether or not he was responsible for his troops' interpreting his laws to mean the extermination of Mexico City's beggars, the facts is that Tornel remained popular where it most mattered—among the property-owning, voting *hombres de bien* who welcomed the attempt to rid the Federal District of the "importunate" plague of beggars:

There is not a branch of the government of the Federal District that has not received the careful attention of the governor. Whether it be the hospice for the poor, the corps of public security or the corps of the local militia, they have all been organized and brought into line in a matter of days, either by magic or thanks to the miraculous work that only a genius is capable of. Mexico [City] owes the safety its inhabitants currently enjoy to his exertions. Tornel lives only to work; he dedicates himself to [the Federal District] night and day.[162]

The point was, in the opinion of the property-owning classes, that by putting into practice such extreme laws as the *ley de vagos*, Tornel was succeeding in creating a sense of security and safety. In other words, by persecuting beggars and imposing tight control over all places generally frequented by thieves and other *maleantes*, he was defending the interests of the *hombres de bien*. A month after the *ley de vagos* was issued, a feeling that law and order had finally become permanent in the capital had overtaken the city: "The governor is to be soundly congratulated, for no disturbances have been observed to affect the public order. The reports of the patrol, public watchmen, mayors and aldermen do not include any news that might upset the citizens."[163] Regardless of whether his measures were extreme, his policing of the Federal District was effective. This success, together with his displays of philanthropy, made him a popular governor among the more affluent members of society. In a way, by combining his ruthlessness with caring philanthropic actions, his humanitarianism counterbalanced the brutality with which his men had dealt with the capital's beggars.

On 3 March, he became the president of his own Junta Superior de Sanidad.[164] His concern over the atrocious condition of Mexico's hospitals was as passionate as his concern over the state of prisons. He insisted that it was his belief that to turn Mexico into a truly civilized nation, it was essential that its prisons and hospitals should be humane, clean and efficient.[165] On 28 May he warned the capital's population of an epidemic that was beginning to spread through the city and called an extraordinary meeting of the Junta de Sanidad to find quick remedies to prevent the cholera outbreak from spreading further.[166] He helped with the organization of the Junta de Beneficiencia.[167] He was also the vice president of the Compañía Lancasteriana and the president of the Junta de Caridad del Hospicio de Pobres. He had all the titles that were needed to be considered a charitable, benevolent, and caring philanthropist.

On 28 March, only twenty-one days after issuing the *ley de vagos*, he established a law by which no audiences whatsoever were allowed to witness executions:

Extremely interested as I am in ensuring that the Mexican people's customs do not undermine the view that Mexicans are of a sweet and compassionate nature, I am concerned that when those criminals who have been sentenced to death are driven to their final punishment, the healthy spectacle of justice is turned into an unpleasant form of entertainment.[168]

To deter audiences from gruesome speculation about the executions, he forbade the presence of carts and horses in the roads through which the prisoner would pass on his way to his execution, the sale of food at the place of execution, and the presence of an audience. Once more, he was popular among the *hombres de bien*, who found this delight in executions immoral. However, the merchants who profited from selling food to the audiences on such occasions and the large crowds who, unable to afford the theater or the bullfights, usually enjoyed such events were not happy. Brief spells of public outrage against his prohibitions followed. However, the *Correo*, as would be expected, praised him for having banned any audience at one Francisco Martinez's execution: "A healthy philosophy condemns turning the sad spectacle of witnessing a man's execution into an object of amusement, whoever that man may be."[169] His law, as far as they were concerned, "will always honor the philanthropy of the current governor of the district."[170]

In spite of the occasional riots or angry demonstrations directed against him, he became firmly established in his position of active head of the police in the capital, energetic in his pursuit of criminals and Spaniards, and succeeded also in being seen as a benevolent governor whose philanthropic concerns were paramount:

A profound wise man, knowledgeable in all the scientific sciences; a studious man who always proposes good laws to benefit society; he is of a sweet, peaceful, kind and courteous disposition when he talks; he knows how to distinguish merit wherever he finds it without discriminating between color or people. He is not one of those judges who favor the powerful delinquents, turning crime into a virtue, lies into the truth; neither does he accept malice as innocence, and he does not expect the rich to pay him for the praise he is prone to offering when he sees fit. He hates the hypocrite, and as he dedicates everything to the happiness of the nation and its constituents, his sleepless nights are incessant, his wakefulness is continuous, always active, always hard-working in defence of the national interests. He is a consummate philosopher when he uses his quill to defend the current system and an intrepid warrior, sword in hand, when he forces the enemies of our federation to bite the dust.[171]

His temporary fall from grace, if that is what it could be deemed, came after he decided to propose offering an amnesty to Bravo and the captive rebels of the Montaño revolt (15 April 1828),[172] and as a result of what initially appeared to be a minor scandal in June concerning his decision to allow the theater to open during the religious *novenario* of the Virgin of Los Remedios.

THE TORNEL-AGUIRRE SCANDAL, JUNE–AUGUST 1828

In 1852, Tornel would reminisce about these days with a certain degree of bitterness and repentance:

If the revolution initiated by Lieutenant Colonel Don José Manuel Montaño, and led by the vice-president, general of division Don Nicolás Bravo had not had the sole purpose of replacing one faction with another, their success would not have been doubted, because the republic was tired and almost lost as a result of the abuses and disorder caused by all of them. However, given that had the *escoceses* replaced the *yorkinos*, the situation would not have improved, and if anything, would have worsened, the people came to side with the faction that was protected by the government, no doubt concerned that both could fall, something that would have caused a complete state of bewilderment and an endless state of anarchy.[173]

He spoke of "the path of perdition that we have all followed" and lamented "the sad fruit of our errors," the bitter consequences of "the hatred and fights that were the cause of such bitter evils."[174] Although he did not express these feelings at the time and was happy to assume his new position of governor of the Federal District, nevertheless he started to moderate his political stance, in the spring of 1828, to the extent that the more radical members of the Rite of York started to suspect him of betrayal.

On 15 April he attended the Chamber of Deputies and made a proposal that must have surprised all the politicians who considered him a passionate *yorkino*. Together with Sabas Domínguez, Manuel María de Llano, José María Bocanegra, and Mariano Escandón, he proposed that an amnesty be granted to all those members of the military who had been involved in the Plan of Montaño, including Nicolás Bravo.[175] As early as 24 February, the *Correo*, suspecting that Tornel might have been considering such a proposal, had written a friendly warning addressed to him, Manuel Gómez Pedraza, and José Ignacio Esteva, listing the dangers of granting freedom to the prisoners of Tulancingo. He ignored the warning. As he went on to record in 1852, Carlos María de Bustamante was wrong when he claimed that he had done everything to condemn Bravo. It was Tornel who was eventually responsible for Bravo's return from exile in 1829:

Bustamante, venting his old rancor against Victoria, has claimed that Victoria was determined to have Sr. Bravo condemned, and that he used his most efficient agent, the president of the chamber [of deputies], Tornel, to do so. All of this is false: the president was very careful not to make such a recommendation and Tornel, who obviously disapproved of the revolution, did not, however, show any hatred towards Sr. Bravo or indeed towards his followers, as he was to prove later by organizing the return to the Republic of those very men who had been exiled because of their involvement in the plan of Montaño.[176]

Surprising as it may first seem, a pamphlet that circulated on 8 December that year, signed by the radical Anastasio Zerecero and that had as its main purpose to justify the Revolt of La Acordada, claimed that one of the rebels' objectives was to bring back Bravo from exile.[177] As would be confirmed in later years, Bravo was not only a close friend of politicians like Tornel, who had fought with the Ancient Patriots and were radicals in the 1820s, but also went on to become a *santanista*, acting as Santa Anna's interim president in the 1840s.

Nevertheless, Tornel proved to be ahead of those radical *yorkinos* who would later rescue Bravo's tainted memory, when he decided to defend him in April 1828. The debate that Tornel started on 15 April began at half past four in the afternoon and did not end until the next morning. The prisoners of Tulancingo were not granted amnesty, but Tornel succeeded in exempting them from the death penalty. Moreover, although they were to be exiled from Mexico, Bravo and Barragán would still receive half of their pay as *generales de división*.[178]

Tornel's proposal of 15 April marked the beginning of what was obviously his realization that things were beginning to go too far. After Tulancingo, the strong *yorkino* hold over government had become so absolute and so corrupt that, although he continued to benefit from their success, it was apparent that sooner or later somebody else would follow Bravo's example, and this time the conflict would be all the more violent: "The *yorkinos*, having triumphed in the election and in the battlefield, thanks to the imprudence and ruin of their rivals, were now in complete control of the situation. They were the regulators of all public business even its most insignificant details."[179] The radical *yorkinos* became complacent, convinced that they were untouchable. Tornel witnessed with disgust the suspension of ministers such as Sebastián Camacho and Miguel Ramos Arizpe, both of whom had openly stated their unease at the way the *yorkinos* were beginning to behave in government.[180]

Tornel and, in fact, Bocanegra's change in stance was not unique. Following the battle of Tulancingo, to quote Enrique González Pedrero, "as is usually the case following such an outright victory, perhaps because this brought an excess of confidence, the *yorkinos* became divided at the height of their strength, and as occurs with overflowing rivers, the events which followed came like a flood of disasters."[181] However, there was more to those divisions than just an "excess of confidence." The *yorkinos*, having based their entire propaganda between 1825 and 1827 on an anti-*escocés/* anti-Spanish platform, found themselves without an enemy and thus in serious need of replacing their offensive politics with beliefs that consolidated their hegemony. This need to define the politics of *yorkismo* once the *escoceses* had been defeated brought to the light the divisions that existed within what had until then been a very loosely defined liberal Masonic faction with radical-populist tendencies. In other words, as long as there was a common enemy, whether it was reactionary proroyalist Spaniards or members of the Scottish Rite of Masons, the *yorkinos* had been able to create a united front between radical and moderate liberals. The absence of a common enemy meant that the *yorkinos* lost the one thing that had previously united them.

By April, coinciding with the vote in the Chamber of Deputies over the fate of the rebels of Montaño, these divisions started to make news in the press as the radical *yorkinos* started to campaign in favor of Vicente Guerrero in the buildup to the presidential elections and the more moderate *yorkinos* turned against their own lodges and joined the ex-*escoceses*, the *novenarios*, and the *imparciales* in supporting General Manuel Gómez Pedraza. Tornel's own actions, together with the turmoil his political career was to undergo in the spring and summer of 1828, are clearly representative of the divisions that started to afflict the members of the Rite of York.

Toward the end of April, Tornel used his position of power to thwart the radical *yorkinos* he had been acclaimed for defending. He expelled Zavala's friend and co-revolutionary, Lissautte. Zavala was deeply offended and shocked by this action, and his account of Lissautte's expulsion illustrates how Tornel was beginning to change:

A newspaper called *El Tribuno* had been published in the city of Guadalajara, that remonstrated with virulence against the pretensions of the church, and was equally unforgiving with the ministers, especially the Minister of Justice, Ramos Arizpe. Although Mr Lissautte did not feature as the author, the government suspected that he was responsible for the stronger and more reasoned articles.[182]

Tornel believed the attacks on Ramos Arizpe were as scandalous as the tricks the *yorkinos* had used to get rid of Camacho. To the surprise of the *yorkinos*, who relied on his passionate stance against the *escoceses*, he had ceased to be consistent with their beliefs. Zavala wrote:

Whilst [Lissautte] stayed in the house of this magistrate [Zavala] he was safe at all times, and on many occasions Tornel and others who were after him came to enjoy his company and even sat at the same table. However, one day when he had to go into the Federal District to deal with some of his affairs, the *jefe político*, Tornel, got hold of him and forced him to go in custody to the port of Veracruz where he was embarked on a boat to New Orleans.[183]

As far as Tornel was concerned, the reasons for the expulsion were clear. Lissautte was responsible for "severe attacks on the Church and on our religious beliefs."[184] If Zavala was angry with him because he had sat down to dinner with him and Lissautte before arresting the Frenchman, it was Zavala's problem: "He makes the ridiculous accusation that he should not have treated Lissautte as he did, because *they had both eaten at the same table in Tlalpan*. What a bizarre piece of reasoning!"[185]

The radical *yorkinos* did not wait long for their retaliation. In June 1828, a pamphlet entitled *Gracias singulares del C. Coronel José María Tornel* started a campaign against him that lasted most of the summer. He was accused of betraying the *yorkinos* by suspending Luis Lozano, an outspoken *yorkino* who had played an active part in the purges following Tulancingo, from the secretariat of the Federal District, portraying Tornel's decision as an injustice and as an example of his treachery:

When the *Licenciado* Lozano has just saved the mother-country from the threat of the Montaño faction, when he had just merited the esteem, trust and gratitude of a Señor Esteva, to whom the mother-country owes so much, especially as he redeemed us during the recent dangerous crisis; it is then that [Tornel] replaces the *Licenciado* Lozano, and instead of rewarding him as would have been expected, even if it was just for his minor services; he subjects him to public embarrassment, separating him from his post.[186]

Although for the author of the pamphlet, Tornel's betrayal of the *yorkinos* was his worst crime, the attack went on to encompass a wide range of criticisms of the way he was governing the Federal District. The riots that had broken out as a consequence of his *Ley de vagos y maleantes* and the brutality with which his men had dealt with the protesters were presented as examples of the tyrannical rule he was imposing on Mexico City:

One singular grace of the current Sr. Gobernador, is that famous, unheard of, scandalous and anti-constitutional general inquisition he ordered to be executed against beggars, on that tragic day in which Mexico found itself in a worse situation than it had been in under the lives of those Caligulas [viceroys] Venegas and Calleja; and which I refrain from describing here so that I do not shock other nations into believing that we are savages.[187]

He was accused of nepotism: "One singular grace of Sr. Tornel is his determination to fill the municipal corps with his creatures."[188] He had replaced
the councillor and lawyer Juan Francisco Azcárate with his godson, and he
had made sure that friends of his such as Bocanegra and his brother-in-
law, the *Licenciado* Bonilla, among others, were all given important positions in the government of the Federal District, either as vice presidents of
the various committees or as councillors, even though none of them had
the necessary qualifications as *letrados*.

The tone of open bitterness of the pamphlet stemmed from the obvious
resentment felt by the *yorkinos* who had considered Tornel to be one of
them and a close friend, but who now believed they had merely been used
and discarded by him: "One singular grace of Sr. Tornel is the painful
oblivion to which he has consigned the old patriots, his brothers of long
ago, and not just from the period that followed the Scottish earthquake,
but from the foundation of the mother-country. We painfully see how he
has offered many of the main posts in the civic militia to repentant *escoceses*."[189] There was a sense of disbelief in the pamphlet at Tornel's betrayal
of the Rite of York and the palpable fear that in changing sides, he had
divided the *yorkinos*. Those who respected him could not help listening to
the reasons for his desertion. He was provoking other members of the Rite
of York to reconsider their affiliation. This was apparent in the way that
the outspoken *yorkino* newspaper, the *Correo*, continued to defend him
throughout the summer of 1828 against José María Aguirre and his supporters, who were attacking him from a *yorkino* point of view: "You do
not change your opinions or your affiliations to a Rite so easily . . . with
such practices the Governor is dividing the patriots. Many have become
cautious and mistrustful. . . . If we the patriots become divided, the *escoceses* and *novenarios* will triumph."[190]

As far as those *yorkinos* who felt Tornel was betraying them were concerned, the only explanation for Tornel's chameleon-like changes was his
insatiable ambition. They interpreted his creation of the local militia as a
means of having his own private army to become the eventual patriarch of
the nation. Moreover, they interpreted his change as an indication that he
wanted to create a new Mexican aristocracy among the wealthy *yorkinos*,
opposed to those *yorkinos* who believed in consolidating a liberal (radical)
Mexico:

He is accused of possessing an excessive ambition, for it is thought that he unlaw-
fully changed the procedures in the foundation of the local militia in order to have
an army made up of his own creatures and to become the Patriarch in the next
elections. It is said that he is trying to get rid of the poor patriots who helped him
rise and that he is aiming to create a [new] aristocracy, offering jobs and favors to
members of the higher classes, . . . thus dividing the Rite of York into two chambers; one made up of the poorer members who will only serve as the obedient

animals of the Apocalypse, acting as blind instruments of their ambitious intentions; and the other made up of people who belong to the higher spheres of the hierarchy, rich even though they are beasts.[191]

Tornel's own account of his so-called betrayal or change of direction was quite different. His defense was that he had never really changed at all. He claimed in 1852 that he was a moderate man all along and that some of the circumstances of history made him sometimes carry out what would appear to be extreme measures. However, whenever it was possible, he would try to find the most reasonable stance within the political frame of the time. Therefore, if he was so severe with the Spaniards, it was not so much his own choice but because he was obeying orders: "Tornel complied with the demands of the time, without exaggerating or ignoring them. . . . [In fact], he softened and sweetened the fate of the unfortunate victims of these circumstances. Regarding the Spaniards he dictated some measures that, although they were seen to be severe, were effectuated in order to help them without raising the suspicions of the *exaltados*."[192] In retrospect, he was not an *exaltado* or a radical, and because of this, he appeared to change, but it was the *yorkinos* who were changing and not him; dizzy with power, they were becoming more extreme in their political stance, and he was not prepared to follow them that far. Therefore, it was the fact that he was a "moderate" that led him to be "severely punished by his party because of the kindness with which he treated the Spaniards, continuously drying the tears of their families."[193]

Ironically, the scandal that led to Tornel's suspension as governor and triggered Dr. Aguirre's attack on him was not directly related to any of the points that have been covered. The conflict arose out of a misunderstanding between Mexico City's main theater and the church, on 13 June. Previously, during what was known as *La Piedad*, which lasted nine days, the theaters had been closed because it was considered disrespectful to distract believers from their religious duties with performances they would be tempted to attend in preference to the long masses the church had on offer. However, the manager of the theater, thinking *La Piedad* started later, had already booked a theater company for the very night on which *La Piedad* started, and he had advertised the show, unaware that he was acting illegally.

The manager, on being told by the priests that he could not open the theater, rushed to Tornel to seek help. He had already paid the actors, who were at that moment rehearsing for the opening performance that evening, and he ran the risk of going bankrupt if he was forced to close the theater. Tornel was faced with an awkward decision; he was a deeply religious man, yet particularly partial to the theater. The determining factor was that *La Piedad* was in honor of the Virgin of los Remedios—the Virgin that Spaniards prayed to rather than the miraculous and very Mexican Virgin of

Guadalupe. Tornel must have weighed the pros and cons, concluded that to allow the theaters to remain open would be a popular decision, especially as the Virgin in question was the Spanish one, and decided that there was no reason for the theater to be considered a threat to the church or the faith of its devoted believers. He argued that, on the contrary, if the theater supported the church by putting on religious plays during *La Piedad*, it would encourage through literature attendance in church. The theater manager, who had only asked for permission to let the production he had advertised for 13 June to go on, found himself suddenly having to put on a show every night during *La Piedad*.[194]

Tornel's reasoning went as follows:

It is very strange that your Excellency, after having allowed a poster to go up announcing to the public the performance of a play tonight, has decided to practice the religious tradition of closing the theater during these nine days that are dedicated to the Virgin María Santìsima de los Remedios. The public has been tricked, something that I cannot allow, in the same way that I cannot allow you to arbitrarily terminate, and without my knowledge, performances that are so important in assisting the maintenance of public order, something I am responsible for. If theater is an innocent pastime in itself, it does not cease to be so on the days when the faithful dedicate themselves to prayer. If it is not innocent it should cease at all times . . . I also know the kind of cult that pleases God; and there is nothing that could please Him more than that crimes are avoided.[195]

He wanted to avoid the risk of riots, and it seemed that the most sensible thing was to allow the theater to open. Francisco Pérez de Palacios, the mayor to whom this letter was addressed, accepted his order, and the *Correo* printed his letter of agreement with Tornel's final decision on the opening of the theater. On 19 June the *Correo* printed the reply in which the town hall celebrated his decision. It appeared that he had found a wise and popular compromise. Before each production, the cast sang a religious composition; no harm was done to the church, and the theatergoers would not resort to rioting because their tickets remained valid as the shows went on.

Much to Tornel's surprise, this incident sparked Dr. José María Aguirre's attack. In the beginning, the dispute was ostensibly minor. Aguirre, a respected priest based in the Church of Santa Veracruz in Mexico City, complained, understandably from a religious point of view, about the moral repercussions of Tornel's decision: "The opera company and the individuals who make up the theater's orchestra cannot sing the 'Salve' with which they wanted to honor María SSma. de los Remedios next Saturday afternoon, because the tradition is that it is sung by one of the religious communities."[196] Initially it appeared that Aguirre was criticizing Tornel from a reactionary and pro-Spanish perspective, and the *Correo* consequently mocked Aguirre's anachronistic pretensions on 21 June: "The priest of Sta.

Veracruz, could not be more extravagant! His whole letter gives off an aristocratic air that belongs to those long days when it was a sin to produce theater for the public."[197] The *Correo*, like Tornel, underestimated the support Aguirre had behind him.

It was not long before Aguirre's attack spread over a wide range of points, and not necessarily from an *escocés* perspective. The reference to the opening of the theater in the pamphlet *Gracias singulares* was not a mere complaint from somebody who believed in obeying the rigors of *La Piedad*; it was a severe condemnation of Tornel's lifestyle:

After the Town Hall had agreed, following a serious discussion, that it was not convenient for it to run the theater, given that this had a ruinous effect on the municipal funds that needed to be spent on much more commendable enterprises, Tornel, in order to have his own way, called an extraordinary meeting, during which he spoke and implored with his usual sweet and enchanting energy. Although the *capitulares* initially resisted the opening of the theater, [Tornel] confused them by saying that the Supreme Government would provide financial assistance for such an enterprise. Therefore, with some regrets they agreed to go back on this previous agreement. The truth is that because of this fatal determination, hospitals do not receive enough support; the cleaning of streets takes place at a snail's pace; in fact, there is not a branch of the city that has not suffered as a result and the city continues to suffer from continuous and enormous losses because this was Sr. Tornel's pleasure; to provide entertainment and a place for idle talk to a small group of men who attend the theater and who represent an insignificant part of Mexico's vast population.[198]

The attack on Tornel had developed from a criticism of his opening the theater during *La Piedad* to one of his actually maintaining it at all, when elsewhere there were insufficient hospitals to deal with the victims of the cholera epidemic, and the poverty of the capital was evident. The attack portrayed him as a member of a pseudo-aristocracy who used public funds to amuse himself and his friends while the rest of the population suffered the hardships caused by the ruined economy.

The pamphlet *Gracias signulares* was followed by the even harsher *Verdadera segunda parte de las gracias singulares*.[199] The whole question as to whether theaters should open during *La Piedad* was by now forgotten. Resentful *escoceses* and radical *yorkinos* joined forces in writing condemnatory attacks on Tornel, illustrating the extremes of his corruption, the extent of his betrayal, his lust for power, and his mishandling of the Federal District. What had started as a minor dispute between Tornel and a reactionary priest had become a major crisis in his political career by the end of June.

On 4 July, Aguirre read out his accusation against Tornel in the Senate, and the senators, instead of rejecting it, officially passed it on to the grand jury to decide whether Tornel was guilty. It seems that a large section of the powerful Rite of York had decided to punish Tornel for his shift in opinion. The *Correo* continued to defend him, showing disgust at the Senate's decision to take Aguirre's accusations seriously and producing satirical poems that mocked the priest. However, his credibility as a politician had suffered a serious blow. On 28 July, during the official preparations for the 16 September celebrations, it seemed as if everybody had forgotten his stirring speech of 1827. He stood as a candidate for vice president of the organizing committee and received only one vote, probably his own.[200]

As July passed, the attacks against and the defenses in favor of Tornel continued to fill the newspapers. On 16 July, his friend Bocanegra gave a moving speech in his defense in the Chamber of Deputies.[201] The dispute, however, continued throughout the summer. On 16 August, the Chamber of Deputies created a committee that had the sole purpose of reconciling Aguirre and Tornel.[202] It would obviously create bad publicity for the members of the Rite of York if they were seen to be divided on the issue or bickering about each other on the eve of the second presidential elections of their new country.

After two months of constant attacks, Aguirre dropped his charges on 19 August. They embraced in Congress as two good friends would do.[203] The reconciliation was achieved. However, although the reconciliation may be interpreted as a gallant attempt by both Tornel and Aguirre to restore the unity the *yorkinos* had experienced only two years before, the divisions that existed in their party were too great to be healed by such a gesture. The growing antagonism between moderate and radical *yorkinos* was not a result of Tornel and Aguirre's dispute. Their dispute was simply an expression of the increasing tensions that had started to develop among the members of the Rite of York since the opposition, as represented by the Scottish Rite Masons, had been swept from the political scene after the battle of Tulancingo. In the buildup to the presidential elections, these divisions became all the greater. Guerreo, who had the support of the more radical *yorkinos* such as Zavala, frightened the predominantly white, landowning Creole families who still believed in the caste system inherited from the colony. He was a *mulato*, not even a *mestizo*. The very color of his skin represented a threat to the Mexican oligarchy.[204] They desperately wanted Gómez Pedraza to be president. Gómez Pedraza was white, he came from the "right" social background, and above all, he was a moderate who was prepared to forgive generals such as Bravo, because they were all from the same class.[205] The growing divisions were so ominous that in an attempt to avoid the conflict that would inevitably break out whatever the outcome of the elections, Tornel "hoping to appease the dissidents and to find a solution to the increasing difficulties, proposed the election of a third candidate, and this was the *general de división* D. Anastasio Bustamante."[206]

This third option did not prosper. By mid-September it became clear that Gómez Pedraza was going to win, and Santa Anna started a revolt on 12

September in Perote, proclaiming Guerrero president of the republic regardless of the outcome of the elections. However, Tornel was suspended from his functions as deputy and governor of the Federal District before news of the revolt reached the capital. On 5 September, in spite of the fact that Tornel and Aguirre had publicly settled their differences, the *yorkino* judge Agustin Pérez de Lebrija accused him in the Senate of neglecting to impose the expulsion laws in the Federal District adequately and of having illegally granted his civic militia certain powers he was not in a position to award. On 13 September, he was found guilty and suspended from both of his public functions. In the wording of the accusation, it was clear that his suspension was due to his betrayal of the radicals; he was to be suspended for "drying the tears [of the Spaniards], on many occasions, . . . protecting them from expulsion, compromising his patriotic reputation."[207] In Tornel's own words, "With a clear conscience he presented himself before the jury to defend himself; however, this was in vain as the hatred of one party had already condemned him from the beginning."[208]

THE REVOLTS OF PEROTE AND LA ACORDADA

Santa Anna's hidden radical *yorkino* sympathies found their most forceful expression on 12 September when he launched the Plan of Perote. Although he had not openly embraced the cause of the *yorkinos* in Xalapa, his political ideas, at a national level, had developed along similar lines to those of his friend, Tornel. Moreover, although the correspondence they maintained during these years (1824–1828) has been lost, it is clear that the writer and the *caudillo* had not lost touch with each other. In fact, it was generally acknowledged by their contemporaries that Tornel and Santa Anna wrote to each other regularly. It is significant that one of the reasons that was given for Tornel's suspension, albeit not publicly, was that since Tornel was known to be a close friend of the *caudillo* and that he had four thousand men under his command, in the form of the civic militia,[209] he had the men and the resources to take over the capital on behalf of Santa Anna if Gómez Pedraza won the elections. This interpretation of Tornel's suspension leads to two conclusions. First, the *gómezpedracistas* in the capital had received prior notification that it was Santa Anna's intention to rebel, should Gómez Pedraza be elected, and, second, regardless of Tornel's "betrayal" and the fact that he had proposed Anastasio Bustamante (a member of the Rite of York, all the same) for president, he was still considered a radical *yorkino* who favored Guerrero's election. Although Tornel went on to join Guadalupe Victoria in the defense of the National Palace during the Revolt of La Acordada, thus resisting "the temptation of actively and openly co-operating with the revolution," renouncing "the opportunity of avenging past feuds and enjoying the bounty which is always shared" among the triumphant rebels, he did explain to the rebels, in secret, that he approved of what they were hoping to achieve.[210] In a clarifying passage of his *Memorias*, Bocanegra (a radical *yorkino*, master of the Federalista lodge in Mexico City, who had also supported granting an amnesty to the rebels of Montaño) noted that by the summer of 1828, the divisions in the Rite of York were such that there was "great ideological confusion and a bitter personality-driven war."[211]

It was clear to Bocanegra, in the same way that it became apparent to Lorenzo de Zavala, that had the 1824 Constitution created a direct system of elections, Guerrero would have won by a landslide victory: "Had the elections [been based] on individual suffrage, [Guerrero] would have received an immense majority [of votes] in his favor."[212] The established indirect system of elections by which, at the end, it was up to the representatives of each state to decide who was elected president, was thus perceived to favor the more moderate of the two candidates—in other words, the *hombres de bien* candidate, Gómez Pedraza. For Bocanegra, Santa Anna's intentions were, if not admirable, "at least justified," given that "the *caudillo* of Perote wanted to protect the triumph of the general will he believed reflected the reality of the nation's desires" against the oppression of a system that had allowed the maneuvers of the parties to place an unpopular candidate on the presidential seat.[213] In Santa Anna's own words, "The people have everywhere made their intentions sufficiently clear . . . , [and] tired of the maneuvers of our despicable domestic enemies, have raised their voice in unison with that of the army . . . presenting this plan."[214]

With Tornel no longer in a position to use the civic militias in the capital to second Santa Anna's revolt, Santa Anna found himself alone at the beginning. He retreated from Perote to Oaxaca via Tehuacán as his very personal enemy, General Manuel Rincón, gave chase with the support of General José María Calderón. Once fortified in Oaxaca, all Santa Anna had to do was wait. In mid-November the radical Juan Alvarez seconded the Plan of Perote from his garrison in Acapulco. Isidoro Montes de Oca followed suit in Taxco. And on 30 November, Lorenzo de Zavala and General José María Lobato, at the head of the barracks of La Acordada, revolted, placing the National Palace under siege.

Although Tornel was a close friend of Santa Anna and sympathized with the rebels, he did not join the revolution. In essence, he could not accept the means by which they were hoping to resist the constitutional election of Gómez Pedraza, and he felt that he had to stand by the government "for the sake of the nation's decorum, and for the sake of his own party," rather than "give the political Pharisees the chance to fill the world with the scandalous thunder [of civil war]."[215] Ultimately, like Victoria, although Tornel personally sympathized with Guerrero's cause and his faction, he could not support a revolt that was undeniably unconstitutional. It was therefore imperative to defend the government and condemn those "who shattered the public peace."[216] Although Tornel thereafter became a fairly regular conspirator and organizer of *pronunciamientos*, he was still a committed constitutionalist in 1828.

Therefore on the night of 30 November, following the first outbreak of gunfire, after a hurried and desperate meeting of several ministers, generals, deputies, and senators, it was agreed that Tornel and General Ramón López Rayón were to go first thing the next morning to the building of La Acordada to try to persuade the rebels to surrender. He wrote that

Rayón and Tornel carried out their mission in good faith as was to be expected; however, this served no use among people who were well aware of the weakness of the government and who thought this was confirmed by its attempts to appease them. At four o'clock in the afternoon they returned to the palace, sadly persuaded that the force of arms, followed by a thousand disasters, would be what would determine the outcome of the conflict.[217]

At the same time, Tornel and Colonel José Ignacio Basadre also saw Guerrero. According to him, they were sincere friends of the general, and because of this, they told him to abstain from getting involved in the conflict, even though the rebels were fighting to place him in the presidential seat, "because of his decency, his known interests, and to avoid a constitutional conundrum, that would form an obstacle if the chamber of deputies had to decide on the validity of the elections."[218] Initially, Guerrero followed their advice and retreated to the mill of Santa Fe "to avoid all compromises, leaving the city which was the theater of war."[219]

After two days of combat, Gómez Pedraza came to the conclusion on the night of 3 December that all was lost. On his own he escaped from the National Palace, fled from the capital, and succeeded in reaching Guadalajara. On 27 December, he renounced all claim to the presidency and on 29 March 1829 left the country. On 4 December, first thing in the morning, the news of Gómez Pedraza's escape spread throughout the National Palace and all over the city. The rebels' march toward the palace started as soon as the news was known. Lucas Balderas, José María Lobato, and Vicente Filisola reached the main square. With the revolution gathering momentum, hundreds of citizens took to the streets. Victoria was furious. He ran down the main central staircase of the palace, sword in hand, followed by Tornel, "ready to die fighting," and he stood in the gaping main entrance, "exposed to the bullets that poured like rain."[220] Tornel insisted that there was no longer any point in fighting, and Victoria realized in the end that it would be a "useless sacrifice" to allow the bloodshed to go on.[221] He told Tornel to go out and persuade Lobato to promise to respect the president (who was still Victoria) and not to harm the men who had defended the palace.

Tornel ran out into the middle of the square amid the gunfire. He spotted Lobato in the corner of the Parián market, nearest to the cathedral, surrounded by an angry crowd, and he rushed toward him to fulfill his duty:

"When by a mistake that could only arise in the middle of the prevalent chaos and confusion, it was thought that I was . . . Gómez Pedraza. There is no need for me to emphasize how dear this could have cost my life."[222] In the midst of the turmoil and when he was convinced that the angry crowds were going to lynch him, a Captain Velasco recognized him, and started shouting to the others that it was not Gómez Pedraza they were about to murder. After this ordeal he succeeded in reaching Lobato, who complied with Victoria's demands.

Although the rebel leaders decided to put down their arms, since Gómez Pedraza had fled and the revolt had triumphed, the violence was not yet over. On 4 December 1828, the sense of exhilaration of the revolt gathered momentum among the leaderless mob that had gathered in the center, and at two o'clock what has come to be known as the Parián riot started. In the words of Costeloe:

During several hours of unrestrained pillage and plunder, shops and warehouses were destroyed and, according to one writer, merchandise worth 2,000,000 pesos were carried off and more than a thousand people "were reduced to destitution." The city was soon overtaken by anarchy and disorder, with crowds of people roaming the streets hungry for vengeance, venting their anger against people and properties.[223]

The situation in the capital quickly deteriorated into a state of complete anarchy. Radical, moderate, and traditionalist politicians alike, the majority of them *hombres de bien*, were horrified by the social dissolution that erupted with the pillage of the Parián, the main market of Mexico City.

THE PARIÁN RIOT

To quote Timothy Anna, "Mexico City now experienced the closest thing to anarchy it had encountered in 136 years, since the great riot of 1692. . . . It lived through what according to all accounts was its worst hour . . . , which more than any other single event galvanized propertied elites to a reborn conservatism."[224] As Silvia Arrom rightly points out, "The riot, though just one episode in one city was a pivotal event in dampening the democratic idealism of early independent Mexico."[225] For Bocanegra, the riot was "a national catastrophe and a veritable calamity."[226] It represented for him, in the same way that it did for all of the *hombres de bien*, a trauma that brought with it a sudden marked fear of the political participation of the masses: "My memory saddens in remembering [these events], and my quill refuses to write about them; . . . attacking order, and even destroying it completely, they left Mexico in the greatest of dangers, whichever way you look at it, because by allowing anarchy to erupt with such strength and resolve, it became obvious that the total ruin of society was inevitable."[227]

In the middle of the chaos, the only representative of the constitutional government was Victoria. He met with Zavala, and they agreed that law and order must be reestablished at all costs. The man they chose to do this was Tornel. At the end of the day, traitor or not, radical or moderate, the fact remained that he had succeeded, in those seven months he had been governor, in gaining the reputation of being a man of action who had the ability and determination to impose law and order in the most extreme of situations. He was found innocent of the charges that had been made against him in September and was renamed governor on 5 December.[228]

Tornel saw his task as one that would involve a great effort on the part of himself and his men: "The irresistible and omnipotent force of anarchy presented itself to my imagination with all the horrors it had caused and all of those it was capable of causing."[229] This image was reinforced when, on his arrival at the government office of the Federal District, he found that there was only one "employee who could assist me with the work that needed to be done without further delay."[230] The public security corps had ceased to exist during the "bloody affray of the past few days."[231]

The situation in the capital could not have been more disheartening: "A part of the Parián was in flames; the rest was the true image of desolation; some of the stalls had been saved from the raid by sheer chance."[232] Tornel assisted in putting out the fire at the Parián, organizing the efforts of those present. He also supervised the owners of the plundered shops in their attempt to save their remaining property. With a small group of *cívicos*, he succeeded in "forcing the mob to retreat" and "to guard [what remained of] the building."[233] After half an hour had passed, his services were no longer necessary in the Parián, and so he moved on. He claims that as he rode through the city, people would call after him, as if he were the savior of their property and of their lives.

One of his next tasks was to reestablish the police force as quickly as possible. While he was doing this, he issued a temporary law, on 6 December, prohibiting more than three people from gathering in any public place, forbidding the carrying of weapons or the sale of alcohol, and ordering that all shops remained closed. He also gave the order that the streets should be constantly patrolled by the local militias who had remained faithful to him.[234] Just as the situation started to return to normal, a sudden lack of flour, maize, and, consequently bread, on the morning of 7 December sparked off another riot. Tornel, terrified of witnessing scenes like those of the French Revolution, ordered all bakers to work, putting them under threat of arrest if they refused to do so, in order to supply the angry and desperate crowds with the basic necessities. He also imposed severe fines on any food merchants who tried to hike the prices in the present situation.[235]

By 8 December, law and order had been restored. Tornel allowed the churches to ring their bells once more and permitted the markets in the squares of El Volador, Jesús Nazareno, and Santa Catarina to reopen.[236] As a sign of confidence and to show that things were back to normal, he allowed the streets to be swept, the lights and pipes to be restored, the bars, societies, and restaurants to open again, and the sale of alcohol and even *pulque* to recommence.[237] Having dealt with any immediate problems, he set himself the task of collecting, at times taking by force, all of the uniforms that had been stolen during the conflict and were being worn by people who were not soldiers. Within a month of his reinstatement as governor, he had succeeded in reorganizing the police force of the Federal District. After the revolt of La Acordada, the police force had lost all of its weapons and had only twelve horses left. When he was made governor again, there were only thirteen men who were willing to continue to police a city of over 220,000. After a month, all of this had changed. Moreover, on 20 December he created a new branch of the police force: a corps of civilians who were elected by their neighborhood and were each responsible for guarding and defending the properties of their block.

His endeavors to restore law and order in the capital were relatively successful, and there was a tight control on places where people gathered, such as marketplaces, bars, and churches. On 5 January 1829, determined to maintain law and order, he issued a decree by which all guns and weapons that had been lost or stolen during the events in December had to be restored to their rightful owners, the army: "Such was the confusion that had taken over things because of those events at the time, that children believed they were authorized to take sides as well and to fight each other in the streets, spilling more blood in a bitter parody of the recent revolution."[238] With children reenacting the past events, using weapons that had been lost in combat, it seemed as if the sound of gunshot would never end. However, according to Tornel, the problem was not so much children imitating the adults' behavior ("What an example we have set!"),[239] but that the adults themselves who had not come to terms with the outcome of the conflict were really threatening the peace and order of the capital.

With weapons widely available, frequent street fights often turned into skirmishes. On one occasion, two different divisions that had fought on opposite sides during La Acordada went into open combat in the capital's Alameda and neighboring streets. Tornel had to take forty dragoons with him to restore order. As he was to write with bitterness, "Unfortunate city! There were so many causes for alarm. It looked like a fortress under siege. The most insignificant of rumors immediately provoked family feuds; and they all feared for their fortunes and their lives."[240] The disorderly situation of the Federal District led to even more drastic measures. On 20 February Tornel issued a decree that basically abolished all gambling in the city, in an attempt to exterminate "idleness, the prolific originator of disorders," persecute all "beggars, the moths of society," and end the "germ of corruption, ruin of all families." He limited the consumption of alcohol, "disgraceful origin of the degradation and depravation of the rabble."[241] His perseverance in striving to clean up the Federal District, together with the relative speed with which he succeeded in restoring law and order in the aftermath of La Acordada, were two aspects of his governorship that inevitably made him popular among the *hombres de bien*. The accounts of the Parián riot that are to be found in the diaries and the memoirs of politicians such as Alamán, Carlos María de Bustamante, Mora, and Zavala, to name but a few, illustrate the extent to which the scenes of anarchy and social revolution disturbed them.[242] Regardless of whether they agreed with Tornel's political beliefs, he had successfully restored law and order in the capital.

TORNEL AND VICENTE GUERRERO

In the wake of the revolts of Perote and La Acordada, General Vicente Guerrero became president of the republic on 12 January 1829. In retrospect, Tornel's evaluation of Guerrero's presidency was one of sadness and missed opportunities. A resolute leader was needed to restore peace and order in the country. With two violently opposed irreconcilable parties, the nation needed "a man who was strong because of his convictions."[243] In his mind, Guerrero was not this man. He relied too heavily on his apparent popularity and in so doing made a fatal mistake. He adopted "middle of the road measures"[244] and infuriated both parties. Although Tornel described him as a moderate, tolerant, and just man, whose generosity went beyond the limits of prudence, he also portrayed him as a man with no education, who was so frightened of doing anything wrong or immoral that he allowed himself to be used and abused by the power mongerers who surrounded him: "In a world without passions, in that . . . ideal world, Señor Guerrero would have been able to figure without any contradiction."[245] Tornel's final verdict is proof of the extent to which he had become a professional politician in all senses of the word: "In the advanced and refined state societies find themselves in, a man without malice is not the most apt to govern them as he will not have the knowledge of experience, he will be easy to seduce and will be sensitive to the suspicious words of the astute flatterer."[246] Guerrero was, in other words, a naive and ignorant man, easily influenced by any politician who flattered him to further his own career.

Although Bocanegra and Tornel supported Guerrero's government (Bocanegra served as his minister of relations [1 April–2 November 1829] minister of the exchequer [3 November–17 December 1829], and interim president [18–23 December 1829]), they already showed signs of their unease toward the middle of 1829 when a number of particularly radical proposals met with the approval of both Congress and the president. For Tornel, the main problem was that by being too "tolerant and fair," Guerrero allowed the radical *yorkinos* he had distanced himself from in the spring of 1828 to abuse his character, all of which resulted in a "shy and hesitant" cabinet dominated by radicals.[247] If he identified himself "with the men of 1829," it was because of "the healthy intentions of the president, my gratitude for his friendship, one which tied me closely to two of his secretaries in particular [Bocanegra being one of them], and my stubborn belief in our popular principles and the sweetness and undeniable tolerance of the government . . . among other considerations."[248] Bocanegra shared Tornel's fears. While in the beginning he believed that Guerrero's presidency "offered the promise of a future which even though it could not be entirely blissful and bountiful, was at least one which could be peaceful and which harbored good hopes for the nation,"[249] by the summer of 1829, he was alarmed at the way in which Zavala succeeded in passing a number of radical proposals and reforms that he thought turned everything upside down, provoking a generalized sense of displeasure and public disapproval throughout the republic.[250] In other words, for both Tornel and Bocanegra, Zavala's reforms as minister of the exchequer—taxing the large landowners, reducing the salaries of both governors and high-ranking officers, abolishing the tobacco monopoly, and expropriating the property of the Jesuits and the Inquisition—were all too radical for their liking.

Nevertheless, they did not voice their unease immediately. On 1 April Guerrero delivered the opening speech with which presidents announce the beginning of their term in office. In the same way that Victoria had asked Tornel to write his speeches, Guerrero also called on Tornel for some help with his use of rhetoric. In response to the accusation that Guerrero was Tornel's puppet (an accusation that echoed the noted view that when Victoria spoke, it was Tornel who was talking), Tornel claimed, in 1833, that when he wrote the president's speeches, all he did was put Guerrero's sentiments into words. It was not "a political romance . . . written to fool and attract the people," "[Guerrero's] heart spoke there."[251]

Having said this, regardless of the fact that he put his prose at Guerrero's disposal, it was not long before Tornel made his unease known. In October 1828, having been elected deputy while he was still suspended, this time for his native state of Veracruz, he displayed in Congress, once it reopened under the new administration in April, the kind of constitutionalist views he had held with such consistency in 1827. In other words, although he was beginning to show signs of disenchantment in the aftermath of the events of the previous year, his faith in the Federal Constitution and constitutional procedures had not faltered. This was to become evident in the stance he adopted over what were two particularly controversial aspects of Guerrero's presidency: the means by which Guerrero's presidency was legitimized and the use of extraordinary powers the president was granted in the summer of 1829.

If the 1824 Constitution was to be abided by, Victoria's successor, once he had completed his four-year term in office, should have been Gómez Pedraza, because he had won the election. The question was how the winning party could fix the situation so that Guerrero's presidency could be interpreted as constitutional. Tornel suggested that the only constitutional solution left to them, after the violent events of La Acordada, was to accept Gómez Pedraza's "resignation, as the most adequate means of ensuring that Señor Guerrero's government is constitutional."[252] His proposal was refused, however, because by accepting Gómez Pedraza's resignation, they would be admitting that he was the constitutional president in the first place, and would have continued to be so, had there not been a coup d'état.

Instead, a grand commission was called to vote on who was to be the next president. Tornel claimed that it had become necessary for them to break the laws of the constitution, "to avoid the disasters of anarchy, further turmoil and the threatening dissolution of the state."[253] Nevertheless, he was disappointed. Although he supported Guerrero, he was disillusioned with the way he had risen to power. In "Federación" he had written that "the moral principle of all revolutions should be to instruct and not to destroy."[254] During the actual revolt of La Acordada he had told Guerrero not to become involved in the conflict and had stayed in the National Palace with Victoria and Gómez Pedraza to defend the constitutional government. He continued to believe in the representative process and opposed the dangerous "right of insurrection" he had warned Landa about two years before. The revolt of La Acordada, and the subsequent rupture with the 1824 Constitution to enable Guerrero to become president of the republic, set a fatal precedent for years to come. Guadalupe Victoria was to become the first and only president to last in power the full four-year term. If Guerrero had succeeded in becoming president of the republic by force, there was no reason why others could not try, as they in fact did, time and again, for the next three decades. As Tornel was to write with foreboding in 1833, "No period in our history started with so many funereal omens as the one that began in January 1829. The parties without retiring from the stage of events, prepared themselves with greater determination for a fierce and long struggle that continues to torment us with its consequences today."[255] The rupture with the constitution and the democratic process inevitably meant that the opposition would no longer consider regaining power exclusively through elections.

The second controversial issue Tornel had to overcome concerning Guerrero's presidency arose on 6 August 1829, at the time of Barradas's expedition, when, as an emergency measure, it was proposed that Guerrero should be granted emergency powers. Tornel opposed the proposal in Congress, arguing that such powers would be a dangerous precedent because they would directly undermine any of the constitutional ideals still remaining in the government. The moment the president had emergency powers, representatives and elections would no longer be necessary because the president could decide what was required. He claimed that "the most gratifying triumph of my life was the one I secured the day I saved the Constitution and perhaps Sr. Guerrero in the national tribunal."[256] However, it was a very brief triumph. By the end of the month, Guerrero was granted emergency powers. Years later, Tornel was to claim that he considered resigning because it was too great a contradiction for him to serve a dictatorship. His friend Bocanegra, however, persuaded him to continue a while longer as deputy for Veracruz and at the head of the Federal District.

THE GLORIOUS VICTORY OF TAMPICO

One glorious event in 1829 at least briefly prolonged that sense of hope that had characterized Mexican politics in 1824 and had almost disappeared entirely by mid-1829, while delaying the traditionalist backlash that was to bring about the overthrow of Guerrero in December: the victory of Tampico (11 September 1829). By all accounts, during the first half of 1829, persecuted Spaniards in Mexico, together with exiled Spaniards in Cuba, started to plan and prepare their revenge. In many senses an illusion was created that all Spaniards in Mexico, together with the overthrown majority who had voted for Gómez Pedraza and the defeated Scottish Rite faction, would fully support a Spanish reconquest of Mexico. The illusion was strong enough to convince the Spanish authorities in Cuba that the time was ripe for the invasion Arenas had talked about as early as 1827. Reenacting Cortés' expedition and yet convinced that the Mexicans would see the Spanish army as "liberating rather than conquering,"[257] General Isidro Barradas, at the head of thirty-five hundred men, landed on the beaches of Cabo Rojo, not far from Tampico, on 27 July. The neighboring villages offered no resistance, and Barradas waited to see the promised counterrevolution begin.

Rumors of the invasion reached the capital before Barradas actually landed in Mexico. Tornel's reaction, as governor of the Federal District, was criticized by the traditionalist opposition as being excessive and unfounded. However, when news of the invasion was confirmed, he became all the more popular for having acted the way he did. On 12 July, he addressed the Federal District with his *aux armes citoyens* speech, *¡Conciudadanos! Los españoles vienen a pisar el suelo sagrado de la república.*[258] He then set about organizing the defense of the capital. The civic militia was called into action. The reserves were brought out into the streets. Suddenly there were troops everywhere in Mexico City, marching back and forth, drilling, and recruiting. The many brigades and divisions in the Federal District showed their support by offering their unconditional assistance and aid to the governor. On 23 July, with confirmation of the imminent arrival of Barradas's expedition reaching the capital, Tornel produced a sharp reply to his critics: *¡Compatriotas! Os anuncié la proximidad*

de la invasión española cuando ya no se podía dudar de ella.[259] On 30
July, Bocanegra printed a letter on behalf of Guerrero praising his preparations to defend the capital. Letters of allegiance to him by the generals
and commanders of the various regiments in the Federal District were also
published in the press. Contrary to what the Spanish agents had told Barradas's superiors in Cuba, "In the capital the definite confirmation of the
long-awaited attack produced an atmosphere of patriotism and national
unity as had not been experienced since the first days of independence."[260]
In the words of Tornel, "The whole nation, without the exception of a
single Mexican, became involved in preparations to defend its dearest
rights."[261]

On 5 August, Tornel demanded that a general amnesty be offered to all
Mexicans and called on the predominant feeling of patriotism, hoping to
end all internal divisions by uniting against the threat of a foreign invasion.[262] As the month went by, he dedicated himself completely to preparing the defense of the capital. He praised and encouraged all of the troops
based in the Federal District and succeeded in granting a provisional amnesty to some of the political prisoners who were incarcerated in the Federal
District, under his jurisdiction.[263] As it happened, none of the preparations
turned out to be necessary. Generals Manuel Mier y Terán and Santa Anna
succeeded in defeating the Spanish invaders.

On 20 September news of the victory reached the capital. The celebrations were spectacular. As Tornel was to recall "In the ever memorable
night in which the decisive defeat of the Spaniards was announced, all of
the inhabitants [of Mexico City] went out into the streets, playing music
and waving flags as they walked; the manifestations of joy had no limits."[264] With Tornel in command of the capital, Santa Anna's victory became a legendary event. He ordered marches, Te Deums, and fiestas and
decreed that 25, 26, and 27 September were to be wholly dedicated to
celebrating the victory.[265] As María del Carmen Vázquez Mantecón rightly
points out, it was Tornel who came up with the idea of calling Santa Anna
the "hero of Tampico."[266] With a propagandist like Tornel at his disposition, Santa Anna started to acquire a mythical status no other general enjoyed. It is no coincidence that Mier y Terán, who played an equally
important role in defeating Barradas, did not feature so prominently in the
celebrations. He did not have someone like Tornel to wax lyrical about his
virtues in the capital. To quote Wilfrid Callcott, "The uncertainties of the
daybreak were now passed. The sun in its full splendor shone upon the
man of destiny as he strode forth with confidence to mold—for good or
ill—his country's future."[267]

THE ABOLITION OF SLAVERY

It was during this brief spell of optimism and unity, and before the news
of Santa Anna's victory reached Mexico City, that Tornel decided to make

the most of Guerrero's emergency powers and asked him to abolish slavery on 16 September 1829, as part of the annual celebrations of independence.[268] Guerrero, a *mulato* himself, sympathized with this cause and decreed that slavery was to be forever banned in the Mexican republic. Tornel's abolitionism would have far-reaching consequences in the 1830s, in particular with regard to the Texan revolt of 1836. Interestingly, although Bocanegra would later write that Tornel was not exclusively responsible for the abolition of slavery in Mexico,[269] as Tornel would have us believe in his *Breve reseña histórica*[270] (although he did recognize that Tornel had played an important part in the deliberations that had led to the decree of 16 September 1829), it is perhaps indicative of the influence Tornel's writings had that to this day, the historiography has tended to view him as the man who inspired this law.[271]

PLAN OF XALAPA, 1829

Although the glorious victory of Tampico and the abolition of slavery delayed the traditionalist backlash that was being plotted in the summer of 1829, they did not succeed in preventing the *hombres de bien* who went on to support the Plan of Xalapa (4 December 1829) from persevering with their aims. It was as the conspiracy started to gather momentum in the fall of 1829 that it became obvious to the ex-*escoceses, novenarios*, moderates, and disenchanted *yorkinos*, who believed the time had come to put a stop to Guerrero's unconstitutional radical government, that a major obstacle to their forthcoming counterrevolution was the power Tornel held as governor of the Federal District. According to Tornel, whoever had control of the troops in the capital was in a position to determine the outcome of a coup: "Two years experience, a practical knowledge of the means of the police, together with the fact that I had created the militia and reorganized the corps of watchmen and that I had won the favor of the people meant that I was one of the general government's best assistants."[272] It thus became imperative to replace Tornel as governor with someone who would support the revolt. On this occasion, rather than organizing a press campaign against him, the more skillful traditionalists who frequented the National Palace found a particularly decorous way of having Tornel removed: they put pressure on Guerrero to send him elsewhere. They initially suggested making him commander general of Yucatán, which had been shaken by a centralist revolt. This would have been a demotion in effect, and Guerrero rejected the proposal. They then proposed an alternative that was in itself an honorable one but would remove him from the scene: they suggested to Guerrero that he promote Tornel by naming him minister plenipotentiary of Mexico in the United States of America. Guerrero, thinking this appropriate and unaware of the conspirators' intentions, agreed.[273] He was to leave at the end of November. Once he was out of the way, on

4 December, the counterrevolution that overthrew Guerrero's administration began.

On 30 November, Tornel addressed the Federal District and the various corps of militias he had created during the past two years. He bade them farewell and prepared to depart.[274] He left all of his family's possessions in the name of his good friend Bocanegra, to take care of them during his absence.[275] As Tornel left the capital in the second week of December 1829, news arrived of the revolt that had begun in Xalapa. He had some doubts as to whether it would be better to stay, but in the end decided to continue his journey to Puebla. On arrival, he went with his secretary, José Antonio Mejía, to the state government to see if they could be of any help. However, the governor told them that the Congress of Puebla had voted to support the revolt. There was nothing for Tornel and Mejía to do: "We decided to leave as nobody was prepared to listen."[276]

The journey from Puebla to Xalapa was full of mishaps. Having almost reached Tepeyahualco, Tornel and his family were surrounded by a cavalry division led by Alvino Pérez who, obeying orders from General Melchor Múzquiz, arrested them. They were thrown into cells in Tepeyahualco, "depriving my family of beds and food."[277] Tornel wrote to Anastasio Bustamante complaining about the way he and his family were being treated. Bustamante, either because he accepted Tornel's claims to his position being "inviolable and sacred" or because he wanted to keep "the attentions of friendship," issued him and his family the necessary passports to continue their journey.[278]

Anastasio Bustamante was the same man Tornel had proposed as president when it had become obvious to him that if either Gómez Pedraza or Guerrero won the elections, war would follow. Bustamante had indeed moved on. He had become vice president under Guerrero's administration. When he was invited to lead the counterrevolution of Xalapa of 4 December, he accepted. With hindsight, Tornel lamented how he had trusted Bustamante before the revolt of Xalapa.[279] When he and his family arrived in Xalapa, Tornel went to look for him in a *hacienda* known as La Joya, where they held a long conversation. He would look back on the encounter in 1833 and thank him for the "humane and caring treatment" they were given. However, they disagreed on everything else. Bustamante, in Tornel's words "believed that he had been called to direct the abandoned machine of the state; he thought that he had to destroy it in order to then own what remained. Without listening to the advice of prudence: i.e. to correct their mistakes, [and] not to become involved in the disturbances, [Bustamante] awarded himself the title of restorer of the laws, disobeying each and every one of them."[280] Tornel tried to persuade Bustamante to abandon the revolt but failed. Although they parted on civil terms and Bustamante allowed Tornel to leave even though he was obviously opposed to his plans, Bustamante would become one of Tornel's worst enemies.

Faithful to their liberal principles and their allegiance to Guerrero's presidency, Bocanegra, Tornel, and Santa Anna all opposed the Plan of Xalapa. Bocanegra defended Guerrero's government by acting as interim president (17–23 December 1829), while Guerrero left the capital to fight the rebels, and Santa Anna opposed the revolt at the head of the state government of Veracruz. It is worth nothing the integrity Santa Anna showed on this occasion by not joining a *pronunciamiento* that had been initiated in his native town of Xalapa and invited him, in its seventh article, to head the rebel army together with Bustamante.[281] However, once Bustamante's military victory was confirmed, Santa Anna decided to distance himself temporarily from national politics by staying in his hacienda, Manga de Clavo, in Veracruz. Nevertheless, as would be confirmed later by Tornel, who saw Santa Anna before departing for the United States, the Veracruzan general was "working on ways in which he could bring about a counterrevolution with uncertain . . . and scarce resources."[282] Santa Anna would have to wait until 1832 before he could initiate this counterrevolution.

On 21 December 1829, Tornel, his wife, María Agustina, and their six children boarded the American vessel *Virginia* and set sail to the United States.[283] The past five years in which Tornel had played such a prominent role in the capital's politics drew to a close, and an uncertain future lay ahead as he and his family sailed up the east coast of the American continent. In those five years Tornel had become a hardened professional politician. He had been the president's secretary, deputy for the Federal District and Veracruz, governor of the Federal District, master of one of the main *yorkino* lodges in Mexico City, and vice president of the Compañía Lancasteriana. His gift with words had been duly recognized as a leading journalist, the president's speechwriter, and even the official orator of the republic during the annual anniversary of independence. From having been a radical federalist, his views had become more moderate, evolving in response to the *yorkinos'* extremism in the aftermath of Tulancingo, and to the way the *exaltados* had abused Guerrero's goodwill. He had also become disenchanted. The bitterness that had come with the expulsion laws, the fact that their constitutional dream had already suffered two significant blows with the unconstitutional rise to power of both Guerrero in 1828 and Bustamante in 1829, and the traumatic experience of the Parián riot, which he had had to quell, all weighed heavily on his shoulders. Nevertheless, Tornel was not altogether downcast. Santa Anna had defeated the Spaniards in Tampico, and he had made an important contribution toward the abolition of slavery in Mexico. It was probably only a matter of time before he and Santa Anna could reverse the current political situation of the mother country. Nevertheless, holding on to power would prove a particularly difficult task for them in the following decade.

NOTES

1. For the Constituent Congress of 1823–1824 and the discussions that preceded the drafting of the 1824 Constitution, see Jaime E. Rodríguez O., "Intellectuals and the Mexican Constitution of 1824," in Roderic A. Camp, Charles A. Hale, and Josefina Zoraida Vázquez (eds.), *Los intelectuales y el poder en México* (Mexico City: El Colegio de México/UCLA Latin American Center Publications, 1991), pp. 63–74; David M. Quinlan, "Issues and Factions in the Constituent Congress, 1823–1824," in Jaime E. Rodríguez O. (ed), *Mexico in the Age of Democratic Revolutions, 1750–1850* (Boulder, CO: Lynne Rienner Publishers, 1994), pp. 177–207; Nettie Lee Benson, *La diputación provincial y el federalismo mexicano* (Mexico City: El Colegio de México/UNAM, 1994); Timothy E. Anna, "Inventing Mexico: Provincehood and Nationhood after Independence," *Bulletin of Latin American Research* 15:1 (January 1996): 7–17; and Timothy E. Anna, *Forging Mexico, 1821–1835* (Lincoln: University of Nebraska Press, 1998), pp. 98–175.

2. Lucas Alamán, *Historia de Méjico*, vol. 5 (Mexico City: Editorial Jus, 1969), p. 510.

3. Lorenzo de Zavala, *Ensayo crítico de las revoluciones de México desde 1808 hasta 1830*, in Zavala, *Obras: el historiador y el representante popular* (Mexico City: Porrúa, 1969), p. 222.

4. José María Bocanegra, *Memorias para la historia de México independiente, 1822–1846*, vol. 1 (Mexico City: Fondo de Cultura Económica, 1987), pp. 410–411.

5. José María Gutiérrez Estrada, *Carta dirigida al Escmo. Sr. Presidente de la República, sobre la necesidad de buscar en una convención el posible remedio de los males que aquejan a la República y opiniones del autor acerca del mismo asunto* (Mexico City: Imp. de I. Cumplido, 1840).

6. Bocanegra, *Memorias*, vol. 2, p. 799.

7. José María Tornel, "A.D. José María Gutiérrez Estrada. O sean Algunas observaciones al folleto en que ha proclamado la destrucción de la república, y el llamamiento al trono mexicano de un príncipe estrangero," *El Cosmopolita* (31 October 1840), p. 2.

8. Ibid., p. 3.

9. Ibid., p. 4.

10. Ibid.

11. José María Tornel, *Breve reseña histórica de los acontecimentos más notables de la nación mexicana* (Mexico City: INEHRM, 1985), p. 9.

12. José María Tornel, "Contestación al artículo comunicado del ciudadano Dr. Joaquín Infante inserto en los números 148 y 149 de este periódico," *El Sol*, 23, 24 November 1823.

13. Anna, *Forging Mexico*, p. 268.

14. Tornel, "Contestación," *El Sol*, 23 November 1823, p. 648.

15. Ibid.

16. Ibid, 24 November 1823, p. 652.

17. Anna, *Forging Mexico*, p. 267.

18. Tornel, "Contestación," *El Sol*, 24 November 1823, p. 652.

19. Tornel, *Breve reseña histórica*, p. 14.

20. Although it is not known when Tornel became an *escocés*, he states that he was one before he became a *yorkino* in 1825: *Breve reseña histórica*, p. 46.

21. Alamán, *Historia de Méjico*, vol. 5, p. 508.

22. Tornel, *Breve reseña histórica*, p. 22.

23. Ruth Solís Vicarte, *Las socidades secretas en el primer gobierno republicano (1824–1828)* (Mexico City: Editorial ASBE, 1997), pp. 73–83.

24. For Guadalupe Victoria, see Elmer W. Flaccus, "Guadalupe Victoria: His Personality as a Cause of His Failure," *Americas* 23:3 (January 1967): 297–311; Arthur L. DeVolder, *Guadalupe Victoria: His Role in Mexican Independence* (Albuquerque, NM: Artcraft, 1978); and Lillian Briseño Senosiain, Laura Solares Robles, and Laura Suárez de la Torre, *Guadalupe Victoria primer presidente de México* (1786–1843) (Mexico City: Insituto Mora/SEP, 1986).

25. Carlos María de Bustamante, *Diario histórico de México. Enero–diciembre 1825*, vol. 3 (Mexico City: SEP/INAH, 1982), pp. 7, 136 (for 1 January and 4 October 1825). See also Solís Vicarte, *Las sociedades secretas*, p. 88.

26. *Justo Simplicio el Tapado, Preguntas al Payo del Rosario, sobre la escandalosa y criminal conducta del señor gobernador* (Mexico City: Imp. de José María Gallegos, 1828), p. 3.

27. Tornel, *Breve reseña histórica*, p. 33.

28. Ibid., p. 35.

29. Ibid., pp. 37, 46.

30. Ibid, p. 24.

31. Solís Vicarte, *Las sociedades secretas*, p. 74.

32. Tornel, *Breve reseña histórica*, p. 24.

33. José María Tornel, *Manifestación del C. José María Tornel* (Mexico City: n.p., 1833), p. 8.

34. El Amigo de la Justicia, *Ultimo golpe de paz al ciudadano Tornel* (Mexico City: n.p., 1826), pp. 7–8.

35. Anna, *Forging Mexico*, p. 176.

36. More recent studies on the First Federal Republic include: Stanley C. Green, *The Mexican Republic: The First Decade, 1823–1832* (Pittsburgh: University of Pittsburgh Press, 1987), and Manuel Ferrer Muñoz, *La formación de un Estado nacional en México. El Imperio y la República federal: 1821–1835* (Mexico City: UNAM, 1995).

37. Michael P. Costeloe, *La primera república federal de México (1824–1835)* (Mexico City: Fondo de Cultura Económica, 1983), p. 63.

38. The Rite of York was formally constituted on 29 September 1825 in Joel Poinsett's house, counting among its founding members Vincente Guerrero, José Ignacio Esteva, Miguel Ramos Arizpe, José María Alpuche, and Lorenzo de Zavala. See Solís Vicarte, *Las sociedades secretas*, p. 109. For a discussion of the ideological banners that differentiated the *escoceses* from the *yorkinos*, see Will Fowler, *Mexico in the Age of Proposals, 1821–1853* (Westport, CT: Greenwood Press, 1998), pp. 18–21, 48–54.

39. Tornel, *Breve reseña histórica*, p. 46.

40. Costeloe, *La primera república federal*, p. 52.

41. *El Sol*, 21 July 1826.

42. Ibid., 31 July 1826. Also see Costeloe, *La primera república federal*, pp. 73–77.

43. Will Fowler, *The Mexican Press and the Collapse of Representative Government during the Presidential Elections of 1828*, Research Paper No. 21 (Liverpool: ILAS, 1996).

44. Lorenzo de Zavala, *Ensayo crítico de las revoluciones de México desde 1808 hasta 1830* in *Obras. El Historiador y el Representante Popular* (Mexico City: Porrúa, 1969), p. 322.

45. José María Luis Mora, *Obras sueltas* (Mexico City: Porrúa, 1963), p. 9.

46. *El Aguila Mexican*, 4 October 1826.

47. Ibid.

48. *El Correo de la Federación Mexicana*, 17 January 1827.

49. See ibid., 27 December 1826.

50. Ibid.

51. Ibid.

52. Ibid., 5 August 1827.

53. Ibid., 21 January 1827.

54. Ibid.

55. Ibid.

56. Ibid.

57. Ibid., 23 March 1827.

58. Ibid.

59. Alamán, *Historia de Méjico*, vol. 5, p. 520.

60. Tornel, *Breve reseña histórica*, p. 165.

61. *El Correo de la Federación Mexicana*, 5 September 1827.

62. Michael P. Costeloe, *The Central Republic in Mexico, 1835–1846. Hombres de Bien in the Age of Santa Anna* (Cambridge: Cambridge University Press, 1993), p. 153.

63. *El Correo de la Federación Mexicana*, 12 September 1827.

64. Ibid., 13 August 1827.

65. Ibid., 10 January 1827.

66. Ibid., 13 March 1827.

67. *El Mosaico Mexicano* 6 (1841): 97–104.

68. For a discussion of Bustamante's *indigenismo*, see Fowler, *Mexico in the Age of Proposals*, pp. 105–107, 116–117.

69. See *El Correo de la Federación Mexicana*, 16, 19, 27 January; 4, 10, 13, 17, 19, 25 February; 2, 4, 5, 9, 17 March 1827.

70. Ibid., 2 March 1827.

71. Ibid., 5, 9 March 1827.

72. Ibid., 24 October 1827.

73. Ibid.

74. Ibid., 23 November 1827.

75. Ibid., 17 February 1827.

76. Ibid., 25 February 1827.

77. Ibid., 5 March 1828.

78. Ibid.

79. For Vicente Rocafuerte see Jaime E. Rodríguez O., *El nacimiento de His-*

panoamérica. Vicente Rocafuerte y el hispanoamericanismo, 1808–1832 (Mexico City: Fondo de Cultura Económica, 1980).

80. *El Correo de la Federación Mexicana*, 2, 19 March 1827.

81. Ibid. 25 April 1827.

82. Ibid., 6 May 1827.

83. Ibid.

84. Ibid.

85. Ibid., 3 April 1827.

86. Ibid., 5 April 1827.

87. Ibid., 13 October 1827.

88. Ibid., 17 October 1827.

89. Ibid., 6 April, 11 May 1827.

90. Ibid., 17 May 1827.

91. Tornel was to claim later that the *comisionado regio* was none other than the notorious Basque adventurer Eugenio de Aviraneta (1792–1872), who participated in a number of conspiracies to reconquer Mexico for Spain, including Barradas's expedition in 1829. Nevertheless, as has been proven in Salvador Méndez Reyes's recent study on Aviraneta, although Aviraneta was working on organizing a Spanish offensive from Cuba at the time, he was not the *comisionado regio* Arenas was alluding to. See Salvador Méndez Reyes, *Eugenio de Aviraneta y México* (Mexico City: UNAM, 1992).

92. Tornel, *Breve reseña histórica*, pp. 86–88.

93. Ibid., p. 114.

94. Ibid., p. 168.

95. *El Correo de la Federación Mexicana*, 4 March 1827.

96. Tornel, *Breve reseña histórica*, p. 168.

97. *El Correo de la Federación Mexicana*, 10 May 1827.

98. Ibid., 14 May 1827.

99. Ibid.

100. Ibid., 24 December 1827.

101. See Harold D. Sims, *La expulsión de los españoles de México (1821–1828)* (Mexico City: Fondo de Cultura Económica, 1984) and *The Expulsion of Mexico's Spaniards, 1821–1836* (Pittsburgh: University of Pittsburgh Press, 1990).

102. *El Correo de la Federación Mexicana*, 14 May 1827.

103. Ibid.

104. Ibid., 15 February 1828.

105. Tornel, *Breve reseña histórica*, p. 171.

106. Ibid.

107. Ibid.

108. Sims, *La expulsión de los españoles*, pp. 120–121.

109. Tornel, *Breve reseña histórica*, p. 171.

110. *Réplica de varios españoles al señor Tornel en su contestación a las cuatro palabras* (Mexico City: Imp. J. M. Lara, 1841), p. 3. This lengthy pamphlet, consisting of eighty pages, was followed by *Varios españoles al señor Tornel. Ultima respuesta* (Mexico City: Imp. J. M. Lara, 1841).

111. Sims, *La expulsión de los españoles*, p. 41.

112. Fowler, *Mexico in the Age of Proposals*, p. 223.

113. Solís Vicarte, *Las sociedades secretas*, p. 154.

114. *El Amigo del Pueblo*, 1 August 1827.

115. Solis Vicarte, *Las sociedades secretas*, p. 155.

116. Josefina Zoraida Vázquez, *Don Antonio López de Santa Anna. Mito y enigma* (Mexico City: CONDUMEX, 1987), p. 16.

117. An excellent study on the political situation in Veracruz during these years, which contains details on the Santa Anna—Rincón rivalry, is Carmen Blázquez Domínguez, *Politicos y comerciantes en Veracruz y Xalapa, 1827–1829* (Veracruz: Gobierno del Estado de Veracruz, 1992).

118. For the *novenarios*, see Fowler, *Mexico in the Age of Proposals*, pp. 53–54.

119. For a fuller discussion of the Plan of Montaño, see Fowler, *Mexico in the Age of Proposals*, pp. 54–56. The plan is included in Tornel, *Breve reseña histórica*, p. 179.

120. *El Correo de la Federación Mexicana*, 4 January 1828.

121. Ibid.

122. Ibid.

123. Tornel, *Breve reseña histórica*, p. 178.

124. Ibid.

125. *Conducta que ha observado el Ayuntamiento de Jalapa desde el 6 al 12 de enero de 1828* (Xalapa: Imp. del Gobierno, 1828).

126. See Fowler, *The Mexican Press*, pp. 1–13.

127. *El Correo de la Federación Mexicana*, 15 February 1828.

128. Ibid., 16, 17 February 1828.

129. Ibid., 22 February 1828.

130. Ibid., 26 February 1828.

131. Mora, *Obras sueltas*, p. 72.

132. Manuel Payno, *Los bandidos de Río Frío* (Mexico City: Porrúa, 1996), p. 213.

133. Archivo General de la Nación (henceforth refered to as AGN), "Expulsión de Españoles," Vol. 5, Expediente 7, ff. 89–108, José María Tornel, *Bando*, 26 February 1828.

134. *El Correo de la Federación Mexicana*, 28 February 1828.

135. Ibid., 26 March 1828.

136. Sims, *La expulsión de españoles*, p. 182.

137. Solís Vicarte, *Las sociedades secretas*, p. 177.

138. Tornel, *Manifestación del C. José María Tornel* (Mexico City: n.p., 1833), p. 14.

139. AGN, "Expulsión de Españoles," Vol. 13, Expediente 2, ff. 17–57.

140. Ibid.

141. Tornel, *Manifestación*, p. 14.

142. AGN, "Expulsión de Españoles," Vol. 5, Expediente 7, ff. 89–108.

143. Ibid.

144. Ibid., letter, 17 June 1828.

145. Tornel, *Manifestación*, p. 26.

146. Ibid., pp. 25–26.

147. Ibid.

148. AGN, "Expulsión de Españoles," Vol. 5, Expediente 7, ff. 89–108.

149. *El Correo de la Federación Mexicana*, 23 February 1828.

150. Ibid., 7 March 1828.
151. Fanny Calderón de la Barca, *Life in Mexico* (London: Century, 1987), p. 94.
152. *El Correo de la Federación Mexicana*, 29 February 1828.
153. Calderón de la Barca, *Life in Mexico*, p. 94.
154. *El Correo de la Federación Mexicana*, 29 February 1828.
155. Ibid.
156. Ibid., 11 March 1828.
157. Ibid.
158. Calderón de la Barca, *Life in Mexico*, pp. 51, 65.
159. Ibid., p. 75.
160. *El Correo de la Federación Mexicana*, 16 March 1828.
161. L. R., *Victoriosa defensa del esclarecido patriota gobernador del distrito, ciudadano José María Tornel* (Mexico City: Imp. de Ontíveros, 1828), p. 6.
162. Ibid., p. 5.
163. *El Correo de la Federación Mexicana*, 1 April 1828.
164. Ibid., 6 March 1828.
165. Ibid.
166. Ibid., 11 June 1828.
167. Ibid., 1 June 1828.
168. Ibid, 2 April 1828.
169. Ibid., 30 March 1828.
170. Ibid.
171. El Pega Recio, *Las tenazas de San Dimas agarran pero no sueltan* (Mexico City: Imp. de Ontíveros, 1828), p. 3.
172. *El Correo de la Federación Mexicana*, 29 May 1828.
173. Tornel, *Breve reseña histórica*, p. 209.
174. Ibid.
175. *El Correo de la Federación Mexicana*, 29 May 1828.
176. Tornel, *Breve reseña histórica*, p. 211.
177. Solís Vicarte, *Las sociedades secretas*, p. 190.
178. *El Correo de la Federación Mexicana*, 29 May 1828.
179. Tornel, *Breve reseña histórica*, p. 266.
180. Ibid., pp. 267–268.
181. Enrique González Pedrero, *País de un solo hombre: el México de Santa Anna* (Mexico City: Fondo de Cultura Económica, 1993), pp. 388–389.
182. Zavala, *Obras. El historiador y el representante popular*, p. 344.
183. Ibid.
184. Tornel, *Breve reseña histórica*, p. 288.
185. Ibid., p. 289.
186. El Patriota Observador, *Gracias singulares del C. Coronel José María Tornel, gobernador del distrito federal que se le recuerdan para que evite su caida y no le suceda lo que a la ilustre víctima de Padilla* (Mexico City: Imp. de José María Gallegos, 1828), p. 2.
187. Ibid.
188. Ibid., pp. 3–4.
189. Ibid., p. 4.
190. Ibid.

191. Ibid.
192. Tornel, *Breve reseña histórica*, p. 284.
193. Ibid., p. 285.
194. *El Correo de la Federación Mexicana*, 13 June 1828.
195. Ibid.
196. Ibid., 21 June 1828.
197. Ibid.
198. El Patriota Observador, *Gracias singulares*, p. 3.
199. *Verdadera segunda parte de las gracias singulares del ciudadano coronel José María Tornel, gobernador del distrito federal* (Mexico City: Imp. de José María Gallegos, 1828).
200. *El Correo de la Federación Mexicana*, 28 July 1828.
201. Ibid., 4 August 1828.
202. Ibid., 4 September 1828.
203. Ibid., 11 September 1828.
204. Jan Bazant, "From Independence to the Liberal Republic, 1821–1867," in Leslie Bethell (ed.), *Mexico since Independence* (Cambridge: Cambridge University Press, 1992), p. 12.
205. For Gómez Pedraza, see Laura Solares Robles, *Una revolución pacífica. Biografía política de Manuel Gómez Pedraza, 1789–1851* (Mexico City: Instituto Mora, 1996).
206. Tornel, *Breve reseña histórica*, p. 312.
207. *El Correo de la Federación Mexicana*, 14 September 1828.
208. Tornel, *Breve reseña histórica*, p. 342.
209. Ibid., p. 339. Also see Solís Vicarte, *Las sociedades secretas*, p. 172, where she quotes Carlos María de Bustamante, who jotted down in his diary, on 1 June 1828, that Tornel was rapidly enlarging his battalion of civic militias to take action should the elections not favor Guerrero. Tornel's militias were "el pie de fuerza principal con que cuentan los yorkinos, y que si Dios no lo remedia nos dará mucho que entender en las próximas elecciones. Con tal objeto ha activado el gobernador Tornel su organización."
210. Tornel, *Manifestación*, pp. 6–7.
211. Bocanegra, *Memorias*, vol. 1, p. 464.
212. Lorenzo de Zavala, *Obras. Viaje a los Estados Unidos del Norte de América* (Mexico City: Porrúa, 1976), p. 11.
213. Bocanegra, *Memorias*, vol. 1, p. 474.
214. Quoted in González Pedrero, *País de un solo hombre*, p. 438.
215. Tornel, *Manifestación*, pp. 6–7.
216. Ibid., p. 7.
217. Tornel, *Breve reseña histórica*, p. 386.
218. Ibid., p. 387.
219. Ibid.
220. Ibid, p. 392.
221. Ibid.
222. Tornel, *Manifestación*, p. 9.
223. Costeloe, *La primera república federal*, p. 207.
224. Anna, *Forging Mexico*, pp. 219–220.

225. Silvia Arrom, "Popular Politics in Mexico City: The Parián Riot, 1828," *Hispanic American Historical Review* 68:2 (May 1988): 267.

226. Bocanegra, *Memorias*, vol. 1, p. 492.

227. Ibid.

228. *El Correo de la Federación Mexicana*, 15 December 1828.

229. Tornel, *Manifestación*, pp. 10–11.

230. Ibid.

231. Ibid., p. 12.

232. Ibid.

233. Ibid.

234. Public Record Office (henceforth referred to as PRO), Exp. 2222, ff. 292–294, *Bando: El gobernador del distrito a sus conciudadanos* (10 December 1828); Exp. 2234, ff. 344–345, *Edicto* (6 December 1828).

235. *El Correo de la Federación Mexicana*, 10 December 1828. Also PRO: Exp. 2237, ff. 350–351, *José María Tornel y Mendívil, diputado al congreso de la unión por el D.F., su gobernador & c* (7 December 1828); PRO: Exp. 2239, ff. 353, *José María Tornel y Mendívil, etc.* (8 December 1828).

236. Tornel, *Manifestación*, p. 13.

237. José María Tornel, *José María Tornel y Mendívil, etc. Diputado y Gobernador . . . sobre el restablecimiento de paz pública que considera el más privilegiado entre sus tareas, para la cual dicta 13 articulos sobre el cuidado de la ciudad, su iluminación, limpieza, empedrado, venta y distribución de alimentos y bebidas, cañerias . . .* (Mexico City: n.p., 8 December 1828).

238. Tornel, *Manifestación*, pp. 20–21.

239. Ibid.

240. Ibid., p. 21.

241. Ibid., pp. 21–22.

242. Fowler, *Mexico in the Age of Proposals*, pp. 20, 23, 43, 55, 57, 65, 115–117, 179, 201, 225, 226, 229, 233, 237, 246, 259.

243. Tornel, *Manifestación*, p. 26.

244. Ibid.

245. Ibid., p. 27.

246. Ibid.

247. Ibid.

248. Ibid.

249. Bocanegra, *Memorias*, vol. 2, p. 6.

250. Ibid., p. 10.

251. Tornel, *Manifestación*, p. 28.

252. Ibid., p. 19.

253. Ibid.

254. Tornel, "Federación," *El Correo de la Federación Mexicana*, 24 August 1827.

255. Tornel, *Manifestación*, p. 18.

256. Ibid., pp. 32–35.

257. Costeloe, *La primera república federal*, p. 222.

258. *El Sol*, 17 July 1829.

259. Ibid., 25 July 1829.

260. Costeloe, *La primera república federal*, p. 223.

261. Tornel, *Manifestación*, p. 30.

262. *El Sol*, 9 August 1829.

263. Ibid., 25, 26 August 1829.

264. Tornel, *Manifestación*, p. 37.

265. González Pedrero, *País de un solo hombre*, p. 535.

266. María del Carmen Vázquez Mantecón, *La palabra del poder. Vida pública de José María Tornel* (1795–1853) (Mexico City: UNAM, 1997), p. 75.

267. Wilfrid Hardy Callcott, *Santa Anna. The Story of an Enigma Who Once Was Mexico* (Hamden, CT: Archon Books, 1964), p. 78.

268. Tornel, *Breve reseña histórica*, p. 85.

269. Bocanegra, *Memorias*, vol. 1, p. 327.

270. Tornel, *Breve reseña histórica*, pp. 85–86.

271. A perfect example is Manuel Rivera Cambas, *Antonio López de Santa Anna* (Mexico City: Editorial Citlaltépetl, 1958), p. 201.

272. Tornel, *Manifestación*, p. 37.

273. Ibid.

274. *El Sol*, 1 December 1829.

275. Archivo General de Notarías de la Ciudad de México (henceforth referred to as AGNCM), Notaría 155, Francisco Calapiz y Aguilar (Escribano Nacional y Público), "Poder general," 23 November 1829.

276. Tornel, *Manifestación*, p. 40.

277. Ibid.

278. Ibid.

279. Ibid., pp. 40–41.

280. Ibid.

281. The Plan of Xalapa is reprinted in Bocanegra, *Memorias*, vol. 2, p. 55–56.

282. Tornel, *Manifestación*, p. 41.

283. Ibid.

3

Snakes and Ladders (1830–1840)

THE AMERICAN DREAM

Tornel celebrated his thirty-fifth birthday in Baltimore. Having escaped from the political furnace of Mexico, he certainly took to the American way of life. Like so many other Mexicans at that time, he found that the United States represented a utilitarian dream that was well worth studying carefully so that a similar utopia could be established in Mexico. At the time, Baltimore was the third largest city in North America, with a population of approximately eighty thousand. It had a large tobacco market and an even larger flour market. However, of its outstanding features, it was those that had been revolutionized by the progress of industry that most impressed Tornel. Modernity was out there, shining in all its glory for Tornel to admire. Baltimore had twelve large textile factories, plus paper, metal, glass, and copper foundries. Wheat was pounded in mills powered by steam engines. He jotted down that they pounded over two hundred barrels a day and wrote with profound admiration: "It is difficult to conceive of a more industrious people or even one that is so dedicated to work as the people of Baltimore."[1]

Baltimore's atmosphere of peace, tranquility, hard work, and prosperity deeply affected Tornel. In his impressions of "La Ciudad de Baltimore en 1831" he repeatedly expressed his amazement at the miracles and wonders of American industry. Baltimore had the best gas factory in the United States, so theaters and streets were impressively lit up at night. He praised the bridges he saw for their "solidity, elegance and extension." He was equally astounded by the speed with which rail tracks were being laid down. The incredible distances they were planning to cover made him exclaim, "What aren't these people capable of?" Any comparison of Baltimore with Mexico City could only conclude that Baltimore excelled because of its "prodigies of industry." He reiterated that "there is not here a form of industry that has been neglected, nor a branch of commerce that has been left unattended." And he particularly liked "the columns of trees that grow in front of the houses," giving the city "an unforgivable grace and beauty" and recommending this example be followed in Mexico. The combination of fresh, green landscapes and wealth, so characteristic of temperate and prosperous northern countries, fascinated him. The "range of green hills . . . particularly on a summer morning," on the one hand, and the beautiful mansions of the "well-to-do families," on the other, created for him an enviable sedate, lush sense of comfort, splendor, and easily attainable abundance.[2]

Tornel and his family enjoyed their stay in Baltimore. They were given a warm welcome by the wealthier families of the city, who, according to him, enjoyed being gracious to foreigners because they belonged to such a distinguished social class. He recorded with gratitude the refined treatment he and his family were given: "My family and I have received from the ladies and gentlemen of this beautiful city such displays of affection, and such delicate gifts that we will never forget them." He became fully immersed in American high society: "Here you find the manners of English high society, and there is nothing more pleasant than the intercourse of these people, who without having lost the simplicity of our American customs, are also educated with all the courtesy and refinement of an older civilization." As well as enjoying the hospitality of Baltimore's elite, the University of Maryland invited him to give a number of plenary lectures, stating that he was "one of [Mexico's] most famous and distinguished diplomats." He enjoyed his stay in Baltimore to such an extent that he was quite prepared to write that "if the tempests of my mother-country ever cast me away to foreign lands, out of gratitude I will look for my home and asylum in Baltimore."[3]

Although he enjoyed the eighteen months he spent in Baltimore, he did not lose sight of the threat that U.S. expansionism posed to his government. In fact, the only aspects of American life he praised have already been mentioned: the American industrial revolution, its prosperity, and the manners of the Roman Catholic upper classes.[4] He was critical of everything else he saw. In many ways, Tornel's response to the United States epitomized the quandary in which the Mexican political class found itself at the time: attempting to emulate its northern neighbor while hoping to retain those contradictory customs and traditions they associated with their national identity. To quote Edmundo O'Gorman, the Mexican political class, regardless of whether they were liberals or conservatives, according to the traditional historiography, wanted "to acquire the prosperity of the United States without renouncing Mexico's traditional character, given that this [was] seen as being the very essence of the new nation. Therefore, they . . . [wanted] the benefits of modernity without wanting modernity itself."[5]

Tornel's actions during his stay in Baltimore can be divided into three different categories: those that he carried out in order to depict himself as capable of making sacrifices to defend Mexico's sacred integrity versus U.S. ambitions; those that he designed to convey the notion that he was detached, far removed from the divisions inherent in party politics; and those meant to appeal to his countrymen's emotions, that is, their emergent patriotic and nationalistic sentiments. The fact that he persevered in his role as minister plenipotentiary in spite of the way Bustamante's new administration ignored and abandoned him during his American stay was definitely used by Tornel to convey the idea that he endured great hardships to defend Mexico's sovereignty and national integrity.

Soon after his arrival in Baltimore, his attempts at fulfilling his duties as minister plenipotentiary became seriously undermined by the policies of Mexico's new government. Because he had been placed in the United States by General Guerrero, Bustamante's new administration chose to ignore Tornel; without actually asking him to resign, which might have caused a scandal, it placed one of its supporters, José María Montoya, in Baltimore and proceeded to deal with the government of the United States through him instead. Montoya was therefore in all senses but name, Mexico's minister plenipotentiary in North America during Tornel's diplomatic mission. Tornel was evidently indignant at the way he was treated by his own nation's government. As he was to recall in 1833, "The government of Sr. Bustamante contented itself by neglecting to use my services and went on to deal with Sr. Montoya, as if I had gone on some strange mission to Algiers or somewhere even further away."[6] Nevertheless, he persevered in trying to work as the official minister plenipotentiary of Mexico even though his government had essentially disowned him.

He eventually succumbed to the pressures arising from the Bustamante administration's abandonment of him. By February 1831, he claimed that Bustamante's government was undermining his position further by delaying and reducing his pay: "I was deprived of the necessary means." His situation deteriorated to the extent that "my financial hardship became extreme, one more week's delay and the abandonment to which I had been so irrationally condemned would have become apparent [to those acquaintances he had made in American high society]." Therefore, in the end, for purely financial reasons, "It was vital to leave a country in which I had lived with honor, especially as my disrepute was inevitable."[7] He gave in to the pressures of not being treated as Mexico's ambassador in the United States and of not receiving his pay. That same February, having spent just over a year in Baltimore, he wrote to Lucas Alamán asking for permission

to resign. On 13 February, Alamán answered his appeal accepting his resignation and saying that he would be relieved of his position by José María
Montoya.[8] On 1 June, Tornel wrote to the minister of relations asking for
permission to give his official farewell.[9] His financial distress was such that,
by June 1831, he was able to leave Baltimore only because the "respectable
and honorable" widow of Iturbide gave him a thousand pesos to get back
to Mexico.[10]

Those last three months of his stay in Baltimore were bitterly humiliating.
He could no longer afford to maintain his family's lifestyle, and it became
impossible for him to hide from his many privileged acquaintances the fact
that he was not being paid by the Mexican government: "It was impossible
. . . for me to maintain a certain degree of prosperity, or to attend the needs
of my numerous family." He was forced to give all his furniture to Montoya because it belonged to the Mexican government. Moreover, Montoya
"mortified me with requests that are not the best proof of his sensitivity."[11]
It is not surprising that as soon as he returned to Mexico, he dedicated
himself to plotting the downfall of Bustamante's government. Nevertheless,
he tried to carry out his obligations as minister plenipotentiary to the best
of his abilities regardless of the absence of any concrete support from his
government. In 1833 the moral of this story was quite clear. Tornel resisted
Bustamante's pressures as long as he could in order to defend his country's
territorial integrity. He was not prepared to accept an early resignation
because he claimed that the interest of his mother country came first in his
priorities.

To defend his country's integrity, he maintained regular correspondence
with American officials such as Martin Van Buren, Anthony Butler, and
David Brent concerning a variety of frontier issues.[12] He also wrote to the
Mexican government and to friends, including Bocanegra and General Manuel Mier y Terán on matters such as the means of preventing the United
States from annexing the northern territories of Mexico.[13] Among all his
diplomatic concerns, his efforts to create a permanent treaty of "friendship,
navigation and commerce" with Washington featured most prominently.[14]

As early as 6 March 1830 he wrote to the Mexican government warning
of what he interpreted to be the beginnings of North American expansionism. He was direct in his assertions: "There is no doubt that the majority
wish to acquire those states that lie to the south and east of the United
States."[15] On 18 March, he wrote to warn of the unsettling news that the
Spanish government was planning to invade Mexico again.[16] For the following fifteen months he continued to write similar letters on a regular
basis, warning his ungrateful government time and again of the imminent
threat of an American or a Spanish military offensive against their country.
However, his most publicized actions during his stay in Baltimore were
those he took in an attempt to prevent his own secretary José Antonio

Mejía and Lorenzo de Zavala from selling large areas of Texas to the Americans.

From the moment of his arrival in Baltimore, he witnessed the rapid and badly organized colonization of Texas, in which the flow of American citizens into Mexican territory was not successfully restricted or controlled. He read firsthand accounts of how the new settlements did not comply with their initial promises to follow the laws and ways of their newly adopted mother country and of how they subsequently proceeded to disobey Mexican law without being punished. It was, in his words, the sad tale of "the unprecedented treachery of the colonists and settlers, and of the generosity of the Mexicans who did not think of imposing any of the restrictions that prudence alone advised they should establish."[17]

It was as minister plenipotentiary that he gained firsthand knowledge of Zavala's entrepreneurial activities. Zavala, ignoring the law of 6 April 1830, which made it illegal for North Americans to emigrate to Texas, became involved in the transactions of the Galveston Bay and Texas Land Company and went on to acquire the handsome sum of $100,000 by issuing an unstated number of certificates for leagues and labor of land of up to 4,428 and 177 acres, respectively.[18] On 5 February 1831, Tornel wrote to Mier y Terán giving him the details of Zavala's actions as well as those of his secretary Mejía. Zavala had committed an act of treachery: "The worst of all." Together with Mejía he had sold "a large part of Texas, towards Galveston Bay" to the Americans.[19] Tornel, acting as minister plenipotentiary despite the fact that his own government had ceased to treat him as such, immediately printed a formal protest in several American newspapers in the name of the Mexican government. Moreover, he forbade his consuls from issuing passports to anybody wishing to travel to Texas. He warned the government of Zavala and Mejía's intentions as well as of "the evident dangers immigration causes." However, as he said to Mier y Terán:

Although I have not disregarded any of the means I have at my disposal to contain the torrent of so many accumulated greedy aspirations, I believe that it will all be ineffective if our government does not oppose the entrance of Americans and if it does not prevent Colonel Mejía from giving away the lands he has sold. . . . Neither the consuls nor I can prevent the Americans from embarking to Texas.[20]

As Pedro Santoni noted recently, "The Law of Colonization [6 April 1830] did not produce the results Alamán had anticipated. . . . Even if this measure had been as Herculean as first envisioned, other circumstances would have sabotaged its effect. Not only was Mexico incapable of enforcing the major stipulations of the accord, but the decree also heightened resentment among American colonists in Texas."[21] In other words, although the government chose to ignore Tornel, there was little they could do to prevent the lands from being sold. Nevertheless, Tornel's endeavors to save Mexico's national integrity did not go unnoticed. As Bocanegra was to record in his *Memorias*, Tornel "protested against any signed contract that was against Mexican law."[22] Tornel and Bocanegra's eventual shift from federalism in the 1820s to centralism in the mid-1830s was in part due to their firsthand experience of the colonization of Texas and the problems this had entailed, in particular from 1829 to 1831. Tornel saw the expansionist fervor of the United States and the anti-Mexican attitudes of the U.S. colonizers who were illegally buying Texan properties during his official stay in Baltimore. Bocanegra had been equally involved in the issue, serving as minister of the interior under Guerrero.[23] It became apparent to them that by the early 1830s, in Texas, where there were eight North Americans to every Mexican, federalism became a first step toward secessionism. In their minds, the only way to prevent Texas from becoming independent would be, by 1835, to impose a centralist system that prevented the Texans from going their own way, using the federalist system, as they had, to ignore and disobey the decrees of the federal government.

The idea that he portrayed himself as detached and far removed from the divisions inherent in party politics is closely linked to what has been seen so far concerning his defense of Mexico's "sacred" integrity. This is apparent not only in the fact that he condemned Zavala regardless of his *yorkino* and *guerrerista* affiliations, but also in the way he condemned U.S. expansionism. This antiparties early brand of Mexican nationalism would become one of the main banners of *santanista* ideology in years to come.[24]

During his stay in Baltimore, he also found time to work on several translations, including T. Joutel's *Diario histórico*, which he printed in New York on 5 June 1831.[25] The reason he chose to translate, of all possible texts, Joutel's *Diario histórico* stemmed from his strong sense of what could be defined as political patriotism. Essentially Joutel's diary was one of the first documents to outline the initial borders between British America and New Spain. Indirectly he was reaffirming his convictions that the border between Mexico and the United States should be the same now as it had been then. It is obvious that during his stay in Baltimore, he became perfectly aware of the ambitions of the United States. As he was to write in 1837 with a certain degree of hindsight, and yet still ten years before the fatal fall of Mexico City: "The dominant thought of the United States of America has been for fifty years, in other words, since its political infancy, to occupy a large part of the territory that was Spanish before, and that belongs today to the Mexican nation."[26] As a preface to the translation, Tornel significantly included a letter addressed to Mier y Terán in which he stressed the importance of Joutel's text, since it demonstrated unequivocally Mexico's rights over those very lands Mier y Terán was trying to control in the face of the increasingly hostile and secessionist behavior of the American colonists.

Tornel had good reason to be concerned. During his stay, he had lived through the violent expulsion and extermination of Indian tribes in Georgia and Alabama. It was evidence, or a sign at least, of the iron will that lay behind U.S. expansionism. If the U.S. government was capable of officially supporting the extermination of Indians who had always lived in the disputed lands, there was no reason that they would necessarily take into consideration the sentiments or rights of the Mexican people if they coveted the lands south of the long-established border. Tornel did not hesitate in drawing the parallel: "In dispossessing the Indians of their lands, it was considered whether the Mexicans could also be dispossessed of theirs."[27]

Tornel enjoyed his stay in Baltimore inasmuch as he enjoyed mingling with the members of civilized high society. However, in political terms, and as the official, albeit abandoned, minister plenipotentiary, his stay made him aware of the threat that lay ahead: war with the United States. Americans, at least those he socialized with, were often genteel and well mannered, kind and generous in the extreme to foreigners who belonged to a similar social class. However, they could also be, in his mind, vile, devious, and extremely ambitious. As he wrote in 1837, concerning the character of the government of the United States as well as that of its people:

To desire, to wait and then to act; this is how the distinctive character of the American government and people can be defined; no other society in the modern world can compete with their untempered ambition. Once they have decided what will most satisfy their greed, they prepare for the right moment to close in on the object of their desire, projecting a certain abandonment and lack of interest that is far from being a true reflection of their real intentions. Once the circumstances seem opportune, they do not think twice about the means they employ to achieve their final end.[28]

This aversion to the United States and his awareness of U.S. expansionist ambitions served two distinct purposes. First, the actions he took as a result of his fear, together with the ideas he expressed in writing and the way that he did not let Bustamante's abandonment undermine his patriotic concern, contributed to the notion he nurtured that he was above the considerations inherent in party politics. Second, by emphatically warning his countrymen of the threat of an American invasion, at a time when Bustamante's sole concern seemed to be to crush his fellow Mexican adversary Guerrero (who had mounted a rebellion in the south of the republic following his overthrow), he made it clear that he was not advocating civil war and factional divisions: on the contrary, he was demanding unity in the face of the danger of foreign intervention. Tornel's belief in unity echoed Santa Anna's own reiterated view that Mexico needed a patriotic government that was above party interests. Santa Anna had already stated in 1829 (possibly in Tornel's words):

[My] heart only seeks peace and unity, it joyfully gives in to the redeeming idea of a general and fraternal reconciliation; that the kiss of true peace amongst Mexicans of all parties, serves as the medicine which may cure all of our ills before they infect us. . . . The ridiculous names, which have so far been given to the parties, tear the nation apart; let there be only one . . . the party of the true Mexican patriots. Let us prepare for a great national reconciliation, because only this will serve as the anchor of our hopes.[29]

A rather startling anecdote worth mentioning here is, according to A. M. Gilliam's *Travels in Mexico*, that "when in the United States in the capacity of Mexican minister, [Tornel] received a horse-whipping before Barnum's hotel in Baltimore."[30] From Tornel's own account we know that he stayed in Barnum's hotel for three months, and that, as far as hotels went, he thought it was "the best, the largest and the most looked after in the whole of the Union."[31] However, Tornel never made any reference to the humiliating experience of a public horsewhipping. Why and by whom he was horsewhipped remains a mystery.[32] However, regarding his aversion to the government of the United States and their disproportionate ambitions, Gilliam claimed it all stemmed from this experience. Although this empirical interpretation of Tornel's motives is perfectly valid, there was clearly a more rational reasoning behind his condemnation of U.S. expansionism. It is specifically the way in which he chose to appeal to his countrymen's emotions, their emerging patriotic and nationalistic sentiments in particular, that suggests that he was more calculating than Gilliam implied.

During his stay in Baltimore he became well acquainted with the Catholic community. In his opinion the Catholic cathedral of Baltimore was one of the city's outstanding buildings; he became a close friend of Father Eccleston, who would later become archbishop of Baltimore. Another distinguished figure of this community was the widow of Agustín Iturbide, who acted as the benevolent and charitable protector of a nunnery and had close ties with Tornel from the early days of independence.[33] It is not gratuitous that in his notes on Baltimore the one thing that merited his utmost disgust with the political system of the United States was the preservation of slavery, and the segregation of whites and blacks. Significantly, it was only in his much-favored Catholic community that this was not the case:

In this very same cathedral I saw with tears in my eyes how Mrs. Carlton, the daughter of Mr. Charles Carlton . . . , received the host with a slave of hers kneeling beside her. In the United States this is an extraordinary event, for colored people are never to be seen mixing with white people. And there, it is only the Catholic faith that allows humanity to maintain its dignity without establishing differences that are based on mere differences in our epidermis.[34]

This question of racism and slavery was to become one of Tornel's main points when attacking or criticizing the United States. In his exhaustive historical account of the events that surrounded the disastrous Texan campaign of 1836, *Tejas y los Estados Unidos*, he wrote with great acrimony: "In no other part of the globe can the hatred of white people against blacks be more accentuated than in the United States." He juxtaposed his views with Zavala's praise of the United States in the travelogue that Zavala had written—"to praise them as high as the stars and to plunge his mother-country into an abyss." Tornel's criticism of the American propagation of slavery was relentless: "The worst scandal of all, the one that has shocked the civilized world is the conservation of slavery in the United States. It is scandalous that they are strongly determined to maintain and propagate it when other nations have arrived at the philanthropic conclusion of ending this cruelty and ignominy to humanity."[35] One of the main causes for discontent among the Texan colonists was the 1829 abolition of slavery, which they went on to ignore and eventually challenge by force in the Texan revolt of 1836.[36]

This is in itself an important point in that it reflects to a great extent the self-serving nature of the patriotism Tornel and Santa Anna displayed on more than one occasion. They claimed to be outside party politics. Their sole interest was, in their words, Mexico. Even when the United States was seen as a close ally and a role model on which they could base the solid foundations for Mexico's new and enlightened political system during the first ten years of independence, neither Tornel nor Santa Anna ever espoused the policies Zavala so fervently praised and proclaimed.[37] In other words, they were never associated with a movement whose ideals could be eventually seen as a vile imitation of the beliefs of the country that was to become Mexico's worst enemy. Even when Tornel praised the United States, he did not do so without highlighting those areas in which Mexico excelled.

He reverted first to the Mexican national sense of philanthropy. Mexicans, he claimed, treated colored people as equals. They had officially abolished slavery. Second, Mexicans were Roman Catholics, devoted to a much more enlightened and worthy church than the majority of Protestant North America. Mexico did not have the industries that were flourishing in the United States or the wealth, but they had a "better" religion and were more dignified as human beings. Of all possible consolations, bearing in mind the violent and humiliating events that lay ahead, Tornel had found what was probably the most appealing one. His assertions granted the material losers the hidden pride of knowing that, in spite of all the defeats, they would remain morally superior.

Nevertheless, at the time, it was difficult for Tornel to do much either to dampen U.S. expansionism or to prevent large chunks of Texas from being sold to North American colonists. Abandoned by his own country's government, he resigned in February 1831 and returned to Mexico in the fall of 1831, after spending the summer in New Orleans, not without having first heard of Guerrero's execution on 14 February.

THE CIVIL WAR OF 1832

The capture and execution of Vicente Guerrero polarized public opinion to such an extent that when Santa Anna launched his federalist revolt of 2 January 1832, Mexico was plunged, for the first time since independence, into a large-scale civil war. The fact that Santa Anna had to defeat the government's regular army with the sole help of the civic militias is indicative of the extent to which the civilian population felt outraged—not only about Guerrero's execution but also by the way Bustamante's cabinet had behaved once in power. From 1830 to 1832 what became known as the party of order (*el partido del orden*) took over the reins of government. Under the guidance of the ideologue Lucas Alamán, Bustamante's government began to implement constitutional reforms that curtailed the power of the federal states and limited the universality of suffrage to more clearly defined property-owning citizens. Although several attempts were made to inject new life into the Mexican economy through the creation of a bank, the Banco de Avío (16 October 1830), Bustamante's government soon became characterized by its repressive nature. Newspapers were forced to shut down or were censored, and a number of leading politicians such as Andrés Quintana Roo found themselves being threatened and even beaten up if they did not comply with the regime's politics. However, the tide of opinion turned against Bustamante's government when it authorized the execution of Guerrero, after he was taken prisoner in highly treacherous circumstances. The execution of a high-ranking officer who was also an ex-mandatory of the republic, an action that had not been carried out since Iturbide's execution in Padilla (19 July 1824), turned the majority of those moderates who had previously supported the party of order against Bustamante's government. It was almost as if now that old royalists such as Bustamante were in power, the time had come to settle old scores with those insurgents who had dominated the political scene since Iturbide's downfall.

For Bocanegra, Bustamante's government was characterized by the vindictiveness with which its opponents were treated and the shamelessness with which its supporters were favored, thus "crowning immorality."[38] Moreover, Bocanegra believed that the government was characterized by its "public disorders," its "violent *pronunciamientos*," and the brutal, severe repression with which all of the regime's critics were silenced.[39] As for the often-celebrated economic progress the republic enjoyed at the time, thanks to Alamán's creation of the Banco de Avío, Bocanegra felt not only that the administration had set out, from the beginning, to fool and distract the Mexican people but also that it complicated the economy by adopting measures that were truly detrimental at a time when consolidating measures were necessary.[40] The execution of Guerrero featured prominently in his condemnation of the regime. Bocanegra did not hesitate to accuse the government of having planned and authorized the treacherous capture and subsequent execution.[41] News of the execution found Tornel still in Baltimore, and he was deeply shocked. It represented "a horrifying scandal, a crime which will be condemned by history so that its repudiation is eternal." Moreover, the fact that it had been "so coldly calculated" confirmed that Bustamante's government could not "*count* [anymore] *with that prestige all governments need to exert* [if they want to be obeyed and respected], *for the loss of credit is irreparable when a government openly assaults public morality.*"[42]

Tornel returned to Mexico bearing two very personal grudges against the Bustamante regime: it had abandoned and thus humiliated him during his diplomatic mission in the United States, and had assassinated one of the heroes of the insurgency, a man he had been particularly close to as both a *yorkino* and his speechwriter during the 1829 administration. The time was ripe for revenge. He arrived in Veracruz at the beginning of December 1831 and was in Xalapa, staying with his friend Santa Anna, by the middle of the month.[43] Although there is no documentary evidence, Tornel and Santa Anna almost certainly must have sat down and plotted the forthcoming overthrow of the Bustamante regime. It was only two weeks after they met, and once Tornel had returned to Mexico City, that Santa Anna launched his Plan of Veracruz of 2 January 1832.

Santa Anna had pretty much kept to himself during the first two years of the Bustamante regime. Although he had refused to serve under the administration though the opportunity was offered to him, he had not immediately taken up arms on hearing of Guerrero's execution. The time was not yet right for an open confrontation with the government. As he noted in a letter to a friend, dated 9 April 1831, he appeared to be quite happy just dedicating himself to running his hacienda, Manga de Clavo, letting time go by:

In regard to my country, I cannot tell you anything, because it is now sixteen months since I have abandoned public affairs and retired to this farm, which is my own property, where I desire nothing but the peace and welfare of the country, and my own tranquillity. I never enjoyed more satisfaction than during the time of my retirement, in the bosom of my adored family. I enjoy the necessary comforts of life, and look with horror upon high stations; so it is that in this corner I am nothing else than a spectator of what is passing in the world.[44]

Nevertheless, as Wilfrid Callcott points out, "by late summer, however, his ambitions were awakening and he was cautiously feeling out the situation and organizing support."[45] However, in the summer of 1831, he was still lacking somebody like Tornel who could orchestrate events from the capital, liasing with the federalists in Zacatecas, where Bocanegra was now based, contributing to turning what would initially start as a regional revolt into a national one. Once Tornel was back, the revolt could get under way.

Before Tornel's importance in the civil war of 1832 is assessed, it is important to note the strength of Santa Anna's position, by the end of 1831, to launch a successful revolt. With the exception of General Manuel Mier y Terán, who committed suicide on 3 July 1832, thus forfeiting, rather dramatically, his chances of becoming president, Santa Anna was probably the only general at the time whose prestige was as yet untarnished. He had succeeded in avoiding sullying his reputation by refusing to become involved in any of the administrations that had governed the country until then. Therefore he had never been in a position to betray his supporters or approve of unpopular reforms to rescue the increasingly bankrupt national economy. He had also avoided becoming closely associated with any of the factions that had become bitterly divided in the capital. Moreover, when he had intervened in national politics, he had shown himself to be invariably a step ahead of the rest, creating the kinds of opportunities the majority of the political class seemed to be hoping to find, without knowing how to. In brief, his *pronunciamientos* until then had successfully initiated major shifts and changes that the majority appeared to want to embrace. Rather than changing sides opportunely, it had been Santa Anna who had sparked off the most significant transformations Mexico's political system had experienced during the first national decade. The fall of Iturbide and the subsequent republican proposal had come about in the aftermath of Santa Anna's Plan of Veracruz (2 December 1822). The adoption of a federal constitution had likewise succeeded Santa Anna's Plan of San Luis Potosí (5 June 1823). And it had been Santa Anna who had first rebelled in Perote (12 September 1828) against those electoral results that the majority had deemed to be an inaccurate interpretation of the will of the people. Moreover, after the glorious victory of Tampico (11 September 1829), Santa Anna had become the most praised general of the period. Furthermore, in a remarkable display of integrity, he had refused to lead the *pronunciamiento* of Xalapa (4 December 1829) and had become significantly detached from a regime that was deeply unpopular by the end of 1831. His military victories during the 1832 civil war added to his legendary status as Mexico's answer to Napoleon, and he would go on to win the presidential elections of 1833 with a landslide victory.

With Tornel back in Mexico City after having been away for two years, Santa Anna joined the Plan of Veracruz, which stated that (1) it was the rebels' intention to support the federal constitution; (2) it was imperative that Bustamante renewed his cabinet, since it was perceived to be dominated by centralists and was considered to be responsible for tolerating unforgivable crimes against the country's civil rights and liberties; (3) Santa Anna would be offered the leadership of the revolt; and (4) the authors of the plan (Ciriaco Vázquez, Ramón Hernández, and Eusebio Flores, among others) would cease to be responsible for the rebels' actions the moment Santa Anna took over the revolt (which he did from Xalapa on 6 January).[46] Initially Santa Anna "took the leadership of the uprising but favored a moderate approach."[47] He wrote to Bustamante in an attempt to persuade him to change his cabinet, thus avoiding the bloodshed that did indeed occur subsequently. He suggested that Bustamante make Sebastián Camacho minister of interior and exterior affairs; Valentín Gómez Farías minister of justice; Melchor Múzquiz minister of war; and Francisco García minister of the exchequer.[48] It is probably no coincidence that Tornel was a close friend of Camacho (he was appalled when Camacho was removed from office by the radical *yorkinos* in 1828), and that he was close to Múzquiz who, like him, had studied in the Colegio de San Ildefonso. It is equally relevant that Bocanegra, who had returned to Zacatecas following the triumph of Bustamante's 1829 revolt and rejoined the Supreme State Tribunal of Justice, was a close friend of Gómez Farías and Governor Francisco García. In other words, Santa Anna's proposal must have been inspired by Tornel and Bocanegra's advice, especially since Santa Anna had not had the chance to have become acquainted with any of these politicians during the first national decade, because he had spent most of the time in either Veracruz or Yucatán. Santa Anna's proposal was unacceptable to those rebels who would not tolerate Bustamante's remaining in office and to Bustamante himself, who refused to implement Santa Anna's suggestions. Almost inevitably, in February 1832, Santa Anna "with some reluctance, launched the armed conflict."[49]

Santa Anna's revolt soon escalated into the most violent civil conflict of this period.[50] Those *yorkinos* who had supported Guerrero's presidency—the radicals, the moderates within the party of order, the growing faction of *santanistas*, and in particular those federalist states that had been threatened by the centralist tendencies of Alamán's administration, most notably Zacatecas (where Bocanegra was based)—under the leadership of Governor Francisco García and Valentín Gómez Farías joined forces to overthrow the Bustamante regime. After the battles of Tolomé (3 March), El Gallinero (18 September), El Palmar (29 September), and the Rancho de Posadas (6 December), Bustamante surrendered, and in the Treaty of Zavaleta (23 December), it was agreed that Gómez Pedraza (whom Tornel had seen in New Orleans on his way back to Mexico)[51] would be allowed to return to Mexico City to complete his term in office as president (the same term that had been interrupted as a result of the Revolt of La Acordada of 1828).[52]

Although the alliance forged between the Zacatecan federalists and the *santanistas* in 1832 was to a certain extent a "marriage of convenience,"[53] to use Frank Samponaro's definition, they shared far more ideological aims and personal ties than has been generally accepted in the historiography. Bocanegra and Gómez Farías had been close friends since their years as deputies for Zacatecas in Iturbide's Congress. Given that the *santanistas* had been federalists since 1823, supported the 1824 Constitution, and had ended up supporting a moderate agenda within the more radical movement that came to power after La Acordada, it is not surprising that they had strong ideological reasons for opposing Bustamante's government and joining forces with politicians such as Gómez Farías, also an ex-*iturbidista*, a federalist, a supporter of the 1824 charter, and a reformist who had opposed the radical *yorkinos* by forming with Francisco García the faction of the *imparciales* in 1828, and who still, in 1832, did not want to be associated with the *exaltados*.[54]

Therefore, while Santa Anna led the campaign against the government in the east of the country, gradually making his way from Veracruz to Mexico City, via Puebla, and Bocanegra assisted García and Gómez Farías with the campaign in the north, Tornel served as a point of contact between the two rebel armies in Mexico City. He deliberately refused to fulfill his duties within the regular army (which on this occasion proved to be loyal to the government), repeatedly claiming throughout 1832 that he was too ill to take up his position as colonel in the 3rd Infantry Battalion.[55]

Although Tornel did not play a key role at the forefront of the revolution, and later claimed that he kept a low profile and did not become involved in the political events that brought about Bustamante's downfall,[56] he nevertheless contributed to the revolt by writing against the regime and liasing between Santa Anna and the Zacatecan federalists. His writings took on two dimensions. On one level he attacked Bustamante directly by writing for *El fénix de la libertad*. On another, he published two translations that included indirect criticisms of the regime.[57] As an example, his rather free translation of Francis Bacon's philosophical thoughts[58] contained a dedication to Bocanegra in which he referred his friend to chapter 3, for it was there, he claimed, that Bocanegra would find the reason for his homage. Chapter 3 was entitled "Misfortune," and in it Bacon argued that true virtue was to be found in those individuals who, against all odds, sacrificed their personal comfort in order to combat adverse circumstances. Out of the agony of misfortunes, true virtue emerged triumphant. With Bocanegra and the Zacatecan federalists under siege from the government's forces, it was not too difficult to ascertain where Tornel's sympathies lay during the 1832 civil war.

Once the Treaty of Zavaleta (23 December 1832) was signed, Bustamante decorously surrendered without having to face any punishment or trial, and General Gómez Pedraza returned to the presidency to complete the four years in office that had been interrupted as a result of the 1828

Revolt of La Acordada. By making Gómez Pedraza president, Santa Anna and the Zacatecan federalists succeeded in giving constitutional legitimacy to their revolt and created the right circumstances for a new round of elections. Not surprisingly, the two favored candidates were Santa Anna and Valentín Gómez Farías, both of whom had played a major role in leading the revolution that had brought down the Bustamante regime. Surprising as it may sound, Tornel also stood for president.[59]

It is surprising for two reasons: it would be the first and only time that he decided to run for the presidential seat (Tornel never appeared to be interested in being head of state; he preferred to enjoy the privileges of power by performing a secondary rather than a leading role in national politics), and it meant that he would be competing with his great friend Santa Anna. The only explanation, albeit a purely speculative one, is that Tornel already knew that Santa Anna did not want to trouble himself with the everyday cumbersome business of running the country. Although there is little doubt that Santa Anna was looking forward to being elected president, he appeared to be more interested in staying in his hacienda in Veracruz. In other words, although Santa Anna appeared to enjoy the idea of holding the prestigious title of president of the republic, he was not keen on moving to Mexico City and having to deal with the administrative burden of acting day to day as the nation's executive. More often than not, Santa Anna preferred to retire to his haciendas in Veracruz rather than govern from Mexico City. More research needs to be carried out into Santa Anna's activities in Veracruz before we can determine whether his reluctance to take on the responsibilities of the presidency was a personal choice (a love of life in the hacienda), or a political choice (based on the belief that it was more important for him to control the political situation of Veracruz than that of the country at large, as long as he had reliable agents like Tornel in the capital who could exert pressure on the national government on his behalf). If Tornel had prior knowledge that Santa Anna was intending to claim sick leave when he was elected president, then it is more than likely that his candidacy was designed so that he could become vice president (Santa Anna's deputy president in the capital). In other words, had Tornel come second in the elections (and thus become vice president), the perfect *santanista* scenario would have come into place. Santa Anna would have been able to retire to Manga de Clavo and ensure the state of Veracruz was run according to his plans, while his closest friend, Tornel, would have looked after the daily business of the national government as Santa Anna's acting president (*presidente interino*) in Mexico City. Unfortunately, this dream was not to be, although Santa Anna won the presidential elections by an overwhelming majority, Gómez Farías came in second.

The possibility of having Tornel as either president or vice president certainly unsettled the editors of the radical newspaper *La Columna* who, unable to forgive him for his 1828 change in stance, went on to publish a series of libelous articles about him, claiming that he had been a royalist until 1821, that it had been Santa Anna who had persuaded him to embrace the Plan of Iguala after he had condemned it, and that he was one of those unpleasant political insects that is always hovering around annoying everybody, making a lot of noise.[60] Tornel did not bother to defend himself publicly on this occasion,[61] although he did publish, in May 1833, his extensive *Manifestación del C. José María Tornel*, in which he accounted for his actions from the Revolt of La Acordada to his return to Mexico in 1831. Instead he went to spend the month of February in Orizaba with his son José María, using the trip to visit Córdoba and Tehuacán, and perhaps Manga de Clavo.[62]

THE RADICAL ADMINISTRATION OF VALENTÍN GÓMEZ FARÍAS, 1833–1834

On 1 April 1833, Valentín Gómez Farías was sworn in as acting president of the republic since Santa Anna, after accepting the post of president, had excused himself from taking up office for alleged health-related reasons. He needed time to recover and thus requested to be allowed to remain in Manga de Clavo. It did not take long for the *santanista*-federalist alliance to break down. However, the animosity that developed between them was not so much the result of Gómez Farías's political agenda as of the way the newly elected Congress started to behave. Even José María Luis Mora, who acted as Gómez Farías's intellectual adviser during the so-called radical administration of 1833–1834, was prepared to admit that "the minority [of the congressional representatives] were worthy men of noted virtue and talent, and the majority, as is always the case, belonged to the rabble [*vulgo*], made up of angry and violent men who lacked any sense of propriety."[63] In essence, the radical Congress of 1833–1834 wanted to reform the nation too fast by the *santanistas'* standards. The *santanistas* were still as reformist in their inclinations as politicians such as Gómez Farías or Mora. However, like the moderates and the traditionalists, they believed that all reform needed to be undertaken slowly. In Bocanegra's words: "There are those who say let's finish with what is old and start everything anew; but these with poor intelligence, or better said, in bad faith, do nothing other than destroy, reaching extremes in which neither men nor God are respected."[64] Tornel, with the experience of two decades of constitutional failures weighing on his shoulders ("we have tried every possible form of government, from an absolute monarchy with its brilliant pomp to a federal republic with its dangerous exaggerations"), stated in 1840 that they had made the mistake of adopting laws that did not conform to the "habits and customs, whose roots are deep and ancient" of the nation. In other words, they had failed so far because they had tried to reform

Mexico too quickly: "Without having prepared the earth first, we have planted exotic plants that died as soon as they were born."[65]

Although Samponaro stresses that the disintegration of the *santanista*-federalist alliance in 1834 was not so surprising given that their union had resulted in 1832 from a pragmatic rather than an ideological need,[66] it nevertheless remains the case that the *santanistas*, who had already expressed their unease with the radical leadership of the Rite of York, first in 1828 and later under Guerrero in 1829, found themselves rejecting and reacting to a Congress that in 1833–1834 was attempting to reform the country overnight. For Bocanegra, Santa Anna had led in 1832 what had amounted to a "truly national" movement united in a bid to crush Bustamante's "strong and really oligarchic party." Furthermore, evidence of the truth of his claim was that Santa Anna had then gone on to win the 1833 presidential elections with a comfortable majority. However, the Congress of 1833–1834 was not, in Bocanegra's mind, representative of the "truly national" movement in the same way as Santa Anna himself was. It was dominated by a gang of demagogues whose politics were aimed at "persecuting certain classes of society." Bocanegra, who joined the government as minister of the exchequer (16 May–12 December 1833), supported Gómez Farías' intentions of "verifying a change in the republic, which varying its political nature, prepared the ground so that in the long run the establishment of true democratic principles would be possible." Moreover, Bocanegra believed that the council of individuals formed around Gómez Farías consisted of individuals whose "respectability and reputation" were well known. However, Bocanegra lamented that "although the principles [the cabinet] was hoping to conquer and establish were . . . very good in themselves, such as introducing reforms which may mend the territorial divisions and [the provision of] public education, these came hand in hand with extremist ideas which were leading us to the precipice." What was required, he believed, was that regardless of "which policy was pursued [what was important was] that its implementation was slow [*mesurada*], thus ensuring the nation's well-being and happiness without leading to those abortions which later result in our ruin." In other words, the subsequent animosity that surfaced between the radicals and the *santanistas* revolved around the impatience of the *exaltados* who dominated Congress, not the nature of the reforms themselves.[67]

With Santa Anna allegedly convalescing in Manga de Clavo and Bocanegra at the head of the ministry of the exchequer, it took only one month for Congress to provoke a major political crisis. In what Reynaldo Sordo Cedeño describes as a chaotic series of proposals that were motivated by political passion rather than serious reflection,[68] Congress put Bustamante's cabinet on trial for the execution of Guerrero (contravening the agreements made in the Treaty of Zavaleta), nationalized the duke of Monteleone's properties, and decreed that the Mexican government, and not the pope, could nominate and verify the appointment of ecclesiastical posts (thus exercising the *patronato*). The press exacerbated the increasing tension by either advocating truly radical measures such as the abolition of military and church privileges (proposing an end to the *fueros*) or embracing an extremely reactionary agenda, inviting the regular army to uphold law and order by closing down Congress in the name of their mother country and their sacred religion.[69] Aware of the escalating discontent and in the hope of pacifying the fast-increasing anger of the factions (whether it was the radicals who wanted Congress to act faster or the traditionalists who wanted to prevent Congress from going any further in its heightened reformism), Santa Anna decided to go to Mexico City and take up his position as president.

Santa Anna arrived in the capital on 15 May, around ten o'clock in the morning, and the next day delivered a speech aimed at reminding the political class of their duties, employing the unequivocal rhetoric and turn of phrase of his good friend Tornel.[70] They owed their allegiance to the nation above all other considerations. It was their duty to respect its wishes. The people were the sole source of authority and power. The politicians were their privileged servants, whose "sublime honor" it was to represent them. It was imperative that they fight against ignorance, tyranny, and immorality. The federal constitution was sacrosanct. He recommended that the legislature showed prudence. There was no reason to fear tyranny, for the 1824 charter ensured that no tyrant could grab hold of Mexico's destiny. He promised to defend liberty, the rights of the individual, and equality before the law, and he argued that religion was the main guarantee of human freedom. He also promised to reorganize and reward the army and to attend to the urgent need of providing a basic education to the masses. These were Santa Anna's (Tornel's) beliefs: "My political faith is simple, and my intentions are straight [and honest]. Grant me your enlightened ideas [*luces*] and the favor of a people you have been chosen to represent, in our attempt to promote, even at the expense of our lives, our liberty and good fortune."[71] As noted by Callcott, "There is every reason to believe that Santa Anna was a real liberal at this time, or was at least glad to see some new experiments tried."[72] With Santa Anna temporarily serving as president, Tornel returned to occupy an important post within the ministry of defense as *oficial mayor*.[73]

Any sense that peace might have been restored with Santa Anna's assumption of his presidential role was soon shattered. Moreover, his apparent aversion to despotism was put to the test when, on 26 May, Colonel Ignacio Escalada launched a *pronunciamiento* in Morelia that demanded, among other things, the defense of the church and the army from the attacks of Congress and the naming of Santa Anna as supreme head of the nation. Santa Anna was quick to reply. On hearing the news of Escalada's plan he issued a circular on 28 May, published in the press the following day, stating that he condemned the uprising and would abide by the law, while reassuring the rebels that the army and religion were not being threatened by the administration.[74] Although rumors abounded that Santa Anna was secretly involved in the conspiracy to close down Congress and make himself supreme dictator of Mexico,[75] he personally set off to quell the growing rebellion, on 3 June, on hearing that it had found a division prepared to second it, in Tlalpan, only a few miles south of the capital, led by their commander in chief Gabriel Durán. He did not leave the capital without first ensuring that Tornel was promoted to the rank of general on 1 June 1833.[76]

It was as a recently promoted general that Tornel first heard the extraordinary news that Santa Anna had been taken prisoner on 6 June by the very division that had gone out with him to repress Durán's uprising. In what must have been a particularly bizarre scene, the high-ranking officer, Tomás Moreno, escorted the captured Santa Anna to Yautepec while his men and those soldiers who welcomed their arrival in the town called him their "hero" to cries of "Long live Santa Anna! The Supreme Dictator of Mexico!"[77] On 8 June, with Santa Anna in captivity, General Mariano Arista launched his own Plan of Huejotzingo in which he proclaimed Santa Anna "supreme dictator" of Mexico and demanded the protection of military and ecclesiastical privileges.[78] According to Bocanegra, Santa Anna, who had already told the rebels that they were mistaken if they thought that he would support their plan (which is why he was made prisoner in the first place; so that he might reconsider his initial rejection of their proposal), refused to budge on his intentions. He was transferred on 9 June to the hacienda Buenavista, from where he escaped, reaching Puebla on 13 June. Once free, he returned to Mexico City on the night of 17 June, where he was given a hero's welcome.[79]

It is still not known whether he initially agreed to second the conspirators' proposals (something they would later claim he had done), or if the whole issue of his captivity was a ploy to allow him to wait and see how the other high-ranking officers reacted to Arista's plan, before he decided whether to become a dictator. Most of the evidence would appear to suggest that he did not want to overthrow the existing constitutional government. As will be seen further on, Santa Anna would be offered on several occasions during his lifetime the opportunity of becoming dictator of Mexico, and invariably, at least until 1853, he did not seize the occasion. Costeloe is right in reminding us that although Santa Anna had the opportunity to impose a permanent dictatorship in 1833, 1834, 1841, and again in December 1842, "he made no obvious or known attempt to establish a permanent military dictatorship. Instead, he always expressed his belief in

the republican and representative form of government, and after each sei-
zure of power and dismissal of Congress, he permitted the election of a
new Congress and the drafting of a new constitution."[80]

Santa Anna thus spent three weeks in Mexico City and then departed,
on 10 July, to crush the remaining rebels in Guanajuato at the head of
twenty-four hundred men. Arista finally surrendered on 8 October, and
Santa Anna returned to the capital on 27 July, occupying the presidency
once more until 15 December 1833, when, claiming ill health once again,
he retired to Manga de Clavo. During these months, Tornel, as *oficial
mayor* in the Ministry of Defense, spent most of his time promulgating the
numerous decrees and reports that circulated concerning Santa Anna's captivity, escape, and campaign against Arista.[81] He also started to make his
displeasure known regarding the extremism of the radical Congress, and
was subsequently attacked with relish by *La Columna*, whose editors accused him of being a power-monger and a vile opportunistic turncoat.[82]

As an *hombre de bien* who had distanced himself from the radicals since
1828, as a high-ranking officer, indeed a general now, who believed in
preserving the army's privileged status in regard to the law, and as a devoted and practicing Roman Catholic, Tornel had good reason to be
alarmed at the way Congress was proceeding. Among the most radical
reforms that were undertaken between 12 June and 6 November 1833, the
following deserve a mention:

12 June: The staff of Mexico City town hall (which was still composed of politicians
who had been named by Bustamante) were replaced with their 1829 predecessors.

23 June: The *Ley del Caso* expelled from the republic fifty-one politicians whose
views were considered to be unpatriotic (including General Bustamante).

17 August: The missions in California were secularized.

31 August: Church property belonging to the missionaries from the Philippines was
expropriated.

14 October: The ecclesiastical Colegio de Santa María de todos los Santos was shut
down.

18 October: The properties of the Philippine and San Camilo missionaries were
placed on auction to the general public.

19 October: The Catholic and church-dominated University of Mexico was shut
down.

21 October: The closed university was replaced by a (secular) Dirección General
de Instrucción Pública.

24 October: The closed Colegio de Santa María de todos los Santos was to become
a national library.

24 October: The Dirección General de Instrucción Pública was to be financed
through the expropriation of the following church properties: the Monastery and
Church of San Camilo, the Hospital and Church de Jesús, the Hospital de Belén,

the Asylum for the Poor de Santo Tomás, the Old Inquisition building, and the Monastery and Church de Espíritu Santo.

27 October: The civil obligation to pay *diezmos* (contributions to the church) was abolished.

3 November: The 16 May 1831 law that granted the church the right to nominate its priests, bishops, and archbishops was abolished.

6 November: The civil obligation to take ecclesiastical vows was abolished.[83]

Tornel was concerned that they were reforming the country too quickly and, like Bocanegra, was alarmed at the violent nature of the Congress. Their initial intention of forming a government that could reconcile the divided factions was being completely ignored by Congress. The *Ley del Caso*, which arbitrarily exiled fifty-one politicians, appeared to Tornel and Bocanegra as a clear example of Congress's despotism. The majority of those victimized individuals were "commendable people of distinguished merit . . . renowned for their past services to the nation."[84] The extreme party interests of the dominant radical faction were being allowed to rule the country. Tornel and Bocanegra might not have believed, for example, in what Bustamante had tried to accomplish during his presidency, and they might have even felt personally insulted by his conduct toward them (especially Tornel), but that did not mean that they approved of exiling individuals who were *hombres de bien* like themselves, fellow members of that political class in which "social assumptions ran deeper than the conservative-liberal divide."[85]

Nevertheless, the *santanistas* had not yet given up on the Gómez Farías administration. Tornel and Bocanegra, like Santa Anna himself, had not supported the attempt to turn the *caudillo* into Mexico's supreme dictator. They still believed, although they had become profoundly disenchanted by now, in their representative federal form of government, and they had not altogether abandoned some of those radical ideals they had embraced in the mid-1820s. The *santanistas* shared, to a certain extent, the anticlericalism of the 1833–1834 Congress. They believed in secularizing education and, like the radicals, were of the opinion that it was the church's obligation to finance the state and the army. What would differentiate the *santanistas* from the radicals would be the way in which they set about securing the financial support of the church. Rather than openly declaring that it was their intention to assault the church, they secured large church grants in 1834 and 1847 by making a slightly less drastic form of amortization a prerequisite for their defense of church privileges. In other words, while *santanista* discourse and rhetoric was all about proclaiming their unconditional support of church privileges and the church's moral importance in society, in practice, they demanded a series of significant loans in exchange for that support and found different ways to ensure that the church financed the resurrection of the army.[86] Given that Congress had mainly focused on attacking the church during the first nine months it had been in place, the *santanistas* did not yet feel the need to use the force of the army to put a stop to Congress's activities. It would be once Congress chose to focus on assaulting the army's privileges that the *santanistas* would finally bring their alliance with the federalists to an abrupt end.

It was therefore coinciding with Santa Anna's return to the presidency on 27 October 1833 that Tornel and the *caudillo* thought of a way of preempting Congress's forthcoming attack on the regular army. Tornel was made minister of war (6–19 November 1833) for the first time, during Santa Anna's brief spell in the capital, and together they instigated the radical reform of 16 November. Adopting extraordinary powers, Santa Anna decreed that the regular army was to be reduced from twelve to ten battalions, from twelve to six regiments, and that the mounted artillery brigade was to be abolished. Moreover, from then on, there could only be eight generals and twelve brigadiers in the entire regular army. There is no doubt that both Tornel and Santa Anna were hoping to anticipate Congress's own proposal and appease the radicals' demands. Not surprisingly, however, Congress accepted the reform but went on to propose its own more draconian rationalization, which would never get as far as being legislated in the wake of the army's reaction in May 1834.[87]

TORNEL, GOVERNOR, AND CONSPIRATOR, 1834

Once the reform of 16 November was in place, Santa Anna placed Tornel at the head of the Federal District before retiring to Manga de Clavo. It is more than probable that he preferred to have Tornel acting as governor then rather than as minister of war, since Tornel would then have the militias of the capital at his orders. This was something that could prove helpful in case it became necessary to organize a coup in order to bring an end to Congress's increasingly radical demands. It can hardly be seen as coincidental that between December 1833 and May 1834, Tornel ensured that the militias of the Federal District were strengthened through a number of laws he proposed and implemented, securing their loyalty by granting them significant financial support (for example, Tornel authorized awarding 300 pesos to the Batallón del Comercio in April 1834).[88] Nevertheless, Tornel enjoyed being governor of the Federal District. He used to say that he felt that he had been born to be governor and, as Bocanegra noted, he was very good at it: "He carried out [the duties of governor of the Federal District] with characteristic skill and efficiency."[89] It is worth noting here that of all the roles he played during his lifetime (insurgent, presidential speechwriter, educationalist, playwright, and minister, to name but a few), it was for his services as governor of the Federal District that he is remembered in Mexico City's street plan. The street that carries his name in the *colonia* San Miguel Chapultepec, between General T. Montiel and General Pedro Antonio de los Santos, carries the title of *gobernador* before it.

As was the case in 1828 and 1829, Tornel proved to be a particularly dedicated governor (19 November 1833–29 November 1834). He also showed what an able conspirator he was. The Plan of Cuernavaca (25 May 1834) and the *pronunciamientos* that ensued leading to the end of Gómez Farías's radical administration were planned, organized, and monitored by Tornel. However, before his role in the Plan of Cuernavaca is analyzed, it is worth noting the laws he proposed and implemented in 1834, since they provide a clear indication of the extent to which he was dedicated, as governor of the Federal District, to ensuring that the capital was a safe place in which to live. His activities from December 1833 to November 1834 were almost exclusively oriented toward guaranteeing law and order and that criminals were caught and persecuted accordingly. His obsession with eradicating crime became almost a personal crusade, one that even led to enemies of his, such as Mora, to praise him for his policing skills. Together with his endeavors to enforce a policy of zero tolerance to crime, he had to orchestrate the response to the cholera epidemic that swept through the capital in 1833–1834,[90] and he displayed the evolved belief that Mexico was not yet ready to enjoy complete and unrestricted freedom of the press, by demanding that certain newspapers be censored and that certain pamphleteers be arrested, thus abandoning his earlier belief that a combative press was a necessary component in a healthy democratic system.

As part of his campaign to clean up the capital, Tornel decreed a conditional prohibition on the sale of *pulque* and forbade certain gambling games such as *bagatela* from taking place.[91] In a bid to exercise greater control over the local army, he forbade soldiers from roaming the streets after curfew if they had no license to do so.[92] He also took a personal role in ensuring that all foreigners who were not in Mexico on a diplomatic mission visited him to account for their movements and to give reasons for their visit.[93] Furthermore, he awarded himself full power and control over the police force[94] and decreed that a census be taken in each area of the Federal District, demanding that all vagabonds and truants from school be reported to the appropriate authorities.[95] He decreed that anybody detained carrying illegal weapons would be imprisoned and made a number of official suggestions to dissuade Mexico's youth from being tempted into crime at a tender age.[96] Once more he banned begging and also banned large groups of people gathering at night, even for a wake.[97] It was also in a bid to make it difficult for criminals to exploit the darkness of night for their own schemes and devices (and probably because the streetlights of Baltimore had made such a deep impression on him) that he proposed and oversaw the making and placing of gas-lit street lamps in the main avenues of the capital.[98] As if all of this were not enough to confirm that he was extremely determined in his bid to clean up the capital, on two different occasions he was reported to have personally given chase to and caught notorious criminals: the thief who robbed José María Martínez's jewelers in May[99] and a gang of infamous bandits who had been terrorizing Mexico City's *gente decente* in October.[100]

Parallel to his endeavors to bring law and order to the capital, Tornel had to find the means of controlling the cholera epidemic from spreading further. He was not only concerned with cleaning up the city in metaphorical terms, but also in the more literal sense of improving the city's hygiene.[101] He banned the burial and burning of corpses within the confines of the capital, forcing them to take place in a cemetery outside the city limits.[102] He proposed the immediate creation of a medical school that could quickly prepare its alumni to deal with the epidemic,[103] and regularly kept the capital's inhabitants informed of the progress they were making against the deadly illness, which started to take effect in April that year.[104] However, regardless of the fact that the epidemic began to recede, Tornel remained vigilant, issuing decrees that determined what was required to become a medic in such a time of crisis,[105] and holding numerous meetings with the Junta Superior de Sanidad throughout the year.[106] By 4 November 1834, Tornel was in a position to state that the epidemic was over, and he proposed a series of measures, based on firsthand experience, to be implemented in order to prevent another one from taking place.[107]

Perhaps the most striking aspect of his activities as governor in 1834 was his determination to ensure that freedom of speech was restricted. For someone who had been so outspoken in the 1820s in his condemnation of any proposal that may have involved censoring the press, Tornel's change in stance was truly dramatic. His return to prominence in the political scene of the capital had been accompanied by a proliferation of articles and pamphlets written against him.[108] There is little doubt that he was reacting to these attacks when he argued that freedom of the press was being abused and that there was a need for some form of censorship.[109] Nevertheless, it was not the first time that he had been the target of severe attacks in the press. During the summers of 1826 and 1828, he had been equally criticized, and yet, even then, in the mid-1820s he was still prepared to defend the freedom of the press in Congress and in the editorials he wrote for *El Amigo del Pueblo*. There was more to his defense of censorship than just a personal displeasure on his part at the way certain pamphleteers were portraying him. Representative of the way the stage of hope (1821–1828) had degenerated into a stage of disenchantment (1828–1835),[110] Tornel, like so many of his contemporaries, had become, by 1833, deeply disenchanted with early republican politics and, hardened by the events of 1828 in particular, was no longer prepared to uphold some of the more idealistic notions he had embraced prior to the Parián riot.

Bocanegra, whose politics evolved parallel to Tornel's, became deeply distressed by the way in which the press shamelessly abused its freedom in

1828.[111] This experience convinced him that the freedom of the press was a double-edged sword, which could be as detrimental as it was useful to a nation's development.[112] Thus, Bocanegra, in the summer of 1829, acting as minister of relations, promoted the decree of 5 September that declared that those authors, publishers, and printers who were deemed responsible for writing, publishing, or printing any antipatriotic texts could be immediately placed on trial. When several states protested at Bocanegra's "unconstitutional" reform, he replied that given that the freedom of the press had been so brutally abused, threatening in the process to destroy the country's internal peace, order, and unity, they had had no choice but to implement the means by which these excesses could be controlled.[113] Tornel, like Bocanegra, had also become convinced that some form of control was necessary after the events of 1828. In fact, in 1829, acting as governor, he had already displayed his developing aversion to the freedom of the press when he censored the authors of a pamphlet that criticized Santa Anna.[114] Nevertheless, by 1834, his endeavors to censor the press were much more forceful. To quote Mora, Tornel "was responsible for destroying the opposition in the press and exiled . . . some of the editors of the newspaper entitled *La Oposición*."[115]

As early as 4 January 1834, he wrote to Gómez Farías demanding that the vice president give him some indication as to what rules could be applied to prevent the freedom of the press from being abused.[116] However, since little was done in response to his plea, Tornel went public and wrote an article condemning the existing freedom of the press in *El Telégrafo* on 22 May. As long as this freedom was abused, there was a need to impose some form of censorship and to punish and imprison those individuals who were responsible for abusing it:

The sheer uncontrolled nature of the press has reached such extremes that we must force the authorities to take action. Congress, the president and the vice-president of the republic, and our very own institutions are attacked with such shamelessness that we cannot but fear the proximity of a horrific crisis. . . . How is it that we allow certain pamphlets to circulate freely when their sole detestable intention is to plunge our mother country into the horrors of anarchy?[117]

On the same day as the Plan of Cuernavaca was launched, Tornel decided to use his power as governor to put an end to what he considered to be the relentless and repeated abuses of the freedom of the press, and he issued a decree by which the press and the publication of offensive posters in the Federal District could be censored and punished.[118] Thereafter he ensured his decree was implemented accordingly and went on to issue a similar decree in October that affected the publication of unlawful pamphlets.[119] While he publicly celebrated his men's victories, such as the arrest of the "liars" of *El Mosquito Mexicano*,[120] he was equally forceful in condemning his men when they failed to fulfill their duties to his satisfaction. Thus, he accused the Federal District censors of being blind and too tolerant in October[121] and went on to argue in November that they were still not doing enough to restrain the disgusting behavior of the press, demanding that new forms of censorship be immediately adopted.[122]

Tornel would never go back on his evolved view that to guarantee the complete freedom of the press, as had been the case in the 1824 Constitution, was a recipe for disaster. There was no space for such a liberal law in a country where a freedom like this one was compulsively abused with libelous and offensive articles that could only contribute toward destabilizing further their young, frail, political system, exacerbating the divisions and the violence that appeared to have become an endemic part of party politics in early republican Mexico. He would never again reiterate the view that a combative press was a prerequisite for a healthy political lifestyle.

Paralleling his disenchanted belief that the Mexican people were not mature enough politically to enjoy a system in which freedom of the press was guaranteed by the constitution, Tornel's unease at the way Congress was behaving led him to conclude that a coup needed to be orchestrated so that its increasingly radical demands and deliberations were abruptly brought to an end. In other words, in stark contrast to the beliefs he had professed in the mid-1820s that elections were the only legitimate means of changing a government, Tornel wholeheartedly embraced the role of conspirator in the first months of 1834. According to Mora, Tornel started to plot the downfall of the Gómez Farías administration as early as January 1834, keeping Santa Anna fully informed of the events in the capital and coordinating "small intrigues" with Francisco Lombardo. It would appear that he was not particularly concerned with disguising his intentions, he openly insulted Gómez Farías and came out to defend Santa Anna publicly from the claim that he was responsible for Congress's banishment of several members of the clergy and the military.[123] Gómez Farías, like Mora, was more than aware of the fact that Tornel was writing regular letters to Santa Anna, keeping him informed of the events in the capital, and that he was involved in a conspiracy to close down Congress.[124]

Santa Anna returned to the capital and occupied the presidential seat once more on 24 April, and although he challenged some of the measures being discussed in Congress, he awaited the forthcoming revolt to exercise his power fully. Meanwhile, Tornel went to Cuernavaca for a few days with his brother-in-law, Miguel Diez Bonilla, and drafted the plan that was proclaimed on 25 May 1834, calling for "Religion, the *fueros* and Santa Anna" and demanding a reversal of Gómez Farías' policies. As Manuel Rivera Cambas rightly points out, "The plan had as its apparent leader the general Don Angel Pérez Palacios, but in reality it was orchestrated by Don José María Tornel and the *Licenciado* Bonilla."[125] Further to writing and preparing the revolt of Cuernavaca, in order to rally widespread support for the plan, he promised, according to Mora, "mountains of gold to those that proclaimed, protected or even just accepted it."[126] Moreover, even after Santa Anna started to reverse the policies of the Gómez Farías administration, Tornel continued to work to ensure that support for the Plan of Cuernavaca was outright, censoring the press,[127] celebrating any news that reached the capital showing how the different garrisons in the republic were declaring their allegiance to the plan,[128] and organizing meetings in his own office with the supporters of the Plan.[129]

The Plan of Cuernavaca was successful. On 17 June, in the wake of the plan, Santa Anna dismissed Gómez Farías' advisers and by the middle of the summer had taken full control of the country, reversing most of the laws that the radical Congress had passed. Tornel's loyalty and success were again rewarded, this time with the Ministry of War on 2 December 1834. Mora bitterly wrote that

the first dictatorial actions of Santa Anna, under the direction of Bonilla, the virgin sword of Tornel, the influence of the privileged classes and the publications of the . . . editor Lombardo, had no other aim but to change all the [political] personnel of the republic; the chambers were dissolved and the same happened to the state Congresses, the governors were also sacked, the town halls were changed, the Court of Justice and a large section of the magistracy had to leave, and all minor judges were replaced except for those who paid homage to the dictatorship.[130]

PLAN OF CUERNAVACA

The Plan of Cuernavaca was not as reactionary as Mora might have led us to believe. Although it was clearly traditionalist in the way that it defended the traditional privileges (the *fueros*) that both church and army had enjoyed since the colony, it did not pretend, as Mora implied, to impose an authoritarian dictatorship that served the interests of the "military and ecclesiastical oligarchy."[131] In other words, while its defenders wanted to protect the army and the church's interests, they did not want to impose a military republic. Evidence of this can be found in the fact that a new Congress was formed that went on to draft a new constitution after it was decided in October 1835 that federalism had failed and a centralist political system needed to be devised. Furthermore, the 1836 Constitution, better known as the Seven Laws (*Siete Leyes*), created a third legislative branch, beyond the Chamber of Deputies and the Senate, called the Supreme Conservative Power (Supremo Poder Conservador), one of the main aims of which was to control the executive and prevent a dictatorship.

According to the plan's five articles, in response to the "atrocious chaos, confusion and disorder" the country was in as a direct result of the legislature's behavior, its advocates (Tornel) wanted to ensure that (1) all decrees issued against individuals (*la ley del Caso*) and the church, and in favor of Masonic sects were abolished; (2) all laws approved that violated the constitution and the general will were reversed; (3) Santa Anna be given the authority to execute these demands; (4) all deputies who favored these deeply unpopular reforms were removed from office and replaced by others following the corresponding procedures specified in the 1824 Constitution; and (5) Santa Anna would have those forces that defended the plan at his service to ensure that the plan was executed accordingly.[132] Although Tornel succeeded in ensuring the plan was supported by numerous garrisons, it was nevertheless extremely popular. The mobilization that took place was such that it would be hard to believe that the fall of the radical 1833–1834 administration was entirely his doing. In brief, Tornel succeeded in voicing what had become a fairly generalized sense of discontent at the way Congress was proceeding. In broad terms, the population as well as the army was not yet ready to embrace or support Congress's radical attack on church and army. As Bocanegra noted, the "innumerable" *pronunciamientos* that were issued in allegiance to the plan of Cuernavaca showed the extent to which a large proportion of the population had come to resent Congress's measures.[133] Although the united front that the regular army presented against the 1833–1834 Congress was one of the clearest examples of there having been a civilian-military divide at a time when this was often blurred (there was no instance of a garrison that opposed the plan),[134] the 316 plans of allegiance it received between May and August 1834 included a high proportion of civilian-led groupings (such as town halls, municipalities, and regional councils).[135]

It is clear that Tornel and Bocanegra's view that Congress had become despotic and tyrannical and that it no longer represented the beliefs or the more traditionalist Catholic tendencies of the majority of the population, found favor, evident in the lack of any significant support offered to Congress when it most needed it. The radicals were thus swiftly ousted from power, without having the resources or the control over the civic militias to be able to defend themselves. A new order was imposed, and the church and the army's *fueros* were preserved. However, the church was made to pay for the support the *santanistas* guaranteed them in imposing the Plan of Cuernavaca. As Barbara Tenenbaum reminds us, "Nine days after the proclamation of the Plan of Cuernavaca, the Church agreed to provide Santa Anna between 30,000 and 40,000 pesos, on a monthly basis, over a period of six months."[136] In other words, the *santanistas* succeeded in achieving what the radicals had failed to do: to force the church to assist the republic's dire economy with its funds and properties. The difference was that they did this by making church loans a prerequisite for their guaranteed defense of church privileges. They did not openly attack the church as the radicals had done.

CHANGE TO CENTRALISM

The Plan of Cuernavaca set the stage for what would become the next major upheaval in the political life of early republican Mexico: the change to centralism. Surprising as it may be, Tornel made known his conversion to centralism as early as July 1834 (a year before the federalist system was formally abandoned by the government).[137] What becomes evident is that the weight of experience was beginning to bear heavily not only on Tornel's shoulders but also on those of the majority of Mexico's political class. As Bocanegra would note years later in his *Memorias*: "I read what I am writing and I become convinced, under the light of truth and experience, that there is an abyss between the theory and the practice, between what is speculated and what is real." The experience of the First Federal Republic appeared to confirm that there was no public spirit and that it was impossible to find a "truly national opinion." After the revolutions of 1828, 1829, 1832, and 1834, it had become clear that the 1824 Constitution had failed to establish a stable, long-lasting political system suited to the needs and customs of the Mexican people. Experience was there to prove that they had made a mistake. The constitution had, in the end, even been one of the causes of the upheavals of the late 1820s and early 1830s:

It had defects, the most important of all being that it represented an attempt to blindly imitate the constitution of the United States of America, without making the necessary distinctions, or the important omissions which should have been incorporated when applying [such a system] to this Republic; whether this nation was or was not in the right situation to adopt the same constitution was not considered, [just as no attention was given to the fact that in the United States] . . . the constitution came from institutions which already existed, which did not replace previous ones; a very different context to that of Mexico.[138]

Without renouncing their liberalism,[139] *santanistas* like Tornel and Bocanegra arrived at the conclusion that the reality of their country—the public events of their conflictive present—demanded that they change its political system. Scenes such as those that had characterized the Parián riot must be avoided. Mexico needed a new constitution that did not go against the general will, did not create a context in which political upheavals were commonplace, and took into account, first and foremost, "the habits, customs and even preoccupations of the people."[140] As was professed in the *pronunciamiento* of Orizaba (19 May 1835), it was essential that they terminate the federal system, "adopting [instead] another form of government more in tune with the people's needs, demands and customs, and which can better guarantee our independence, internal peace and the Catholic religion we believe in."[141]

Tornel became a committed centralist and did not defend federalism ever again, even when Santa Anna joined forces with Gómez Farías and the *puros* in 1846 and contributed to the reestablishment of the 1824 charter. For Tornel, the experience of the First Federal Republic demonstrated that federalism weakened rather than strengthened the nation. In 1842 he argued that "the centralization of power is not just a tendency, it is a need in any democratic country," and he defended his views by extensively citing Alexis de Tocqueville, who had argued previously that "the equality of men amounted to having a strong, uniform and single government." Faced with the imminent loss of Texas and fearing U.S. expansionism, Tornel rejected the federalist inclinations of the 1842 Constituent Congress, stressing that if they reinstated a federal system, "the republic will become weaker, at a time when she needs to be stronger to oppose the ambitions of a powerful nation."[142]

Although Santa Anna allowed the change to centralism to take place, he was not in Mexico City either while the discussions got under way or when the change was implemented (23 October 1835) or, in fact, when the new constitution was finally approved (29 December 1836). Instead he was either resting in his hacienda, at the front of the troops that went to quell the revolts in Zacatecas (April–May 1835) and later Texas (December 1835–April 1836), or a prisoner of war in the United States. Nevertheless as Reynaldo Sordo Cedeño's research has shown, Santa Anna, unlike Tornel, remained notably ambivalent over the entire issue during the year in which federalism was abandoned.[143] Although he took it on himself to crush Governor Francisco García's federalist revolt in Zacatecas, ending it with the battle of Guadalupe (11 May 1835), he did so not so much because he supported the change to centralism but because he saw it as his duty to ensure that public peace was not disturbed by any armed insurrections. Clearly more research needs to be done regarding Santa Anna's activities in Veracruz before we can start to understand his position on the thorny federalist-centralist divide. However, with hindsight and bearing in mind his predisposition to join the federalists in 1846, and the fact that as someone whose interests were deeply rooted in his home province, it would have been natural for him to defend a federalist system (as he had done initially in his 1823 *pronunciamiento* of San Luis Potosí), it is worth wondering whether he was a federalist at heart who was prepared to go along with centralism as long as the central government was run by *santanistas* who would leave him alone to do as he pleased in Veracruz. Unlike Tornel, whose political ideas evolved in such a way that he became a committed centralist after 1834, Santa Anna remained a federalist who could live with centralism as long as it did not interfere with his activities in Veracruz. When he joined the federalists in 1846, it was at a time when the *santanistas* were not in control of the government, and when he joined the Alamán's centralist conservatives in 1853, it was with the prior knowledge that supporters of his like Tornel, Antonio Haro y Tamariz, and Juan Suárez y Navarro would be running the show in the capital.

The change to centralism, according to Costeloe, "if we are to accept contemporary opinion, excluding liberals like Mora, . . . did reflect Mexican public opinion of the time. The word federalism has lost its magic appeal, as one writer put it and the experience of the past decade has brought disillusion and a desire for change."[144] Over four hundred petitions and *pronunciamientos* were written and proclaimed between May and October 1835, and "centralism was in the air and a large number of Mexicans had reached the conclusion that federalism had failed."[145] With Santa Anna away, the presidency was occupied first by Miguel Barragán (28 January 1835–26 February 1836) and later by José Justo Corro (27 February 1836–1 April 1837) after Barragán died. Although Corro was "alleged to be weak and indecisive, and throughout most of his year in office the man believed to be in control of the government was Tornel,"[146] the faction that actually dominated both Congress and the government was, to use Sordo Cedeño's definition, the centralist party,[147] which, although containing some *santanista* politicians, tended to represent a more traditionalist agenda than that sustained by the *santanistas* in general. Evidence was that in the wake of Santa Anna's Texan disaster, Anastasio Bustamante won the presidential elections of 1837. Further evidence is that although Tornel tried to prevent the newly formed Constituent Congress from creating the Supreme Conservative Power because it would restrict the actions of the executive, strutting and shouting for over an hour and a quarter, according to Carlos María de Bustamante, in the session of 14 December 1835, Congress went on to sanction its creation on 16 December.[148]

Nevertheless, although Tornel was not as firmly in control of the government as he might have hoped when he instigated the Plan of Cuernavaca, it is nonetheless evident that he supported the change to centralism and overall was satisfied with the political system that was created with the Seven Laws, even though he feared the Second Law could weaken the executive. In the words of Bocanegra, the success of the *santanista* revolt of 1834 brought with it "a satisfactory state of peace," and 1835 began with some hopes for "an improved political situation."[149]

TORNEL, MINISTER OF WAR

As the change to centralism started to be formulated, Tornel became minister of war for a second time. Regardless of the fact that he is remembered in Mexico City's street plan today for having been governor of the Federal District, Tornel is primarily known in the historiography for his work as minister of war during Santa Anna's repeated periods in office. According to Fernando Díaz Díaz, "An analysis of the list of ministers during the eleven occasions in which Santa Anna formally assumed the presidency of the nation offers us the following result: José María Tornel: six times [minister of war on each occasion]."[150] Jan Bazant confirms this view: "Santa Anna found him very useful, especially as his minister of war and marine. . . . Tornel was the closest collaborator of the president; he was also his friend and his favorite."[151] There is good reason for him to be associated with the Ministry of War; he went on to hold this position for approximately eight years, excluding interruptions.[152]

A study of his role as minister of war is fundamental in any appraisal of his life, as he dedicated a great deal of time and effort to the restructuring and improvement of the armed forces. Indeed, it is impossible to give an accurate analysis of the essential aspects of his beliefs without looking carefully at the proposals he made, as well as at those he carried out in his ministerial capacity. The decisions he arrived at and were forcefully expressed in the annual ministerial reports he wrote (1835, 1839, and 1844) contain the essence of his views on the formation of the army. A detailed study of them, as well as of his actions as minister, enables us to understand with greater clarity the following points and aspects of his political and military career: (1) that he was minister not only because of his friendship with Santa Anna, although this obviously helped, but because of his own proved skills as minister of war; (2) that he was consistent in his ideas on the army throughout his life, thus disproving the repeated allegation of inconsistency in his beliefs; (3) that his political success can be attributed in no small degree to the way he pleased the military; and (4) his views on society, like his ideas on the army, were to a great extent, a reflection of his opinions of Mexico's political life. Although his reports of 1839 and 1844 will be looked at separately further on, it nevertheless remains the case that the essence of his military reformism was present in his 1835 report. To explore these ideas, Tornel's views will be analyzed thematically, following a similar division of topics to the subheadings in his reports: education and the corps of engineers, the medical corps, and systems of recruitment and discipline.

Education was one of Tornel's main concerns throughout his life. His involvement in the Compañía Lancasteriana, his active participation in the creation of the Instituto de Ciencias, Literatura y Artes (1825), his directorship of the Colegio de Minería (1843–1853), and his occasional interventions in the Colegio de San Ildefonso are all proof. Similarly, he took it upon himself to enforce a basic education on his soldiers each time he was in office.

When he became minister of war in 1835, one of the main problems he encountered was the army's general lack of education.[153] Because most soldiers were recruited from the peasantry, the working classes, and the marginal sectors of society, few men could read or write: "Having destined members from the most ignorant and lowest sectors of society to make up the ranks of the army, there have been cases where in certain corps there was not a single individual who could be promoted to the rank of corporal or sergeant, given that nobody satisfied the requisites specified in the ordinance." He did not hesitate to pin the responsibility for their impoverished and ignorant state on the Spanish government: "The Spanish government opposed the idea of providing an elementary education to the people." Moreover, "education was so poor that a man who knew the first letters of the alphabet became the wise man of the village, the perpetual secretary of the town hall and the assessor of the municipal authorities." However, by 1835, fourteen years had passed since independence had been achieved. Tornel was aware of this and made a point of admitting that little had been done to improve this Spanish legacy of illiteracy and ignorance: "Having achieved our independence, education did not receive the attention, which was to be expected." He argued in the true spirit of the enlightenment that a primary education was the foundation of all sciences and that it was "necessary to improve the social condition of the people."[154]

To support his views, he referred his audience to the resolutions made by the duke of Kent to combat the ignorance that characterized his Royal Scottish Regiment. Apparently, according to Tornel, the prince "of sweet and pleasant memory to all philanthropists and lovers of knowledge"[155] had founded a school for his soldiers that was run by a sergeant who had been educated with the Lancasterian methodology.[156] Furthermore, in November 1811, "the Duke of York, general and head of the British Army, established regimental schools, by order of the government, awarding the teachers the salary and privileges of a sergeant." Tornel argued that they ought to follow this example: "Mexicans are convinced . . . of the need to adopt this happy policy in all of the corps of the army." Therefore, he proposed on 23 March 1835 that a sergeant be made responsible for teaching the alphabet to the soldiers in each company. Initially this sergeant would teach eight soldiers at a time. Moreover, these soldiers would not be expected to perform any other duty while attending classes, and he proposed that, as an incentive, those who made the most of these lessons—"the most hardworking"—could be promoted to either corporal or sergeant. He offered twenty-five pesos as a monthly payment to each corps in order to cover the expenses of this educational program. Books were to be provided separately by the serving minister of war, who was obliged to inform Congress of the progress of these schools, making any necessary observations rising from the experience as a whole.[157]

His concern about education was not limited solely to the teaching of the elementary principles required to achieve a basic level of literacy. In the same report he showed concern over what he defined as "military scientific education." This referred mainly to the corps of engineers he had helped to create in 1827 and also to the training of the medical corps, as will be seen further on. The engineers' corps, founded in 1827, had never become the thriving scientific division he had hoped for in his initial proposal of 5 November. In fact, on 16 November 1834, the small number of existing engineers had been further reduced. Tornel stated that this was scandalous if Mexico was to become a truly civilized nation, it was imperative to be able to boast of a functional engineers' corps. To achieve such an aim, it was essential for the army to have an efficient and fully organized school that could provide sufficient trained engineers.

One of the initial problems was that since the engineers' corps had been created, there had been little incentive for bright students to enroll. The reason was obvious: "A young educated man finds better and more stimulating prospects in any other career than in the army. It is fundamental, if we want to count upon the services of worthy men, to ensure that their future is . . . secure in the army." In other words, it was absurd to expect to have an engineers' corps made up of volunteers with no stable income and no pension guaranteed. The military hospitals were suffering from an identical problem. Doctors, like engineers, made a better living outside the army than in it. For this reason, Tornel advocated a well-organized school that guaranteed a complete apprenticeship in the army as well as a respectable wage that would encourage those who had plans of becoming either engineers or doctors to do so within the military profession. For this to happen, some essential reforms were needed to complete the organization of the existing school of engineers. Tornel stressed that no soldier could become an officer within the engineers' corps without being examined first. Until 1835, the situation was still one in which personal contacts were almost officially recognized and valued more than the knowledge required to achieve promotion, and the engineers' corps was consequently in danger of being run by completely ignorant and incompetent officers.

The second reform he proposed regarding the engineers' corps was also a display of common sense. Until 1835, the lack of funds had meant that the school of engineers was based exclusively on theoretical lessons. Tornel emphasized that this was not enough to create a practical and technically minded functional and serviceable corps of engineers: "Scientific principles are not enough in themselves to form officers in engineering; without practice they are as useless as isolated theories are." Consequently he proposed that the school be established in the old fortress of Perote, which would enable the students to put their theories into practice:

It is essential that we establish a school of [engineering] practice, in which the exactitude of the rules can be measured and where what has been learnt through calculations can be executed in practice. The school of practice could be established in the Fortress of Perote, and there, the engineers could carry out all the necessary exercises to enable them to develop their skills in preparing either the attack or defence of fortresses.

Once more, Tornel referred his audience to the successful example of the British Army. In 1771 the Academy of Artillery and the Academy of Engineers had been united in Woolwich. Because these two forces were complementary they could aid each other with their education. He argued that this example merited replication: "Allowing our officers from the two separate corps to study together those subjects they share in common." For those few outstanding students, he suggested the incentive of sending them for a brief spell of time to West Point Academy in the United States and the French Polytechnic School of Paris.[158]

In theory, the time was ripe to execute all of these reforms. The only obstacle that could prevent their successful execution was the disruption that came with war—either internal or against a foreign power. Tornel made a point of remarking on the way internal turmoil had consistently thwarted the implementation of idealistic plans: "If the political turmoils had not distracted our young engineers from their studies, our expectations, which seemed to be so well-founded in 1831, would have been fulfilled." He lamented, "It is and will always be regrettable that our constant political earthquakes prevent us from consolidating those establishments in which the honor, utility and glory of the nation are best served."[159]

The fact that Tornel was influenced by the views and beliefs expressed by the benevolent and philanthropic *philosophes* and *enciclopédistes* of the Enlightenment is apparent not only in the way he consistently stressed throughout his life the need for a general and effective educational program. There is further evidence of his liberalism in the way he also emphasized in each one of his reports the need for functional and well-maintained hospitals together with an equally well-trained medical staff.

In his 1835 report, he strongly advocated rescuing the medical corps from oblivion. The Cuerpo de Sanidad Militar, founded in 1829, had suffered a similar fate to the engineers' corps due to political upheaval following the Plan of Xalapa and Bustamante's rise to power. Limited resources and too few medical staff had led the Bustamante regime to reduce the medical corps' funds in order to finance other enterprises. Tornel thought that it was fundamental "that such a branch that is as important and worthy of our consideration as the health of those who fight to defend the nation, is put right, not only to show that our nation is a munificent one, but to prove that it does not affect ignorance of the fortunes of those who risk their lives for it and serve it so advantageously." The two main problems were the lack of funding and the absence of a significant number of fully trained medics or nurses. The result was that "medical assistants and practitioners full of ignorance form the majority of a medical corps that has inflicted worse wounds on our troops than enemy bullets have!" Returning to his firm beliefs in the benefits of investing in an efficient educational program, he reminded his audience that "ignorance in this art has always figured in our catalogue of plagues." Funds allotted to the medical corps being negligible, fully trained medics preferred to make a living outside the military profession—not only because they were better off as civilians but also because there was no incentive for them to abandon their "comforts to follow the departing troops and to participate in their dangers."[160]

However well intentioned, Tornel's plans to regenerate the medical corps were limited in their effectiveness. While he had insisted that education needed funds urgently and went on to demand them, he was more prepared to accept that the severe economic crisis Mexico was undergoing meant that its economy could not be further taxed at present; therefore, little could be done other than voice concern and distress. He succeeded in obtaining an increase of 4,600 pesos on the budget of 1833, but admitted that this was "a very small increase if one considers those improvements which our corps and hospitals need." Essentially all he claimed he could do at the time was to promise to allocate whatever funds might be necessary to regenerate the medical corps whenever they were made available: "The government abstains for the time being, albeit with regret, from adopting the aforementioned project, because it requires funds which cannot be obtained without further crippling the treasury."[161] Faithful to his promise, a year and a half later, on 6 August, the Cuerpo de Sanidad Militar was formed "with the aim of providing hospitals and troops with medical assistants." Tornel succeeded in creating a corps that consisted of one director general, two inspectors, a director in charge of each hospital, with a surgeon allocated to each corps of the permanent and active militia, and with "the respective medical assistants, to work in regular hospitals as well as in blood hospitals." If in 1835 the medical corps could not rely on a competent number of medical and nursing staff to serve their provisional and permanent hospitals, by 1839, "both kinds have been generally provided for; the majority of corps have medical assistants now and for the troops the necessary number of practitioners has been supplied." Furthermore, those who had chosen to follow a medical career in the army had not abandoned their corps on becoming qualified doctors or surgeons. In spite of the "renowned dire straits of the treasury," he claimed that their newly trained medics had at last been rewarded. The government had succeeded in providing them with "general and particular power for each class, their corresponding privileges and the right to a pension." Moreover, in the existing hospitals they had found the resources to provide the "wages of the employed medical assistants and domestic staff." At the time, on 7 January 1839, this was the one part of his report with which he could allow himself to be, to a great extent, satisfied. What in 1835 might have been received as a politician's empty promise was by 1839 a project that had been fulfilled in more ways than one. If there was one thing he considered could produce "the most healthy effect on the good of humanity and more specifically on that of the worthy troops" at such a time of war and turmoil it was definitely the Cuerpo de Salud Militar.[162]

As Cambas rightly points out, Tornel, once he became minister of war, "always believed in having a large army."[163] In 1835 he opened his ministerial report with a long exposition on the need to have a well-kept army.[164] He challenged the view that appeared soon after independence was achieved that it was a contradiction to be a free country and have a regular army. He agreed that war was clearly a despicable evil, and that ideally, in a world in which such horrors could be avoided, armies would then no longer be necessary. However:

if evil exists, if men cannot find a way to ensure that everybody is fair, respecting each other's rights, then it cannot be denied that to repel a force it is essential that another force is created. Defence is a natural and justifiable right of nations in the same way that it is of individuals. To order and regulate this defence is not only a question of prudence, it is a necessity.[165]

These considerations appeared fourteen years after the war of independence had ended—fourteen years in which every conflict that had taken place, with the exception of the Barradas expedition, had been the direct result of military interventions and uprisings. Although Tornel insisted that "our army is the organized defence of a nation," it was clear from the experience of the past few years that the army had been responsible for most of the wars and conflicts the country had witnessed since independence. Tornel refuted this fact with the allegation that the army had not been the perpetrator but the victim of these internal turmoils: "Those very ones who are probably the true instigators of the disasters our nation has suffered in so many upheavals, claim that the army, that has been either the victim or an unwilling instrument in all of these events, has been responsible for these casualties." He blamed the factions and the parties and cleared the army of all blame. He stressed, moreover, that of all of their institutions, it was the army they were indebted to: "The Mexican army conquered independence; the nation owes its freedom to its efforts; and the federation was proclaimed and established by the army." Therefore, in order to consolidate peace and harmony in the republic, it was fundamental to ensure that the army was not alienated from society. This was a direct allusion to the reforms the Gómez Farías administration had started to impose, limiting the privileges of the army as well as the clergy, and that had eventually provoked the Plan of Cuernavaca. The army, as well as being necessary, should be well kept and the military should be treated as a respected and integral part of society: "to separate the soldiers from the interests of society is to fight society; it means to turn into enemies those who are awarded a privileged condition so that they can better serve society." If the army's main purpose was to protect the integrity of the nation and preserve society as it was versus the constant threats of the forces of anarchy, it was foolish to criticize and attack it. Without the army, "society would have been dissolved, property would not have been protected, roads would not have been used except by bandits." Therefore, in Tornel's mind, the need for an army stemmed from the notion that it was essential to the safekeeping of society as it had developed after independence. The army deserved to retain its privileged condition because it was the sole force that could protect the properties of the landowning and propriety classes from the ever-present threat of banditry and social unrest.[166]

The other reason Tornel offered to justify his belief in maintaining a large regular army was that Mexico had to contend with the dangers of foreign ambition. He reminded Congress of the proximity of Cuba, the Arenas conspiracy, and the Barradas expedition. Although after Ferdinand VII had died, there was the possibility that relations between Spain and Mexico could change for the better, a renewed attempt to reconquer Mexico was not out of the question. Given that it was likely that Mexico would have to confront a foreign invader, not to have a regular army would be a recipe for disaster. An untrained popular army made up of volunteers on the spur of the moment could never defend a country adequately:

When the people rise en masse to fight a war against a foreign invader or a domestic tyrant, all of their labors are abandoned, labors that constitute the true wealth of a nation, that provide it with its substinence. Hordes of shapeless masses with no guns or discipline, do not have either caution, confidence or a sense of subordination to the leaders who are unfortunately destined to command them.[167]

On the one hand, the land would be deserted by this method of emergency recruitment, leaving the country without an adequate means of sustaining itself financially or any means feeding its people. On the other hand, these improvised troops, having had no military training, would not know how to obey their superiors' orders. When the actual battle began and it was essential that the troops could immediately act on command with an awareness of strategy and war tactics, their complete ignorance in military matters would inevitably lead to chaos and defeat. Tornel emphasized this point in arriving at the conclusion that a regular and disciplined army was what Mexico needed to guarantee its independence: "In these circumstances defeat is inevitable and independence, in other words the very existence of a nation, depends on the success of only one battle. The superiority of a disciplined and hardened army over a force made up of irregular masses is as clear as that of light over darkness."[168]

Therefore, having established that Mexico needed a large and regular army, he focused on two aspects that were clearly related to the means of achieving this: the system of recruitment and the control of desertions. In his opinion, the system of recruitment was catastrophic because it sent criminals into the army as a form of punishment, and there was no consistency in it. The consequence was that the army was composed of bandits and assassins nobody would want to entrust with the defense of the nation, and because there was no regular system of recruitment, it counted in its numbers men of all ages and occupations who either could not survive a day's combat or whose talents were being wasted having been taken away from their valuable professions in civilian society through arbitrary and forced levies. Desertions were quite understandably a probability; those who had decent professions were propelled to leave by a sense of injustice; the criminals chose to escape, taking with them stolen supplies, only to become even more dangerous and successful as bandits on Mexico's highways.

The reforms Tornel proposed in 1835 were enlightened in comparison with the recruitment methods of the time. He proposed the enforcement of military service. It would be carried out by all men with the exception of "the physically impaired, and those individuals whose professions or jobs are more useful to the nation in postings that lie outside the military profession." Moreover, he stated that military service would have to have a time limit. It could not last indefinitely, as had been the case until then, inspiring many to desert. Because it would now be a service the majority of men would have to carry out, the period of time each individual would have to serve would be the minimum: "The law must lay out that by affecting a larger number of men, the service will be all the lighter and more tolerable."

To avoid arbitrary decisions and personal feuds, recruitment was to be effected with a form of lottery. Each year the local authorities would recruit sufficient soldiers, taking into consideration the population size of their community, by drawing lots, starting with men who were between eighteen and twenty-two years of age, and moving on to the twenty-three to twenty-six age group if there were not enough men in the first group. Eight days were to be allocated for these men to check whether their names had been drawn; they could make an appeal for exemption if they believed they were unfit for military service for medical or other reasons. Those who had no address or property did not participate in this lottery and were sent to serve the coasts and the frontier posts,[169] and were used, although this was not made explicit, as cannon fodder.[170]

Tornel's new system of recruitment, at least on paper, supplied the army with a constant, large number of men. It pleased the generals who had seen their troops reduced by the law of 16 November 1833; it pleased the nation, granting it an army that was not exclusively made up of criminals and would be disciplined; and it pleased the working population because it only took men away from home for a maximum period of two years and from a limited age group. The large Indian population who had no property and no choice in the matter did not benefit from Tornel's proposal.

Regarding the problem of desertions, Tornel hoped that these reforms would reduce considerably those cases in which the motivation for leaving the army was based on the previous arbitrary process of selection and the fact that service could go on interminably without any consideration given to the individual's age, marital status, or professional background. However, to ensure that desertion was controlled, in his 1835 proposals he advocated sending to frontier posts those deserters who were caught. He also recommended this same destination for criminals. It was important that the army be made up of "useful and principled people."[171]

Tornel's plans were not fully implemented in the years following his proposal due to internal conflicts and the wars that erupted almost immediately after the publication of his report. The Texan campaign as well as the French Pastry War were important factors in determining that these reforms were not properly implemented. In 1839, Tornel lamented the fact that "the 1835 administration dedicated itself constantly to achieving the resurrection of the army; however, its work could not be perfect because the corps it created one day had gone to fight the enemy on the next."[172] He argued that they had not had the time to implement the reforms adequately. Given a long period of peace and political stability, he was convinced that the Mexican army would be more than ready to go to war: "A long period of peace would result in the establishment of an army that was worthy of its objectives, and the most suited to ensure the progress and stability of wishes that may be deemed to be the true pleasure of the people."[173] This amounted to the following truism: "In order for an army that is useful in war to be organized, it is essential that it is formed in times of peace and stability."[174] As was soon to become evident, these times of peace and stability were not yet there to stay.

THE TEXAN CAMPAIGN

In the fall of 1835, news of a secessionist *pronunciamiento* in Texas reached the capital, and Tornel and Santa Anna, far from hoping only to achieve a moral victory, threw themselves into the conflict determined to preserve Mexico's sovereignty over Texas. A brief account of Tornel's activities during the Texan campaign illustrates how he tried to appeal to his countrymen's emerging patriotic sentiments. What could have been seen as a Mexican federalist rebellion against the repercussions of the October change to centralism was portrayed by Tornel from the very beginning as a war between Mexico and the foreign American intruders who were trying to steal Texas for the United States. From the beginning of the conflict, Tornel consciously turned what might have been an internal crisis into a patriotic crusade to save Mexico's national integrity from U.S. expansionism.

On 30 and 31 October 1835, he sent two long letters—one to the governors of all the provinces of the republic, and the other to all of the generals, inspectors, and directors in positions of authority—stressing that the time had arrived for them to prepare for combat and that the Americans would not be forgiven for interfering in Texas. He was confident as minister of war that the victory would be theirs: "If the supreme government were to request your patriotic services, it will do so with the confidence that victory will always follow the flags of those who fight valiantly for a good cause." On 7 November, the *Diario del Gobierno* printed an *oficio*, signed by Santa Anna and Tornel, that on behalf of Mexico's true patriots declared war on the Texan "adventurers."

Santa Anna, faithful to the notion that he was ready to sacrifice his life to defend Mexico's integrity, set off to Saltillo that month to prepare his army for war. Tornel stayed behind in the capital and dedicated his time to boosting the morale of the nation as well as of the army with regular speeches and announcements full of patriotic fervor. He praised the active militia; proclaimed his gratitude to all the generals who were offering to go and kill the rebellious Texans; thanked the active battalion of Tehuantepec; praised Mexico, encouraged by the fact that it was obvious to him that everybody wanted to give those foreigners in Texas a good and thorough lesson; issued security and defense measures intended to protect Mexico from the threats of foreign invasion;[175] and according to Mora, "as a result of General Barragán's death, Tornel was left as the sole man running the government."[176]

Santa Anna reached San Antonio Béjar toward the end of February 1836. Despite his presence in the area, on 2 March 1836 the solemn declaration of the independence of Texas was proclaimed. David L. Burnett was elected president of Texas, and Zavala was named vice president. Nevertheless, on 6 March Santa Anna orchestrated the triumphant battle of the Alamo. Determined to punish the Texan rebels, he decreed that he would not accept the surrender of any of the foreign adventurers and had all of those who were taken prisoner executed. Tornel was convinced that Santa Anna would conclude the war with a much-celebrated Mexican victory. As Mora wrote in 1837: "Tornel and the *hombres de privilegio* were convinced that in a battle between Mexican soldiers and Texan settlers, the advantage would always be with the former." Nevertheless, Mora believed that "this was a misguided assumption; [since] the Mexicans were fighting in a foreign land."[177]

Santa Anna's forces nevertheless went on to defeat the Texans again, this time at Goliad on 18 March. According to military historian William A. DePalo, Jr., "To this point, Santa Anna's military planning had been reasonably sound. But his decision to disperse his forces violated the principles of concentration and economy of force and gave a beaten enemy the opportunity to recover."[178] Lulled, according to DePalo, into "a sense of complacency and overconfidence that affected his subsequent tactical decision-making . . . [he pursued] the rebels along four separate axes of advance with only vague knowledge of their strength and disposition."[179] The advantage he had, and which could have allowed him to defeat Samuel Houston and suppress the Texan revolution, was thus lost, and on 21 April, Santa Anna was defeated in particularly humiliating circumstances[180] at the battle of San Jacinto and taken prisoner. Mora could afford to be ironic: "The result was the one we most naturally feared; the invincible Santa Anna was defeated and to save his life and that of his friends he signed, without the authority to do so, several treaties in which the independence of Texas was recognized. Here we have examples of patriotism and valor to be emulated in the years to come!"[181]

In the first instance, Tornel's reaction was one of reluctance to accept the meaning of the news of the defeat. On 20 May he passionately argued to the nation that the war must continue, with or without Santa Anna, that it was their mother country that was being divided by foreign ambitions, and that they could not possibly conceive of surrendering. However, this was only his public reaction. According to Fuentes Mares, on 15 May, he despatched to General Vicente Filisola the order that he was to act "with 'extreme prudence', in order not to endanger in any way the life of the illustrious General Santa Anna."[182] He apparently rectified this decision on 19 May, ordering Filisola to maintain his position "while the government sent indispensable reinforcements to resume the offensive."[183] What becomes clear, as has been noted in a recent study by Sordo Cedeño on his role during the Texan campaign,[184] is that Tornel found himself suddenly in the uncomfortable situation of having to be congruent with the nation's needs while hoping to save Santa Anna's person and image at the same time. To satisfy both of these needs, one personal, the other national, was an impossible task. This was not only because Santa Anna had been taken prisoner but because he had allegedly, once in captivity, ordered Filisola to retreat and had signed an agreement on 14 May by which he promised to end the hostilities and order the evacuation of the Mexican troops south of the Río Grande.

Tornel thus attempted to perform an extraordinary double-act by ordering Filisola and the generals in the area to ensure that no harm came to Santa Anna while asking them to maintain their strategic positions, resisting the captive president's order that they should retreat south of the border.[185] On 19 May he stressed to Congress that the war must go on and decreed that none of the orders Santa Anna had issued, and none of the treaties he had signed once in captivity, could be obeyed, since they had been issued and signed by a man whose very imprisonment prevented him from acting freely and of his own accord.[186] Nevertheless, on the same day, he also wrote a private letter to Filisola in which he emphatically ordered him not to place Santa Anna's life at risk.[187]

Equally representative of Tornel's balancing act was the way he decreed on 20 May that as long as Santa Anna remained in captivity, the army would mourn the situation by flying the national flag half-mast and placing a black knot on it.[188] While he publicly argued that the war should go on and that any statements the captive president might make should be ignored, he attempted to portray what many came to see as an act of betrayal, as a tragic situation in which Santa Anna was a victim rather than a criminal, whose condition should be mourned rather than condemned. However, it soon became impossible for Tornel to defend Santa Anna. He must have sensed this since he asked for permission to resign as minister of war on 6 June.[189] His wish was not granted, and Tornel was faced with what Sordo Cedeño is probably right in describing as his worst hour.[190] Filisola, either ignoring Tornel's decrees or obeying his private letters, accepted on 26 May Santa Anna's order that he should retreat and left Béxar (San Antonio), moving his troops south of the Río Bravo. News of the retreat, of Santa Anna's agreement to sign a peace treaty with the Texans, and of the consequent defeat reached Tornel on 13 June. He was uncertain as to the best course of action in the circumstances, since it took him ten days to inform Congress of what had happened in the wake of Santa Anna's defeat at San Jacinto.[191] Once he did so, it nevertheless remains clear that he finally decided to defend his friend, whatever the cost, rather than join the rest of the political class in condemning his actions in captivity. On 23 June, in the words of Carlos María de Bustamante, he "shamelessly" defended Santa Anna, going to the extreme of arguing that the treaties Santa Anna had signed were not as detrimental as they had been made out to be. Nevertheless, although he was subsequently accused in *El Cosmopolita* of having placed his personal interests before those of the nation,[192] he continued to work as minister and vowed to recover Texas. The government-funded *Diario del Gobierno* supported him: "The services that this illustrious Mexican has carried out for his mother-country from the moment he became minister, a post he performs with so much skill in the present, will be among those that will always, always, be listed as having been distinguished."[193] It praised the government for rejecting his resignation and praised him for the way he had lightened the burdens of the crisis.

On 26 June, the *Diario* printed a long letter by Filisola in which he explained the reasons for his retreat. In the same paper Tornel's reply appeared, condemning Filisola for abandoning Texas and obeying the orders of Santa Anna who, having been taken prisoner, was no longer in a position to give commands to his troops. However, rather than blaming his own men, Tornel blamed the defeat on the fact that the Mexican soldiers had suffered from a lack of food and provisions once they had reached Texas.

Furthermore, in order not to lose the sympathy of the *hombres de bien*, he continued to thank them for their contributions and their donations during the campaign.[194]

His efforts to soften the impact of the defeat did not go unnoticed. The *Diario* reported all of the actions he had carried out to prevent the loss from developing into a full-scale revolt against the government. He created a fund for the families of the men who had been captured, wounded, or killed in the Texan campaign.[195] He argued that they should continue with the Texan campaign as long as the majority seemed to believe that Mexico could afford to reconquer Texas. Once it became obvious to him that the majority thought otherwise, he argued that the war could not be fought forever: "Sr. Tornel already said in the discussion that was included in yesterday's issue that an eternal war cannot be carried out except in hell."[196] According to the *Diario* he could do nothing wrong; he was even described as being a saint![197] According to *El Cosmopolita*, Tornel was "the man who is universally responsible for everything that goes wrong in the world."[198]

Accused and defended, hated and adored, Tornel continued in the position of minister until 22 April 1837. Surprisingly, his reputation was not seriously damaged by the Texan disaster. Moreover, he returned to hold the post of minister on 17 December 1838. In a bid to defend Santa Anna and himself, Tornel opted to do what he knew he could do best: he wrote *Tejas y los Estados Unidos de América en sus relaciones con la república mexicana.*

Tornel's account of the conflict deserves a detailed analysis not only because of the insight it provides into the war, but also because it is representative of the manner in which he used his intellectual powers to pave the way for his rise and his continuation in a position of influence. The thesis of *Tejas y los Estados Unidos* is essentially that the Texan war was an international conflict, and the outcome was not the result of Santa Anna's military incompetence, but the inevitable and tragic result of Mexico's careless generosity.

The treatise starts with a clear indictment of U.S. expansionism. Tornel does not limit his critique to his own subjective views of the Americans; instead he consistently refers to concrete historical events to justify his beliefs. He reminds the reader of Jefferson's plan to occupy Panama and describes in great detail the way the United States acquired Florida and bought Louisiana from Napoleon Bonaparte. His evidence can lead to only one conclusion: "Selfishness is a vice that cannot be separated from the character of the Anglo-American people." Furthermore, he states that the only reason the United States supported the various independence movements in Latin American countries was to occupy them later. Once he has established that the U.S. government intends to expand throughout Latin America and that its support of the various wars of independence has always had a very concrete ulterior motive, Tornel introduces the theme of Texas. The implications of the introduction are immediately obvious: the United States intended to occupy Texas, and this is why it supported the Texan struggle for independence.

From the moment Texas is mentioned, Tornel establishes the facts that it belonged to Spain, and its frontier was always known and respected by France. He bases this point on two documents: a letter by Luis de Onís and Joutel's *Diario histórico*. The conclusion he arrives at is evident: "With this it can be demonstrated that the continuing French presence in Spanish territory cannot determine any claim or title for domination." This is supported by an exhaustive chronology of the Spanish explorers and settlers who from 1512 onward discovered and established themselves in Texas. To give his argument even greater conviction, he quotes a passage from the memoirs of the American general Wilkinson, who quite explicitly criticized his own government and country for "several aggressions against the province of Texas." Therefore it is clear from his account that Texas was Spanish originally and Mexican as a result. In other words, the Americans had never had any legitimate claim on the land. Thus, any conflict or dilemma could only be the result of U.S. expansionism:

We must agree that it is fatal for us to have as our neighbors such a destructive race that intervenes in all of the transactions of America, that proclaims that its political school is a unique and complete system, that claims as its own anything that may make its republic stronger and larger, without paying any attention to ancient and accepted rights or even to the peaceful possession of several centuries.

To confirm this view, Tornel quotes Tocqueville, who argued that the ambitions of the United States would know no limit: "Those limits established in treaties will not contain them; wherever it pleases them they will jump the imaginary barriers." However, the loss of Texas was due not only to U.S. expansionism. In Tornel's mind, one of the determining factors in the defeat was the way American citizens were allowed freely to colonize Texas: "It was a grave mistake to open the door to the Americans, and this grave mistake was not corrected until we were suddenly faced with all of its consequences." The ambition of the Americans and the generosity of the Spaniards and then the Mexicans were a recipe for disaster: "How much we have contributed ourselves to our own ruin and dishonor!"

Tornel continues his account with a detailed history of the American colonization of Texas, including brief biographies of Moses and Stephen Austin and the actual *Informe del Gobierno Supremo de Coahuila*. What is immediately apparent from the latter document is that as a result of the lack of any form of restriction, allegedly 10 percent of the population of the United States moved to Texas in the first thirteen years of independence. This point had two serious implications. First, with the constant flow of

American colonizers, land in Texas started to be bought and sold in the United States, and the Mexican government had no voice in the matter. Second, the large numbers of American colonizers who settled in Texas did not share "either the inclinations, or the customs, or the language, or the politics" of their newly adopted country. In short, the Mexican government did not profit from the sale of land that belonged to its national territory, and it was alienated from the large communities who bought these domains for they were foreigners who were living as if Texas already belonged to the United States.

Tornel mused that considering the eventual outcome of the Texan campaign, in the long run it would not have been such a bad idea to sell it to the United States rather than give it away:

We could have learnt from this example and aided the treasury, selling what we did not want to keep anyway. Yet our blindness has been such that we have given away the lands of a paradise, we have given them away without making any profit or gain to our very own enemies. We believe what I am saying because we are seeing it and because it is now that we receive the punishment we deserve for our lack of foresight.

However, as he went on to point out, they could not have foreseen such a loss, because they had made the initial mistake of considering the United States an ally. He argued that, unaware as they were at the time of the expansionist plans of the Americans, it was easy for them to be generous and welcome the Americans into their country.

Having described the treachery of the Americans and illustrated their deviousness with a concise portrait of U.S. ambassador Joel Poinsett's role in Mexico, Tornel makes his criticism more general. Therefore, not only is the reader given a vitriolic depiction of American ambition but a full account of the injustices and inhumanities characteristic of American society. He criticized racism and slavery in particular, and claimed they were two of the most appalling aspects of American society.

Tornel reserved some praise for General Mier y Terán, who in 1831 tried to control the entrance of Americans into Texas, and he lamented his suicide. In contrast, he dedicates over eight pages to condemning Austin, Mejía, and Zavala for their treachery. It is after he has established that the instigators of the Texan revolt were motivated purely by the mercenary desire to make a quick personal gain, that he analyzes the official reasons that were given to justify the rebellion.

The Texans argued that they were becoming independent (1) in the name of freedom; (2) because they were federalists and opposed the government's move toward centralism; (3) because the government had neglected the improvement of education in Texas; (4) because its army had committed acts of oppression and tyranny in Texas; and (5) because the Texans were not allowed to practice any religion other than the Catholic faith. Tornel looks at each one of these points and attempts to show how some of these assertions are simply excuses and others are completely false, returning to the point that the Texan campaign was an international war from the very beginning. Regarding the Texan idea of freedom, Tornel's response deserves to be quoted:

What causes amazement is their audacity, first, to proclaim their freedom when they have opened a new market of human meat in Texas, in defiance of all Mexican laws; second, to proclaim their rights when having lived entirely how they pleased, they have not respected any of the laws that give society a sense of order; third, to speak of property when it is they who have usurped a sovereign dominion, and finally, to rise and cry for a war to the death against these very people who gave them a country to live in, such homes, hospitable laws and their own civilization.

As for the claim that the Texans were opposed to a centralist system, he pointed out that the American colonizers had not previously objected to Spanish colonial rule, or Iturbide's empire, or the triumvirate, none of whom had in fact been federalist. It was clear to him that the federalist stance was an excuse and the fact that proclamation of Texan independence had been pronounced in the capital of the United States was more significant than any pretense of political discontent.

He considered that the allegation that they had neglected the improvement of education in Texas was in bad faith. It was generally accepted that the local town halls were responsible for taking care of education in their respective communities with the funds they obtained through municipal and regional taxes and contributions. In other words, "If they did not allocate the funds to the education of their children, the fault was theirs." Furthermore, the Texans had two representatives in Congress, and they never voiced this concern. Tornel strongly objected to the accusation that the Mexican army had committed unnecessary acts of oppression and tyranny in Texas. In his mind, the reality of the situation had been quite the opposite: the American colonizers had come to Texas armed, they had challenged and attacked the government representatives of law and order, and they had refused to pay any taxes to the national exchequer. Regarding religion, he argued that the Americans knew when they came to Texas that Catholicism was the only faith in the land. If they objected to this, "why did they not stay in their own country, or construct temples in the solitude of the West?" When they settled, they conformed to the church. To argue that the defense of Protestantism was a valid justification for the revolt was in Tornel's mind irrelevant and, if anything, another excuse to disguise what was in essence a war born of U.S. expansionism.

Tornel provides a tragic account of the war; the Mexican economy and the Mexican army, crippled by debt, could not save Texas from the claws of prosperous America: "How could we make war without funds, in such a distant land where it was even necessary to transport the provisions of the soldiers?" The account is full of praise for the heroic Mexicans who fought the war and made extraordinary sacrifices to finance the campaign. Significantly, he condemned Mexicans who were using the outcome of the war to create further divisions within Mexico, antagonizing the parties and the factions with unnecessary criticisms, especially when it was so obvious that the Texan war had never been simply a national issue: "I condemn more than anything the anti-philosophical attitude of those who encourage out of habit national hatreds."

At the end of *Tejas y los Estados Unidos*, Tornel concludes that there is no doubt that the United States intended to appropriate Texas and that Mexico must regain Texas. Finally, he reflects on the possible outcomes of a direct war between Mexico and the United States. He stated that they had to continue the war in Texas not only because it was their national duty, but also because the definitive loss of such an extensive area of Mexican territory would inevitably lead to a further loss. In short: "The loss of Texas would inevitably be followed by that of New Mexico and that of the Californias; and little by little the whole of our territory would be taken until we were reduced to becoming an insignificant expression." His historical treatise concluded with a defiant refusal to accept that the war was over. Moreover, Tornel was convinced that if the conflict escalated into an open war between Mexico and the United States, Mexico would be the victor:

The war of independence and the subsequent civil conflicts have meant that in one form or another the whole of the Mexican population has come to know how to use guns and our nation has become an entirely warring one. This is not the case in the United States. . . . The national militia is very useful for the Americans to defend their homes, but it is not to attack the homes of others. Making an impressive effort the United States could form a regular army of around 6,000 men, and no more (and these would not be able to pass). Would the Mexicans allow such a small contingent to impose itself upon them? No; they have beaten 20,000 Spanish veterans in their own country when they were fighting against a government that relied on long-established customs and advantages, and an extensive time in power.[199]

Tornel was mistaken in his forecast of the outcome of a war with the United States. However, in 1837, he was demonstrating quite convincingly that the Texan campaign and its immediate outcome had had little to do with Santa Anna and his management of country and army. By focusing his readers' attention on the threat of U.S. expansionism, he succeeded in diverting any criticisms that he and Santa Anna might have received from the opposition. The enemy was foreign. Santa Anna and Tornel were beyond party politics; they had done everything to defend Mexico's national integrity, and they were true patriots.

Regardless of Tornel's intentions in publishing his *Tejas y los Estados Unidos*, the fact remains that by 1837, Santa Anna had become a *persona non grata* as a result of the Texan debacle, and the government was following a political path that, led by the traditionalists and the centralists in Congress, did not reflect Tornel's own ideals. In other words, although the *santanistas* had succeeded in rising to a position of considerable power as a result of the 1834 Plan of Cuernavaca, they had failed to consolidate a dominant role in government. In part this had been the result of the traditionalist factions' hold over Congress and in part because of the way Santa Anna had fallen from grace in the battle of San Jacinto. The first truly coherent and representative *santanista* proposal would have to wait until the 1841 Triangular Revolt overthrew Bustamante.[200] Tornel persevered in his attempts to rescue the *caudillo*'s reputation, but to little avail. As well as writing the apologetic *Tejas y los Estados Unidos*, he issued a circular on 12 January 1837 that rejoiced at the news that Santa Anna had been set free by the Americans,[201] and on 23 February, he solemnly welcomed the return of the *caudillo* by ordering the church bells to toll on his arrival in Veracruz, an order that the ecclesiastical authorities solemnly ignored.[202]

Santa Anna, more than aware that he was perceived to be a traitor (to quote Callcott, his "brilliant star . . . [appeared to have] been only a meteor that had flown its course and had been permanently extinguished")[203] and that it was not the right time to attempt a return to national politics, retired quietly to Manga de Clavo, where he passed "in peace and quiet the remainder of 1837, and spring, summer and autumn of 1838."[204] Tornel, who in 1834, at the height of his shared *santanista* triumphalism had celebrated Santa Anna's rising star by decreeing that 11 September (the day on which Santa Anna defeated the Barradas expedition in 1829) should become an annual national holiday,[205] became less prominent in his public role as minister of war, concentrating on the day-to-day business of managing the national army, attempting to implement the reforms he had proposed in 1835. However, the daily attacks to which he was subjected in the press became increasingly hard for him to ignore, and, in the end, he resigned on 22 April 1837,[206] following Anastasio Bustamante's electoral rise to the presidency. Since the Texan debacle, Tornel was consistently portrayed in the press as having stolen government funds, placing Santa Anna's personal interests before those of the nation, and having been a particularly ruthless and sanguinary minister of war.[207] Nevertheless, unlike Santa Anna (some wanted to put him on trial for his behavior in captivity), Tornel was able to survive the Texan disaster with greater success. Regardless of the role he had played during the campaign, he was invited to form part of the Supreme Conservative Power in May 1838, after one of its members died.

Coinciding with Santa Anna's retirement in Manga de Clavo, Tornel kept a low profile during the latter half of 1837 and for most of 1838, even though he became a member of the Supreme Conservative Power on 15 May 1838, following the death of José Ignacio Espinosa.[208] With more time on his hands, he went back to writing and translating. He discussed Michel Chevallier's depiction of Mexico,[209] translated Napoleon's notes on his military campaigns,[210] and translated King Frederick the Great's secret instructions to the Prussian army.[211] There is little information available regarding his activities as a member of the Supreme Conservative Power in 1838, except that in a secret session held at the beginning of December, he favored allowing Bustamante to remain in the presidential seat vis-à-vis the proposal that he should be asked to resign since his handling of the French blockade of the Gulf Coast was perceived by some as having been entirely inappropriate.[212] Adopting what was by now a fairly familiar argument, Tornel believed that under threat of foreign aggression, it was not the right time to destabilize what was already an increasingly disunited government by demanding the president's resignation. Of course, there was probably a good reason for the fact that the press had forgotten him and thus left him alone during most of 1838. Having left the government in April 1837, he had not been in a position of power during what had become Mexico's third major international crisis since independence: what is popularly called the French Pastry War.

THE FRENCH PASTRY WAR

With the defeat of San Jacinto, the stage of profound disillusion began. The centralist Constitution of 1836, formally adopted on 29 December 1836, did not bring the expected respite or recovery hoped for by its leading authors and intellectuals: Francisco Sánchez de Tagle and Carlos María de Bustamante. Although Corro's presidency was followed by General Anastasio Bustamante's second government (1837–1841), the traditionalist factions were soon to discover that the man they had elected president during the spring of 1837, and in whom they had placed the few hopes they had of imposing order and stability with a long-lasting constitutional framework, was neither as dynamic as had been previously thought nor as traditional in his political beliefs. By 1838, the rumor became widespread that Bustamante, while serving as president, was conspiring to overthrow the centralist constitution in order to replace it with a federalist one by joining forces with Manuel Gómez Pedraza and the moderates. Although he never actually executed such a proposal, the traditionalist and centralist factions became divided between those who supported Bustamante and those who thought a different leader was required; and so did the liberals, with Valentín Gómez Farías becoming the leader of the more radical *puros* and Gómez Pedraza, leader of the *moderados*.

Moreover, while the political class's divisions became increasingly more acrimonious, the French government demanded the immediate payment of 600,000 pesos in compensation for the damages that had been inflicted on a number of French shops (including a bakery—hence, the name the conflict was given) during the 1828 Parián riot. Given that the Mexican government was not in a position to pay the extortionate amount of money the French government was demanding, nor did it believe that the demands were justified, Bustamante's government found itself becoming unexpectedly involved in an international conflict that resulted in particularly damaging consequences for the republic's economy. The French response was to send its fleet to the Gulf of Mexico and blockade the key ports of Tampico and Veracruz for over a year. Since the Mexican government refused to pay the required sum of money, the blockade escalated into a war, culminating in the bombardment and invasion of Veracruz on 27 November 1838.

Santa Anna rose to save the day. Having returned to Mexico in disgrace and retired to a secluded life on his hacienda, giving up any hope of regaining the population's trust and support, he led the attack of 5 December 1838 that forced the French invading army to retreat to their ships and leave the port of Veracruz. The heroism and selflessness of his action were enhanced in the eyes of the public by the fact that as he galloped down the main street of Veracruz toward the port, a cannonball hit his leg and seriously wounded him. His leg was amputated on the following day. Making the most of the situation, he published a farewell letter that was widely circulated at the time in which, feigning to be on his deathbed, he succeeded in portraying himself as a man who was above politics and whose sole concern was the good of the nation. First, he depicted himself as having sacrificed his life to defend Mexico's sacred integrity against the French aggressors: "I was wounded in this last effort and probably this will be the last victory that I shall offer my native land." Second, he conveyed the notion that he was far removed from the divisions inherent in party politics; like a benevolent father figure, he was glad that as he died, there might be an end to the disruption for which such factions were responsible: "On closing my career, I cannot refrain from expressing my joy at seeing the beginning of reconciliation among the Mexican factions." And finally, he appealed to the people's patriotism by asking his countrymen to forgive him for his mistakes and not deny him the one title he wanted to honor his children with—that of having been "a good Mexican."[213] Almost overnight, from having become Mexico's worst general after San Jacinto, Santa Anna was once more that warrior of Napoleonic stature who had defeated the Spaniards in 1829 and now the French in 1838.

With Santa Anna's reputation on the mend, Tornel was called in to serve as minister of war again, on 17 December. The *Diario del Gobierno* enthusiastically celebrated his return to office.[214] Energetic as ever, Tornel set about organizing the country's defense. Between 19 and 31 December he decreed that all men were eligible to fight against the French, offered a general amnesty to all political prisoners, presented a plan of action for the transport of gunpowder and 100 boxes of cartridges from Santa Fé to Veracruz to the area of conflict, forbade the ports of the Gulf Coast from giving the French fleet any assistance, rallied support among the capital's *gente de bien* so that they assisted the army's endeavors with all-important financial donations, issued a series of laws to control the way soldiers were being conscripted as well as to ensure that all desertions would be duly punished, ensured that fifty thousand pesos were allocated to the regiments stationed in Veracruz, and finally called an end to the use of forceful conscriptions (the *leva*) since these were beginning to turn the affected communities against the national government.[215]

On 7 January 1839 he presented his second ministerial report. Although most of it was understandably concerned with the war, he nevertheless recounted the ways in which his 1835 reforms had progressed since then. With regard to his concern with providing the rank and file with an education, although the economic constraints on the country had meant that Chapultepec Castle had not been converted into a military school as foreseen in 1833, and the "regular school of the army" had suffered the temporary blow of being closed down on 2 May 1837, some progress had been made since 1835. In January 1838 the regular school had been reopened, and Congress had agreed to spend thirty-six thousand pesos every year on Tornel's educational reforms. The number of soldiers learning to read and write had increased from the initial figure of eight at a time to two hundred in each company. Moreover, not only were "endowed individuals" being educated, but "the military's orphans and children." Tornel used this fact to defy all criticism; even when wars were crippling their country, "the unjust enemies of our national representation will take back their criticisms, in spite of themselves, when they see that never before have the soldier's conditions been better served than they are now." Although the plans of 1835 had not been completely put into practice, soldiers were being educated. Tornel did not allow the main preoccupation of Congress—that of ending the existing wars—to prevent him from reminding them that "to educate the people results in securing its firm and permanent happiness." Regarding the medical corps, by January 1839 this was the one part of his report with which Tornel could allow himself to be satisfied to a great extent. What in 1835 might have been received as a politician's empty promise was by 1839 a project that had been fulfilled. If there was one thing that he believed could produce "the most healthy effect on the good of humanity and more specifically on that of the worthy troops" at such a time of war and turmoil, it was definitely the Cuerpo de Salud Militar.[216]

Tornel's 1835 proposals to change the system of recruitment had not been fully implemented due to the internal conflicts and the wars that erupted almost immediately after the publication of his report. The Texan campaign as well as the French Pastry War were important factors in determining that these reforms were not properly implemented. In 1839, Tornel lamented the fact that "the 1835 administration dedicated itself constantly to achieving the resurrection of the army; however, its work could not be perfect because the corps it created one day had gone to fight the enemy on the next." He argued that they had not had the time to implement the reforms adequately. Nevertheless, they could not afford to waste any more time lamenting the impact the different conflicts had had in undermining his attempts at resurrecting the army. In January 1839, at war on two fronts (parallel to the French blockade the government had to contend with an ongoing federalist uprising that had erupted in October 1838 in Tampico), the main priority was to crush General José Urrea and José Antonio Mejía's federalist rebellion and to repulse the French offensive. Considerations as to how recruitment could be improved were secondary to winning both wars. Therefore, rather than obey laws that had been legislated during a time of peace, it was important for them to adapt to the existing context and act accordingly without allowing previous theories to obstruct their actions: "It is always very useful to adapt to the circumstances of war." Therefore, although there were already allegedly 32,442 men recruited under the terms passed in 1835, the emergency demanded an urgent increase to ensure a Mexican victory. According to Tornel, they needed to be able to create a temporary army of civilians quickly in case the French launched another offensive and proceeded to move inland. In order to achieve this, he created an emergency corps of urban militias and gave them the name *defensores de la patria*. He estimated "in a month 50 thousand men from the urban militias can be called to arms" if such a measure became necessary. These urban militias were to be made up of civilians of all ages who were to be given basic military training so that they could provide an effective defense against any foreign invaders. However, their military contribution would be necessary only in time of war. In peacetime these civilians could go back to their everyday activities. The *defensores de la patria* were civilians who had been drilled to be able to survive a military attack and combat it if such an event occurred in the very specific context of 1839. Although this latter appendage to Tornel's reforms in recruitment contradicted his belief in maintaining one permanent, regular, and disciplined force, he had no qualms in embracing it if it meant repelling the French: "When forces are organized according to the rules, the results are all the more important and fewer sacrifices are needed;

however, if all of our efforts are necessary to win this ignoble war which the French have provoked, then the whole nation will be armed."[217]

While Santa Anna had regained his mythical status by losing his leg while forcing the French to retreat to their ships, Tornel proceeded zealously with his organization of the defense of Mexico's national integrity. A brief look at the *Diario del Gobierno* from 11 January to 23 February 1839 finds him frantically issuing decrees and orders to ensure a Mexican victory. He organized the army's urban squadrons and vanguard divisions, initiated a blockade of Santa Ana de Tamaulipas where the federalist rebels were based and reorganized the postal service around the area, ordered that all weapons belonging to the army that were in the possession of civilians should be returned, decreed that the newly created militias, the *defensores de la patria*, were entitled to be protected by the *fuero militar*, circulated the decrees by which all those soldiers who participated in the action of 5 December 1838 would receive a reward, and by which pensions would be awarded to the widows and children of men who died in combat, and implemented a further series of laws condemning deserters to the death penalty.[218] Even his wife, María Agustina, joined the patriotic effort, presiding over the Hospital de Sangre and organizing fund-raising events such as the charity opera of 1 February 1839.[219] Although the French demands were met behind the scenes and an agreement was reached through mediations carried out by the British minister plenipotentiary, Richard Pakenham, by which the Mexican government agreed to pay the demanded 600,000 pesos in three installments,[220] to the general public, a Mexican victory had been struck by Santa Anna's heroic charge of 5 December and Tornel's gifted running of the Ministry of War. Evidence of this is that when Bustamante requested from the Supreme Conservative Power, permission to leave the presidential seat temporarily to lead the campaign against the federalist rebels, the interim presidency was offered to Santa Anna.[221]

Thus on 20 March 1839 Santa Anna returned to the capital to hold the post of president. Only three years after having been deemed responsible for the humiliating defeat of San Jacinto, Santa Anna was once more at the head of the nation. The fact that he had essentially lost the Texan campaign through military incompetence and had gone on to sign (treacherously, in terms of how his actions had been seen at the time) a treaty with the Texans in which he had formally acknowledged their independence, appeared to have been either forgotten or forgiven. In the aftermath of the glorious 5 December, Santa Anna regained his mythical status.

The popular cult of the figure of Santa Anna was unique during this period. The fact that entire communities went on long pilgrimages during the early 1840s to visit the cemetery of Santa Paula to adore and venerate his buried leg can be understood only if we accept with Justo Sierra that "the masses . . . were determined to see him as a Messiah."[222] His extraordinary appeal was not simply based on his extraordinary charisma or personal idiosyncrasies. As Michael Costeloe reminds us regarding Santa Anna's victory over the French, "There is no doubt that Santa Anna used his interim presidency very astutely to restore and enhance his reputation, above all with the army. He had done in a few weeks what Bustamante had failed to do in two years."[223] Moreover, he consolidated the restoration of his reputation by going on to silence the radical press, "publicly but obtusely" backing constitutional reform, and defeating the main federalist revolt.[224]

BATTLE OF ACAJETE

Once the French Pastry War was over, the army's efforts were channeled into crushing Urrea and Mejía's revolt in Tamaulipas. On this occasion Tornel played an active part in the events and went to Acajete to confront Mejía who had mobilized his troops to Veracruz. There was probably a personal feud involved, dating back to Tornel's days in Baltimore. Otherwise, it is difficult to explain his sudden desire to defy danger on the firing line. The Mejía in question was the very same Mejía who had been his secretary in Baltimore and with whom he had fallen out when Mejía had joined Zavala in selling large areas of Texas to the Americans.

Paying no attention to protocol and making the most of the fact that Bustamante appeared to be stalling in his offensive against the federalist rebels who had gathered in Tampico by mid-April, Santa Anna left Mexico City at four o'clock in the morning on 30 April, accompanied by Tornel, and set off at the head of one thousand five hundred men to end the federalist revolt. While Congress and the Supreme Conservative Power found themselves in the situation of not knowing where the president was or what his intentions could be, discussing, with a certain sense of indignation, whether they had been ridiculed by the way Santa Anna had clearly decided to act without consulting them, the intrepid *caudillo*, the gifted writer, and General Gabriel Valencia destroyed the rebellion in the bloody battle of Acajete (3 May 1839).[225]

According to Rafael Muñoz, Santa Anna "has . . . the good idea of not directing the battle personally. General José María Tornel, as his second in command, gives the orders." The showdown took place on 3 May in the hacienda of San Miguel La Blanca, and is significant because of the light it casts on Tornel as a general in combat: "Before the battle began, the minister of war [Tornel] had given the order that all of the [rebel] commanders who were taken prisoner would be killed by a firing squad."[226] The brutality of this order is all the greater when it is contrasted with the general practice of internal warfare of the time in which, "contrary to the rule elsewhere Mexican revolutions were seldom sanguinary."[227] His ruthlessness even contradicts in one sense his constant lament over the tragic manner in which they continued to kill each other in civil wars. However, it must not be forgotten that he firmly believed that law and order was to be maintained whatever the cost. The following details are clearly an example of this. In Muñoz's account of the battle there was "cannon fire, rifle fire, bayonet charge, escape of the rebel commanders and surrender of the troops."[228] Over six hundred soldiers died. Mejía was captured and executed three hours later. In Muñoz's account, Mejía's famous line—"Tell General Santa Anna that if the positions of captor and captive had been reversed I would have allowed him only that number of minutes, not hours—"[229] was misdirected; his execution was in fact ordered by Tornel. Moreover, Tornel forced Valentín Gómez Farías to witness Mejía's execution so that he learned a lesson and saw the fate awaiting those who rebelled, if he had his way: "Not satisfied with asking him to deliver the order which specified that Gómez Farías's military ally should be executed immediately, he asked him not to return until he had witnessed the event."[230]

As Sordo Cedeño fully confirmed the consequences of Acajete were extremely important. The federalist movement was crushed, and it would take over a year before it could gather momentum once more, in the albeit unsuccessful coup of July 1840. Perhaps more important was that it confirmed in the eyes of many the futility of the Supreme Conservative Power and gave Santa Anna's legendary status a further boost. Compared to Bustamante, who was now perceived to be hesitant and indecisive, Santa Anna emerged as a triumphant energetic leader, capable of crushing the most resilient of rebels, even though he was now a cripple.[231] Whether or not Santa Anna deserved the praise he received, it was Tornel who, acting once more as the *caudillo*'s propagandist, ensured, through the speeches he delivered and published in the spring of 1839, that Santa Anna's glorious actions were known and celebrated by the entire republic.[232] Once again, having reached the heights of power, Santa Anna decided to retreat to his hacienda in Veracruz. In spite of the fact that there were calls for him to become dictator of Mexico, he withdrew from the political arena of the capital on 11 July, leaving Nicolás Bravo at the head of the country while Bustamante made his way back to Mexico City from the north.

THE ABANDONED CICERO

Although Tornel was probably basking in the glory of Acajete and must have thought that his political career was on the ascendant following Santa Anna's interim presidency, it is evident that he was extremely distressed when, on 27 July 1839, only eight days after Anastasio Bustamante had returned to assume the presidency, Bustamante asked Tornel to resign as minister of war. Bustamante wrote a long letter to him explaining that he was doing it for Tornel's sake. Wilfrid Callcott's translation retains all of the irony of the original text and is thus worth quoting in full:[233] "The apoplectic fits to which you are subject being so frequent, I believe it indispensably necessary, to avoid a recurrence of them, that you separate yourself from the immense toil of the ministry, and dedicate yourself exclusively to the re-establishment of your health, which as your sincere friend, I cannot behold with indifference."[234]

Tornel, indignant, refused to resign. In the words of Manuel Rivera Cambas, "The departure of Tornel provoked a scandal, as this gentleman would not leave his post, and he accused Bustamante of ingratitude."[235] On the day of his expulsion, he printed the aggressive complaint *El General José María Tornel a sus amigos*, stating that the reason for his removal was that he was Santa Anna's friend: "I am General Santa Anna's friend, this is the reason for my fall." He argued that he was refusing to resign because he was an "enemy of hoaxes" and would not allow his past illness to serve as an excuse.[236] Although this pamphlet was followed by several more,[237] Bustamante did not falter in his resolution.

Abandoned by Bustamante for a second time, Tornel's resentment was indeed great. To add insult to injury, the circumstances in which Tornel was snubbed in 1839 mirrored those of his American adventure. Bustamante was, in his mind, a deeply ungrateful individual. In spite of the fact that he had proposed him for president in 1828, Bustamante had deserted Tornel in 1830. In spite of the fact that Tornel had, as a member of the Supreme Conservative Power, defended him in December 1838 against the move to force his resignation, Bustamante was ostracizing him again in the summer of 1839. (Ingratitude was to feature as one of the key themes of the play he was to write in 1840: *La muerte de Cicerón* [*The Death of Cicero*].)

At least in theory, Tornel's political career was not yet over. During the time he had served as minister of war, he had had to withdraw his membership of the Supreme Conservative Power temporarily, since the 1836 Constitution prevented any of its five members from holding a cabinet position at the same time. Now that he had been forced to resign from the ministry he could return to the Supreme Conservative Power. Therefore, it came as a blow to him that the four individuals (and his substitute) who made up the Supreme Conservative Power, although unable to prevent Tornel from rejoining them, decided that he could not have a voice in any of the three matters they were deliberating at the time. Tornel took it upon himself to publicize his anger. He was not only being marginalized by the president but by the Supreme Conservative Power as well.

In the first of two lengthy pamphlets he published in the fall and winter of 1839 against the behavior of the Supreme Conservative Power, he stated that its members were avoiding him and deliberately preventing him from fulfilling his duty to the nation because they feared his influence and ideas; he hinted, as he had with Bustamante, that they despised him because he was Santa Anna's friend. With a good dose of irony, he asked himself a number of rhetorical questions as to the possible reasons for his exclusion. Although his friendship with Santa Anna was the probable cause of his marginalization, he noted that this could not be the case since the four individuals in question had hoped to proclaim Santa Anna dictator in December 1838. And although his support during Santa Anna's interim presidency for the constitutional reforms that had been proposed in 1839 (that threatened the existence of the Supreme Conservative Power) was another probable cause for the way he was being ostracized, he noted that this could not be the case since the four individuals in question (and his substitute) had allegedly approved of them at the time. And finally, using the same irony, although they probably envied his success as minister of war, he noted that this could not account for their behavior since they had approved of his rise to the ministry in the first place. In the end, although Tornel adopted the mask of a naive (albeit extremely talented), victimized politician who could not understand what was happening, his *Protesta* proposed in almost unequivocal terms that the four individuals in question (and his substitute) did not want him to join their discussions because they were opposed to reforming the constitution. He concluded by provocatively stating that as long as he was not a part of their deliberations, whatever they decreed would be null and void, since all five members were needed to be present for any decisions to be approved, according to the constitution.[238]

Of those five men, it was Manuel de la Peña y Peña who took it upon himself to refute Tornel's allegations in his equally lengthy reply, the *Dictamen de la comisión del Supremo Poder Conservador*. According to de la Peña y Peña, Tornel was excluded from participating in the discussion of the three issues because they concerned legislative matters in which Tornel had already been involved in his capacity as minister of war. In other words, they were not consciously or illegally ostracizing him; they were simply preventing him, as specified in the constitution, from influencing decisions in which it was a well-established fact that he had a personal stake; he had promoted the unconstitutional (the Supreme Conservative Power was not consulted) law of 8 April 1839 by which the freedom of the press was restricted; been involved in the 19 April transactions that resulted in a loan of £130,000 (in which the Supreme Conservative Power was not consulted); and openly defended, as minister, the proposals made to reform the constitution (which only now were being considered by the Supreme Conservative Power). Once they moved on to discuss issues in which he had not had a voice as minister, he would be more than welcome to return to his post in the Supreme Conservative Power. Nevertheless, the apparent common sense of de la Peña y Peña's assertions was not devoid of an equally ironic and vitriolic use of language. The fact that Tornel had said that they were hoping to impose a dictatorship with Santa Anna was a provocation and a lie. Moreover, the notion that without Tornel there was no quorum was equally absurd. To Tornel's assertion that the Supreme Conservative Power was committing political suicide by excluding him, de la Peña y Peña noted that the contrary was true: Tornel was committing political suicide by making such a fuss.[239]

Tornel replied to de la Peña y Peña's response to his protest in February 1840 with a particularly vitriolic condemnation of the Supreme Conservative Power and of its members, and without the naive tone of his earlier pamphlet. Most of the detail of the pamphlet is not relevant to the present discussion. Suffice to say that Tornel took de la Peña y Peña to task, in excruciating detail (the pamphlet is seventy-seven pages long), over just about every statement he made, even questioning his choice of quotations and, in the process, his understanding of writers such as Tacitus, Jeremy Bentham, and Benjamin Constant. It was probably fairly evident to Tornel that he was fighting a losing battle and that he would return to prominence only once the current administration, Supreme Conservative Power included, was overthrown. His *Respuesta* was more than anything an exercise in erudite terrorism. Nevertheless, a passage that deserves mention is one in which Tornel attacked the members of the Supreme Conservative Power from a regional and class perspective. In spite of all of the years Tornel had now spent in the capital, he remained (like Santa Anna) a *veracruzano* at heart. Moreover, it also shows that however much he had risen up the social ladder, he remained the resentful son of a shopkeeper in the eyes of a longer-established Mexico City–based pseudo-aristocracy:

In this capital of the republic there remains an old political class that learnt its science of government in the school of the viceroys and of those semi-gods that were known as *oidores*, that practices its art and plays with us, the men of the revolution, helping us to rise to then overthrow us, depending on its selfish interests. This brotherhood, as invisible as it is successful in its calculations, is the same one that for different reasons, and depending on the circumstances, has maintained a constant and decisive influence in the affairs of state. It pleases it, for instance, to praise and call for General Santa Anna? We then have him turned into a Cirus, the glorious restorer of the temple; another Constantine, founder of the cult; a great and noble hero capable of impersonating all alone the glory of the nation. It is in its interest to destroy him and insult him? Then we are told he is a traitor, the one who lost Texas, one of those tiring tyrants that exhausts human patience.[240]

As Michael Costeloe has confirmed in a recent study, a significant proportion of politicians born and bred in the provinces found, during the early national period, that the elites of the capital could be, as well as a tight and impenetrable set, a particularly influential force in national politics.[241]

In brief, after Bustamante forced Tornel to resign in July 1839, his political activities were restricted to writing complaints about the way Bustamante had abandoned him (again) and the way the Supreme Conservative Power had ostracized him. In June 1840 he received enough of an apology from a probably fearful (and threatened) Supreme Conservative Power that he published a pamphlet acknowledging his predisposition to put aside the anger he had felt for the better part of a year.[242] This meant that he was able to return to fulfill his duties in the Supreme Conservative Power for the rest of 1840. However, it would appear from the available information that he did not take a major role in their discussions thereafter. While Santa Anna distanced himself from politics, enjoying life on his hacienda, offering to come back to Mexico City only during the failed July federalist *pronunciamiento* in which José Urrea stormed the National Palace and took Bustamante prisoner, only to surrender once it became clear that neither he nor Gómez Farías could muster any support, Tornel adopted a similarly low profile, concentrating mainly on the Compañía Lancasteriana.

With more time at his disposal, Tornel went back to writing. Apart from writing a powerful indictment of Gutiérrez Estrada's monarchist proposal, it was in the fall of 1840 that Tornel wrote two of his most outstanding literary pieces: the oration he wrote for the 1840 celebrations of independence and his play *La muerte de Cicerón*. Both works were deeply imbued with the resentment he had come to feel toward Bustamante and his administration. Because this is mainly a biography of Tornel that pays close attention to his relationship with Santa Anna and the politics of *santanismo*, I will not offer an in-depth analysis of his writing. Nevertheless, since he was considered at the time as one of the leading intellectuals and writers of the period, it is worth examining how Tornel used language to put across his ideas.[243]

By the time he wrote his *Discurso* of 1840, his style had matured, and his use of what could be described as manipulative objectivity was at its most persuasive (the adoption of what is an ostensibly objective ideological stance with the aim of converting the unconverted to a particularly subjective or partisan one). Its passages of despair, with their passionate condemnation of Mexico's internal turmoils and civil wars, are among the most emotional and stirring pieces of the period; they also contain one of the most damaging attacks on Bustamante's regime of the time.

As an example of the way Tornel wrote, his 1840 *Discurso* is an ideal piece to analyze. In order to illustrate the way Tornel succeeds in affecting the audience's sensibility and as a result succeeds in converting what is a general lament into a direct condemnation of Bustamante's regime, the passages contained in pages seven to sixteen deserve detailed attention. On page seven, he describes and explains what the past nineteen years have been like:

Hesitant and uncertain have been the nation's steps, from the dawn of its political existence. We have tried all possible forms of government from the absolute monarchy with its brilliant pomp to the federal republic with its dangerous exaggerations. In the adoption of the laws, customs and traditions that have old and strong roots have been tenaciously undermined; without preparing the field, we have sown exotic plants that died when they were born. Maintaining the old legislation of our elders we have deformed it with extravagant appendices that have altered the plan without improving it. The general movement of spirits, marked by the achievement of independence, demanded more analogous institutions and an education that were proper to the new being or life that the nation had acquired at such a high cost. A luxury of words, dishonest phrases, vain promises, confused designs, poor means; such has been the fleeting nature of our political systems and governments, which, piling up one after another, have all disappeared without leaving behind one single and solid memory of any use or profit.

Tornel's use of imagery is particularly evocative in this passage. The nation's steps (the nation is compared to a toddler) are described as having been hesitant and uncertain from the dawn of its existence. The parallel drawn between Mexico and a young infant inevitably supplies the sentence with an element of affection. The use of the word *dawn* (*albor*) adds to that sense of hope—a reminiscence of the early days of independence seen in the first light of morning, with the rose-tinted expectations of a glorious sunrise. However, those expectations were frustrated. Devoid of imagery, the following sentence appears all the more bold and striking. All forms of government were tried, and none of them had worked. Once the theme of failure has been emphatically established, without any baroque illustrations, he introduces the use of emotive imagery. He says that they tried to adopt laws, which went against the strong and ancient roots of Mexico's traditions and customs. He develops this image of the land, of the earth, with the striking metaphor that they planted exotic plants that died on being born. They had forgotten to prepare the ground and give the fields the right conditions for them to live in. The use of the word *exotic* provides the emotional charge of the sentence. Tornel thus conveys both the beauty and the strange nature of the original ideals he shared with his countrymen when independence was achieved. It is both evocative of what at the time were completely new concepts of life and government, as well as of the delicacy with which they needed to be handled. In this one image he compresses with pathos the whole experience of the years following independence.

Tornel's regular use of parallel alternatives or synonyms is as present as ever, emphasizing, through the repetition of concepts, the degree to which the dreams of 1821 had gone astray: "hesitant and uncertain," "customs and traditions," "old and strong," "new being or life," "dishonest phrases, vain promises," "use or profit." Moreover, he accentuates the emotional value of these contrasting and complementary concepts by replacing facts with sensations:

Long civil wars have exhausted, in a sense, the enthusiasm that accompanies the regeneration of the people; the cold selfishness that abandons our fate to the whims and passing fancies of a handful of audacious individuals aspires to replace that unselfish feeling that is always the hope and a help during the great crises of the state. I am not exaggerating, fellow citizens.

The concrete and factual results of long-lasting civil wars can include a ruined economy or a high rate of mortality. However, he replaces such details with an abstract sensation: "enthusiasm." The use of the word *enthusiasm*, as opposed to figures or statistics, offers a much more emotional portrayal of the outcome of the troubles. It even implies, because enthusiasm is a sentiment inherent to hope, that Mexico has reached a dead-end. To stress this sense of despair, he describes the selfishness of Mexico's rulers as being "cold" and, by association, calculating.

On page nine, he supports this allegation with a device characteristic of romanticism; he becomes empirical and appeals to the audience's memories of the recent events that had disturbed the peace of the capital:

Two months ago cannons roared in the streets and squares of the opulent capital. We have not come to this pleasant location without noticing the rubble and ruins of those majestic buildings that we could have inherited and yet which we have been unable to respect. As you have walked here from the temple of the august ceremonies, you observed that the avenue was stained with Mexican blood; blood shed to bitterly lament and not to celebrate in triumph.

The destruction in Mexico City might not be connected with either the people's alleged loss of enthusiasm or the cold selfishness of Mexico's political leaders, but Tornel introduces the ideas consecutively, with the added emotional weight of going from the abstract to the personally concrete— from words such as *enthusiasm* to the specific reference to the devastation caused by Urrea and Gómez Farías's unsuccessful uprising two months before.

On page thirteen is a further example of how Tornel combines political theory with his own personal emotional interpretation of history:

It is not the implementation but the oblivion of our republican principles that has caused us so many disasters. If we leave the narrow path of virtue the republic will only exist as a fantastic name; if personal ambition replaces the useful desire to strengthen the prosperity of the mother-country, the republic will be immolated in the dirty honor of a small citizen; if the political parties place themselves in the catalogue of factions, the republic, ceasing to be a lady in control of her actions, will but obey the whims and evil aspirations of a few; if the progress of healthy reason is stopped or prevented from developing, the Republic becomes chaotic; it is in limbo, without hope of improvement; if privileges damage common interests the Republic becomes the inheritance of the exclusive classes; if, in the end, each citizen ceases to be a bastion of independence and freedom, an invincible supporter of the rights of the nation, a more or less perfect model of political morality, then the Republic is destined to collapse as Rome collapsed when corruption flattened all paths and provided facilities for the most degrading slavery.

Tornel presents the following ideas: that republicanism, if obeyed, is a virtuous system of government; that patriotism should be upheld before personal ambition; that party factionalism divides the country instead of supporting it; that any form of privilege turns the republic into the property of the landed classes and goes against the grain of the general prosperity of the nation; and that it is necessary for every individual to defend the political morality of the country and strive to maintain its freedom and independence. He adorns these ideas with emotional terms. He uses subjective and abstract concepts such as "the paths of virtue," "healthy reason," "chaos," "in limbo," and "the political morality" to convey them. He supports these personal beliefs with arbitrary adjectives—"*fantastic* name," "*dirty* honor," "*small* citizen"—generally placing them before the noun in Spanish for greater emphasis. He supplies a forceful and at times grotesque imagery: the selfish dictator or conspirator is short and dirty; the nation is a lady who is no longer in control of her actions or her destiny. Moreover, he uses terms that are unambiguous, such as "whims and evil aspirations." He concludes the paragraph with a comparison that carries the conviction of culture and knowledge, stating that Mexico is about to become like ancient Rome, ridden with corruption and guilty of encouraging slavery.

The 1840 *Discurso* is first and foremost a tragic lament of Mexico's ill fortune and an indictment of factionalism and civil war. However, it is also a subversive piece of anti-Bustamante propaganda. From the very beginning of the speech, there is an indirect criticism of Bustamante's regime in that it is evident that the horrors of the past nineteen years have not been overcome. In fact, as the speech progresses it becomes clear that the situation has become worse. On page fourteen there is a good example of this:

At this point in time the responsibility of those who are expected to direct the fortunes of our famished and ailing nation, that could die and will die if great efforts are not employed to save her from the greatest dangers, is very grave indeed. With our old society in ruins, we sit calmly on the debris and we do not think of constructing a new one in which beliefs are not at war with the most urgent needs of the period.

Where are we then? We are in a violent and whimsical situation. *The characteristic sign that the social state is infallibly declining and becoming corrupt is the progressive increase in the stress we place on our passions and the parallel decrease in the faith we place in our rights.*

The majesty of law is replaced by the fleeting prestige of some groups or individuals. The sovereignty of the people is proclaimed and in a monstrous change of direction, there is the hope of preventing the people from exercising their rights, the most sacred and inviolable of their attributes. I discuss and allow my heart to bleed in the presence of the Supreme Magistrate and before the most notable citizens of the Republic, for as long as I can speak freely, I have the courage to publish my convictions, which are the convictions of the masses who are more than aware of who they are and what they deserve.

The emphasis is Tornel's. It is clear from this passage that he takes a step away from the general lament and directs his criticism at the men currently responsible for running the country. If they do not do something soon, Mexico will die. He asks, "Where are we then?" The answer is short and consequently emphatic: "In a violent and whimsical situation." So that this is understood, he emphasizes the next sentence. The obvious sign that Mexico is in decline and ridden with corruption is the rise in internal conflicts (what he describes as "passions") and the lack of commitment of the government to solve the country's problems. Moreover, he claims that under the current administration, law has been substituted by ineffective politicians who have been distracted by prestige. He also states that the sovereignty of the people has lost its right to be represented.

The mention of censorship is another astute piece of manipulation. He draws attention to the fact that he is criticizing the government on a day of celebration and ensures that his audience is aware of his courage as he proclaims the faults of the regime. Although he is clearly free to declaim his beliefs, the fact that he needs to be brave to express them contains the obvious implication that the freedom of speech he is making use of is only relative, and that it is not thanks to Bustamante's tolerance that his voice can be heard, but thanks to his courage.

The concluding paragraph of the speech is a disguised call to arms:

Courage Mexicans; there is still time to save what has been lost . . . to save your beautiful country from a despotism that debilitates everything, from an anarchy that consumes everything. However grave the circumstances may be, there is nothing superior to the firm and enlightened resolution of a magnanimous people. Mock the designs of the incorrigible enemies of the American regeneration. . . . There is no hope for you, no future, no happiness in store, unless the Republic is consolidated and triumphs.[244]

The implications of this paragraph are evident. The enemies of the nation are incorrigible. The Mexicans' duty is to rescue the country from despotism. The incorrigible enemies of the nation are the despots who are allowing anarchy to prevail. Because they are incorrigible, they will not change. At present there is no hope, no future, no happiness. The logical conclusion is that the only answer to Mexico's crisis is to remove the government by force; because they are incorrigible, they will never adopt the measures the country needs to prosper. By stressing that it is imperative that the republic triumphs, Tornel is also indirectly accusing the administration of having monarchist sympathies.

Having already claimed in his 1840 *Discurso* that Mexico was about to become like ancient Rome, ridden with corruption and guilty of encouraging slavery, in *La muerte de Cicerón* he illustrated this point further by setting his play in the year after the death of Julius Caesar. A close look at the play shows that it is as much about Bustamante's regime as it is about the death of Cicero. Faithful to one of the classical unities, the action of the play takes place in one day. It tells the story of how Mark Antony tries to persuade Octavius to have Cicero executed and how he eventually tricks him into doing so. The action of the play follows the discussions between Mark Antony and Octavius over whether a confident government should need to purge its enemies and whether certain influential figures, capable of urging the people to revolt, must of necessity be killed to preserve law and order. Characters such as Fulvia, Mark Antony's wife, and Octavia, Octavius's sister, add an emotional dimension to this debate, with Fulvia advocating Cicero's death to promote her husband's career and Octavia begging for mercy on moral and essentially Christian grounds. By way of contrast, the play follows Cicero's escape to the island of Caieta, where the discussions between Cicero and Atticus, his loyal friend, center around the validity of Cicero's surrendering to his enemies to die, thus proving through his martyrdom the tyrannical nature of the government. Atticus's lack of confidence in the people leads him to try to persuade Cicero to escape and continue the struggle in exile. However, Cicero's determination to die for the people of Rome is fulfilled in Act Three, when the betrayal by one of his supposed friends, Philologus, leads Cicero's murderers to find and execute him in the forest.

Thematically, this play offers two interesting debates concerning authority and freedom that that are still relevant today. In Act One, the debate, with all its possible repercussions, evolves around the justification of murder as an acceptable political measure. The other debate, which takes place in Act Two, concerns sacrifice and death and to a certain extent the notions of sainthood and martyrdom, as conceivable means of progress. Cicero believes in his death as a means to provoke a positive reaction. *La muerte de Cicerón* is also about tyranny and its manifestations. However, the main theme of the play is clearly ingratitude and betrayal. Octavius is ungrateful and betrays Cicero because he is young and lacks the maturity to challenge Mark Antony. Laenas was once a slave Cicero freed. Philologus was once educated by Cicero. They both betray Cicero. In contrast, Atticus, Tirus, and Febronius are manifestations of loyalty.

To a certain extent, Mark Antony and Fulvia are not as despicable as Octavius, Philologus, or Laenas, in that they were never in debt to Cicero, and as far as the play recalls, were always his enemies. Tornel obviously condemns their brutality and ruthlessness, although there is a certain integrity in their resolutions. Above all, the play condemns Octavius's weakness and the corruption and ingratitude of the other two. As for the condemnation of Mark Antony and Fulvia, it is to be found in Octavia's demands. As Octavius says, a confident government, a stable government, does not need to execute its enemies. Julius Caesar is portrayed as a hero precisely because he was prepared to forgive his critics. Mark Antony, in contrast to the memory of Caesar and Octavia with her angelical pleas, appears as a cold-blooded, pragmatic, and ruthless tyrant who believes in death as a necessary political means of survival. Fulvia is much less rational; she just wants Cicero to die out of malice and to help her husband's political career to prosper.

Cicero plays a relatively minor part in the play. As the title suggests, the play is about his death—the reasons for his death and the circumstances in which it took place. It is not about Cicero himself. However, when he does appear on stage and when he is described by the other characters, he has the characteristics of a hero. Nevertheless, it is an example of Tornel's move away from neoclassicism that his Cicero is not a true Aristotelian tragic hero—one who, having been noble and great, suffers a fall because of fate or his own mistakes. In other words, classical and neoclassical tragedy narrate the story of a fall. Cicero, however, finds greatness in his death; he becomes heroic. He does not suffer from a fall. There is no decline in his position or status. He is never seen as having committed any mistakes of horrendous proportions or suffering any repercussions. Cicero is an admirable orator at the beginning and continues to be so at the end. He is a man of principles. He agrees to escape only out of kindness to his loyal friends so that they do not die for him. When he dies, we are told that he opens out his arms. In more senses than one, Tornel's Cicero is more similar to the figure of Christ than he is to a neoclassical hero. The tragedy is that of Rome, which will be left without one of its greatest spokesmen.

Within its historical context, *La muerte de Cicerón* is a clear attack on Bustamante. Tornel in the summer of 1839 had accused Bustamante precisely of ingratitude and treachery. There is no doubt that these are the main themes of the play. Moreover, parallels are drawn between the events and characters in the play with those of Mexico's political stage. Cicero, for instance, is an idealized alter ego of Tornel. He is an orator. He is accused of being a turncoat, of having changed sides from opposing to supporting Caesar, and from supporting to opposing Catilina. He is victimized by an unsympathetic regime. The Roman rulers are either weak or evil. The result is that they are tyrants. The events in the play are a metaphor of the decadence Mexico has fallen into, governed by despots like Mark Antony—ungrateful traitors who have been corrupted by power and money.

La muerte de Cicerón was dedicated to Andrés Quintana Roo, who was prepared to say in print that "so many merits contained in just one work make the dedication with which you have honored me, captivated by a friendship that is as blind as love, all the more worthy. Please accept my most expressive thanks with which I proclaim myself your passionate friend and loyal servant."[245] It is a play that certainly deserves to be reprinted in an annotated edition because of its literary and historical value.[246] It would be interesting to analyze the play in greater depth (his portrayal of women, the use of prose and theatrical speeches, the parallels he establishes between ancient Rome and Mexico in the 1840s, his use of imagery, etc.). Such an exhaustive study would probably deserve a separate book in its own right.

Therefore, having succeeded in confirming his well-established reputation as one of Mexico's leading literati, Tornel started plotting the downfall of that "Roman" administration that, in his mind, had so unjustly betrayed and abandoned him. Unlike his Cicero, however, Tornel was not intending to become a martyr to save his mother country. It made far more sense to overthrow the regime and return to the corridors of power.

Since his stay in the United States, power had proved to be difficult to hold on to. Had Tornel looked back on New Year's Eve at the past decade of the 1830s, he would no doubt have had the impression that it had been a decade of repeated rises and falls. From having been abandoned in Baltimore, he returned to Mexico in 1831 to form part of a political movement that succeeded in overthrowing the Bustamante regime in 1832 and rising to power in 1833. However, when the *santanistas'* control of the government could have been consolidated, he found this control was taken away by the radicals who came to dominate the 1833–1834 Congress. Nevertheless, he orchestrated the 1834 *pronunciamientos* that brought an end to the Gómez Farías administration and succeeded, once more, in forming part of the government that was subsequently formed. This turned out to be another lost opportunity. By 1836 Congress was dominated by centralists and traditionalists, and Santa Anna was a fallen hero in the wake of the Texan debacle. His political prominence thus faded again as Bustamante returned to hold the presidential seat in 1837. Ironically, it was a major international crisis with France that allowed Tornel and Santa Anna to return to power in 1839, following the victory of 5 December 1838 and Santa Anna's subsequent return to the presidency. With the added victory of Acajete (3 May 1839), Tornel must have been convinced that at last, the *santanistas'* hold on government would be more permanent. And yet, at the height of his power, Tornel sank back down again with Bustamante's return to the presidency in July 1839, only to find himself ostracized from the National Palace for the better part of the last year of the decade. In many ways, Tornel and Santa Anna's experience of the 1830s had been like that of the board game *snakes and ladders*, where you can as easily reach the top by climbing up a *ladder* as you can find yourself back down at the beginning again by sliding down a *snake*. In his own words, he had, on three occasions in one decade, been "led to the peak of the rock of

Tarpeya to be subsequently thrown off it, from the greatest of heights into the abyss of ignominy."[247]

Yet Tornel was a survivor. The first national decade had turned him into a hardened professional politician. The second had made him even harder. Organizing revolutions was no longer problematic. While in 1822 and 1828 Tornel had been unsure about the means adopted to overthrow the existing ruler (Iturbide, first, and Gómez Pedraza, second), he had shown no qualms about supporting the 1832 revolution or about organizing the 1834 Plan of Cuernavaca. The end justified the means. Experience had also come to affect the way he saw Mexico. It made sense to limit the suffrage. He supported the 1836 Constitution for the way it had addressed this issue. Thereafter only property-owning citizens could have a voice in choosing who governed the nation. Federalism had failed. In 1834 Tornel became a centralist, and he would remain one until he died. Censorship was also a necessary method of control. The people were not yet ready to be exposed to an entirely free press (especially since this freedom was repeatedly abused). Nevertheless, in spite of his profound disillusion, he remained a committed republican. All that was needed was a government that could grab hold of the country's destiny and give it order, stability, and peace and impose a long-lasting centralist constitutional system that without bizarre inventions such as the Supreme Conservative Power would enable the executive to be strong and decisive. It was important to have a large army. Tornel was more than aware of the potential threat the United States posed to the republic. It was important that Mexico had a strong government that was not divided by the kind of factionalism that had weakened the First Federal Republic and was now weakening the First Centralist one. In brief, the *santanistas* needed to ensure the next time they rose to power that they truly consolidated their position in power, so that it would be possible for them to impose once and for all their very own national project on the nation.

NOTES

1. José María Tornel, "La ciudad de Baltimore en 1831 (Sacado de los apuntes del Escmo. Sr. General D. José María Tornel, sobre los Estados Unidos)," *El Mosaico Mexicano* 3 (1840): 330–334.

2. Ibid.

3. Ibid. Most of the information on Tornel's stay in Baltimore is based on the noted article, "La ciudad de Baltimore." His descriptions are supported by another account he wrote, printed by the *Diario del Gobierno*, 26 February 1837.

4. The affluent households he frequented, such as those of Charles Carlton, or that of the archbishop of Baltimore, Father Eccleston, all belonged to Catholic families.

5. Edmundo O'Gorman, *México. El trauma de su historia* (Mexico City: UNAM, 1977), p. 33.

6. José María Tornel, *Manifestación del C. José María Tornel* (Mexico City: n.p., 1833), p. 46.

7. Ibid., pp. 57–58.

8. AHM: Exp. XI/III/I-Lucas Alamán to Tornel, 13 February 1831.

9. Ibid., Tornel to Alamán, 1 June 1831.

10. Tornel, *Manifestación*, p. 58.

11. Ibid., p. 57.

12. A complete and detailed account of this correspondence can be found in Carlos Bosch García, *Documentos de la relación de México con los Estados Unidos (31 de diciembre 1829–29 de mayo 1837)*, vol. 2 (Mexico City: UNAM, 1983).

13. José María Bocanegra, *Memorias para la historia de México independiente. 1822–1846*, vol. 1. (Mexico City: Fondo de Cultura Económica, 1987), pp. 548–553.

14. Bosch Garcia, *Documentos*, p. 221.

15. Ibid., p. 189.

16. *El Registro Oficial*, 24 April 1830.

17. José María Tornel, *Tejas y los Estados Unidos de América en sus relaciones con la república mexicana* (Mexico City: Imp. de Ignacio Cumplido, 1837), p. 41.

18. Margaret Swett Henson, *Lorenzo de Zavala. The Pragmatic Idealist* (Fort Worth: Texas Christian University Press, 1996), pp. 47–51.

19. Bocanegra, *Memorias*, vol. 1, p. 550.

20. Ibid., p. 551.

21. Pedro Santoni, *Mexicans at Arms. Puro Federalists and the Politics of War, 1845–1848* (Fort Worth: Texas Christian University Press, 1996), p. 25.

22. Bocanegra, *Memorias*, vol. 1, p. 548.

23. Will Fowler, *Mexico in the Age of Proposals, 1821–1853* (Westport, CT: Greenwood Press, 1998), p. 234.

24. Ibid., pp. 241–243.

25. T. Joutel, *Diario histórico del último viaje que hizo M. de la Sale para descubrir el desembocadero y curso del Missicipi*, trans. José María Tornel (New York: Imp. José Desnoues, 1831).

26. Tornel, *Tejas y los Estados Unidos*, p. 1.

27. Ibid., p. 46.

28. Ibid., p. 10.

29. *Proclama* of 10 February 1829, reprinted in Bocanegra, *Memorias*, vol. 1, pp. 489–492.

30. A. M. Gilliam, *Travels in Mexico during the Years 1843 and 44* (Aberdeen: George Clark & Son, 1847), pp. 112–113.

31. Tornel, "La ciudad de Baltimore," p. 332. Zavala also stayed in Barnum's hotel, otherwise known as the City Hotel, stating that it was central, on the corner of the square in which the monument to the heroes of 1814 was built. He also noted that it was busy and that the waiters and chambermaids were mainly black, with some of Irish origin. See Lorenzo de Zavala, *Obras, Viaje a los Estados Unidos del Norte de América* (Mexico: City: Porrúa, 1976), p. 107.

32. In my unpublished Ph.D. dissertation, "José María Tornel y Mendívil, Mexican General/Politician (1794–1853)," (University of Bristol, 1994), pp. 134–135, I suggested that the horsewhipping may have been the result of one of Tornel's adulterous relationships. Gilliam makes a reference on p. 87 of his *Travels in Mex-*

ico to the extraordinary fact that Tornel adopted a young American teenager in 1843, just after his wife, María Agustina, had died (October 1843). Gilliam is not the only American who recorded meeting Tornel's adopted son. Waddy Thompson, who served as minister plenipotentiary of the United States in Mexico, wrote in his *Recollections of Mexico* (New York: Wiley & Putnam, 1847), p. 77: "The boy was sent to the house of General Tornel, the Minister of War, and was really, as I know, adopted on a full footing of equality in his family, and treated with the most parental kindness." It is commonly accepted that adoptions in nineteenth-century Mexico, especially among the more distinguished families, were not a question of charity but a way of patching up any traces of adultery. The adopting father relieved the single mothers of the economic and social burden of bringing up an illegitimate child and purged whatever guilt they might have had by becoming responsible for the education of the offspring of their adventures without openly admitting them as being their own. Executing a rather fanciful leap of the imagination, I went on to propose that young John Hill was probably Tornel's bastard son, one he must have conceived in the United States, since he was taken prisoner coming into Mexico from America. Given that, according to Thompson, John Hill was a "handsome boy, of about fifteen years of age," I stressed the use of the term *about* and taking two years away from his age, arrived at the conclusion that the year of his conception was 1830. In other words, I argued that if John Hill was Tornel's son, then the horsewhipping scene at Barnum's hotel conjured up images of an American father, perhaps husband, punishing the randy Mexican for sleeping with Miss or Mrs. Hill. I at least noted that the anecdote remains a mystery and that any such theory as the one exposed could only be a guess. Since then, María del Carmen Vázquez Mantecón has amply illustrated the extent to which my early interpretation was a touch farfetched and that Tornel's horsewhipping was due to the fact that he made the mistake of insulting a rather highly strung American. See María del Carmen Vázquez Mantecón, *La palabra del poder. Vida pública de José María Tornel (1795–1853)* (Mexico City: UNAM, 1997), p. 90. Having said this, one still wonders why he decided to adopt John Hill (that is, if he did adopt him, something that Vázquez Mantecón doubts, since no legal documents have been found to confirm that the adoption took place). And if it was not a case of adultery, we are then left with the question of what he actually did say to inspire the offended *gringo* to give him a serious horsewhipping. We will probably never find out what actually happened outside the Barnum hotel the day Tornel was beaten and humiliated in public.

33. Tornel, *Manifestación*, p. 58.

34. Tornel, "La ciudad de Baltimore," p. 332.

35. Tornel, *Tejas y los Estados Unidos*, p. 47.

36. Josefina Zoraida Vázquez, *La intervención norte-americana 1846–1848* (Mexico City: Secretaría de Relaciones Exteriores, 1997), pp. 37–38. See as well Josefina Zoraida Vázquez and Lorenzo Meyer, *México frente a Estados Unidos (Un ensayo histórico 1777–1988)* (Mexico City: Fondo de Cultura Económica, 1989), pp. 42–43 and Josefina Zoraida Vázquez, "México y la guerra con Estados Unidos," in Josefina Zoraida Vázquez (ed.), *México al tiempo de su guerra con Estados Unidos (1846–1848)* (Mexico City: Fondo de Cultura Económica/El Colegio de México, 1997), p. 29.

37. For a discussion of Zavala's views on the United States, see Fowler, *Mexico in the Age of Proposals*, pp. 185–188.

38. Bocanegra, *Memorias*, vol. 2, p. 196.

39. Ibid., pp. 156, 159, 204–205.

40. Ibid., p. 162.

41. Ibid., p. 190.

42. Tornel, *Manifestación*, p. 55.

43. Vázquez Mantecón, *La palabra del poder*, p. 93.

44. Quoted and translated into English in Wilfrid Hardy Callcott, *Santa Anna. The Story of an Enigma Who Once Was Mexico* (Hamden, CT: Archon Books, 1964), p. 87.

45. Ibid.

46. The plan of Veracruz is reprinted in Bocanegra, *Memorias*, vol. 2, pp. 265–268.

47. Anna, *Forging Mexico*, p. 247.

48. Mariano Riva Palacio Archive (henceforth referred to as MRP), Nettie Lee Benson Library, University of Texas at Austin, 203, Santa Anna to Bustamante, Veracruz, 4 January 1832.

49. Anna, *Forging Mexico*, p. 247.

50. See Will Fowler, "Civil Conflict in Independent Mexico, 1821–1857: An Overview," in Rebecca Earle (ed.), *Civil War in Nineteenth-Century Latin America* (London: Macmillan, in press).

51. Although one wonders whether it might have been Tornel who came up with the idea of bringing back Gómez Pedraza so that the revolt could become a legitimate one in constitutional terms, by 1831, Tornel and Gómez Pedraza were far from being on good terms. In late 1831 Tornel published a vitriolic condemnation of Gómez Pedraza's *Manifesto que Manuel Gómez Pedraza, ciudadano de la república de Méjico, dedica a sus compatriotas; o sea, una reseña de su vida pública* (Guadalajara: Imp. de Brambila, 1831), in which he lamented the ex-president's lack of patriotism. See José María Tornel, *Carta del Sr. Tornel sobre el manifiesto del señor Pedraza* (Mexico City: Imp. del Aguila, 1831). It is still possible that Tornel suggested that they demanded the return of Gómez Pedraza since bringing him back did not entail supporting him. After all, elections were held during the three months in which he occupied the presidency, and it was clear to Tornel (who did not like him) and Santa Anna (who had actively fought to depose him from the presidency in 1828) that it was a temporary measure that would give their revolt constitutional legitimacy while allowing Santa Anna to rise to power through electoral means in 1833.

52. For the 1832 Federalist revolt, see Frank Samponaro, "La alianza de Santa Anna y los federalistas, 1832–1834. Su formación y desintegración," *Historia Mexicana* 30:3 (1981): 359–380; Jaime E. Rodríguez O., "The Origins of the 1832 Rebellion," and Josefina Zoraida Vázquez, "Los pronunciamientos de 1832: aspirantismo político e ideología," both in Jaime E. Rodríguez O. (ed.), *Patterns of Contention in Mexican History* (Wilmington, DE: Scholarly Resources, 1992), pp. 145–162, 163–186, respectively.

53. Samponaro, "La alianza de Santa Anna y los federalistas," p. 359.

54. See Fowler, *Mexico in the Age of Proposals*, pp. 230–231. See also Will

Fowler, "Valentín Gómez Farías: Perceptions of Radicalism in Independent Mexico, 1821–1847," *Bulletin of Latin American Research* 15:1 (January 1996): 39–62.

55. AHM: Exp. XI/III/I-93, see letters by F. Cacho, José Ignacio Ormachea, Ignacio Alas, and Tornel, 1, 2, 9, 12, 21, and 24 May 1832.

56. Tornel, *Manifestación*, p. 58.

57. Francis Bacon, *Pensamientos filosóficos, del canciller Bacon. Traducidos por el coronel José María Tornel* (Mexico City: Imp. de Alejandro Valdés, 1832), and *Discurso sobre la influencia de la filosofiá en las costumbres y en la legislación de los pueblos: o sea Manifestación de los beneficios de que le es deudor el género humano. Tradujo del francés el coronel José María Tornel* (Mexico City: Imp. de Galván, 1832).

58. Vázquez Mantecón highlights only too well the extent to which Tornel's *Pensamientos* was far from being an accurate translation of the original in her *La palabra del poder*, p. 94.

59. *La Columna*, 20 February 1833.

60. Ibid., 20, 27 February 1833.

61. As he noted in an undated letter (in response to the articles in *La Columna*) addressed to an unspecified high-ranking officer in the Ministry of Defense, although he was clearly displeased with what was being said about him, he did not want to engage in a heated discussion over his past services with people (like General Pedro Lemus) who did not deserve to be answered: "Aunque me sería muy fácil sostener la odiosa lucha que ha provocado el Sr. Lemus, considero que este medio es indigno de mis principios, de mi constante moralidad, y propio solamente para envilecer más y más la libertad de prensa, de que tanto se abusa por desgracia. Yo tengo la satisfacción íntima de mi conciencia." He did, however, request that the Ministry of Defense do something to silence Lemus: "Para que estas garantías de la inviolabilidad de mi honor sean completas, es necesario que . . . el gobierno se explique, que dicte cuantas providencias estime convenientes al esclarecimiento de la verdad para mi defensa o para mi castigo." See AHM: Exp. XI/III/I-93, letter by Tornel, n.d. (c. 1833).

62. AHM: Exp. XI/III/I-93, letter by Tornel, 17 January 1833, requesting leave and permission to spend a month in Orizaba, Córdoba, and Tehuacán with his son José María Tornel y Bonilla.

63. José María Luis Mora, *Obras sueltas* (Mexico City: Porrúa, 1963), pp. 46–47.

64. Bocanegra, *Memorias*, vol. 2, p. 379.

65. José María Tornel, *Discurso que pronunció el Exmo. Señor General D. José María Tornel y Mendívil, individuo del Supremo Poder Conservador, en la Alameda de la Ciudad de México, en el día del solemne aniversario de la independencia* (Mexico City: Imp. de I. Cumplido, 1840), p. 7.

66. Samponaro, "La alianza de Santa Anna y los federalistas," p. 386.

67. Bocanegra, *Memorias*, vol. 2, pp. 383–385, 417–418, 421–422, 447.

68. Reynaldo Sordo Cedeño, *El congreso en la primera república centralista* (Mexico City: El Colegio de México/ITAM, 1993), p. 25.

69. Michael P. Costeloe, *La primera república federal de México (1824–1835)* (Mexico City: Fondo de Cultura Económica, 1983), pp. 383–385.

70. Vázquez Mantecón, *La palabra del poder*, p. 97.

71. Quoted in Bocanegra, *Memorias*, vol. 2, pp. 434–435.

72. Callcott, *Santa Anna*, p. 99.

73. *La Columna*, 26 May 1833.

74. *El Fénix de la Libertad*, 29 May 1833.

75. *La Columna*, 1 June 1833.

76. AHM: Exp. XI/III/I-93, "Hoja de servicios," n.d. (c.1845).

77. Bocanegra, *Memorias*, vol. 2, p. 441.

78. Both the Plan of Escalada and the Plan of Arista are reprinted in Bocanegra, *Memorias*, vol. 2, pp. 485–486 and 486–491, respectively.

79. Ibid., pp. 441–444.

80. Michael P. Costeloe, *The Central Republic in Mexico, 1835–1846* (Cambridge: Cambridge University Press, 1993), p. 214.

81. See *La Columna*, 15, 23 June; 3, 17, 24, 29 July; 14 August; 25, 28 September; 21 October 1833. Also see the circulars he promulgated on 13, 28 June; 21 July; 12, 24 October 1833 in the Colección Lafragua (henceforth referred to as CL), Fondo Reservado, Biblioteca Nacional de México.

82. *La Columna*, 21, 22, 25, 28, 30 September; 16 October 1833.

83. Fowler, *Mexico in the Age of Proposals*, pp. 194–195.

84. Bocanegra, *Memorias*, vol. 2, p. 445.

85. Charles A. Hale, *El liberalismo mexicano en la época de Mora, 1821–1853* (Mexico City: Siglo XXI Editores, 1987), p. 303.

86. Fowler, *Mexico in the Age of Proposals*, pp. 244–245.

87. Costeloe, *La primera república federal*, p. 407.

88. *El Telégrafo*, 11 April, 24 May 1834.

89. Bocanegra, *Memorias*, vol. 2, p. 472.

90. For the 1833–1834 cholera epidemic, see: Donald F. Stevens, "Temerse la ira del cielo: los conservadores y la religiosidad popular en los tiempos del cólera," in Will Fowler and Humberto Morales Moreno (eds.), *El conservadurismo mexicano en el siglo xix (1810–1910)* (Puebla: BUAP/University of St Andrews, 1999), pp. 87–101; and Charles A. Hutchinson, "The Asiatic Cholera Epidemic of 1833 in Mexico," *Bulletin of the History of Medicine* 32 (1958): 160–173.

91. Manuel Dublán and José María Lozano (eds.), *Legislación Mexicana. Colección completa de las disposiciones legislativas expedidas desde la independencia de la república ordena por los licenciados Manuel Dublán y José María Lozano*, vol. 2 (Mexico City: Imp. del Comercio, 1876), pp. 643–644, 650–651 (includes Tornel's *Bandos* of 8 December 1833, 9 December 1833, and 18 December 1833).

92. Ibid., pp. 677–678 (includes Tornel's *Bando* of 27 February 1834).

93. Ibid., pp. 672–673 (includes Tornel's *Bando* of 3 February 1834).

94. *El Telégrafo*, 3 August 1834.

95. Ibid., 13 August 1834.

96. Ibid., 21 September, 15 October 1834.

97. Ibid., 25 October 1834.

98. Ibid., 19 December 1834. Also see *Al público* (Mexico City: Imp. de Tomás Uribe, 1835), which in ninety pages contains a lengthy account of how the noted streetlamps were devised and set up by the town hall, with reprints of the relevant documents and correspondence that were written by and to the *ramo de alumbrado de esta ciudad*, featuring Tornel as one of the key instigators of the plan.

99. *El Telégrafo*, 5 May 1834.

100. Ibid., p. 7, October 1834.

101. See as an example: *Manifestación que el Escmo. Ayuntamiento hace al público de esta capital de las últimas ocurrencias sobre las contratas de limpia de ciudad* (Mexico City: Imp. de Tomás Uribe y Alcalde, 1834).

102. Dublán and Lozano (eds.), *Legislación Mexicana*, pp. 647–650 (includes Tornel's *Bando* of 15 December 1833).

103. Ibid., p. 654 (includes Tornel's *Bando* of 21 December 1833).

104. *El Telégrafo*, 17 April 1834.

105. Ibid., 28 April 1834.

106. Ibid., 10, 14, 15, 26 July; 24 October; 6, 12 November 1834.

107. Ibid., 4, 12 November 1834.

108. See *La Columna*, 25, 28, 30 September; 16 October 1833; see also Cayetano Romero Ávilez, *Cuando hay modo de tener, nada detiene a Tornel* (Mexico City: Imp. de Antonio Alcalde, 1833); Juan Piña, *Pascuas al Gobernador* (Mexico City: Imp. de Manuel Fernández Redondas, 1834); and Quien todo lo huele, *Luego que Gómez Farías se informe de este papel, le da la cholera morbus al gobernador Tornel* (Mexico City: n.p., 1834).

109. See note 61.

110. Fowler, *Mexico in the Age of Proposals*, p. 5.

111. Bocanegra, *Memorias*, vol. 1, p. 393.

112. Ibid., vol. 2, p. 33.

113. Ibid., pp. 34–38.

114. The pamphlet was entitled *Grito del general Santa Anna contra su supremo gobierno, y pobre del Sr. Guerrero para de aquí al mes de enero*. The measures Tornel took can be found in *El Sol*, 30 October 1829.

115. Mora, *Obras sueltas*, p. 162.

116. Valentín Gómez Farías Archive (henceforth referred to as VGF) (Nettie Lee Benson Latin American Collection, University of Texas at Austin), no. 244, Tornel to Valentín Goméz Farías, 4 January 1834.

117. *El Telégrafo*, 22 May 1834.

118. Ibid., 25 May 1834.

119. Ibid., 14 October 1834.

120. Ibid., 4 September 1834.

121. Ibid., 25 October 1834.

122. Ibid., 19 November 1834.

123. Mora, *Obras sueltas*, pp. 153, 155.

124. See VGF: Nos. 267, 271, letters by Joaquín Huarriz (30 January 1834) and Anonymous (5 February 1834) warning Gómez Farías of Tornel's sedition and reactionary conspiracy.

125. Rivera Cambas, *Santa Anna*, p. 30.

126. Mora, *Obras sueltas*, p. 155.

127. *El Telégrafo*, 25 May 1834.

128. Ibid., 15 June 1834.

129. Ibid., 26 June 1834.

130. Mora, *Obras sueltas*, p. 156.

131. Ibid., p. 81.

132. The Plan of Cuernavaca is reprinted in Bocanegra, *Memorias*, vol. 2, pp. 573–574.

133. Bocanegra, *Memorias*, vol. 2, p. 547.

134. Will Fowler, *Military Political Identity and Reformism in Independent Mexico. An Analysis of the Memorias de Guerra (1821–1855)* (London: ILAS, 1996), pp. 21–22.

135. All plans are listed in Fowler, *Mexico in the Age of Proposals*, pp. 281–282.

136. Barbara A. Tenenbaum, *México en la época de los agiotistas, 1821–1857* (Mexico City: Fondo de Cultura Económica, 1985), p. 64.

137. *El Telégrafo*, 20 July 1834.

138. Bocanegra, *Memorias*, vol. 2, p. 557, vol. 3, pp. 38–39, vol. 1, p. 329.

139. Bocanegra says that the 1835 government "continuó su marcha cumpliendo con el ofrecimiento de no hacer retroceder las instituciones liberales." Ibid., vol. 2, p. 600.

140. Ibid., pp. 613–614.

141. The *Pronunciamiento* of Orizaba is reprinted in ibid, p. 633.

142. José María Tornel, *Discurso pronunciado por el Exmo. Sr. General Ministro de Guerra y Marina, Don José María Tornel, en la sesión del 12 de octubre de 1842 del Congreso Constituyente, en apoyo del dictamen de la mayoria de la comisión de constitución del mismo* (Mexico City: Imp. de I. Cumplido, 1842), pp. 6–8, 27.

143. Sordo Cedeño, *El congreso en la primera república centralista*, pp. 61–106.

144. Michael P. Costeloe, "Federalism to Centralism in Mexico: The Conservative Case for Change, 1834–1835," *Americas* 45 (1988): 184.

145. Josefina Zoraida Vázquez, "Los primeros tropiezos," in Daniel Cosío Villegas (ed.), *Historia general de México*, vol. 3 (Mexico City: El Colegio de México, 1977), p. 28.

146. Costeloe, *The Central Republic in Mexico*, p. 78.

147. Reynaldo Sordo Cedeño, "El pensamiento conservador del partido centralista en los años treinta del siglo xix mexicano," in Fowler and Morales Moreno (eds.), *El conservadurismo mexicano*, pp. 135–168.

148. Sordo Cedeño, *El congreso en la primera república centralista*, pp. 205–207.

149. Bocanegra, *Memorias*, vol. 2, p. 557.

150. Fernando Díaz Díaz, *Caudillos y caciques: Antonio López de Santa Anna y Juan Alvarez* (Mexico City: El Colegio de México, 1972), p. 151.

151. Jan Bazant, "José María Tornel, Mariano Riva Palacio, Manuel Escandón y la compraventa de una hacienda," in Alicia Hernández Chávez and Manuel Miño Grijalva (eds.), *Cincuenta años de historia de México*, vol. 1 (Mexico City: El Colegio de México, 1991), p. 389.

152. (1) 6–19 November 1833; (2) 2 December 1834–22 April 1837; (3) 17 December 1838–27 July 1839; (4) 11 October 1841–19 September 1843, 26 October 1843–26 March 1844, 11 April–10 June 1844; (5) 21 February–31 July 1846; and (6) 20 April–11 September 1853.

153. For a study on military education during these years see Anne Staples, "El impulso al conocimiento académico, 1823–1846," in *La evolución de la educación militar en México* (Mexico City: Secretaría de la Defensa Nacional, 1997), pp. 113–134.

154. All quotes are taken from José María Tornel, *Memoria del secretario de estado y del despacho de guerra y marina, leída en la cámara de representantes en*

la sesión del día veinte y tres de marzo, y en la de senadores en la del veinte y cuatro del mismo mes y año de 1835 (Mexico City: Imp. de I. Cumplido, 1835), p. 21.

155. Ibid.

156. For the Lancasterian methodology see: Will Fowler, "The Compañía Lancasteriana and the Elite in Independent Mexico, 1822–1845," *TESSERAE Journal of Iberian and Latin American Studies* 2:1 (Summer 1996): 81–110.

157. Tornel, *Memoria. . . . 1835*, pp. 21–22.

158. Ibid., pp. 23–25.

159. Ibid., pp. 24–25.

160. Ibid., pp. 29–30.

161. Ibid.

162. José María Tornel, *Memoria de la secretaría de estado y del despacho de la guerra y marina, leída por el Escmo. Sr. General D. José María Tornel, en la cámara de diputados el día 7 de enero de 1839, y en la de senadores el 8 del mismo* (Mexico City: Imp. de I. Cumplido, 1839), pp. 23–24.

163. Cambas, *Antonio López de Santa Anna*, pp. 200–201.

164. This exposition entitled "Necesidad del ejército" was used with an introduction in a beautifully bound and handwritten commemorative book that can be found in the Edmundo O'Gorman Collection at the Nettie Lee Benson Latin American Collection, University of Texas at Austin: *Ejército Mexicano. Memoria sobre la organización que se dió al ejército mexicano, y que se dedica al Excmo. Sr. Benemérito de la Patria, General de División, Presidente de la República Mexicana, D. Antonio López de Santa Anna, constante defensor de sus compañeros de armas* (Mexico City: n.p., 1853).

165. Tornel, *Memoria. . . . 1835*, p. 3.

166. Ibid.

167. Ibid., p. 5.

168. Ibid., p. 6.

169. Ibid., pp. 14–15.

170. Ruth R. Olivera and Liliane Crété, *Life in Mexico under Santa Anna, 1822–1855* (Norman: University of Oklahoma Press, 1991), p. 162.

171. Tornel, *Memoria . . . 1835*, p. 15.

172. Tornel, *Memoria . . . 1839*, p. 12.

173. Ibid.

174. Ibid., p. 16.

175. See *Diario del Gobierno*, 3, 6, 9, 12 November; 25, 27, 31 December 1835.

176. Mora, *Obras sueltas*, p. 165.

177. Ibid.

178. William A. DePalo, Jr., *The Mexican National Army, 1822–1852* (College Station: Texas A&M University Press, 1997), p. 61.

179. Ibid.

180. For a particularly colorful account of how Santa Anna's troops were taken by surprise after they had all settled down to enjoy a siesta, see Enrique de Olavarría y Ferrari, *Episodios históricos mexicanos*, vol. 4 (Mexico City: Fondo de Cultura Económica, 1987), pp. 1802–1817.

181. Mora, *Obras sueltas*, p. 167.

182. José Fuentes Mares, *Santa Anna, aurora y ocaso de un comediante* (Mexico City: Editorial Jus, 1956), p. 139.

183. Ibid.

184. Reynaldo Sordo Cedeño, "El general Tornel y la guerra de Texas," *Historia Mexicana* 42:4 (1993): 919–953.

185. Vicente Filisola, *Representación dirigida al Supremo Gobierno por el general Vicente Filisola, en defensa de su honor y aclaración de sus operaciones como general en jefe del ejército sobre Tejas* (Mexico City: Imp. de I. Cumplido, 1836), pp. 66–70.

186. Dublán and Lozano, *Legislación mexicana*, vol. 3, p. 142; contains Tornel's law of 20 May 1836.

187. Tornel to Filisola, 19 May 1836, in Filisola, *Representación*, pp. 76–77.

188. Vicente Filisola, *Memorias para la historia de la guerra de Texas*, vol. 2 (Mexico City: Editora Nacional, 1968), pp. 504–505.

189. *Diario del Gobierno*, 7 June 1836.

190. Sordo Cedeño, "El general Tornel," pp. 948–950.

191. See *El Cosmopolita*, 15 June 1836, for suspicions that Tornel was not telling the nation everything he knew about the state of affairs in Texas.

192. *El Cosmopolita*, 4, 5 July 1836.

193. *Diario del Gobierno*, 17 June 1836.

194. Ibid., 8 July 1836.

195. Ibid., 17, 31 July 1836.

196. In the *Diario* on 12 August 1836, Tornel was praised for his "Iniciativa de regularizar la campaña de Tejas." In the *Diario* on 6 September 1836, he was praised for arguing the contrary. In the end, he advocated continuing the war until Texas was regained. As can be seen in Vázquez and Meyer, *México frente a Estados Unidos*, the continuation of the war with Texas became a matter of much debate: "Para México el asunto se convirtió en una obsesión política que a veces resulta difícil de comprender" (p. 49). It was a difficult choice. If the government accepted the reality of the defeat and loss, abandoned the war, and dedicated itself to restoring the national economy, it ran the risk of being condemned by a patriotic population, reluctant to be humiliated by one of its states. On the other hand, if the government continued the war in order to continue receiving the support of the nation, it ran the risk of ruining the already distressed economy forever.

197. *Diario del Gobierno*, 16 August 1836.

198. Ibid., 10 November 1836.

199. All quotes taken from Tornel, *Tejas y los Estados Unidos*, pp. 12, 19, 23, 24–26, 42, 62, 66, 67, 69, 77, 90, 95–96.

200. Fowler, *Mexico in the Age of Prospals*, p. 235

201. *Diario del Gobierno*, 12 January 1837.

202. Fuentes Mares, *Santa Anna*, p. 154.

203. Callcott, *Santa Anna*, p. 153.

204. Ibid.

205. Vázquez Mantecón, *La palabra del poder*, p. 100.

206. *Diario del Gobierno*, 24 April 1837.

207. To sense the widespread criticism he was subjected to, all that is needed is to sample the numerous articles that were printed in the *Diario del Gobierno* to defend him. See *Diario del Gobierno*: 18, 26 July; 3, 7, 14, 16 August; 6, 13 Sep-

tember; 1, 29 October; 10, 22 November; 17, 24, 30 December 1836; 9, 18, 20 March; 11, 15, 23 April 1837.

208. Ibid., 21 May 1838.

209. Ibid., 29 January 1838. His article on Chevallier was later praised in the same newspaper, 26 February 1838.

210. "Máximas de Napoleón sobre el arte de la guerra, con notas muy interesantes apoyadas en las campañas de Tirena, Conde, Montecuculli, Gustavo Adolfo, Federico, Napoléon y otros grandes capitanes, traducidas por el general J. M. Tornel," *Diario del Gobierno*, 24, 26, 28, 30 April; 2, 4, 6, 8, 10, 12, 14, 18, 20, 22, 24, 26, 28, 30 May 1838.

211. "Instrucción secreta que dió el gran Federico a sus oficiales, particularmente de caballería, para su gloriosa campaña de Baviera, traducido por el general José María Tornel," *Diario del Gobierno*, 22, 26, 28 August; 1, 11 September; 16, 19, 21, 26, 29 October 1838.

212. Vázquez Mantecón, *La palabra del poder*, p. 110.

213. Quoted and translated into English in Callcott, *Santa Anna*, p. 159.

214. *Diario del Gobierno*, 22 December 1838.

215. Ibid., 19, 20, 23, 24, 28, 29, 30, 31 December 1838.

216. Tornel, *Memoria . . . 1839*, pp. 4, 18–20, 23–24.

217. Ibid., pp. 16–17.

218. *Diario del Gobierno*, 11, 12, 14, 21, 22, 27 January; 14, 23 February 1839.

219. Ibid., 25 January, 2, 9 February, 10, 20 April 1839.

220. Sordo Cedeño, *El congreso en la primera república centralista*, pp. 314–315.

221. Costeloe, *The Central Republic*, p. 148

222. Quoted in Enrique Krauze, *Siglo de caudillos* (Barcelona: Tusquets Editores, 1994), p. 139.

223. Costeloe, *The Central Republic*, pp. 154–155.

224. Ibid.

225. Sordo Cedeño, *El congreso en la primera república centralista*, pp. 319–321.

226. Rafael F. Muñoz, *Santa Anna. El dictador resplandeciente* (Mexico City: Fondo de Cultura Económica, 1983), p. 174.

227. Olivera and Crété, *Life in Mexico*, p. 167. Also see the section entitled "Civilised Warfare" in Fowler, *Military Political Identity*, pp. 16–21.

228. Muñoz, *Santa Anna*, p. 174.

229. Quoted as well as translated in Callcott, *Santa Anna*, p. 167.

231. Sordo Cedeño, *El congreso en la primera república centralista*, p. 322.

232. Ibid., pp. 324–326; see also *Diario del Gobierno*, 13 May; 2, 19, 26, 30 June 1839.

233. The original text can be found in José María Tornel, *El general José María Tornel a sus amigos* (Mexico City: Imp. I. Cumplido, 1839), pp. 3–4.

234. Callcott, *Santa Anna*, p. 165.

235. Manuel Rivera Cambas, *Los gobernantes de Mexico (1822–1843)*, vol. 4 (Mexico City: Editorial Citlatépetl, 1964), p. 505.

236. Tornel, *El general José María Tornel a sus amigos*, pp. 1–2.

237. José María Tornel, *Carta del general José María Tornel a sus amigos, sobre*

un artículo inserto en el Cosmopolita del día 17 de agosto del presente año (Mexico City: Imp. de I. Cumplido, 1839).

238. José María Tornel, *Protesta del general José María Tornel y Mendívil, individuo propietario del Supremo Poder Conservador, contra el decreto espedido por éste en 9 del presente mes sobre reformas de la constitución* (Mexico City: Imp. de I. Cumplido, 1839), pp. 3–4, 6–7, 14–16.

239. Manuel de la Peña y Peña, *Dictamen de la comisión del Supremo Poder Conservador, aprobado por éste, contestando a la protesta de Tornel, que se publica por acuerdo del mismo Supremo Poder* (Mexico City: Imp. de I. Cumplido, 1839), pp. 7–8, 11–17, 39–49, 69.

240. José María Tornel, *Respuesta del general José María Tornel y Mendívil al escrito que formó el Escmo. Sr. Lic. D. Manuel de la Peña y Peña, que acogió el Supremo Poder Conservador, e imprimió y circuló el gobierno como suplemento de su diario, contra la protesta que el espresado publicó en 30 de noviembre del año anterior, sobre el decreto espedido en 9 del mismo mes, acerca de las reformas de las constitución* (Mexico City: Imp. de I. Cumplido, 1840), p. 10.

241. Michael P. Costeloe, "Mariano Arista y la élite de la ciudad de Mexico, 1851–1852," in Fowler and Morales Moreno (eds.), *El conservadurismo mexicano*, pp. 187–212.

242. José María Tornel, *Manifestación de la validez del decreto de 13 de mayo de 1840, espedido por el Supremo Poder Conservador, y satisfacción a los reparos hechos por el Supremo Gobierno en el 5 del corriente* (Mexico City: Imp. de I. Cumplido, 1840).

243. A more in-depth study of his literary style can be found in Will Fowler, "José María Tornel y Mendívil, Mexican General/Politician (1794–1853)" (Ph.D diss., University of Bristol, 1994), pp. 192–206.

244. José María Tornel, *Discurso que pronunció el Escmo. Sr. General D. José María Tornel y Mendívil, individuo del Supremo Poder Conservador, en la alameda de la ciudad de México, en el día del solemne aniversario de la independencia* (Mexico City: Imp. de I. Cumplido, 1840).

245. José María Tornel, *La muerte de Cicerón*, printed in the journal *El Mosaico Mexicano*, vol. 5 (Mexico City, 1841). Quintana Roo's words serve as the preface to the publication.

246. A photographic reprint of the play is included in Vázquez Mantecón, *La palabra del poder*.

247. Tornel, *Protesta*, p. 6.

4

"So Many Hopes of a Blissful Future" (1841–1844)

THE *SANTANISTAS* IN POWER, 1841–1844

Although Gutiérrez Estrada's 1840 monarchist proposal did not inspire much enthusiasm at the time, it did reflect the sense of profound disillusion that had come to characterize Mexican politics after two decades of perceived instability and failed constitutional systems. By 1841 it became clear to the *santanistas* that the time was ripe for a military uprising. The *santanistas* were still republicans, and their populist patriotism prevented them from wanting to invite a European prince to take the Mexican throne. Nevertheless, they shared Gutiérrez Estrada's profound disillusion and were beginning to consider the possibility of imposing an enlightened dictatorship in Mexico, which, without being in any way permanent, might succeed in granting the country a much-needed spell of order and stability during which the political class would have the time to consider what kind of constitution could best serve a nation with the problems and traditions of Mexico.

Bustamante had lost the support of the party of order and the centralists since he had flirted with the moderate federalists in 1838 and showed himself indecisive during both the conflict with France and the federalist revolts of 1839. He was hated by the *puros*, who had seen his government crush all of the rebellions they had organized, including the July 1840 coup in the capital. The moderates felt betrayed after they had been led to believe that they would play an active part in his government and that he would bring back an amended version of the 1824 Constitution. The abysmal state of the economy had lost Bustamante any support he might have had from the more affluent landowners. In brief, the majority of the political class appeared to be reaching the conclusion that the centralist 1836 Constitution had been as much of a failure as the imperial proposal of 1822 and the federalist one of 1824.

Therefore, it came as no surprise that when Generals Mariano Paredes y Arrillaga, Gabriel Valencia, and Santa Anna orchestrated the Triangular Revolt of the summer of 1841, with the corresponding *pronunciamientos* of Guadalajara (8 August), Ciudadela, Mexico City (4 September), and Perote (9 September), Bustamante's government surrendered without presenting any significant opposition. According to the Scottish-born wife of the Spanish ambassador, Fanny Calderón de la Barca, the Triangular Revolt was, more than a revolution—"like a game at chess, in which kings, castles, knights and bishops, are making moves, while the pawns are looking on or taking no part whatever."[1]

The result of the Triangular Revolt was the signing of the *Bases de Tacubaya* (6 October), which created a temporary dictatorship with Santa Anna as president (1841–1843) and was intended to restore order and stability in the republic while a new Constituent Congress was formed to deliver a new constitution. As several recent studies have shown, the *santanistas* Santa Anna, Tornel, and Valencia, together with Paredes y Arrillaga, misjudged the general mood of the electorate and found themselves faced with a hostile Constituent Congress in which the majority of newly elected deputies were federalists, both moderates and radicals.[2] Faced with a Congress hoping to draft a new and progressive federalist constitution that threatened to curtail the privileges of both church and army, Santa Anna retired to his hacienda in Veracruz and ordered his interim president, Nicolás Bravo, to dissolve Congress (19 December 1842) and start all over again.

After the Constituent Congress had been closed, the press censored, and a number of outspoken federalists imprisoned, a handpicked *santanista*-traditionalist Junta of Worthies (Junta de Notables) set about creating a new centralist constitution, which was finally approved on 8 June 1843: the *Bases Orgánicas*. Although Santa Anna remained president of the republic, he gave up the dictatorial powers he had been awarded in the 1841 *Bases de Tacubaya* by accepting the 1843 Constitution, which again created a strong legislative branch in order to control the executive.

Santa Anna's government from 1841 to 1844 represented the first occasion on which the *santanistas* were able to demonstrate the content of their political thought through the policies and reforms they pursued in power. The *santanista* government, formed in 1841 as a result of the *Bases de Tacubaya* (6 October), was one of the most stable governments of Independent Mexico. This can be seen particularly in the continuity that characterized various ministerial posts at the time. As an example, the three most important ministries did not change hands between 1841 and 1844: Bocanegra (minister of the interior, 18 October 1841–21 September 1844), Tornel (minister of war, 11 October 1841–10 June 1844), and Ignacio Trigueros (minister of the exchequer, 21 November 1841–28 October 1844). In Bocanegra's mind, the *Bases de Tacubaya* initially established a government in which Santa Anna "could exercise a real dictatorship," and it was thanks to this dictatorship that "peace and public order [were restored] and all the advances a properly constituted society aspires to acquiring" were obtained.[3] Tornel, in his 1844 annual ministerial report, was proud of the progress achieved during the three years the *santanistas* had been in power; the 1841 political plan, which "was ardently received by the nation," had already "provided [the nation] with so many hopes of a blissful future."[4]

The success of Santa Anna's government, according to Tornel and Bocanegra, was due first to the *Bases de Tacubaya* but above all to the 1843 Constitution: the *Bases Orgánicas* (12 June 1843). The *Bases de Tacubaya* had created the peaceful and orderly conditions that had made possible the drafting of a liberal and pragmatic constitution, which reflected the customs of the nation:

The nation's discontent and the sad embarrassing way in which we lived required and demanded the adoption of more sensible policies, and these were the ones this government adopted without hesitating. The administrations created by the 1824 and 1836 constitutions went against [public] opinion, and their situations were as a result weak and inadequate. It is not possible to provoke the conditions of the masses. It is useless to challenge what are natural tendencies. In our republic the secret for ensuring that there is peace and that order is maintained, rests on a sound knowledge of [the country's] needs, and a general disposition to attend them, without forgetting the true and not fictitious state of society. The main aim of the provisional government [1841–1843] was to bring about progress, and its main rules were obeyed so that this progress was achieved without any precipitation; the kind of precipitation which in the history of nations always leads to major disappointments.[5]

For Bocanegra the sanction of the *Bases Orgánicas* represented "one of those events, which considered [in historical terms] . . . , must be no doubt seen as one of those [fundamental turning points] which forms [and even characterizes] a period in a nation's history."[6]

The *Bases Orgánicas* illustrate quite clearly the nature of the *santanistas* constitutional ideas by 1843. Although the *santanistas* supported the creation of a dictatorship in 1841, it was not their intention to impose a long-lasting authoritarian state. The *Bases de Tacubaya* were a temporary measure. Santa Anna recognized this in his speech of 13 June 1843, when he admitted that the *Bases de Tacubaya* had served to create the stable conditions that had allowed Mexico's political class to find a "political organization suited . . . to the needs [of Mexico] and which strengthened its liberal principles." Now that the *Bases Orgánicas* had been completed and approved, Santa Anna celebrated that his "conditional dictatorship was coming to an end" and that he could thus "bury his discretional faculties" forever. Santa Anna was unequivocal in stressing that he had used the dictatorship to ensure that Mexico's political class could find the most appropriate constitution without suffering the interruption of repeated conflicts, of those "so many contradictions and unheavals" that had characterized national politics until then. He had not, however, at any point, abused the extraordinay power he had been given, even if "absolute power is a perpetual temptation to he who exercises it."[7]

It is evident from the closure of the Constituent Congress in December 1842 that the *santanistas* believed in a representative system so long as it conformed to their political ideas. Faced with a hostile Congress with a majority of federalists, moderates, and radicals, the *santanistas* decided to dissolve it and start all over again, this time ensuring that the constituent Junta de Notables which they went on to form with a selection of hand-picked individuals, created a representative system that did not challenge or contradict the main principles of early 1840s *santanismo*. After all, as was stated in Tornel's 1842 *Acta* and Plan of Huejotzingo, the deputies of the 1842 Constituent Congress either had not understood or refused to understand the general desires and will of the nation by adopting a constitution that was "diametrically opposed to its will and interest." Mexico needed a *Junta de Notables* that could present "a constitutional project suited to the country's circumstances . . . saving in so doing principles such as the popular representative republican system, independence, national integrity, the religion of our forebears without tolerating any other, and the division of powers."[8]

The *Bases Orgánicas* consolidated a centralist republic with the usual division of powers, abandoning the fourth power (the Supreme Conservative Power) created in the 1836 Constitution. The government was to be elected, and thus the electoral system had to be both popular and representative. However, the *santanista* use of the term *popular* was not an accurate one, given that suffrage was further restricted in the 1843 charter. Voters now not only had to be male, but also needed to earn over 200 pesos a year (100 more than under the 1836 charter). Congress was to continue to have two chambers, one of deputies and one of senators. However, the *Bases Orgánicas* went on to ensure that only the elite could become members of the Senate: large landowners, mine owners, proprietors or merchants, industrialists whose property was worth over 40,000 pesos or at least someone whose social position was clearly perceived to be privileged (such as a general, bishop, governor, or former senator). Freedom of the press was allowed but controlled. The constitution explicitly forbade the publication of literary or journalistic texts that attacked the Catholic faith. Catholicism was once more formally named as the official religion of the state. The military and ecclesiastical *fueros* were also explicitly guaranteed.[9]

For the *santanistas* the *Bases de Tacubaya* and the *Bases Orgánicas* resulted in three years of progress and good administration. Bocanegra asserted in his memoirs that each of the ministerial reports presented in 1844 accounted for the hard work they had carried out in improving the country's situation and reflected the pride they felt at having done a good job.[10] Before analyzing Tornel's own contribution to the 1841–1844 administration, it is worth outlining the *santanistas'* ideology as it was reflected with regard to issues such as the protection awarded to the church, economic policy, and the beliefs sustained regarding a moderate freedom of the press. Once a more general portrait of the politics of the 1841–1844 government has been drawn, Tornel's own actions will be looked at in detail: his role in the 1841 Triangular Revolt and the 1842 closure of Congress, and the proposals he promoted in terms of supporting the regular army and promoting education with relation to the 1843 limitation of suffrage.

While *santanista* discourse and rhetoric was all about proclaiming unconditional support of church privileges and the church's moral importance in society, in practice they demanded a series of loans in exchange for that support and found different ways to ensure that the church financed the resurrection of the army. Therefore, the *santanistas* were like most other factions in that they were intolerant Roman Catholics; they were like the traditionalists in the way they paid lip-service to defending church privileges, but they were like the radicals in the way they believed in expropriating church property if the financial needs of the state and the army demanded such a measure to be taken. In brief, although they appeared to share the views of the traditionalists in their rallying to the defense of church privileges in 1834 and in 1847, it nevertheless remains true that the amortization laws that provoked the proclerical backlashes of Cuernavaca (1834) and *los polkos* (1847), albeit effected by radical administrations, were originally consented to by the *santanistas*. In other words, the *santanistas* blackmailed the church in both 1834 and 1847 by allowing a radical administration to assault church property. By ensuring that the church promised financial support in exchange for the overthrow of those radical administrations they had assisted in their rise to power in the first place, the *santanistas* secured significant loans from the church. Therefore, the *santanistas*, like the radicals, believed that it was the church's obligation to finance the state and the army. However, unlike the radicals who openly declared their intention to assault the church, the *santanistas* succeeded in obtaining large church grants by making a slightly less drastic form of amortization a prerequisite of their defense of church privileges. In 1834, the church agreed to provide Santa Anna with between 30,000 and 40,000 pesos monthly over a period of six months, in the wake of the Plan of

Cuernavaca. In 1847, this arrangement was repeated. After the revolt of the *polkos*, Santa Anna forced Gómez Farías to resign "in exchange for a Church loan of 1,500,000 pesos," which was added to a further 20 million pesos the church had previously agreed to cover with its properties.[11] Although in 1841, the *santanistas* were not in a position to blackmail the church in the same way they had done in 1834, or in the same way that they would do in 1847, their attitude toward the church remained the same. To quote Costeloe, in 1843, Santa Anna's message "seemed to be that the army, personified by himself, would impose order and protect the status of the Church and all those other economically and socially privileged groups, but at a price, and that price was to be ever-rising cash contributions. There was no attempt on his part to negotiate any deal or pact as Paredes had advised. In short, if they wanted his protection, they were going to have to pay for it."[12] This philosophy, which granted greater importance to the needs of the army and the treasury than to those of the church or the great landowners, continued to be formulated in the *santanista* newspaper *La Palanca* in 1849. With evident populist overtones, *La Palanca* on 3 May 1849 stated that "if the clergy [like] . . . the rich, using [religious] pretexts hope[d] to [prevent] . . . any reforms from taking place . . . forcing the proletariat to continue suffering as a natural slave," they were inciting the masses to revolt.[13]

Ignacio Trigueros's economic reforms during his term as minister of the exchequer (1841–1844) illustrate only too well the extent to which the *santanistas* were particularly pragmatic in terms of the economic policies they supported. Trigueros's own down-to-earth approach mirrored the way that the *santanistas* and the church struck a pragmatic relationship where they conditionally supported each other, the state vowing to protect the church in exchange for ready supplies of cash. In terms of economic policy, Trigueros carried out a rather complex balancing act between free market economics and committed protectionism. As Torcuato Di Tella has noted recently, the interests of the businessmen and manufacturers of the states of Mexico, Puebla, and Veracruz were in themselves opposed and contradictory. For example, while the commercial interests of Puebla tended to be favored by protectionist legislation, the opposite was the case with Veracruz. However, even then, it was impossible to argue a case for imposing different economic strategies for each separate state or department when in Veracruz itself, for instance, the cotton and tobacco growers were threatened by foreign competition and would benefit from some state protection. As Lucas Alamán was already aware in 1830–1832, and as Trigueros went on to discover in 1841–1844, for a political coalition to survive, it needed to be able to please the conflicting needs of the key states of Puebla and Veracruz. In other words, "it was often necessary to combine, or assuage, both protectionist and free-trader interests, a next to impossible task."[14]

Under Trigueros the following protectionist reforms were put into effect:

Mexican mints were established in Chihuahua and Oaxaca; the colonial monopoly over the production of cards, salt, and sulfur was reestablished; and all import taxes were raised by 20 percent. In contrast, his laissez-faire reforms included establishing a British mint in Zacatecas, offering all railway construction contracts to British firms, authorizing Sres. Aguero González y Compañía to import up to 60,000 quintals of string, and imposing a new tax on the export of all national produce.

What characterized the economic policy of the *santanista* 1841–1844 government was the vigor with which it attempted to raise funds for the treasury. Trigueros was particularly thorough in the way he systematically sought different ways of raising existing taxes or inventing new ones. He imposed a whole range of new taxes on "urban properties, rustic properties, industrial establishments . . . salaries, professions . . . luxury items, and a monthly direct tax of half a real."[15] The amortization tax went up 15 percent; indirect taxes were imposed on the sale of cart wheels, the use of outside drainpipes, and postal services; direct taxes were extended to include a monthly contribution (to be paid in advance) from all established businesses in the country, the notorious *alcabala* (a direct tax on any form of sale); and on 20 April 1843 the richest proprietors of the nation were forced to pay an emergency tax that in just nine days raised 270,000 pesos. There was also a strong push to promote the growth of Mexico's nascent industry, and the Banco de Avío was replaced with a new Junta de Industria.[16]

According to Tenenbaum, "the [santanista] tax reform created a system not that different from any modern tax system," which meant that the *santanistas* succeeded in raising in both 1843 and 1844 the highest income for this period through taxation (19.6 million pesos in 1843 and 20.6 million pesos in 1844). If the *santanista* economic project failed in the end, it was because such a tax system, in order to function properly, required a well-organized and efficient administrative system, which did not exist at the time; and the spectacular rise in taxes was counterbalanced by an even more dramatic rise in expenses, which meant that at the end of the day, the nation's deficit continued to increase regardless of the large sums of money the state was raising through taxation.[17]

An analysis of the *santanistas'* economic program shows that they were determined to impose a new, effective tax system and that they believed, like the radicals, in creating a strong state. However, their program was also characterized by its pragmatism. Where local commercial interests were better served by free market economics, there was an attempt to pursue laissez-faire policies, and where the opposite was the case, protectionist proposals were supported. Above all, what predominated was the view that it was necessary to create more taxes and that both the church and the landed classes needed to pay more in order to rescue the national economy.

As for the freedom of the press, reflecting Tornel and Bocanegra's own noted evolved view on the need to control it, although the *Bases Orgánicas* went on to support it (with conditions and reservations), in practice, the 1841–1844 administration was characterized by its use of censorship. Not surprisingly, once the *santanistas* consolidated their hold on power in 1841, they exercised some censorship over publications that criticized their administration or that, in their view, abused the freedom of the press that, in theory, they claimed to believe in. Thus, on 14 January 1843, the law of 8 April 1839 (which heavily fined those editors or printers who were found guilty of disturbing the public peace with their publications in the Department of Mexico) was reinstated. On 16 January, it was given national status, applying to the entire republic. Newspapers such as *El Cosmopolita*, *El Restaurador*, and *El Voto Nacional* closed down. The editors of *El Siglo XIX* suspended the publication of their newspaper for two weeks in protest. Although a group of federalists attempted to make up for the sudden absence of an opposition newspaper by creating *El Estandarte Nacional*, the government forced them to close it down only a few days after it was launched.[18] From this it can be assumed that although the *Bases Orgánicas* guaranteed the freedom of the press (except in religious matters) on paper, the reality was that the *santanistas* became increasingly heavy-handed with newspapers that were critical of their politics and policies.

The *santanista* administration of 1841–1844 was also characterized by the way it reformed the army and promoted education. It was Tornel, in both cases, as minister of war and president of the Compañía Lancasteriana, who was mainly responsible for these two all-important aspects of the regime. The attention the *santanistas* gave the army was one that clearly differentiated their political proposals from those of the other factions— the radicals, the moderates, and the traditionalists. As for education, although all of the factions would in one way or another defend its importance in improving the state of society,[19] it was the *santanistas*, in 1841– 1844, who would, perhaps surprisingly, turn out to be the political group that did the most for promoting it during the early national period. However, before Tornel's roles as minister of war and educationalist are analyzed in depth, it is worth noting the ways in which he had become Santa Anna's very own particularly adept conspirator and manipulator.

TORNEL, MASTER MANIPULATOR

As the decline of the Bustamante government entered its final stages, Tornel went back to conspiring. Having written the condemnatory *Discurso* of 1840 and *La muerte de Cicerón*, he threw himself into the conspiracy that led to Bustamante's downfall. Although he continued to find time to write erudite articles such as "La providencia en el Nuevo Mundo" and "Historia. Bosquejo de la Administración de los Incas en el Perú," and went on to translate a Mr. Courtin's treatise on eloquence as well as Byron's Napolitan stanzas, Tornel also started to make time to prepare for the forthcoming overthrow of Bustamante.[20] On 12 April 1841, Tornel, representing the tobacco growers of Xalapa and Orizaba (*diputaciones de cosecheros de tabaco de las cuidades de Jalapa y Orizaba*), officially presented their complaints and reservations against Bustamante's regime to the Senate. It can be deduced from the fact that he was speaking in the name of the landowners of the province of Veracruz that he had spent some time back in his home town. It would therefore not be farfetched to suggest that he must have seen Santa Anna in Xalapa during this time. More significant, there was a threat implicit in his *Manifestación* that signaled to Congress that if Bustamante did not give way to their demands, his days as president could very well be numbered. The landowners would not tolerate becoming "slaves without a will of their own or rights," and "an orderly society" which should come with "impartial laws," could easily be altered if the Senate did not oppose the plans that favored foreign companies.[21]

By the summer of 1841, Bustamante was under attack from all sides. Finding that the time was finally right to intervene, after repeated consultations with various delegations of cotton planters and tobacco farmers, Santa Anna joined the so-called Triangular Revolt in August. The province of Veracruz, homeland of Tornel and Santa Anna, immediately rallied to Santa Anna's support, with the authorities of Xalapa, Orizaba, and Córdoba asking Santa Anna to back their demands.[22] Although the revolt was mainly led by Santa Anna, Paredes y Arrillaga, and Valencia, Tornel was not far from the scene. In fact, he acted as Santa Anna's representative at the Hacienda de los Morales, on 29 September, during the negotiations that followed Bustamante's downfall and was one of the authors of the *Bases de Tacubaya*, which on 6 October awarded Santa Anna, in Richard Pakenham's words, "almost absolute power."[23]

In recompense for his unfailing friendship and for having, no doubt, succeeded in guaranteeing the financial support of the wealthy landowners of Veracruz, Tornel became minister of war on 11 October 1841. It is evident that he also profited financially from their victory, purchasing the Hacienda de San Juan de Dios, in Chalco, for 25,500 pesos in May 1842.[24] However, Santa Anna's power was not as yet as absolute as he would have expected it to be. As Costeloe points out, he "was required under the *Bases de Tacubaya* to make arrangements for the election of a national congress to begin its sessions in June 1842, its principal business being to draw up a new constitution. It is reasonable to suppose that Santa Anna did not look with favour on the idea of another congress."[25] The result of the elections came as a blow the moment it became evident, on 11 April 1842, that Congress was to be made up mainly of federalists who would clearly be hostile to the *santanistas'* autocratic style of government. Letters came and went between Santa Anna, Paredes y Arrillaga, Valencia, and Tornel discussing the actions that could be taken to reverse a situation that Tornel considered had arisen partly because they had not been vigilant and because "their attempts to intervene were clumsy and too late."[26]

The actions carried out to dissolve Congress were drastic and characteristic of the resolution the *santanistas* were starting to show when it was imperative to consolidate autocratic rule. It comes as no surprise that a great deal of the groundwork needed to achieve this was covered by Tornel. On 11 April, with a fabricated allegation of insubordination, he arrested General José Joaquín de Herrera, a well-respected federalist of the time, who had become one of the leaders of the moderates. The protests that followed meant that Herrera was eventually released. However, the resolution of the *santanistas* remained unchanged, even if the tactics that were used were different as a result. Following a parallel strategy to that adopted in 1834, the *santanistas* and the military took to starting revolts throughout the country soon after Congress met in June. Tornel not only worked hard to encourage these *pronunciamientos*, in the same way he had done in 1834, but actively led the revolt of the garrison of Huejotzingo, on 10 June 1842, demanding the dissolution of Congress and the creation of a *Junta de Notables*.[27] Once the situation was ripe for direct intervention, to use Josefina Zoraida Vázquez's words, Santa Anna "requested the election of Nicolás Bravo as interim president and the unenviable task of dissolving congress was left to him."[28] Congress was closed in December. Tornel again ensured that any protest was silenced by arresting politicians such as Melchor Alvarez, José Mariano Michelena, José Ignacio Ormachea, Cirilo Gómez Anaya, and Gregorio Gómez, with the pretext that they had indirectly recognized the independence of Texas[29] and by punishing journalists who were in any way deemed to be subversive.[30]

While Santa Anna retired to the quiet life on his hacienda Manga de Clavo, Tornel became a member of the Junta de Notables whose main task was to draft the new constitution. According to Costeloe, "although [Santa Anna] did not return in person to the capital until 5 March, he maintained his usual vigilance, and with Tornel . . . was able to direct affairs from his country estate."[31] On 13 June, the new constitution, known as the *Bases Orgánicas*, was adopted with all due ceremony, and in Callcott's words, "For the promulgation of the new instrument, Santa Anna of course came out of his retirement. With much éclat he appeared as master of ceremonies."[32] The new Consejo de Gobierno included personalities such as Gabriel Valencia, José María Bocanegra, Carlos María de Bustamante, Crecencio Rejón, and Tornel. Their power was consolidated in the buildup to the inauguration of the new constitution, by Tornel's discovery of a conspiracy to overthrow their government, and his immediate action, which was to arrest Manuel Gómez Pedraza and Mariano Riva Palacio in the spring of 1843. In fact, whether they were involved or not in a conspiracy, most of the leaders of the moderate liberal federalists "were kept imprisoned until the constitution was sanctioned," giving no opportunity to the opposition to voice its dissent.[33]

In brief, by the early 1840s Tornel had become one of Santa Anna's most useful and influential players in the capital. Not only was his eloquent prose of great assistance to the *caudillo* in the way that Tornel served him as a particularly articulate and persuasive propagandist; not only was he essential to Santa Anna in the way that he was there to inform the *caudillo* of events in the capital whenever he decided to retire to Veracruz: he was also crucial to Santa Anna's success in the way that he was a hard-working conspirator and manipulator. It was Tornel's links with the landowners of Veracruz that led to their agreeing to finance the Triangular Revolt that overthrew Bustamante. It was Tornel who orchestrated and coordinated the *pronunciamientos* that went on to "legitimize" the closure of Congress in 1842. And it was Tornel who, based in the capital, ensured that the opponents of the regime were either imprisoned or silenced. More than "Santa Anna's butler (*lacayo*)" as Mora called him, Tornel had become his master manipulator in the capital by the early 1840s.[34] Tornel was also instrumental to Santa Anna in the way that he gave *santanismo* its very own ideological voice. Tornel became one of the main ideologues of the *santanistas* in the way that, as minister of war, he turned their defense of the army into an early example of what became in the twentieth century, in the words of Brian Loveman and Thomas Davies, the militaristic philosophy of "antipolitics,"[35] and in the way that he gave a strong populist slant to the extraordinary educational reforms for which he was responsible.

TORNEL, MINISTER OF WAR

In Tornel's 1844 ministerial report, after three years of being in power, he made it more than apparent that he was deeply satisfied with the progress that had been made in the army. Regarding education within the military profession, three years of uninterrupted work in the ministry meant that he had been able to ensure personally the implementation of his reforms.[36] The schools he had talked of as a desirable aim in 1835 were now a concrete part of military life to which he could refer in the present tense: "A regular school is for the Mexican army a good, liberal and philosophical plan; the chosen means by which it has been established and developed have been appropriate and effective."[37]

The only improvements he considered could be made to the system were relatively minor. He stated that their methodology could be revised; that it would be worth finding out whether the teachers were all capable abecedarians, that it would also be recommended to find a means of ensuring that time was not wasted; and that one would hope that all instructors followed the glorious example of the ex–deputy director of the school who was now involved in even greater concerns of public interest.[38] The fact remained that after three years with Tornel at the head of the armed forces, everything possible was being done "to achieve perfection in primary education."[39]

This same sense of achievement and fulfillment applied to the education of the corps of engineers. In fact, there was more reason for him to be satisfied with the improvements that had been carried out in this force, as it had been the one to suffer most directly from the previous years of wars and revolts. In March 1839 there were only five students. In subsequent years, once he had returned to assume the ministry of war, the number of students had risen to 234. They had a good pass rate as well; 203 of their students had gone on to become officers. There were currently 62 students in the process of taking their exams, showing very promising work. The exams taken in December 1843 had been highly satisfactory. Tornel was confident: "In the years to come this national creation will provide even more abundant and reasoned fruits, and it will be considered one of the glories of independent Mexico."[40]

The only branch of the army, in fact, that had not benefited from Tornel's reformism was the medical corps. Whereas in 1839, at a time of deep crisis, he had been able to produce a satisfactory report on the reforms that had revitalized it, in 1844, when there had been the time and the continuity to allow such reforms to flourish, the opposite had been the case: "All the attempts and efforts of the legislature and the government to reform this corps have by one fault or another come to nothing, and our soldiers continue to lack that necessary assistance which they so deserve as they shed their blood in defence of the nation during campaigns." He offered no explanation. His concern was nevertheless expressed in the same usual terms of disappointment and disgust, and he reiterated the need to rescue this all-important and neglected corps. He stated that the government had succeeded in establishing the law of 6 August 1836 once more, as it had been cancelled on 25 February 1843, and hoped that this would help the medical corps to recover. Although he deplored the lack of attention given to the medical corps, nevertheless there were still working hospitals, where there had not been any only ten years earlier.[41] Where it was necessary to overcome this neglect with a certain degree of urgency was out in the desert lands of the north. Soldiers who were wounded in the constant skirmishes that took place against the Comanche and the Apache had to be attended by any nearby settlers. The divisions that departed to face the hardships of a campaign were still in desperate need of doctors and nurses who were prepared to go with them. Tornel emphasized again the urgency with which Congress must address this problem:

This is an evil which requires an immediate and effective remedy, because it is painful and a matter of concern to the troops who suffer the fatigues and hardships of service, that they lack the adequate assistance. Specifically in the case of those divisions who march to fight it is fundamental that they are provided with a cohort from the medical corps, with the adequate number of surgeons, first aid kits and all the necessary medical instruments to ensure that our troops can be cured.[42]

The root of all this evil, according to Tornel, was the same as it had been in 1835: lack of funds. In Mexico City's General Hospital, patients were not being attended adequately because doctors were not being paid regularly. There was a very damaging moratorium in the payment of their wages. Tornel hoped that by handing the doctors' wages over to the director of the medical corps to give to them on his obligatory daily round of visits, further bureaucratic delays could be avoided, thus making their pay readily available.

As for the internal conflicts the army had been involved in between 1841 and 1844, these had been minor. Although there had been skirmishes in Yucatán, Sonora, and the south of Mexico, and the revived campaign in Texas was still consuming lives and forces, these had been years of peace compared to the previous decade. Tornel's 1844 ministerial report clearly reflected this. He could afford the time to look back and refer his audience in Congress to the report he had delivered in 1835: "It was ten years ago now, that standing in this august building, reading another report, I insisted on proving the need for an army." He remained convinced of this need. Moreover, he claimed that had there not been "a more or less organized force," Mexico would have disintegrated either from its internal conflicts or as a result of the French Pastry War. He was full of praise for the army, which "in spite of the fact that it has not yet been possible to raise it to a state of absolute perfection, due to the continuous civil conflicts Mexico has suffered, [the army] has been loyal to its mother-country, has gone to look for its enemies in remote and deserted frontiers, has marched to the extremes of the republic, and is always ready to expose itself to danger."[43]

Regarding the campaign in Texas, one of Tornel's priorities on becoming minister of war in 1841 had been to resume the war to recover it. In his 1844 account of the events, he argued that only in 1836 was there a serious plan to send a second expedition to regain Texas: "which failed for causes and reasons which remain incomprehensible." After that, several other conflicts had distracted the attention of the army, and once the government was handed over to the Bustamante administration of 1839–1841, "There was not even the thought by then of launching another offensive. . . . The cause of the nation was so badly defended that it was thought . . . that [Texas] had been lost." According to Tornel it was only once the *Bases de Tacubaya* replaced Bustamante with Santa Anna and his interim presidents that it became a main concern of the government to recover Texas. With Tornel at the head of the Ministry of War, "aid of all kinds was immediately sent; the number of forces was increased considerably, those that existed were reorganized, and they were all made to advance to the frontier." On 5 March 1842, the first fruits of these endeavors became apparent. General Rafael Vázquez succeeded in taking San Antonio Béjar. According to Tornel, the enemy started to retreat after this victory "and to fear constantly for its safety." On 7 July, Colonels Antonio Canales and Cayetano Montero defeated the enemy at Lipantitlán. Moreover, from June to December, General Woll kept the Texans at bay in their attempts to settle in the lands near Béjar, south of the border. On 26 December 1842 in a battle between the Texan settlers and General Ampudia's troops in the town of Mier, in which the Mexican soldiers, in spite of the torrential rain, "marched and fought in the mud, [and] defended their positions with extraordinary valor," the Texans were repulsed. According to Tornel, it was thanks to these valiant efforts that since December 1843, discussions were under way concerning the future of Texas between the Mexicans and the Texans in the town of Sabinas; and Tornel hoped that after these three years of renewed combat in which they had demonstrated what they were capable of, the Texans would reconsider their position, because "the government knows of no other rule than that it is its duty to always and forever save the rights and honor of the nation."[44]

As for the conflict in Yucatán, the beginning of the troubles broke out in May 1839, when some local *caudillos* started a revolt that proclaimed the province's independence. Although this particular revolt was crushed almost as soon as it began, it served, in Tornel's words, as the spark that set the region on fire. On 18 February 1840, the garrison in Mérida proclaimed the independence of Yucatán, and by June, the separatist fervor that was triumphing in Yucatán spread to Tabasco. Bustamante's administration did not find the means, the resources, or the will to confront the Yucatecan crisis. It despatched three hundred undisciplined men who simply joined the rebels on arrival. Tornel, in 1844, asked with a certain amount of rhetorical theatricality:

What did the government then in office do to remedy the loss of a province which was so advantageously located in the Republic? Did it attempt to use the many resources of politics; did it talk to the *yucatecos* with the language of reason; did it even propose possible means of reconciliation and compromise? Did it prefer to use the resources of brutal force, opportunely employing the army with which the nation had trusted it, to maintain the integrity of its territory?[45]

The answer to his questions was clearly that they had done nothing at all. Action was taken only once the *Bases de Tacubaya* awarded Santa Anna the presidency and Tornel returned to the Ministry of War. Initially, several attempts were made to end the troubles through negotiation. From the outset, it is evident that Tornel knew that it would be a difficult war to win considering that Yucatán is a dense, tropical rainforest, where a regiment of men who were neither used to the climate nor acquainted with the terrain would be clearly at a disadvantage and would almost certainly fail. However, these attempts at negotiation failed and, on 31 May 1842, the Yucatecan secessionists defied the Mexican government by adamantly rejecting all calls for reunification. Given no other choice but war, Tornel was prepared to adopt whatever measures were required to crush the Yucatecans: "Given that the political horizon of Yucatán was dark, and that the government's hopes of reaching a happy end through such generous concessions had been dissipated; the thought of war was not only justified, it was an essential necessity to defend the nation's honor and to protect its rights, giving at the same time an energetic and worthy lesson which will avoid the consequences of a bad example being set."[46]

On 22 June 1842, the Margarita left Veracruz with the first of what would be many expeditions to end the Yucatecan revolt. Not all of these expeditions were successful or even returned. The pamphlet entitled *Desahogo de D. José María Tornel, bajo la firma de José López de Santa Anna*, printed in Mérida in 1843, exemplifies the extent to which the Yucatecans were convinced that they would win the war, as well as the way they viewed Tornel's attempts to suppress their revolt:

Another surrender! Holy Brígida! . . . It is not surprising that at this point the minister's bile started to boil; it is not surprising that he has snapped. . . . He calls us *traitors, ignorant people, insurgents*, and we cannot remember whether he even said we were heretics. . . . In spite of everything, Your Excellency will have seen that your forecasts that the army would surrender a second time have been proven wrong. . . . The government forces left at full steam and thank God went back to where they came from.[47]

Nevertheless, at the time of his report in January 1844, it appeared as if an end to the Yucatán war was possible. A new set of concessions had been drafted on 15 December 1843 and were awaiting their approval from the Yucatecan *caudillos*. Tornel liked to be optimistic: "The reincorporation of the province of Yucatán into the community of the republic is an event which will be written in the brightest page of the provisional government's history."[48] Peace was in fact established but did not last long. In 1847 the Maya rose and fought their way across Yucatán, driving the whites out of the peninsula. This second war, however, was of a different nature from the one Tornel had had to contend with as minister of war. While the first war was mainly led by the Creoles in Yucatán who wanted power to rest with them rather than with someone in a capital 1,510 kilometers away,

the Maya uprising in 1847 had all the characteristics of a social and political revolution as well as those of a racial war.

During his years in office, however, he did have to make decisions on
policy regarding the caste wars in Sonora and the south of Mexico. In
Sonora the frequent raids perpetrated by the Yaqui and Mayo Indians
meant that the Mexican settlers of the region were in a constant state of
emergency. Adding to the turmoil that arose from these confrontations,
Manuel María Gándara and his brother Juan became the leaders of an
army of Yaqui Indians in 1842 and started to terrorize the communities of
the region, leaving a trail of destruction, "with deeds that are so barbarous
and atrocious that one cannot believe that they were actually carried out
in this century of benevolence and philanthropy." Tornel responded with
vigor, sending men and ammunition. However, even though the government troops inflicted severe casualties on the Yaqui armies of the Gándara
brothers, Tornel could see no end to the conflict in 1844, because "these
triumphs and those that will follow do not and will not solve the problem
in Sonora, for the turbulent and bloodthirsty Gándara has started a savage
caste war, thus killing any hopes of there being a speedy end to such a
scandalous extermination." Although he vowed to double the men, the
resources, and the efforts to bring peace to the region, the only way he
really believed the troubles could be brought to an end was through organized colonization.[49]

In the south of Mexico, following an indigenous revolt in March 1842
in the town of Tecoanapa, Indian uprisings became rife. There were important revolts in Ayahualulco, Acapulco, Chilapa, Hueycantenango,
Tlapa, Huetano, Quechultenango, Iscatepec, Tosaltepec, Zochicalco, San
Miguelito, Zochitepec, Tulantengo, Almolaya, Santo Tomás, Guamusti-
tlán, Chiusingo, Patlicha, and Ostocingo, all in the *departamentos* of Oaxaca, Puebla, Michoacán, and even Mexico. Although Generals Juan
Álvarez, Nicolás Bravo (until he became interim president), and Luis Pin-
zón, with the support of many other outstanding colonels and officers of
the Mexican army, endeavored time and again to repress the Indians, when
one revolt was crushed, another one started. As Tornel was to say in 1844:
"The government has repressed by force all of these excesses. . . . However,
I must confess that the fire is still very much alive, and that although it is
covered with ashes, all it needs is an unexpected gush of wind to rekindle
the flames and the fire will then spread to the south east of the province
of Mexico, and perhaps even further beyond." His recommendation was
that they ensured all insurrections were crushed immediately and that "the
punishment must be as quick as awards are quick to be given for acts of
valor, honor and virtue."[50]

It is evident from his reactions to all of these conflicts that, with the
exception of the Yucatán war in its initial stages, he was no believer in
appeasement. He believed that an immediate and vigorous response, as

soon as it was known that there was any form of trouble, was the only way to achieve a peace that was permanent and that could effectively protect the properties of the landowning and proprietary classes. The zeal with which he ensured that the Mexican army was constantly safeguarding the peace and order of the republic and the interests of these classes gained him the respect of his political adversaries to the extent that he was asked to serve as minister of war even by somebody as improbable as Mariano Paredes y Arrillaga.

Although he constantly lamented the use of force, he did not fail to point out that it was fundamental for democratic life that the country benefited from the advantages of a healthy, peaceful, and stable situation, which was, after all, what the army was hoping to achieve through its ceaseless exploits. Moreover, he was convinced that the army was not only the guarantee of democracy; it was also the most democratic of all institutions in a republic: "The most democratic part of a republican nation is the army which guards its frontiers, repels the invasion of foreign enemies and which ensures that the peace and safety of the country remain undisturbed."[51]

Moreover, after three years of relative peace in which his system of recruitment had been given time to develop, certain results were clearly visible, albeit not to the extent that would have been expected. In the infantry there were 20,700 men—8,378 more than in October 1841. In the cavalry there were 8,693 men—3,663 more than in 1841. Although he was hoping to have an infantry of 52,983 men and a cavalry of 19,940 men, he was pleased to see the increases during his time in office.

Many of the problems he had hoped to cure with his 1835 reforms nevertheless remained unresolved. His lottery system of recruitment, "the most liberal and republican system," was not working as he had intended it to: "The lottery finds in the Mexican Republic a constant and open opposition, which has not been appeased either by the philosophy of its legislators or by the active efforts of the governments." The major problem was that the local authorities continued to accept the appeals for exemption from those "useful and hardworking men" among their acquaintances with whom they sympathized, exempting them from doing their military service. On the other hand, they continued to send "beggars, depraved individuals and criminals" to swell the ranks of an army that was meant to be made up of all of Mexico's sons. Tornel exclaimed, "How can we expect the Mexican army to be a paragon of virtue and morality when it is made up of the scum of the people?" Desertion remained as much of a problem as it had been in 1835. Tornel asked the local authorities to recruit "good citizens" and to prevent criminals from infecting the army, giving them the "prostituted title of defenders." What was apparent was that in war and in peace, the system of recruitment Tornel had designed in 1835 was still not working in 1844.[52]

Waddy Thompson's recollections of the Mexican army in 1843 are certainly worth noting here. In terms of discipline, he believed that "the inequality between disciplined and undisciplined troops is estimated by military men as one to five," making a mockery of Tornel's attempts to enforce discipline and instruction on all regular soldiers. Regarding the system of recruitment as it was practiced in reality rather than as Tornel had intended it to be:

The soldiers of the Mexican army are generally collected by sending out *recruiting* detachments into the mountains, where they hunt the Indians in their dens and caverns, and bring them in chains to Mexico; there is scarcely a day that droves of these miserable and more than half naked wretches are not seen thus chained together and marching through the streets to the barracks, where they are scoured and then dressed in a uniform made of linen cloth or of serge, and are occasionally drilled.[53]

Desertions were to continue into the next two decades in such a way that it comes as no surprise that Ignacio Altamirano's novel *El Zarco*, one of the best exponents of the nineteenth-century novel in Mexico, was about an army of deserters, *los plateados*, "[who] had organized themselves into parties of a hundred, two hundred and even five hundred men . . . who roamed the province, living off the land, imposing high taxes on the *haciendas* and the villages, establishing tolls in the roads and practising kidnaps every day; in other words, the kidnapping of people they did not release unless they received a very large ransom."[54] In the words of Olivera and Crété, "Discipline was poor; desertion commonplace."[55]

Tornel's failure was highlighted when war broke out with the United States in 1846. It might have been presumed, taking into account his intentions and the results they were meant to achieve, that after approximately nine years of his active involvement in the Ministry of War, the outcome of the war would be different. Regardless of the increased numbers of emergency militias, of the constant endeavors to drill, train, and prepare Mexico's soldiers and civilians for war, General Winfield Scott and his comparatively small army in 1847, succeeded in defeating

the whole Mexican army of (at the beginning) thirty-odd thousand men—posted, always, on chosen positions, behind entrenchments, or more formidable defences of nature and art; killed or wounded, of that number, more than 7,000 officers and men; taken 3,730 prisoners, one seventh officers, including 13 generals, of whom 3 had been presidents of this republic; captured more than 20 colors and standards, 75 pieces of ordinance, besides 57 wall-pieces, 20,000 small arms, and immense quantity of shots, shells, powder, etc.[56]

Nevertheless, from the perspective of 1844, Tornel appeared to have made significant progress with his reforms, and it remained equally clear that he was hoping to reform the army further. Successful in the end or not, what becomes clear is that Tornel's endeavors to professionalize the army, educate it, and improve the soldiers' conditions were consistent enough to ensure that the military became Santa Anna's most faithful and important pillar of support after 1835. The success of *santanismo* as a political ideology, paired with its strong commitment to defending the regular army's institutional interests, was key to Santa Anna's repeated rise to power and, by default, Tornel's own successful career, but also to the emergence of a corporate military identity among the high-ranking officers of the period.

This was achieved through Tornel and Santa Anna's presentation of themselves and, by association the army, as defenders of an antipolitical and patriotic movement. Bocanegra, as a *santanista*, was forceful in presenting the view that "the crises our mother country has suffered . . . have resulted . . . from the ambitions, clashes and recklessness of our parties." Political parties were thus capable of creating feuds, recriminations, and upheavals, provoking the kind of divisions and revolutions that could quite easily end "with the better established nations," without taking into consideration either "the well-being of a newborn nation" or that fragile independence that was threatened at all times: "That is how blind the party spirit is!"[57] Echoing Bocanegra's condemnation of party politics, Tornel and Santa Anna endeavored to present themselves and the army as belonging to a national movement that was outside or above party interests.

Santa Anna's own autobiography is exemplary of the way he depicted his actions as having been selfless and patriotic. He argued that he preferred "the sweet aspects of family life, with no other distraction than my own affairs," and yet he had sacrificed his quiet retirement and led the army, whether it was against foreign invaders or a "despotic" government, because he had been invited to intervene time and again, and he had felt it was his patriotic duty to do so. The following lines from his memoirs illustrate this point clearly: "I believed that it was my honor to lead the avant-garde of the defenders of the Mexican nation," "I could not be indifferent to the pleas of my fellow-countrymen," "with a love of the *Patria* deeply engraved in my heart since I was of the tenderest age . . . I ran frantically to the place of combat," "My voice would then be confused with the roar of the cannons: there where it was imperative to defy death, for her, there was I. . . . My mother-country has always been my idol; and her soldiers, my brothers."[58]

At a time when the concept of nationhood was as yet unclear and when many Mexicans felt that they owed their loyalty more to their province or region rather than to the new and abstract concept of Mexico as a single and indivisible country, Santa Anna and Tornel's patriotic rhetoric was probably not as appealing to the troops as they believed it to be. However, it can be presumed that it had a certain resonance among the high-ranking officers who belonged to the generation that had embraced the cause of independence in 1821. If in France in the post-Napoleonic years memory became militarized with the romanticization of the past war experience,[59] in Mexico there was a similar idealization of the war of independence that inevitably paid tribute to the patriotism of the military. As can be seen in the annual ministerial reports of the Ministry of War throughout the period, the chambers of deputies and senators were reminded time and again that they owed their independence to the army.[60] If there was not a consciousness of patriotism among the troops, there was one among the high-ranking officers. In the same way that they congratulated themselves on being the authors of independence, they also prided themselves on being the one institution that could safeguard Mexico's national integrity against any form of foreign aggression. In the midst of this romantic notion that the officers belonged to a privileged elite that had been responsible for the existence of their *patria*, the *santanistas'* particular rhetoric was effective.

More significant, Tornel and Santa Anna were able to turn this notion of patriotic responsibility into one of political responsibility, which had as its premise that the army did not belong to the factionalist and divided world of the civilian politicians. The army was above politics. Its sole concern was Mexico rather than the political success of one faction or another. This belief, defined as antipolitics, was one of the immediate results of early military professionalization in the Hispanic world. In Spain, for instance, one of the military bulletins argued in 1841 that "we cannot and will not say 'we are the state,' but we do say, 'We are the nation,' or if you prefer, 'the most pure part of the nation.' "[61] In cynical terms, this detachment from civilian politics or pose of nonalignment with any of the parties allowed the *santanistas* to claim that their uprisings and *pronunciamientos* were carried out for the sake of the nation rather than for themselves. However, it also appealed to a wide spectrum of high-ranking officers, traditionalists and moderates. There was a curious romantic dignity for professional officers in adopting this stance of political detachment or even political superiority. They intervened as an arbitrating force when civilian politicians reached a dead end, without, in theory, becoming sullied in the bickering inherent in constitutional debate. What is more, officers were justified in being proud that it had been thanks to them that independence had been achieved. Like Santa Anna, clearly the most popular general of the period, the army, associated with him, represented the *patria*, or, to echo the view of the Spanish officers, the "parte más pura de la patria."

Tornel was consistent in the way that he presented this view. Moreover, he stressed that the army was not a passive or isolated institution; its history, its story, was that of the country: "Its history is that of the politics of the nation to which it belongs."[62] Tornel's views on the army were a reflection of his views on politics and society. What he attempted to achieve as minister of war was not dissimilar to what he hoped to achieve in society. In summarizing the essence of his reforms and demands throughout his career as minister of war, the following points can be seen to emerge.

Tornel wanted Mexico to have (1) a large army made up of honorable, hard-working young men, that is, members of the middle class; (2) an army with fully qualified doctors and engineers who would contribute in assisting the civilian community with good hospitals and modern roadworks; (3) an army with educated and literate troops, instructed through the Lancasterian method of teaching; (4) an army with an effective system of pensions for the widows and orphans of the dead; and (5) a large and civilized army whose main priority would be to maintain law and order in Mexico and to protect its national integrity. These ideals were respected by the most influential core of the army. Evidence of this is that they stood behind Santa Anna and Tornel for most of this period. Once the *Santanista* party was formed in 1849, Tornel went on to stress that this antiparties platform was not just one upheld by the army, but by the *santanistas* as a whole, whether they were members of the military or civilians.

However, the army was supportive of the 1841–1844 government not only because of Tornel's reforms and patriotic ideology. It benefited considerably in financial terms from Tornel and Santa Anna's largesse. Vázquez Mantecón quite clearly states that one of the main reasons that the military supported Santa Anna time and again in spite of his many changes and misfortunes was that he always ensured, on rising to power, that they were rewarded: "The duration of the government depended on the loyalty of the military, and this in turn depended on a regular pay and the concession of multiple privileges."[63] One of the consequences was, as Waddy Thompson sharply pointed out, that "they have more than two hundred generals, most of them without commands."[64]

Tornel clearly aimed to please the military throughout his life. The fact that he was in a position of power more often than not following independence would appear to suggest that he succeeded in pleasing, at least for most of the time, those members of the military who had a voice in who was allowed to continue in government. Nevertheless, although Tornel ensured that the regular army was duly rewarded for its loyalty with prizes and promotions, on paper, he was consistent in his condemnation of such a practice. In his 1835 report he attacked the systems of promotions and prizes as they had developed since 1821. He considered that not only was it damaging to Mexico's frail economy to squander vital funds on awards and award-giving ceremonies, but also detrimental to military discipline. Furthermore, "so many posts of commanders and officers have been created that there is enough of them to form an army. Moreover, it is worth noting that with the exception of the glorious and national campaign of Tampico, these prizes, awarded with such prodigality, have not been given to reward the military merit of the soldiers. They have been bestowed for political reasons, and as a result the germ of civil war has been kept alive."[65] He condemned all promotions and prizes based on a soldier's questionable merits in fighting his own countrymen. The only truly honorable military feat accomplished after the war of independence was the successful repudiation of Barradas's expedition. To congratulate soldiers for courageously entering into combat for one party or another was morally wrong and encouraged further divisions and resentment among the armed forces whose sole function should be that of defending their national integrity from foreign aggression and not that of attacking members of their own Mexican family. They were in danger of perpetuating the opposition between the factions and granting continued motives for further revolts and uprisings.

Moreover, the ease with which prizes and promotions had been awarded meant that what were intended to be exceptional rewards for men who had carried out exceptional deeds in the name of the nation had lost all real sense of value. They had created a privileged class that, due to its lack of true merit, would appear to the people as a false meritocracy that would never be able to represent them or deserve their loyalty in times of war: "the crosses, braids and distinctions of these orders were seen by the people as frivolous attributions that together with the pomp of the uniforms and other adornments served but to dress up the privileged classes." Therefore, Tornel not only stressed that as a "philosophical and republican government" it was their obligation to prevent the creation of "military orders that form within the state a new privileged corps," alerting Congress to the fact that "the military aristocracy is the most dangerous one," but also proposed to forbid "from now on and forever, the granting of rewards for services carried out during civil wars."[66]

This was quite a drastic proposal, especially considering that it was coming from somebody who knew that it was not wise to upset the military. What is surprising is not only the proposal in itself but also the radical wording of it. Tornel was extremely emphatic in the way he condemned these privileges, using terms such as "the blind obsequiousness of preferences" to describe the inevitable consequence of allowing a select military class to develop, talking about their very respectable military decorations as if they had been completely debased and degraded. As if this were not enough, he also proposed that future prizes should not involve a pay raise or any other form of monetary gratification: "so that this does not mean a further cost to the public treasury." Future prizes were to be based exclusively on their moral value. Therefore, in 1835 Tornel recommended, as an incentive and a means of encouragement, the intangible award of due recognition and moral applause to those men who excelled in their military actions. He did, however, give himself some leeway in the wording of the actual *iniciativa*, which contained the essence of this proposal. In it he stated that "the government is entitled to award a distinction of honor to those soldiers whose actions deserve to be considered distinguished." If he needed to award prizes in the future that did not quite conform to the beliefs inherent in his proposal, the government had the right to make whatever decisions it thought appropriate to reward any outstanding feats the army might have accomplished. On 1 August that year he awarded, in person, prizes and other rewards to all of those soldiers who had displayed courage in resisting the call for Texan independence.[67] And these awards were being given at a time when the Texan campaign was in its early stages.

On 27 April 1836, he issued a circular incorporating the congressional decree sanctioned by José Justo Corro that established an order of merit for army and navy distinguished service. On 15 July, he followed this up by awarding funds to aid the families of soldiers who had been captured, wounded, or killed in the Texan campaign and provided further funds in his circular of 25 July. On 16 August, he clearly stated that all of the heroes who had fought in Texas would be awarded prizes and that if this had not happened yet, it was not the government's fault and would be corrected in time. On 13 March 1837, he addressed a letter to the minister of the exchequer, printed in the *Diario del Gobierno* three days later, demanding more money to be awarded to soldiers who had behaved admirably under the tight pressures of the rationing imposed by the war.

When he returned to assume the Ministry of War on 17 December 1838, he did not appear to hesitate in promoting all proposed incentives and means of encouragement. On 27 December, he allocated 50,000 pesos for the soldiers who were resisting the French blockade in Veracruz.[68] On 11 February 1839, he issued two circulars: one incorporated the congressional decree sanctioned by Bustamante, which ordered rewards for all soldiers who had participated in the action of 5 December in Veracruz, and the other approved the awarding of pensions to the widows and orphans of the deceased. And on 11 May, following Santa Anna's acceptance of the interim presidency, during Bustamante's campaign in Tamaulipas against Urrea, he ordered payments to be made to all military units in the capital.

In January 1844, Tornel offered a few insights into how he had approached the question of promotions and incentives during the three years he had been responsible for the ministry following the Triangular Revolt. To correct the problem he had condemned in 1835, of there being too many officers and *jefes* as a result of the prodigality of promotions awarded in the past, reflecting Thompson's previously mentioned comment, on 9 March 1842, he had presented a project, subsequently approved, that served to state in writing "the duties and attributions" of all ranks and classes in the army. Theoretically, outlining the duties of each rank would force those who were in possession of military sinecures to serve their country. However, in direct contrast with his 1835 views, he had also approved the "establishment of the cross of constancy which prizes and stimulates the servants of the nation" for their loyalty rather than any particular heroic feat carried out against a foreign aggressor. Nevertheless, in the conclusion to his 1844 report he stated that apart from having given the soldiers a larger army to serve in, an education, good training, better weapons, a pantheon for the martyrs of the mother country to rest in peace, and the prestige and honor of belonging to the Mexican army, he had helped them serve in a force in which prizes and decorations were not given for actions carried out during Mexico's civil wars: "This very government has forbidden awarding prizes and decorations for actions taken during the civil wars, offering with this decree alone a high lesson of morality that will not be lost because the Mexican heart always welcomes and nurtures the seeds of virtue."[69]

Therefore, in theoretical terms Tornel's views in 1844 appear to be consistent with those he expressed in 1835. In other words, prizes should be awarded only to men who courageously fought for Mexico against a foreign enemy. The fact that he prided himself on having abolished easy promotion and party-based prizes ten years after having initially proposed such a reform was a clever way of disguising the reality that he had in fact guaranteed the regular army's support by awarding them prizes and distinctions over the years, regardless of the rhetoric. It was Mora who argued quite forcefully (and perhaps quite rightly) that Tornel was mainly preoccupied with creating a privileged military aristocracy that indulged in self-congratulation and prize giving: "Among the projects of Don José Tornel, one of them was to create a legion of honor to reward the services (revolts) of our honorable soldiers. A legion of honor created by Tornel! Tell me, what does Tornel have in common with honor? These two ideas surely exclude each other! . . . Sad fate of Mexico to have ended up in such hands!!"[70]

TORNEL, THE EDUCATIONALIST

In addition to shaping the army (or, at least, the majority of its high-ranking officers) into an all-important bastion of *santanista* belief,[71] Tornel further contributed to Santa Anna's success by promoting education in a way no other general or politician did during the first national decades. Waddy Thompson, one of Tornel's fiercest critics, surprisingly attributed to him and praised him for the notable achievements made in the area of education:

I had not a servant during my residence in Mexico who did not read and write— neither very well, it is true, but quite as well, or better, than the same class in this country. I often observed the most ragged léperos, as they walked down the streets, reading the signs over the store doors. How this happens, I know not, unless it be the effect of Lancasterian schools, which are established all over the country, chiefly I think, through the instrumentality and exertions of General Tornel, a noble charity which should of itself cover a multitude of sins much greater than those his enemies impute to him.[72]

Thompson was conveying two important points. First, the development, progress, and success of the Lancasterian schools in Mexico was largely due to Tornel's lifelong dedication to promoting education among the less privileged sectors of society as well as among the wealthier classes. Second, this dedication was in itself a quality in his character that was recognized and respected at the time by even his most passionate enemies. The implication of this latter point is clearly that such a regard or consideration, if it existed, would have made his permanence in a position of power more tolerable to those who opposed him and what he represented. Moreover, if this was the case, it begs the question whether this commendable philanthropy was an expression of Tornel's character or whether it was in fact just another of his ploys to continue benefiting from the privileges of having a place at the top of the sociopolitical hierarchy. Regarding this last point, what will also be seen in the following pages is that the extraordinary educational boom experienced between 1841 and 1844 was an example of Tornel's (and the *santanistas'*) populist politics.

Nevertheless, regardless of these considerations, it was specifically Tornel's role in the area of education, in the first three decades following independence, that markedly differentiated him from all the other influential generals of the period. A brief outline of the other more well-known generals' exertions in the field of culture confirms this. Santa Anna prided himself on not reading books. Vicente Guerrero was barely literate. Guadalupe Victoria relied on Tornel to write his speeches. Gabriel Valencia was "an uneducated, somewhat primitive man."[73] Mariano Paredes y Arrillaga left school at the age of fifteen and never showed any interest in promoting education or culture. He was "proud, arrogant and extremely quarrelsome."[74] Anastasio Bustamante, although more cultured than Valencia or Paredes, was also a military man who showed little interest in encouraging education or culture. In spite of Alamán's efforts, it is significant that the one time the Compañía Lancasteriana was forced to close down, in 1832, was under Bustamante's presidency. Tornel, on the other hand, "enjoyed the reputation of an enlightened man";[75] he was that "tall, pale, impeccably dressed literary man . . . nicknamed Lorenzo the Magnificent";[76] "an eloquent orator and a very notable writer who was deservedly called a man of letters;"[77] he was "a lover and protector of the arts,"[78] a "learned writer,"[79] "who, having a great deal of classical learning,"[80] "devoted his leisure to aristocratic pastimes; translating Byron and writing plays."[81] Carlos María de Bustamante was prepared to say that he had "a beautiful way with words."[82] As Mario Moya Palencia rightly points out: "He was very different from the other generals."[83] In order to offer an accurate analysis of Tornel's role in the area of education, his different appointments and efforts will be divided into the following categories: the Colegio de San Ildefonso; the Instituto de Ciencias, Literatura y Artes; the

Compañía Lancasteriana; and the Colegio de Minería. (His endeavors to promote education in the army have already been noted.)

Tornel was a student at the Colegio de San Ildefonso, initially sent there by his father, Don Julián, and later interned as a prisoner by Viceroy Calleja. The Colegio de San Ildefonso, already considered as one of the best schools of further education in New Spain, became, with the Colegio de San Gregorio, the Eton or Harrow of Independent Mexico. However, although he never graduated and even spent two months in the colegio as a prisoner in 1814, Tornel became involved in the Colegio's curricular activities once independence was achieved. In 1825, there is a good example of this involvement. On 7 February, *El Aguila Mexicana* published an article he wrote recommending that certain changes be carried out to improve the organization and the criteria of the literary prizes the Colegio was planning to award that spring. Not only was he listened to, he was also invited to be one of the members of the jury who selected the winners of these prestigious prizes. On 17 April, the *Aguila* offered a detailed report of the ceremony. Guadalupe Victoria was present and delivered a speech. Tornel was also reported as having given an eloquent oration, and "in the evening a splendid array of lights decorated the building, in which a truly national party, which was very pleasurable to all of the lovers of good literature, ended with fireworks."[84] Bocanegra described this event in his *Memorias* because he was one of the writers who won a prize for his "dissertation in defence of the federal system."[85] Nevertheless, in comparison with his roles in the other three educational institutions, Tornel's involvement in the Colegio de San Ildefonso was minor, limited to guest appearances such as his participation in the literary prizes of 1825.

In the case of the Instituto de Ciencias, Literatura y Artes, Tornel's involvement was fundamental to its creation. As early as 10 December 1823, *El Sol* printed an article by Tornel entitled "Palabra y Escritura" in which he wrote that Mexico was in need of an academy of rhetoric. To his mind, the written word was the true expression of civilization. Words were capable of forming an ordered and moral society: "Men united to form a society because they spoke. Our needs are met because we communicate them. Thus there are governments and there is order in the world." Therefore, it was a logical and just demand to make:

Now that we begin to exist politically, should we not cultivate and improve our use of the spoken and the written word, which is how nations become eternal? And now that we are called to attend the tribune and our wide forum, should we not encourage the study of oratory and writing to fulfil these demands that are made on us? In order to provide this service I invite all Mexicans to establish one or more academies of humanities, given that we still need orators and poets.[86]

A year and a half later, Tornel took his proposal a step further and started to work on the foundation of an academy or society that could encourage and produce the orators and poets Mexico, as a civilized nation, required to sing its praise and express its needs. His endeavors found nothing but applause. On 2 June 1825, the *Aguila* stated that it was proud to print the *Reglamento* of the new Instituto de Ciencias, Literatura y Artes: "This establishment will honor Mexican culture and its worthy founders, among whom we have the pleasure of recognizing its main promoter: the citizen and Colonel José María Tornel."[87] Tornel, according to the *Aguila*, had not only originally conceived of the idea of creating the Instituto, but had also been involved in the long, hard process of finding funds to be able to finance its existence: "He himself wandered around looking for signatories, asking those individuals he considered most suited to found this enterprise; there were then people who said the project was not practical." Against what the *Aguila* liked to emphasize were great odds, Tornel, "resolute in his purpose, ... continued with his work" and succeeded in creating the Instituto. Moreover, as the patrons of the Instituto were still not as many or as forthcoming as would have been hoped for in 1825, Tornel had in fact financed the project mostly with his own money: "paying from his own pocket some of the necessary expenses."[88]

The Reglamento del Instituto de Ciencias, Literatura y Artes was printed in the *Aguila* on 13, 14, and 15 June 1825 and is worth looking at in some detail as it offers a clear insight into Tornel's cultural and pedagogical aspirations and beliefs. The main objective of the Instituto was to "promote and to perfect the sciences, literature and the arts." To achieve this, there would be three different classes or schools: one of mathematical science, concentrating on subjects such as geometry, mechanics, astronomy, geography, navigation, and physics; one of natural science, concentrating on subjects such as chemistry, mineralogy, botanics, rural economics, zoology, and anatomy; and one of literature, concentrating on subjects such as grammar, poetry, eloquence, history, and ancient Mexican history. Ideally the Instituto would serve the governments of the nation as a potential think-tank "and it will focus on certain questions or relevant problems, especially in the discipline of political economics."

It is significant, especially in the way it compares to the philosophy of the Compañía Lancasteriana, that the Instituto, rather than having students, would be made up of members. To be a member, certain prerequisites were essential: "they need to be well-known for their integrity and good name." Moreover, all members were expected to have a "scientific, literary or artistic reputation, well-known for their ability and constant dedication, for their discoveries, speeches or other useful works." The maintenance of the Instituto would consequently depend greatly on the fees paid by the members. Therefore, there were to be four levels of members. The *socios de número* had to live in Mexico City permanently, were expected to attend most classes, sessions, and seminars, had a voice in the Board of Study, and were the main patrons of the institution. The *socios honorarios* did not have to live in the capital, were always welcome to attend the sessions because of their celebrity, could advise rather than vote on boards, and the payment of any fees was left entirely "to their generosity and patriotism." The *socios de mérito* were members whose intellectual ability and prowess was such that they were invited to attend the sessions. These members were not expected to make any financial contributions to the Instituto and definitely had a voice in the boards. The *socios corresponsales* did not live in the capital and could advise rather than vote on the boards, but were expected to pay a minimum fee.

The Instituto was to have a library and a museum that kept all discoveries and exhibits related to natural as well as ancient Mexican history. All ordinary sessions were to take place once a month and needed to have at least thirteen members present to be considered viable. Any extraordinary sessions would clearly take place when the occasion required it, and these could be open to the general public.

It is evident that the Instituto was more like a society of scientific, literary, and artistic studies rather than a teaching institution. It was reserved for the social and intellectual elite of the nation, and was to be a place where the erudite and privileged of Mexico's haute culture could have a platform to discuss all matters of importance related to developments and research in mathematical science, natural science, or literature. As well as it being possible to graduate from the Colegios de San Ildefonso and San Gregorio, there was also the prestigious University of Mexico, founded in 1554, which, although suffering decline in the initial years of the republic,[89] still offered graduates the opportunity to continue their studies. Consequently, the Instituto was not so much an institute of higher education as a circle of science, literature, and arts.

The Instituto clearly appealed to the Mexican intelligentsia. On 1 August 1825, the members voted on who was to form its presiding committee. Lucas Alamán was voted president; Andrés Quintana Roo vice president; Vicente Cervantes treasurer, and Tornel's brother-in-law, Manuel Díez Bonilla, secretary. It is significant that *escoceses* and *yorkinos* such as Alamán and Tornel were at the time, albeit theoretically opposed in politics, united by their interests in culture and education. In the words of Olivera and Crété, "If anything could be called a unifying force in nineteenth-century Mexico, it was surely devotion to the Lancasterian ideal."[90] Nevertheless, the basic ideal of promoting culture, whether at the basic levels catered for by the Compañía Lancasteriana or at the clearly outstanding level of the Instituto, was a common goal of intellectuals of all factions.

On 2 April 1826, the Instituto was officially inaugurated with the expected pomp and circumstance. The *Aguila* praised Tornel for this "grandiose idea."[91] The Instituto appeared to encapsulate the achievement of one of Mexico's most treasured dreams. In his inaugural speech, Quintana Roo stated with much enthusiasm his faith in there being a glorious future ahead of them and that education would free Mexico's population from its backward customs and bring the long-awaited progress the nation was due. He was convinced that they already had "all the vigor, strength and consistency of those societies of old that were governed wisely."[92]

Tornel's most important role in the area of education was that of vice president and then president of the Compañía Lancasteriana, an institution that revolutionized education throughout Mexico in the nineteenth century. He was vice president from 1826 to 1829 and served as president in 1840–1847, 1850, and 1851.[93] Between its foundation in 1822 and the *santanistas'* rise to power in 1841, the Compañía Lancasteriana experienced mixed fortunes, mirroring the ups and downs of the republic. This is not the place to offer a narrative of the adventures and misadventures of the Compañía Lancasteriana during these years.[94] Suffice to say that after an exhilarating beginning in which the Compañía benefited from having the president's secretary, Tornel, as its vice president,[95] it was forced to close down under the Bustamante regime in 1832. Coinciding with the overthrow of Bustamante, it resurfaced and by 1837 appeared to be thriving once more, running twelve schools in the capital for the children of the less privileged classes of society. However, Bustamante's return brought with it a further spell of decline.

By the time Tornel became the Compañía's president in 1840, it was in severe financial distress. Not only were there only four schools left, but the state of these schools was a matter for concern:

When I visited the schools I found that they had no books; there were no reading boards; there were no signs on the doors so that the people only found out where to send their children by chance . . . there was not even a table to write on, and the schools were lacking in blackboards, pencils and even paper, quills and ink, to the extent that I felt that I had to provide them with the necessary utensils from my own pocket, even though this does not now mean that they have everything they need in abundance or that they even have enough equipment to function satisfactorily.[96]

Tornel was faced with a difficult task, especially because he was no longer in a position of power and did not have the favor of Bustamante's regime.

In January 1841, however, he became *alcalde* of Mexico City. Furthermore, on 28 January he was voted chairman and spokesman of the *Junta de Instrucción Primaria*. Every Thursday at noon, he attended meetings for the junta and voiced the concerns of the Compañía. He insisted on the establishment of a code of practice that formally extended the Lancasterian system to all public schools in the capital.[97] The Lancasterian method of education appealed to Tornel and the *hombres de bien* who became concerned with providing "children and the poorer classes [*clases desvalidas*] of society with a [free] primary education"[98] because it was cheap. The reason was simple: according to the system designed in eighteenth-century England by Joseph Lancaster and Dr. Bell, five hundred pupils could be taught to read and write by one teacher alone. The more advanced or older pupils arrived half an hour before the school day began, and the teacher taught them the day's lesson. Once the other pupils arrived, they were divided into semicircles of ten, and the older pupils spent the day teaching what they had learned to the ten students allocated to each of them. They were all put together in one huge room, and the teacher's main priority was to ensure discipline. Only a select number of advanced pupils used expensive utensils such as quills, ink, blackboards, and chalk. The majority were given boxes of sand in which they practiced writing using a stick.[99] As *alcalde*, Tornel urged the *Ayuntamiento* to find ways of financing the Compañía. Although the Bustamante administration provided no or very little support, Tornel succeeded in ensuring that no more Lancasterian schools were closed.

After Bustamante's downfall in October 1841, and benefiting from Santa Anna's rise to power, the fortune of the Compañía changed. The figures given by the Ministry of Justice and Public Education in 1845 clearly illustrate the extraordinary influence Tornel had on the Compañía and primary education once he was in a position of power, working for a government that favored him and his projects. In just under four years he succeeded in promoting the Lancasterian system throughout the country. By 1845 there were 2,200 children in Zacatecas attending 56 schools and 3,260 students in Puebla attending 38 schools. In the state of Mexico alone, there were 46,698 students going to 960 schools.[100] According to Mary Kay Vaughan, in Puebla "the council's budget for education increased from 3,744.8 pesos in 1838 to 4,912.8 in 1844, when the council administered ten schools with 1,082 students." The U.S. invasion of 1847, together with the subsequent political economic deterioration of Mexico, brought this boom to an end. However, it is no coincidence that the deterioration of the Compañía began in 1844, following Tornel's resignation from the Ministry of War. In Puebla, "between 1844 and 1852, the number of state schools in the city declined by one, and enrolment fell from 1,054 to 764."[101] The most active and prosperous years of the Compañía were those in which the *santanistas* were in power, especially between 1841 and 1844.

This revolution that transformed the Compañía came about as the result of two legislative reforms Tornel effected in 1842. On 6 October he printed his *Reglamento de la Compañía Lancasteriana*, which made it possible for the Compañía to expand. On 26 October, he decreed that the Compañía was to take over the *Dirección General de Instrucción Primaria*, transforming overnight all the schools in Mexico that were not private (only a fifth of them were private)[102] into Lancasterian institutions.[103]

The *Reglamento* provides the organizational reasons for the Compañía's rapid and effective expansion. In 1822, anybody could sign up to be a patron member of the Compañía and get his name in the papers. For this reason, there was no guarantee that the patron members, after benefiting from the publicity of their benevolence, would regularly provide the much-needed monthly donations they had vowed to provide the institution. In 1842 Tornel established a series of conditions that meant that before becoming a member of the Compañía, certain prerequisites needed to be satisfied. In one sense, the "moral and civic virtues which constitute a good citizen" were secondary to the other requirements. To become a member, it was necessary to be proposed by a member. Only after the board had considered the person's merits and financial situation did it vote on whether he could become a member. All members had to attend the Compañía's meeting and carry out whatever tasks were expected of them. To ensure that this was the case, attendance would be taken at each meeting, held every Monday. By requiring all the members who were residents in the capital to attend the Compañía's meetings, Tornel was ensuring that they would not fail to pay their monthly contributions, because he would have the chance to remind them of this obligation. All members had to provide a monthly contribution that could not be less than 1 peso but could be more if the member desired to increase his donation.[104] It was also the members' duty to "extend and promote education to wherever they live." For this to be effective Tornel created committees within the Compañía that were allocated different responsibilities such as the "vigilance of each school; propaganda; funds; the examination of teachers; and a visiting [committee] for ill members, assisting in the funerals of those who may die."[105]

Tornel's organizational skills were effective in reshaping the Compañía and ensuring that it was a successful and viable institution that could expand throughout the republic. The control of the membership and the outline of the members' duties were fundamental in guaranteeing its economic boom during the 1840s. In 1842, there were over 630 patrons throughout the country. Having put in place a system that forced the *socios* to make their monthly donations, the Compañía was able to prosper without depending entirely on the National Treasury's incomplete payment. A careful look at the list provides an accurate idea of who among Mexico's famous patriots was supporting the Compañía at the time.[106]

While all of this would appear to indicate that Tornel was a determined philanthropist who was committed to improving the education of the masses in the 1840s, there were other reforms he carried out as president of the Compañía that highlight only too well the extent to which his motives were not entirely altruistic. In terms of their private lives, Santa Anna and Tornel showed little concern for schools when they had vested interests in the buildings where classes were given. On 18 April 1843, for example, Santa Anna decreed that the Colegio Mayor de Todos los Santos was to become a private property of his loyal *santanista* supporter Manuel Eduardo Gorostiza.[107] Even the dedicated Tornel, in October 1829, rented out the Hospicio de Pobres in which there were five patios belonging to the Escuela Patriótica, as if it were his own property, to Francisco Marián y Torquemada and several other businessmen who made a living selling tobacco, paying little attention to the concern of the pupils.[108] It can thus be argued that the *santanistas* advocated the dramatic expansion of the Compañía as a means of indoctrinating the *clases desvalidas*, displaying in the process an example of what can only be defined as Mexican nineteenth-century populist politics. As Anne Staples has noted in a recent study, education was very much used as an ideological instrument in the nineteenth century.[109]

Tornel's conscious attempt to use primary education as a vehicle by which he could influence the political beliefs of the masses is particularly evident in the 1842 *Reglamento*. In it Tornel stated that boys would learn reading, writing, arithmetic, Spanish grammar, morality and urbanity, history, religion, and the social charter; girls would learn reading, writing, arithmetic, Christian doctrine, manners and urbanity, and sewing.[110] The significant changes he introduced are to be found in the way he omitted the study of the constitution and included history as a subject instead. Given that the *Bases de Tacubaya* had awarded Santa Anna dictatorial powers and that Congress was to be closed later that year, the fact that no existing or past constitution was being taught suggests that it was Tornel's intention to bring up the children of the poorer sectors of society without a strong sense of constitutional rights. Moreover, taking into account that Tornel manipulated history to suit his political needs, the addition of history as a subject, taught according to Tornel's view of Mexican politics, would inevitably serve to glorify Santa Anna and his regime. The further emphasis on morality and urbanity was clearly intended to imprint in the children's minds an awareness of the virtues of preserving law and order and of respecting the rules of society as established by the *hombres de bien*.

What also becomes evident is that the *santanistas*' drive to promote free education was an integral part of their political populism. The fact that Santa Anna and the *santanistas* adopted populist strategies has already been noted. In the words of Angel Calderón de la Barca, Santa Anna was the "most popular *caudillo* of the country."[111] Apart from depicting himself as a true patriot who intervened in politics only for the good of his country, retreating to his *hacienda* in Veracruz once he had allegedly restored order in the country, "his addiction to his fighting cocks and to that national passion of gambling, his many conquests of the opposite sex, his flamboyant display from military parades to Te Deums, his regal demeanour on public occasions always surrounded by brilliantly dressed and obsequious courtiers—all added up to a public image of larger-than-life proportions."[112] The populist cult of his personality went hand in hand with certain populist political promises on behalf of the *santanistas*. Tornel's promotion of free education represents this.

Although there is no written evidence that Tornel and the *santanistas* were promoting free education for populist reasons, it becomes obvious that the extraordinary support they awarded the Compañía was part of this general tendency toward populism. It is not surprising, if this point is accepted, that Tornel played such an active role, visiting all the main schools of Mexico City whenever examinations were held or prizes were awarded. There are in fact numerous leaflets in the Archivo del Ex. Ayuntamiento de México announcing Tornel's appearance at the different events the Compañía organized during the 1840s. The school uniforms, the music, and the guest appearance of one of the leading politicians of the period must have impressed not only the children who were benefiting from this boom of free education but also the parents, who could proudly see their children receiving awards from a man of such celebrity.

As was the case with the army, the *santanistas* were ensuring they had the support of the populace by flamboyantly promoting free education. How could those children who benefited from the healthy expansion of the Compañía and their parents complain of the *santanistas'* corruption or their political changes or even of their despotism, when they were learning to read and write thanks to them? Moreover, although the 1843 Constitution limited the suffrage to citizens who earned over 200 pesos a year, it stated that in seven years, it was to be hoped that the suffrage would be opened up to anybody who could read and write regardless of their financial situation. The boom that primary education enjoyed under the *santanistas* would suggest that this constitutional promise was being taken very seriously by them, aware, almost certainly, that in seven years a grateful literate populace would vote for that very faction that had enabled them to learn how to read and write.

Evidently the nation did benefit from the *santanista* educational revolution of the 1840s even if their motivation was not as altruistic as they claimed. In the words of Lucas Alamán, "no country even the most advanced in Europe dispensed free education in all its forms more abundantly than did Mexico."[113] This was in no small degree due, as Thompson said, "to the instrumentality and exertions of General Tornel."

Another instance of the way Tornel remained a committed educationalist until he died was his involvement in the Colegio de Minería. He was named its president on 4 July 1843, a post that he retained until he died ten years later.[114] The Colegio de Minería was founded during the reign of Charles IV, and unlike San Ildefonso or San Gregorio, it had a long tradition of lay directors and teachers.[115] According to Fanny Calderón de la Barca, it was based in one of the city's most beautiful buildings: "Nothing could be more splendid than the general effect of this noble building" with its "noble court which was brilliantly illuminated with coloured lamps, hung from pillar to pillar," and where even "the supper tables were very hand-some."[116] Even Waddy Thompson was impressed: "The only institution of any character in the city is the Minería—the College of Mines, as its name implies. The building itself is altogether magnificent. It is very spacious, and built of hewn stone in the most perfect architecture."[117] It was a center of higher education of undeniable prestige, and its students could study varied topics: Spanish grammar, ideology and logic, modern languages (French, English, and German), botanics, mathematics, physics, chemistry, geodesy, mineralogy, geology, zoology, geography, cosmography, astronomy, mining, and draughtsmanship. There were also days dedicated to "gymnastic exercises," which the students were expected to attend. The main objective of the Minería was to create experts who would promote Mexico's mining industry.[118]

Tornel's involvement in the Minería was not as demanding or as time-consuming as his presidency of the Compañia Lancasteriana. Thompson argued that with all his other responsibilities, he could not possibly or realistically make a noticeable contribution to the Minería: "General Tornel, the President, is as I have always said, an accomplished man and an elegant writer. But his whole life has been spent in the excitement and bustle of politics, and of Mexican politics, and it is altogether impossible that his scientific attainments can be even respectable."[119] However, each year he awarded students who passed their exams their well-deserved honors. He was also editor of the yearly *Anuario del Colegio Nacional de Minería*, in which the professors and lecturers of the institution printed articles and essays that reflected the results of their research and studies:

The present Director *Excelentismo* Sr. Don José María Tornel, hoping to edit in a volume these interesting works, and to provide the lecturers of the school with a periodical publication in which they can include their articles and the observations they have arrived at following their scientific investigations, on a yearly basis, has had the happy idea . . . of publishing this journal at the end of the school year.[120]

As well as founding this academic journal, he made contributions to it such as his speech of 16 November 1845, *En la solemne distribución de premios de sus alumnos*,[121] and the article, "Elogio del Libertador de México," which was printed in the *Anuario* for 1848.[122] Although the day-to-day running of the Minería was left to the Junta Facultativa of the school, Tornel was considered to have the appropriate credentials to retain the title of president until he died.

The reasons for the satisfaction that Tornel, Bocanegra, and Trigueros expressed in their ministerial reports at the beginning of 1844 can be easily understood. Apart from the controversy that had surrounded the closure of Congress in 1842, the *santanistas* had succeeded in imposing, first through the 1841 *Bases de Tacubaya* and later through the 1843 *Bases*

Orgánicas a relatively stable government. Regardless of whether Santa Anna was in Mexico City or in his hacienda in Veracruz, Trigueros had managed to levy a new range of taxes that had given the treasury more funds than any other government in Independent Mexico, Bocanegra had succeeded in controlling the many affairs of the interior to his satisfaction, and Tornel had significantly reformed the army and improved the conditions of the soldiers, while launching a major boom in primary education.

These three years of *santanista* administration provide the clearest evidence of what politicians like Tornel and Bocanegra believed in after two decades of independent life. In their minds, the stages of disenchantment (1828–1835) and profound disillusion (1835–1847) showed that the Mexican people were not mature enough to be governed by the principles they had in fact embraced, like the majority of the political class, in the 1820s. Just as the people were not ready to be exposed to certain publications, the majority was not ready to participate in the political process. Mexico needed to be governed by a select minority of enlightened *hombres de bien*. The masses needed to be pacified, educated, and controlled, and as long as they did not display sufficient political maturity, it was essential that they were not included in the electoral process. The populism of the *santanistas* was emphasized precisely so that the masses felt included in the political process even though their right to vote was taken away from them. They believed in establishing a strong government with a strong state that defended the Catholic customs of the nation, and they imposed a definite sense of order and stability, whatever the cost. In order to do this, they advocated the temporary creation of a dictatorship in 1841, the resurrection of a particularly large and formidable army, and the consolidation of a centralist system where the executive was not weakened by an arbitrating Supreme Conservative Power. In economic terms, the *santanistas* sought to finance their project by imposing a wide range of taxes and encouraging both protectionist and laissez-faire legislation, depending on the region concerned. Furthermore, in a bid to strengthen the government, the *santanistas* came to defend a philosophy that argued that political parties should be replaced by a national movement like their own, concerned with the welfare of the republic rather than the interests of their party. This patriotic ideology was enhanced by the militarism of the *santanistas*, who came to view the regular army as the true, pure representative of the mother country, identifying themselves with a movement, rather than a faction, that sought to establish peace, order, and unity by avoiding the acrimonious divisions of party politics. Like the majority of the political tendencies of this period, especially once the stage of hope was over, the *santanistas* also came to believe that the only progressive reform was the slow one—the one that paid great attention to the importance of education and the country's culture and customs. One day it was to be hoped that the Mexican people would be ready to be governed by a democratic political system. In the words of Santa Anna, according to Joel Poinsett, who visited him during his captivity in the United States:

It is true that I placed my bets on liberty with great ardor and perfect sincerity. However, I soon realized how foolish I was. Give them one hundred years and the Mexican people will still not be ready for liberty. Their ignorance is such that they do not know what liberty is. Given the influence the Catholic Church still has, despotism is the only kind of government which will work. Of course there is no reason why this despotism cannot be wise and virtuous.[123]

The last *santanista* proposal of 1853 reflected Santa Anna's own despotic tendencies more clearly than did the 1841–1844 administration. In part this was because the stage of despair had not yet arrived. In spite of all the disenchantment and disillusion, the *santanistas* were still constitutionalists in the early 1840s. As can be seen in the *Bases Orgánicas*, they did not yet believe in imposing a long-lasting permanent military dictatorship. The 1846–1848 war had to take place before *santanista* political thought evolved yet again and came closer to advocating the enlightened yet authoritarian principles of a section of Lucas Alamán's Conservative party.

DIVISION AMONG THE *SANTANISTAS*, 1844

For reasons that still need to be researched, there was an important schism toward the middle of 1844 between Santa Anna and his ministers. Tornel, Bocanegra, and Trigueros all decided to resign in circumstances that lead us to believe that a serious conflict of interests emerged in 1844 between what the *santanista* intelligentsia wanted for Mexico (and themselves) and what Santa Anna wanted. Tornel was the first to enter into a bitter dispute with Santa Anna. According to Carlos María de Bustamante, Santa Anna turned against his ever-loyal adviser and propagandist because Tornel gave himself certain presidential airs when he presented himself in Puebla in April 1844, having gone there to buy some haciendas in San Martín Tesmelucam. The main plaza of Puebla filled with a jubilant crowd who cheered him and celebrated his arrival, by waving flags and throwing flowers, and the local authorities welcomed Tornel by offering him a guard of honor to accompany him during his visit. In Bustamante's words, Santa Anna was livid on hearing about this event and immediately asked Tornel to resign because "he is very jealous of his authority and will not admit any rivals."[124]

Apart from Bustamante's interpretation, no other documents have been found that can account for the fact that Tornel and Santa Anna became estranged in 1844. María del Carmen Vázquez Mantecón suggests that there were deeply personal reasons for this rupture. Following the death of his wife, María Agustina in October 1843, Tornel had married, in March

1844, the actress Catarina Silva, with whom he had been having a notorious affair since 1839. Vázquez Mantecón hints at the possibility that Santa Anna might have been jealous of Tornel's relationship with the actress and that their marriage was the final straw that led the *caudillo* to order his resignation.[125] However, the fact that Bocanegra and Trigueros also resigned suggests that there must have been other reasons for the schism—reasons that must have been of a more general nature, more political and less personal.

Although Bocanegra alleged in his letter of resignation of 16 August 1844 that his ill health prevented him from continuing at the head of his ministry, in his *Memorias* he noted, albeit in passing and without elaborating, that one of the reasons he had opted to resign was "the awful political outcomes he feared [were about to erupt] . . . against the well-being of the republic." At a time when the *santanista* administration appeared to be well consolidated, it is difficult to assess what these "awful political outcomes" could be or who was preparing the ground for them to erupt. Santa Anna's reply to Bocanegra's resignation suggests that he knew perfectly well that health was an excuse, not the real cause of his desertion. Without using explicitly political arguments, Santa Anna nevertheless begged Bocanegra not to abandon him and hinted that he was aware that an ideological schism was developing between him and his ministries: "I do not ignore your powerful reasons for wanting to abandon such an arduous and complicated post; but men who love their mother-country and who are, like yourself, useful to her, commit an unforgivable fault by abandoning her when she most needs them."[126]

Tornel, still loyal, did as he was told and resigned, claiming he was ill, and did not challenge Santa Anna as he had done with Bustamante in 1839. However, as Niceto de Zamacois poignantly points out in describing Santa Anna's return to the capital on 3 June 1844: "That night there were fireworks in the main square, and Santa Anna must have been very satisfied with a welcome which his supporters insisted was spontaneous. . . . However, the minister of war, Don José María Tornel did not join the festivities."[127] The policies of the 1841–1844 *santanista* government degenerated after Tornel, Bocanegra, and Trigueros resigned, to the extent that the so-called Revolution of the Three Hours, which erupted in the capital on 6 December, was characterized by scenes of virulent popular hatred toward Santa Anna. The *caudillo*'s statue in the Plaza del Volador was destroyed, and an angry mob went as far as disinterring the remains of Santa Anna's leg from the cemetery of Santa Paula, dragging them through the streets of the capital to the cry of, "Kill the lame bastard [*cojo*]! Long live Congress!"

Tornel and Santa Anna's friendship was not immediately renewed. Santa Anna, without Tornel to organize his mandate in the capital or to control the dictatorial excesses he was prone to, found himself forced into exile a year later, after a period in which, to use John Lynch's words, "excessive spending and venality proved too much."[128] As Josefina Zoraida Vázquez correctly states, "The people were fed up of so many excesses and they applauded the change, and although Santa Anna still had the army he accepted his defeat."[129]

Tornel spent the remaining months of 1844 in his hacienda in Chalco. There is little record of his activities, except that he translated M. Fourier's "Los misterios de la Rusia" and M. Guibert's "Cuadro del arte de la guerra desde el principio del mundo."[130] No doubt he felt bitter about the way Santa Anna had treated him. Since 1820 Tornel had dedicated most of his energies to helping the *caudillo*—keeping him informed of events in the capital, defending him in the press, publicizing his virtues and achievements in speeches and pamphlets, and organizing his return to the presidency. Tornel's political career had been inextricably linked to Santa Anna's for over two decades. Not only had he considered him to be the most adept leader for the country, Santa Anna had been, together with Bocanegra, one of his closest friends. Because Tornel had played such a fundamental role in the 1841–1844 administration, the sudden demand for his resignation must have represented a particularly harsh blow. This becomes evident if one considers that at the beginning of 1844, Tornel appeared to be convinced that in the midst of a period of generalized disillusion, there was some hope of a blissful future—that after three years of *santanista* government they were on the road to consolidating a stable, long-lasting, orderly, and progressive political system. Of all the years Tornel was in a position of power, there is no doubt that the period 1841–1844 was his finest hour. A well-established writer and intellectual, his personal wealth had grown in tandem with his influence in politics. He had finally had the chance to impose some of his most cherished reforms, especially regarding the army and education. And yet, just when he had started to enjoy the fruits of his endeavors, his much-admired friend, the *caudillo* himself, had turned against him. Considering that he had felt quite strongly about Bustamante's ingratitude, one can only guess what he must have felt about Santa Anna's unexpected betrayal. Nevertheless, Tornel was a survivor. With or without Santa Anna he was to remain a key player in national politics.

NOTES

1. Fanny Calderón de la Barca, *Life in Mexico* (London: Century, 1987), p. 412.

2. For the events that led to the closure of the Constituent Congress in 1842, see: Cecilia Noriega Elío, *El constituyente de 1842* (Mexico City: UNAM, 1986), and Michael P. Costeloe, "Generals versus Politicians: Santa Anna and the 1842 Congressional Elections in Mexico," *Bulletin of Latin American Research* 8:2 (1989): 257–274.

3. José María Bocanegra, *Memorias para la historia de México independiente, 1822–1846*, vol. 3. (Mexico City: Fondo de Cultura Económica, 1987), pp. 15, 17.

4. José María Tornel, *Memoria del secretario de estado y del despacho de guerra y marina, leída a las cámaras del congreso nacional de la república mexicana, en enero de 1844* (Mexico City: Imp. de I. Cumplido, 1844), p. 6.

5. Ibid., p. 8.

6. Bocanegra, *Memorias*, vol. 3, p. 35.

7. The *Discurso pronunciado por el Exmo. Sr. Presidente Provisional, Gral. Antonio López de Santa Anna, el 13 de junio de 1843* is reprinted in ibid., pp. 123–127.

8. *El Acta y Plan de Huejotzingo* is reprinted in Bocanegra, *Memorias*, vol. 3, pp. 107–108.

9. See *Bases de organización política de la república mexicana, de 12 de junio de 1843*, reprinted in Boletín de la Secretaría de Gobernación, *Leyes fundamentales de los Estados Unidos Mexicanos y planes revolucionarios que han influido en la organización política de la república* (Mexico City: Imp. de la Sec. de Gobernación, 1923), pp. 213–229. For an analysis of the *Bases Orgánicas*, see Michael P. Costeloe, *The Central Republic in Mexico, 1835–1846. Hombres de Bien in the Age of Santa Anna* (Cambridge: Cambridge University Press, 1993), pp. 226–227; Linda Arnold, *Política y justicia. La suprema corte mexicana (1824–1855)* (Mexico City: UNAM, 1996), p. 125; Carmen Vázquez Mantecón, "Las Bases Orgánicas y la danza de los caudillos en los cuarentas" (paper presented at the Archivo General de la Nación, 13 March 1997); and Will Fowler, *Mexico in the Age of Proposals, 1821–1853* (Westport, CT: Greenwood Press, 1998), pp. 234–238.

10. Bocanegra, *Memorias*, vol. 3, p. 194.

11. Barbara A. Tenenbaum, *México en la época de los agiotistas, 1821–1857* (Mexico City: Fondo de Cultura Económica, 1985), p. 95.

12. Costeloe, *The Central Republic*, p. 225.

13. *La Palanca*, 3 May 1849.

14. Torcuato S. Di Tella, *National Popular Politics in Early Independent Mexico, 1820–1847* (Albuquerque: University of New Mexico Press, 1996), pp. 189–190.

15. Manuel Dublán and José M. Lozano, *Legislación mexicana o colección completa de las disposiciones legislativas expedidas desde la independencia de la república*, vol. 4 (Mexico City: Imp. del Comercio, 1902), pp. 94–97, 134–144, 147–150.

16. Costeloe, *The Central Republic*, pp. 208–209, 223–225.

17. Tenenbaum, *México en la época de los agiotistas*, pp. 85–86.

18. *El Aguila Mexicana*, 25 January 1843; *El Cosmopolita*, 31 May 1843. Also see Costeloe, *The Central Republic*, p. 216.

19. See Anne Staples, *Educar: Panacea del México Independiente* (Mexico City: SEP, 1985).

20. For those articles and translations Tornel published in 1841—"Noticias sobre las poesías aztecas," "Consideraciones sobre la elocuencia de Mr. Courtin," "La providencia en el Nuevo Mundo"—see *El Mosaico Mexicano*, vol. 5 (1841), pp. 143–144, 361–376, 529–534, respectively; and for "Beneficencia para con los animales," "El Lord Byron a los napolitanos en 1823. Estancias," "Historia. Bosquejo de la administración de los Incas en el Perú," see *El Mosaico Mexicano*, vol. 6 (1841), pp. 57–66, 73–75, 97–104, respectively.

21. José María Tornel, *Manifestación presentada a la cámara de senadores por*

el general José María Tornel, apoderado de las diputaciones de cosecheros de ta-
baco de las ciudades de Jalapa y Orizaba, pidiendo la reprobación del acuerdo
sobre amortización de la moneda de cobre, por medio del estanco de aquel ramo
(Mexico City: Imp. de I. Cumplido, 1841), p. 24.

22. See Michael P. Costeloe, "The Triangular Revolt in Mexico and the Fall
of Anastasio Bustamante, August–October 1841," *Journal of Latin American Studies* 20 (1988): 337–360.

23. Ibid., p. 360.

24. Jan Bazant, "José María Tornel, Mariano Riva Palacio, Manuel Escandón
y la compraventa de una hacienda," in Alicia Hernández Chávez and Manuel Miño
Grijalva (eds.), *Cincuenta años de historia de México*, vol. 1 (Mexico City: El Colegio de México, 1991), pp. 389–400.

25. Costeloe, "Generals versus Politicians," pp. 259–260.

26. Ibid., p. 269.

27. See María del Carmen Vázquez Mantecón, *La palabra del poder. Vida
pública de José María Tornel (1795–1853)* (Mexico City: UNAM, 1997), pp. 130–
131.

28. Josefina Zoraida Vázquez, *Don Antonio López de Santa Anna. Mito y
enigma* (Mexico City: CONDUMEX, 1987), p. 27.

29. *El Siglo XIX*, 25 December 1842.

30. Ibid., 29 December 1842.

31. Costeloe, *The Central Republic*, p. 216.

32. Wilfrid H. Callcott, *Church and State in Mexico, 1822–1857* (New York:
Octagon Books, 1965), pp. 132–133.

33. Costeloe, *The Central Republic*, pp. 222–226.

34. José María Luis Mora, *Obras sueltas* (Mexico City: Porrúa, 1963), p. 115.

35. See Brian Loveman and Thomas Davies (eds.), *The Politics and Antipolitics:
The Military in Latin America* (Lincoln: University of Nebraska Press, 1978).

36. Although Tornel left José María Díaz Noriega in charge of the ministry for
just over a month in 1843, and then again for a fortnight in the spring of 1844,
from October 1841 to June 1844, he was responsible for the Ministry of War
without interruption.

37. Tornel, *Memoria . . . 1844*, p. 75.

38. General Pedro García Conde was now director of the School of the Corps
of Engineers.

39. Tornel, *Memoria . . . 1844*, p. 75.

40. Ibid., p. 76.

41. In 1844 there were military hospitals in Veracruz, Tampico, San Luis Po-
tosí, Chihuahua, Matamoros, Tabasco, Perote, Acapulco, Guadalajara, Xalapa, and
Mexico City. There were also three provisional hospitals in Mazatlán, Bravos, and
Chilapa.

42. Tornel, *Memoria . . . 1844*, p. 63.

43. Ibid., p. 60.

44. Ibid., pp. 32–36.

45. Ibid., p. 13.

46. Ibid., p. 17.

47. *Desahogo de D. J. M. Tornel bajo la firma de J. López de Santa Anna*
(Mérida: n.p., 1843), pp. 23–24.

48. Tornel, *Memoria . . . 1844*, pp. 29–30.

49. Ibid., p. 52.

50. Ibid., p. 59.

51. Ibid., p. 5.

52. Ibid., pp. 90–91.

53. Waddy Thompson, *Recollections of Mexico* (New York: Wiley and Putnam, 1847), pp. 170, 172–173.

54. Ignacio M. Altamirano, *El Zarco. La Navidad en las montañas* (Mexico City: Porrúa, 1984), p. 5.

55. Ruth R. Olivera and Liliane Crété, *Life in Mexico under Santa Anna, 1822–1855* (Norman: University of Oklahoma Press, 1991), p. 161.

56. Quoted in ibid., p. 166.

57. Bocanegra, *Memorias*, vol. 1, p. 492, vol. 2, p. 17.

58. Antonio López de Santa Anna, *Historia militar y política*, in Genaro García (ed.), *Documentos inéditos o muy raros para la historia de México*, vol. 59 (Mexico City: Porrúa, 1974), pp. 2, 12, 15, 22, 76.

59. Alfred Vagts, *A History of Militarism: Civilian and Military* (London: Blackwell, 1959), p. 19.

60. Will Fowler, *Military Political Identity and Reformism in Independent Mexico. An Analysis of the Memorias de Guerra (1821–1855)* (London: ILAS, 1996), p. 42.

61. *El Archivo Militar*, 30 September 1841.

62. Tornel, *Memoria . . . 1844*, p. 2.

63. Carmen Vázquez Mantecón, *Santa Anna y la encrucijada del estado. La dictadura (1853–1855)* (Mexico City: Fondo de Cultura Económica, 1986), p. 25.

64. Thompson, *Recollections of Mexico*, p. 169.

65. José María Tornel, *Memoria del secretario de estado y del despacho de guerra y marina, leída en la cámara de representantes en la sesión del día veinte y tres de marzo, y en la de senadores en la del veinte y cuatro del mismo mes y año de 1835* (Mexico City: Imp. de I. Cumplido, 1835), p. 16.

66. Ibid., p. 17.

67. *Diario del Gobierno*, 12 November 1835.

68. Ibid., 17, 31 July, 21 August 1836, 16 March 1837, 30 December 1838.

69. Tornel, *Memoria . . . 1844*, pp. 61, 100.

70. Mora, *Obras sueltas*, p. 167.

71. As argued in Fowler, *Military Political Identity*, p. 54: "The regular army in independent Mexico was traditionalist yet reformist in its political ideology in the broadest sense possible of the term, and *santanista* in practice."

72. Thompson, *Recollections of Mexico*, p. 152.

73. Manuel Moya Palencia, *El México de Egerton 1831–1842* (Mexico City: Porrúa, 1991), p. 206.

74. Michael P. Costeloe, "Los generales Santa Anna y Paredes y Arrillaga en México, 1841–1843. Rivales por el poder o una copa más," *Historia Mexicana* 39: 2 (1989): 420.

75. Moya Palencia, *El México de Egerton*, p. 206.

76. Callcott, *Santa Anna*, p. 287.

77. Manuel Rivera Cambas, *Antonio López de Santa Anna* (Mexico City: Editorial Citlaltépetl, 1958), pp. 200–201.

78. Niceto de Zamacois, *Historia de Méjico desde sus tiempos más remotos hasta nuestros días*, vol. 12 (Barcelona: J. F. Parres y Compañía, 1880), p. 47.

79. Rafael F. Muñoz, *Santa Anna. El dictador resplandeciente* (Mexico City: Fondo de Cultura Económica, 1983), p. 218.

80. Calderón de la Barca, *Life in Mexico*, p. 415.

81. Stanley C. Green, *The Mexican Republic: The First Decade, 1823–1832* (Pittsburgh: University of Pittsburgh Press, 1987), p. 83.

82. Carlos María de Bustamante, *Apuntes para la historia del gobierno del general don Antonio López de Santa Anna* (Mexico City: Fondo de Cultura Económica, 1986), p. 239.

83. Moya Palencia, *El México de Egerton*, p. 206.

84. *El Aguila Mexicana*, 17 April 1825.

85. Bocanegra, *Memorias*, vol. 2, pp. 383–386.

86. José María Tornel, "Palabra y escritura," *El Sol*, 10 December 1823.

87. *El Aguila Mexicana*, 2 June 1825.

88. Ibid., 13 April 1826.

89. Olivera and Crété, *Life in Mexico*, p. 227.

90. Ibid., p. 221.

91. *El Aguila Mexicana*, 13 April 1826.

92. Quoted in Anne Staples, *Leona Vicario* (Mexico City: SEP, 1976), p. 48.

93. Archivo Histórico del Exmo. Ayuntamiento de México (henceforth referred to as AHEAM), Exp. 2444, Instrucción Pública. Cía Lancasteriana, 1822–1886.

94. For a narrative of the Compañía's ups and downs during this period, see Will Fowler, "The Compañía Lancasteriana and the Elite in Independent Mexico, 1822–1845," *TESSERAE Journal of Iberian and Latin American Studies* 2:1 (Summer 1996): 81–110.

95. Ibid., pp. 84–86.

96. AHEAM, Exp. 2479, Instrucción Pública. En General, vol. 5, 1837–1847, "Exposición hecha por el Sr. Baz."

97. Ibid., "Actas de la Junta de Instrucción Pública," 1840–1842.

98. José María Tornel, *Reglamento de la Compañía Lancasteriana de México* (Mexico City: Imp. de Vicente García Torres, 1842), p. 3.

99. See Fowler, "The Compañía Lancasteriana," pp. 82–84. Also on the Compañía Lancasterina see: Dorothy Tanck de Estrada, "Las escuelas lancasterianas en la ciudad de México, 1822–1842," *Historia Mexicana* 23 (1972–1973): 494–513; and Dorothy Tanck de Estrada, *La educación ilustrada 1786–1836* (Mexico City: El Colegio de México, 1984).

100. Olivera and Crété, *Life in Mexico*, p. 219.

101. Mary Kay Vaughan, "Primary Schooling in the City of Puebla, 1821–60," *Hispanic American Historical Review* 67:1 (1987): 45, 49.

102. Olivera and Crété, *Life in Mexico*, p. 219.

103. Fowler, "The Compañía Lancasteriana," p. 95.

104. In the "Lista de los Sres. Socios que han contribuido en el mes vencido en 15 de enero de 1844 para los gastos de las escuelas de la Compañía Lancasteriana," AGN: Exp. *Compañía Lancasteriana*, there are instances of members donating more than 1 peso, such as Fagoaga, who gave the generous sum of 5 pesos, or Cayetano Rubio who gave 4 pesos, as did Juan de Mier y Terán, the Archbishop

Posadas, and Miguel Arias. In this list, Tornel donated only 1 peso, but his sons Agustín and Manuel gave 1 peso each.

105. José María Tornel, *Reglamento de la Compañía Lancasteriana de México* (Mexico City: Imp. de Vicente García Torres, 1842), pp. 1–19.

106. Members included celebrities such as: Manuel Altamirano, Juan Nepomuceno Almonte, José María Bocanegra, Agustín Buenrostro, Ignacio Basadre, Anastasio Bustamante, Ignacio Cumplido, José María Díaz Noriega, Manuel Diez Bonilla, Joaquín Escandón, Juan Espinosa de los Monteros, Rafael Espinosa, Francisco Fagoaga, Isidro Gondra, Manuel Eduardo Gorostiza, Manuel Gómez de la Cortina, Manuel Larraínzar, José María Lafragua, Manuel María Lombardini, Mariano Michelena, Francisco Molinos del Campo, Manuel de la Peña y Peña, the Archbishop Posadas, Guillermo Prieto, Andrés Quintana Roo, Manuel Crecencio Rejón, Ignacio Serra y Rosso, Ignacio Trigueros, Guadalupe Victoria, and Gabriel Valencia. In Orizaba, Tornel's brothers were both members. In Veracruz, Santa Anna was a member.

107. Bustamante, *Apuntes*, p. 137.

108. AGNCM: Exp. Notaría Núm. 158, José Ignacio Cano y Moctezuma, 1826–1833 (Escribano Real), doc. 23 October 1829, Tornel (Arrendamiento).

109. See Anne Staples, "La educación como instrumento ideológico del estado. El conservadurismo educativo en el México decimonónico," in Will Fowler and Humberto Morales Moreno (eds.), *El conservadurismo mexicano en el siglo XIX (1810–1910)* (Puebla: BUAP/St. Andrews, 1999), pp. 103–114.

110. Tornel, *Reglamento*, p. 17.

111. J. de Malagón Barceló (ed.), *Relaciones diplomáticas hispano-mexicanas: Documentos procedentes del Archivo de la Embajada de España en México*, vol. 1 (Mexico City: Editorial Jus, 1949), p. 28.

112. Costeloe, *The Central Republic*, p. 137.

113. Lucas Alamán, *Historia de Méjico*, vol. 5 (Mexico City: Editorial Jus, 1969), pp. 572–573.

114. *El Mosquito Mexicano*, 18 July 1843.

115. Tanck de Estrada, *La educación ilustrada*, p. 130.

116. Calderón de la Barca, *Life in Mexico*, pp. 177–179.

117. Thompson, *Recollections of Mexico*, p. 147.

118. These details can be found in the *Actas del Colegio de Minería* for the years 1845, 1849, and 1851, held in the Colección Lafragua.

119. Thompson, *Recollections of Mexico*, p. 147.

120. *Anuario del Colegio de Minería Año de 1845* (Mexico City: Imp. de I. Cumplido, 1846), p. 1.

121. José María Tornel, "Discurso pronunciado por el Exmo. Sr. General José María Tornel y Mendívil, director del colegio de minería, en la solemne distribución de premios de sus alumnos, que se verificó el día 16 de noviembre de 1845," *El Museo Mexicano* 1 (1845), pp. 179–184.

122. *Anuario del Colegio de Minería Año de 1848* (Mexico City: Imp. de I. Cumplido, 1849), pp. 88–99.

123. Quoted in Enrique Krauze, *Siglo de Caudillos* (Barcelona: Editorial Tusquets, 1994), pp. 143–144.

124. Bustamante, *Apuntes*, p. 250.

125. Vázquez Mantecón, *La palabra del poder*, p. 144.

126. Bocanegra, *Memorias*, vol. 3, pp. 209–210, 309–310.

127. Zamacois, *Historia de Méjico*, vol. 12, p. 330.

128. John Lynch, *Caudillos in Spanish America, 1800–1850* (Oxford: Clarendon Press, 1992), p. 344.

129. Josefina Zoraida Vázquez, *Don Antonio López de Santa Anna. Mito y enigma* (Mexico City: CONDUMEX, 1987), p. 29.

130. Vázquez Mantecón, *La palabra del poder*, p. 145.

5

"Ploughing the Sea": The Mexican-American War and Its Aftermath (1845–1853)

TORNEL AND PAREDES Y ARRILLAGA

Following the Revolution of the Three Hours on 6 December 1844, the moderate faction, for the first time, took hold of the reins of government, bringing General José Joaquín de Herrera to the presidency. Although Santa Anna was forced into exile and the moderates appeared to offer a political platform that could have united the opposed radical and traditionalist factions, they failed to consolidate a stable government. Their pursuit of middle-of-the-road policies that entailed reforms that were of a radical nature and yet conservative in their proposed gradual implementation, met with the opposition of those very factions they were hoping to bring aboard their project. Even before the end of its second month in office, Herrera's government was being virulently attacked by all factions and was crippled by internal divisions. The radical *puros* condemned them because they hesitated in replacing the centralist 1843 Constitution with the federalist 1824 charter, they were slow to replace the large regular army with civic militias, and they started to consider the possibility of recognizing the independence of Texas. The traditionalists attacked them for attempting to dissolve the army and trying to impose a federalist economic policy that clashed with the centralist state Mexico had been since 1835. In brief, rather than achieving a consensus among the different factions, the moderates succeeded in alienating them all. Nevertheless, if any one thing sealed their fate, it was their attempt to find a peaceful solution to the Texan question by acknowledging the state's independence in exchange for some form of payment.

Texas became the burning issue of 1845 and an equally ardent symbol of the dangerous situation in which Mexico found itself after two decades of independent life. With a certain element of pragmatism, moderates like Herrera and Manuel Gómez Pedraza, together with traditionalists like Lucas Alamán, came to the conclusion by 1845 that Mexico would never succeed in reconquering Texas. Confronted with the increasingly effervescent expansionism of the U.S. government, it made sense to them to discuss the British ambassador's suggestion that Mexico recognize the independence of Texas in exchange for the guarantee that the British government would prevent the United States from annexing the northern Mexican territories of California, Arizona, and New Mexico.

However, the patriotic populism of the *puros* and the *santanistas* made such considerations appear to the public at large as nothing other than treason. To make matters worse, on 15 July 1845, Texas became part of the United States. While Herrera's government should have benefited from the support of the *puros* (considering their federalist sympathies and the way they reduced the regular army), it found itself divided and weak against the imminent threat of a war with the United States. The fear of having to wage a war against the powerful expansionist northern neighbor, and of losing it, finally inspired traditionalists, together with some *santanistas*, to sidestep the *puros* and overthrow Herrera's government, replacing it with an allegedly strong dictatorship. On 14 December 1845, General Mariano Paredes y Arrillaga launched the *pronunciamiento* of San Luis Potosí that finally brought him to power.

With Santa Anna in exile, Tornel returned to the political scene, this time backing Mariano Paredes y Arrillaga's coup of December 1845–January 1846. Albeit abandoned by Santa Anna, Tornel had nevertheless defended him prior to his departure to Havana, during the trial the *caudillo* was subjected to in the wake of the December revolution, arguing that he should be granted the amnesty that allowed him to go into exile rather than condemn him to imprisonment.[1] Partly as a result of this and partly because it was believed that he had probably had some involvement in General Joaquín Rangel's failed 7 June *pronunciamiento* to bring back Santa Anna, Herrera's government, fearful of Tornel's die-hard *santanismo*, decided to send him to a frontier post in the northern territories of the republic under the orders of General Mariano Arista. Unable to evade the order, Tornel found himself leaving the capital with his new wife on 8 June 1845. He did not leave, however, without first publishing an angry letter in which he stressed that he was innocent, that he had not been involved in any conspiracy to bring Santa Anna back to power, and that Herrera's government was being unjust and cruel in sending a sick man to fight in Texas.[2] On his way north, he stopped in the hacienda del Cubo; aware that Paredes y Arrillaga was now stationed in San Luis Potosí, he wrote him a letter asking to be exempted from serving at the Texan frontier since he was suffering from a particularly bad lung infection. He also reiterated to Paredes that he had not joined any conspiracy to bring back Santa Anna and that his services were at Paredes's disposition. Paredes sent Tornel a coach, and they met in San Luis Potosí in July, where they no doubt discussed the possibility of organizing a revolt that would bring an end to Herrera's government. One way or another, Tornel did succeed in stalling the order to join Arista's regiment in the north and was back in Mexico City by October, at the head of the Colegio de Minería.[3]

His sudden rapport with Paredes y Arrillaga was both surprising and unexpected. The men were not the best of friends. Although they had worked together to bring Santa Anna to power in 1841 and had maintained a fairly extensive correspondence in 1842 regarding the federalists' control of Congress,[4] their relationship had been a strictly pragmatic one. Only two years earlier, Tornel had tried to have Paredes y Arrillaga sent to Yucatán,[5] and after the discovery of his conspiracy of 1843 to overthrow Santa Anna, Tornel had urged Santa Anna to imprison him and was furious when he let him off.[6] There were also marked differences in their ideological standpoints. Paredes y Arrillaga was an ardent centralist and a passionate reactionary; from as early as 1832 he had expressed the view that only a monarchy could save Mexico from degenerating into the kind of anarchy that would be exploited by the United States in its expansionist bid to conquer Mexico.[7] He was also extremely proud of his military career and the importance of the army, and he hated the "terrible and destructive proletariat." He believed that a liberal democracy that embraced a federal system was completely inadequate for a country like Mexico whose stage of development meant that its people were not ready to be governed by such principles.[8] To quote Michael Costeloe, Paredes y Arrillaga was convinced that Mexico "could and needed to be governed exclusively by . . . the army and the rich and powerful classes, including the clergy, whose education, properties and honor would allow them to impose that political stability without which the country would never progress."[9] As he had noted in a letter to Santa Anna in 1842, the "affluent [acomodadas] classes are to politics what generals are to war."[10] In the same way that he believed that the rank and file should not make decisions in battle, Paredes y Arrillaga believed that the proletariat should not make any decisions in politics.

Evidently Tornel's ideas had evolved to the extent that by 1845, he did share a number of Paredes y Arrillaga's beliefs, albeit in more moderate terms. He identified with Paredes y Arrillaga's centralism, his militarism, and his mistrust of the masses. Nevertheless, having been one of the leading voices in the 1843 Junta de Notables, Tornel was still a committed constitutionalist. His populism, as evidenced in his promotion of free education to the masses, also distanced him from Paredes y Arrillaga's outright hatred of the populace. Tornel believed in restricting the suffrage to property-owning citizens, and even in imposing a temporary dictatorship, but he did not share Paredes y Arrillaga's commitment to banishing the masses completely from the political scene or in completely abandoning a constitutional representational system. It would only be after the 1846–1848 war that Tornel's belief in the need for a long-lasting dictatorship would become apparent. Above all, Tornel was a republican, and it would be this republicanism that prevented him from fully supporting Paredes y Arrillaga once he came to power.

Nevertheless, in the context of 1845, in pragmatic terms, it made sense for Tornel to join forces with Paredes y Arrillaga. Santa Anna had ungratefully turned against him and was in exile, far removed from the political theater of events. Their differences had not yet been resolved, and it was unlikely that the *caudillo* would be in a position to return to power in the wake of the Revolution of the Three Hours. Interestingly, there is evidence that in spite of their estrangement, Tornel and Santa Anna were still writing to each other during the *caudillo*'s exile, even if it was to accuse each other, in a particularly animated correspondence, of not having acted accordingly in power.[11]

Without Santa Anna, and bearing in mind that General Anastasio Bustamante's star had fallen since the collapse of his government in 1841, the only high-ranking officer, together with General Gabriel Valencia, who stood any chance of successfully overthrowing Herrera was Paredes y Arrillaga. Tornel was clearly aware of this. Otherwise it is difficult to understand how he came to support Paredes y Arrillaga's revolt, joining Valencia's mutiny of allegiance in the capital. Paredes y Arrillaga must have known that Tornel's apparent commitment to serving him in the summer of 1845 was not the result of a sudden change that had converted the gifted writer into one of his most ardent defenders. It was in Paredes y Arrillaga's interest to have Tornel working for him in the capital. He could not ignore what Tornel had succeeded in doing for Santa Anna, through his writings and by orchestrating events in Mexico City. This becomes apparent in the way that once Herrera had been overthrown and Tornel's function as a conspirator in the capital was over, Paredes y Arrillaga did not reward him with the Ministry of War but instead offered the post to General Juan Nepomuceno Almonte. Tornel was initially furious at the way Paredes y Arrillaga had used him, and it was only after he made his case well known that Paredes y Arrillaga grudgingly decided to offer him the Ministry of War on 21 February 1846.[12]

Although he served as minister of war under Paredes y Arrillaga's dictatorship from 21 February to 1 August 1846, he was disillusioned with the regime from the beginning, especially since the dictator's monarchist sympathies became known almost from the outset. On 12 February 1846 Lucas Alamán's newspaper, *El Tiempo*, having eulogized the principles of the revolt of San Luis Potosí in its previous issues, stated, "We want a representative monarchy."[13] Tornel was quick to respond, and in an article published in *El Memorial Histórico* on 19 February, he attacked the monarchist proposal in the same way that he had done in 1840, arguing on this occasion that Ferdinand VII's rule provided sufficient evidence to confirm that all monarchies, constitutional or not, were tyrannical. Much to Paredes y Arrillaga's displeasure, paralleling the reaction Gutiérrez Estrada's *Carta* had received in 1840, the majority of the press condemned *El Tiempo*'s monarchic proposal. It is clear from *El Tiempo*'s subsequent about-face over its monarchic principles that Alamán's emergent Conservative party was not a monarchist one. Although there were a number of highly influential politicians within Paredes y Arrillaga's entourage who had become monarchists by 1846,[14] the majority of Mexico's early conservatives were still republicans or were still pragmatic enough to realize that the nation was not yet ready to embrace a monarchic form of government in which a European prince would be invited to take the Mexican throne.

This became all the more evident in terms of the way in which Paredes y Arrillaga started to reconsider his monarchist affiliations. Pedro Santoni asserts that "in the light of the uneasiness that these developments created, Paredes abstained from making public statements that might link him to the monarchist plot. . . . Congress, he said, would determine whether Mexico should adopt a monarchical regime. Paredes clearly did not wish to make such a controversial and unpopular decision by himself, and sought to delegate to the legislature some of the burden."[15] Moreover, the declaration of war with the United States in April 1846 did not unite the conservatives. They became increasingly divided between those who wanted to press on with the monarchist proposal and those who, like Paredes y Arrillaga, became increasingly aware of the extent to which the majority of the political factions, traditionalists, moderates, radicals, and *santanistas* alike were strongly in favor of preserving a republican political system and would not allow a monarchy to be imposed. When Paredes y Arrillaga's Congress finally convened on 6 July 1846, he openly "embraced republicanism in a desperate bid to retain power . . . [and] confirmed that Mexico hungered to preserve republican institutions, and that the legislature would earn Mexico's gratitude if it acquiesced."[16]

In many ways, Paredes y Arrillaga's dictatorship was doomed from the beginning, in part because of the extent to which his closet monarchism divided the very factions that had brought him to power. However, equally important was the unexpected indecision he displayed once the Mexican-American War began in April. Faced with the fear of losing Mexico's sovereignty to the United States or even to a European power (should the monarchist plot have prospered), the *puros* found themselves joining forces once more with a significant number of *santanistas*, in spite of the memory of the events of 1834. Although the moderates did not participate in the conspiracy that led to the federalist revolt of 6 August 1846, which brought an end to Paredes y Arrillaga's dictatorship and to the Central Republic (1835–1846), ushering in the reinauguration of the 1824 Constitution, neither did they rally to the defense of Paredes y Arrillaga, for the obvious reason that he had led the movement that had overthrown Herrera's previous administration.

Tornel, having fulfilled his duties at the head of the Ministry of War for five months while showing no sign of actively supporting the government he was serving,[17] resigned on 1 August 1846, five days before the *puros'* revolt erupted. Although he was not prepared to rally to the defense of the dictatorship, neither did he take part in the revolt that brought back Santa Anna. There were three reasons for this: (1) Tornel was a committed centralist who could not, by 1846, join Valentín Gómez Farías's *puro* federalists; (2) having been the author and instigator of the Plan of Cuernavaca, he was at least consistent enough in his beliefs not to ally himself to those very individuals he had worked so hard to overthrow in 1834; and (3) he and Santa Anna had not yet overcome their differences. This becomes patently clear from the way Salas, Gómez Farías, and Santa Anna decided to ostracize Tornel from the corridors of power once the *caudillo* arrived in the capital on 14 September. It is worth noting that in the many letters that exist in the Valentín Gómez Farías Archive in Austin, Texas, dating from the buildup of the conspiracy to after the revolution that brought about Santa Anna's return, Gómez Farías's *puro* supporters, while prepared to accept that Santa Anna believed in upholding the federalist cause, were nevertheless extremely wary of bringing Tornel on board. In several letters José Eduardo de Salas and Ventura de Mora wrote to Gómez Farías, they alerted him to the risk of involving Tornel, who, like Alamán, "owned the forces of reaction,"[18] and, perhaps, most significant, could influence Santa Anna to turn their government into a dictatorship.[19] Santa Anna was also wary of the ideas and actions of his old friend. He had not yet got over the causes of their estrangement in 1844. As María del Carmen Vázquez Mantecón has noted, it was on Santa Anna's orders that Salas ordered Tornel to leave the Colegio de Minería and go to Tehuacán in late September. Tornel reached Tehuacán on 5 October and spent two months there before he went back to his home town of Orizaba,[20] where he remained until late February, claiming he needed to recover from a chest ailment.[21]

THE MEXICAN-AMERICAN WAR, 1846–1848

In what have been perceived as highly suspicious circumstances, the U.S. fleet allowed Santa Anna to return to Mexico from his exile in Cuba (16 August), and he went on to win the presidential elections in the fall of 1846 under the temporary presidency of General José Mariano Salas. Paralleling the events of 1833–1834, Santa Anna left the vice president, Valentín Gómez Farías, in charge of the government while he organized the defense of the republic and departed to fight the Americans in the northern towns of Saltillo and Angostura. With the Mexican economy in complete disarray, Gómez Farías attempted to raise the revenue to finance the war by demanding a forced contribution of 15 million pesos from the church (11 January 1847). The church responded by financing the Revolt of the *Polkos* (February 1847), which resulted in Santa Anna's removal of Gómez Farías from office in circumstances that mirrored those of 1834.

Although Santa Anna's intervention secured the army a loan of 1.5 million pesos from the church, with the understanding that Gómez Farías's line of thought would not be pursued any further, the country's political class remained as divided as ever, even after General Winfield Scott had landed in Veracruz (9 March 1847) and the U.S. forces were fast approaching the Valley of Mexico. The moderates had in fact participated in the Revolt of the *Polkos* and were subsequently involved in a power struggle with the *santanistas*. Radical federalist states such as Zacatecas, in response to Gómez Farías's dismissal, refused to support the government either by sending troops or providing funds to assist the war effort. By July the U.S. forces were already in Puebla, and by August they had reached the Valley of Mexico.

Although Santa Anna was president (December 1846–September 1847), he did not spend much time concerning himself with the political disputes in the capital. Instead, he concentrated his efforts on the war, leading the Mexican troops in the battles of Angostura (22 and 23 February), Cerro Gordo (18 April), and Amozoc (12 May). In the meantime, Tornel was asked to return to the capital in January; he replied that he would come back, although he claimed that his health was still frail.[22] He arrived in the capital in February and still needing time "to recover," awaited the outcome of the Revolt of the *Polkos*. He did not resume his military service until March, by which time General Scott had disembarked south of Veracruz.[23]

Coinciding with Santa Anna's brief return to the capital in March and a few days before his dismissal of Gómez Farías, Tornel and the *caudillo* met and succeeded in overcoming their differences after three years of estrangement. One can only guess at how Tornel and Santa Anna were able to reestablish their old friendship. Tornel must have felt particularly offended by the way the *caudillo* had forced him to resign in 1844 and then ordered his exile from the capital in 1846. Nevertheless, although their old personal ties must have played a significant part in the renewal of their friendship, politics was also on the agenda. Considering the dislike Tornel felt for Gómez Farías, one wonders whether he was the one who finally persuaded Santa Anna to drop his association with the *puro* federalists, in the wake of the Revolt of the *Polkos*. The way Santa Anna turned against Gómez Farías would certainly appear to suggest that Tornel had some influence on his actions, with the result that Ventura de Mora's fears came true. In José Fernando Ramírez's words, Santa Anna turned against the Gómez Farías administration because Tornel "perverted him with ideas that were entirely contrary [to what was expected], convincing him to march to take over the government because *his personal security and the salvation of the republic depended upon this step.*"[24] Tornel went on to create a *liga* (league), while Santa Anna set off again to fight the invaders at Cerro Gordo in order to consolidate the *santanistas'* power over the federalists, by silencing the moderate and radical enemies of the president.[25] Nevertheless, by August 1847, Tornel, like most other high-ranking officers, found that he had no alternative but to leave politics aside and fight the invading U.S. Army.

General Scott's army left Puebla on 7 August and reached the outskirts of the capital on 16 August, whereupon he moved one division to Tlalpan and the other to the proximities of San Angel. The first two defeats in the campaign of the Valley of Mexico came on 20 August, when, after two days' fighting, General Gabriel Valencia's troops were crushed in Padierna and Generals Pedro María Anaya and Manuel Rincón's forces were beaten in Churubusco. On 19 August, while Valencia's division were engaged in battle, Tornel wrote to the minister of war, unable to hide the fact that before him were the advancing troops of General Scott. He argued that his men were not only discouraged; they had received no pay since 10 August. Tornel wrote that they had reached "the extreme of not having provisions either to feed the troops or the horses."[26] Should they be ordered into action, it would be difficult to summon the required energy and enthusiasm. He insisted that his soldiers were given their 50 pesos pay. He argued that he would be responsible for supervising their pay, not including the pay of two of his sons whom he had with him as *ayudantes.*[27]

Following the U.S. occupation of Churubusco, Santa Anna attempted to bide his time by negotiating an armistice with Scott. When news of the proposed armistice reached Tornel on 22 August, with the order that while it lasted he was not to open fire on the Americans, he wrote back reassuring the minister of war that "Your Excellency's order will be fully implemented."[28] On 24 August, with the armistice now in place, he wrote another letter to the minister of relations, to inform him that although he had taken up his position in the *ejéricto de vanguardia,*[29] he had been made governor of the Federal District. Once more in the position of governor, albeit posted at the outskirts of the capital, it seemed important to him that confidence was restored in the capital. It was fundamental that they make the most of the armistice. His letter stated, "In my mind, if carts are allowed to use the streets and if at the same time shops are allowed to open during the armistice, I am sure that this will create a sense of relief in the city together with a sense of confidence, two things I am constantly working to achieve."[30]

On 25 August, however, the armistice started to take an unexpected direction. Not everybody was abiding by the rules of nonviolence. Since the armistice had been declared on 23 August, U.S. soldiers had started to move around freely on the outskirts of the capital, looking for beds and provisions in the neighboring haciendas. It was on 25 August that one of these soldiers got lost. He followed the path to Tacuba and asked for help from a priest, Manuel Reyes de Mendiola, who passed him on to his neighbor, one Pedro Zalacán, telling him to direct the man back to his camp. On his way back, three men on horseback tied a noose around his neck and dragged him from Xolalco to the Chapel of Santiaguito, where he had come across Manuel Reyes in the first place. By the time they got there, the soldier was dead. The three men took his clothes, his spurs, and his guns and left him lying dead on a tombstone in the graveyard.

On 26 August Captain Charles Ruff, at the head of sixty cavalrymen, followed by ten to twelve carts, rode into the graveyard of Santiaguito and demanded an immediate explanation of what had happened. Ruff said that if the three men responsible, the two Ponce de León brothers and one López, were not punished and hanged for breaking the armistice, he would be forced to punish the whole community of Tacuba with gunfire. The *Alcalde 1°* of Tacuba ran to tell Tornel of what had happened, pleading him to "take the necessary actions so that the aggressors give what is asked of them and as a result save the community from a catastrophe." Tornel passed the problem on to the minister of war. However, he added to the *alcalde*'s account his own view that these three men were innocent because in Azcapozalco, which is where they came from, nobody had yet heard of the armistice. He implied as well that it would not be a good idea to start executing their own fellow countrymen just because the Americans made such demands. Moreover, he returned the dead soldier's possessions to Ruff, but he made sure López and the Ponce de León brothers were safe from the captain's anger, sending them to the capital while reassuring Ruff that they would be dealt with accordingly.[31]

On 26 August he wrote another letter to the minister of war in which he noted that he had discovered that on the way to the hacienda of San Antonio, various of their own carts had been abandoned. He emphasized the vital importance of these carts. They were the only means of transporting the wounded back to safety. They were required for transporting food for the troops as well as to soldiers who had fallen prisoner.[32] However, on 27 August, apart from ceasing to serve as governor after having been only two days at the head of the Federal District, another incident distracted him from carrying out the plan to recover the carts or his more ambitious intentions of fortifying his defense of the capital. The armistice had given the U.S. soldiers opportunity to go into certain parts of the capital to obtain food and provisions for the troops. He gave specific orders to Colonel Joaquín García Luna that any American entering the capital must be fully escorted by Mexican troops. However, when Emile Votz told Captain Juan Palacios that he wanted to go to the Plaza Mayor to get provisions, Tornel was not informed. Furthermore, Palacios, having been given extraordinary powers by García Luna, told Votz that they could go in whenever they wished. By the time Tornel was informed of what had happened, Votz's men were in Mexico City.

As the U.S. carts moved freely into the main square, the Mexican civilians panicked. Seeing the American troops unescorted, the crowds thought it was an invasion. Understandably, the American soldiers were not a popular sight. The crowds started to gather around the carts. When Tornel was informed of Palacios's grave mistake of letting Votz's men march into the capital unescorted, he immediately feared the worst. If the Mexicans killed Votz's men, the armistice would be over. Fully aware of how much they needed the armistice to prepare for combat, he and some of his men galloped into the capital. By the time they reached the main square, the crowds had already gathered around the carts, and it appeared that violence was imminent. He immediately ordered his men to force the U.S. soldiers to retreat to the Plazuela de las Vizcaínas, where there would not be so many people. The crowd did not hesitate. They threw themselves at the carts. Tornel ordered his men to fend off the angry crowd for as long as they could and set off to get Santa Anna and a squadron of cavalry. By the time he returned, the carts were trying to retreat as they were being chased and pelted with stones. Seven of the drivers were seriously injured, and one of the carts had been destroyed. However, he and his men succeeded in getting all of the other carts out of danger. General José Joaquín de Herrera and Tornel agreed that it was not wise to open fire on their own people or to punish them. During the retreat, they were joined by General Joaquín Rangel and his brigade. General Denis Quijano led the retreating procession, with Tornel and Herrera at the rear. The leading American driver was prepared to acknowledge Tornel and his men's merit in having rescued them. As soon as they got back to their camps, Tornel had Colonel Joaquín García Luna arrested for giving Palacios the power to make such important decisions without consulting him first.[33] At half past ten that night, he wrote a second letter to the minister of war, demanding, "so that today's scandals are not repeated and our national pride is not wounded any further," that all provisions be hidden far from any place that might affect public security. However, he remarked that he did not understand why they had to supply the Americans with provisions.[34]

For the next eleven days, similar incidents continued to take place. The preparations for the defense of the capital were not satisfactory. On 6 September, the armistice was broken. General Scott's army moved closer to the capital and succeeded in taking Casa Mata and Molino del Rey on 8 September, suffering heavy losses in the process. On 11 September, Tornel, believing that the Americans had virtually taken Mexico City, gave a general alarm calling civilians to arms in his desperate attempt to organize the defense of the capital, an action that panicked the city. In a letter to Francisco Elorriaga, José Fernando Ramírez described him as "rash and foolish."[35]

On 12 September, he organized the transport of sandbags and barrels of *aguardiente* to the fortress of Chapultepec,[36] where General Nicolás Bravo was based with Santiago Xiconténcatl's national guard and the adolescent cadets of the Colegio Militar. All attempts to hold Chapultepec proved to be futile. The next day it fell to the Americans, and, with it, the last military focal point of resistance. Santa Anna told his war council that all was lost; the best course of action was for the army to leave the capital. On 14 September, General Scott marched into Mexico City. Without an army to defend Mexico City, the people took it upon themselves to fight the U.S. army withy sticks, stones, and whatever else they had. They were mowed down by U.S. artillery. After another day of street fighting, on 16 September 1847, the American flag was seen flying high in the Zócalo.[37] The war was over. Santa Anna resigned as president. On 2 November Tornel, claiming he was suffering from a lung affliction, asked permission to spend four months in Morelia, far from the political and military scene. In fact, he stayed for just under seven months.

The Mexican-American War of 1846–1848 ended formally with the Treaties of Guadalupe Hidalgo (2 February 1848), in which a defeated moderate Mexican government, led by Manuel de la Peña y Peña and constituted after the capture of Mexico City and subsequent resignation of Santa Anna, agreed, in spite of the vociferous opposition of the *puros*, to grant the United States half of Mexico's national territory (Texas, Alta California, and New Mexico, which included parts of Colorado, Utah, Arizona, and Nevada) in exchange for $15 million. Having experienced a stage of hope, a stage of disenchantment, and a stage of profound disillusion, Mexico now entered its final stage of despair.

As had been the case following the defeat of San Jacinto in 1836, the natural assumption would be that after such a colossal fiasco, Santa Anna's political career would have been forever over, and as a consequence, Tornel's career would also be over. Nevertheless, they managed to recover again. On 25 May 1853, just under five years after the debacle, Antonio Haro y Tamariz, minister of the exchequer, wrote to Tornel to inform him that

the *Excelentismo* General *Señor Presidente*, satisfied with your distinguished and very important services against the invading army during the hostilities in the Valley of Mexico, has thought it right to award you the badge of honor as decreed by the National Congress; a just tribute to your many and commendable merits during the defense of the capital.[38]

The president at the time was once again Santa Anna. Tornel was minister of war. Back in power, albeit for a last time, they succeeded in turning one of the greatest defeats in Mexican history into a cause for self-congratulation; they had fought with honor even if they had lost half the nation's territory.

With the fall of Mexico City, Santa Anna "wandered itinerant in the south."[39] He went from Tehuacán to Oaxaca, was expelled from Oaxaca by Benito Juárez, found himself fleeing from a squadron of vindictive Texans, moved to Perote, from there to Xalapa, and with the U.S. authorities' permission finally left the country in 1848 for Jamaica, and later Turbaco, Colombia, where he went into exile for a second time and did not return until 1853. Tornel hung on in Morelia, out of sight (out of mind), claiming ill health, while de la Peña y Peña was faced with the unenviable task of signing away half of Mexico's territory to the United States.[40] The humiliation was such that five years passed before the return of Santa Anna could be organized once more. As Tornel traveled to Morelia, an anonymous letter from Querétaro appeared in *El Monitor Mexicano* conveying a vision of Tornel that probably expressed a view that had become widespread following the debacle of the invasion:

A demagogue, a turn coat, a centralist, a federalist, he has been everything he could be; he has become a general without ever fighting; he has left his public post with a fortune; his children . . . and his relatives are a weight on the treasury and after he demoralized and corrupted the army which has gone and lost the war, it is very natural that he continues to conspire against any government he does not lead.[41]

Nevertheless, unlike Santa Anna, Tornel did return to the capital in July 1848[42] and worked his way slowly back into the corridors of power by initially dedicating himself to a quiet life concentrating on presiding over the Colegio de Minería.

TORNEL AND THE *SANTANISTA* PARTY

Class and ethnic tensions started to erupt in a wide range of minor and major agrarian revolts that spread throughout the republic in the latter half of the decade. One of the larger and more violent of these revolts was the so-called Caste War fought in Yucatán (1847–1852). Unlike all the previous secessionist revolts that had taken place in Yucatán before 1847 and that had been led by the Creole elite, the Caste War of 1847 was a bloody and devastating racial, social, and political revolution in which the Maya almost succeeded in driving the white minority out of Yucatán. Other major agrarian and indigenous revolts surfaced in the central Sierra Gorda and in the southern present-day states of Oaxaca, Guerrero, and Morelos, reaching the State of Mexico in 1849.[43]

If news of the French Revolution of February 1848 was celebrated by the Mexican intelligentsia at first, as it brought an end to the regime that had inflicted the French Pastry War on Mexico ten years earlier, it was not long before the events in France came to be perceived as an ominous prophecy of the chaos that lay ahead for lesser "advanced" republics like their own. Fear of the kind of social dissolution and anarchy that the press reported to have taken over "civilized France," with the resulting inauguration of the "Republic of the Peasants" (1848–1851), polarized the beliefs of the different political factions even further. The Mexican political class—regardless of whether they were traditionalists, moderates, *puros*, or *santanistas*—became convinced that Mexico was about to suffer an even worse revolution than the French one of 1848, especially given that the agrarian revolts that were spreading rapidly throughout the republic had a racial dimension that had not been an issue in France.

A strong sense of despair started to pervade the writings of most, if not all, of the politicians and intellectuals of this period. The sense that Mexico was heading for a cataclysmic social and racial revolution that would result in the complete destruction of society tarnished and affected the views of all of the political factions. This sense of despair was intensified by the equally strong fear that in less than four years, the United States would end up annexing the remaining half of Mexico's national territory—that is, the half that had not already been taken in the Treaties of Guadalupe Hidalgo. Thus it was during the moderate presidencies of Generals José Joaquín de Herrera (June 1848–January 1851) and Mariano Arista (January 1851–January 1853) that the different factions organized themselves into more formal parties in an attempt to come to grips with the defeat of 1847 and the resulting loss of territory and to prevent the escalating agrarian and racial revolts from destroying what was left of civilized society, while they still harbored the hope of finding the means of preventing a future U.S. intervention from finally bringing Mexican sovereignty and independence to an end.

Therefore, 1849 witnessed the creation of Lucas Alamán's Conservative party, the Moderate party, the *Puro* party, and José María Tornel and Juan Suárez y Navarro's *Santanista* party. With the despair so widespread, Tornel's *santanista* proposals had evolved yet again, to the extent that Tornel had ceased to believe in constitutional projects, in the need for a Congress, or in the need for elections. The despair of the 1848 loss caused him to advocate the creation of a dictatorship that would benefit from having a small council of enlightened individuals to advise its executive and control it. Nevertheless, like Alamán, Tornel still believed that the executive, however strong it was, needed to respect certain "principles and responsibilities."[44]

In fact, by 1849 *santanista* political thought had evolved in such a way that it shared many of Alamán's conservative principles. They supported the Catholic faith in that it represented one of the fundamental defining characteristics of Mexican nationality and identity—what Alamán described as "the only tie left that unites the Mexican people."[45] They ostensibly defended the church's privileges, something that could be proved by their reversal of Gómez Farías's administrations reforms in 1834 and 1847. Moreover, as stated in the *Bases Orgánicas*, they did not believe in granting freedom of the press to those writers, publishers, and printers who published attacks on the church. They also believed in creating a strong centralist state with a large army and a modern system of taxation. Santa Anna's flirtation with the federalists in 1846 was representative of neither the *santanistas'* beliefs nor probably those of Santa Anna himself, who at the time needed to find the means of returning to Mexico from his exile in Cuba. If there was a difference between Alamán's 1853 proposal and that of the *santanistas*, this revolved around two issues: the unstated monarchism of one of the factions within the Conservative party clashed with the *santanistas'* republicanism, and the *santanistas'* populist tendencies did not rest easily with the conservatives' public scorn for anybody who was not *gente decente*.

While it is clear that the *santanistas* still believed in a representative system in 1843 and that a dictatorship, such as that created in the *Bases de Tacubaya*, was perceived to be a temporary measure, the same could not be said for their stance in 1849. By the end of the decade, after all the upheavals that had taken place and weakened the defense of the nation to the extent that a smaller U.S. Army had succeeded in taking the capital, resulting in the loss of half of the national territory, the *santanistas* had come to see a dictatorship as the only means of establishing long-lasting order, peace, and stability. Tornel's speech during the annual celebrations of independence in 1850 reverberated with this contagious and generalized sense of despair: "If we meditate on our situation and how we have arrived here after a prolonged series of disputes, it will not be strange if we qualify [our history so far] as deplorable and desperate, and that if the republic is still alive we owe it to some miraculous concession from heaven."[46]

Tornel and the *santanistas* who came to form their 1849 *Santanista* party, with its corresponding newspaper, *La Palanca*, had come to view Congress as one of the main culprits of their previous disasters: "Mexico needs a government in which strength may be concentrated and which occupies only a handful of men, a government that thinks, [in a system] in which the majority are not expected to participate in public matters: which may govern over the departments, which obeyed by these may ensure local well-being."[47] Their despair had led them to abandon their previous belief in a representative system, even one restricted even further to wealthier property owners. It was no longer the case that Mexico's political factionalism, heightened in systems that promoted dialectic, was responsible for the nation's instability. A weak representative system had brought with it disunity and in the end the loss of "half our territory . . . *the wasted legacy of our elders*." For Tornel, the Mexican reality in 1850 was one in which "the worst misfortunes have weighed on our young republic, and its sweetest illusions, its greatest and most glorious hopes have all vanished like smoke."[48]

In its despair, *La Palanca* presented the people as a sick man. One of the lessons they needed to learn after three disastrous independent decades was that this "sick man," while aware of his illness, had not known how to cure himself and had been ill advised and chosen the wrong doctors. The "sick man" needed a dictatorship: "not just a doctor, but a guardian who ensures the prescribed medicine is taken. . . . The people, thus need a man who can guide them by the hand along the right path so that they can be cured of their illnesses, diseases caught thanks to the errors of twenty lost years."[49] The man they wanted to name dictator was Santa Anna, for he was "the Only general who in Tampico, Veracruz and Angostura has measured his sword with Spaniards, Frenchmen, and Anglo-Saxons. The Only one who has abandoned the big stick of authority and left the mother country because of his love for the mother country."[50] However, this dictatorship need not involve "absolute despotism, for although we believe this nation is still far from reaching its period of political perfection, it is nevertheless well beyond that of oppression."[51]

The *santanistas* shared Alamán's view that their dictatorship needed to be controlled by select members of the intelligentsia. Where they did not necessarily agree was on the *santanistas'* insistence that the dictatorship had to guarantee the "conservation of our republican institutions."[52] For José María Bocanegra, it was a case of being pragmatic. The Mexicans had little choice in the matter. Mexico was not ready to live according to democratic principles. They had tried hard to consolidate them, and yet had failed time and again. It was absurd to go on formulating new representative constitutions when they always ended up becoming dictatorships anyway. It was preferable to establish a dictatorship that consolidated "a well-constituted society" once and for all, by responding to "the reality of things" rather than choose another constitutional system that, although beautifully adorned with "magical words" and "promises," would prove once more unworkable, "having no echo or support amongst the majority of the population of the republic."[53]

Perhaps what differentiated the proposals of the *Santanista* party from those of the Conservative party in 1849 was that they incorporated in their ideology a committed defense of antipolitics, a defense that they had succeeded in associating with the army and Santa Anna's own past involvement in the nation's politics. *Santanismo* was therefore presented from the beginning as a national movement rather than a political party or faction. For this reason *La Palanca* claimed that it was natural that the *Santanista* party should be made up of "men who have previously been monarchists, *puros* and moderates." If "persons of such different political inclinations [*comuniones*]" had joined under the *santanista* banner, this was precisely because their party represented a national patriotic movement.[54] The *San-*

tanista party was opposed to "party hatreds and the blows different factions give each other,"[55] it was made up of "men who ardently desire UNION NATIONALITY."[56] What Mexicans needed to do, following the *santanistas'* example, was to "have a mother country [*tener patria*]," to have a strong sense of what that mother country was, what it represented, what it meant, and to create a government in which Santa Anna could rule "our destinies" with a "wide base, in which there may be space for all the factions." This could be possible given that a *santanista* government would not represent "a faction but the people." Still faithful to their liberal origins, the *santanistas* were not seeking to impose a tyranny but a strong and enlightened government that would "strictly obey the resolutions of our eminent men."[57]

Nevertheless, although Tornel and Suárez y Navarro kept the *santanista* flag flying in the daily editorials of *La Palanca* up until November 1850,[58] the time was not yet right for the *santanistas* to stage a successful comeback. Only in 1853, after three more years of instability, would it be possible for Tornel and the *santanistas*, in tandem with the Conservative party, to organize the return of the *caudillo*. Although a major takeover of the government in 1850 was unfeasible, Tornel did succeed in returning to the corridors of power by becoming a senator on 17 January 1850, a post he was to hold until 8 January 1853.

TORNEL, SENATOR

By the time of Tornel's fifty-fifth birthday (1 March 1850), he could at least feel some comfort at having made a significant political recovery from the 1847 debacle. Although the *santanistas* were not in power and Santa Anna was far away in Colombia, he had succeeded in being elected senator. Moreover, he was still at the head of the Colegio de Minería and had been elected president of the Compañía Lancasteriana on 4 January that year (a position he would continue to enjoy until 8 January 1852). He appeared to be happily married to Catarina Silva and had seven children (José María, Agustín, Manuel, Guadalupe, María Trinidad, Victoria, and Mariana).[59] His prestige as a writer and an intellectual remained untarnished. A year earlier, Tornel had written the first and most eloquent critique of the first volume of Lucas Alamán's *Historia de Méjico*, condemning the way that the leader of the Conservative party had presented the figure of Miguel Hidalgo.[60] Together with his review of Alamán's voluminous history, he had also found the time to publish a number of articles in *El Album Mexicano* on a series of authoritarian historical figures he clearly associated with Santa Anna, such as Louis Philippe of Orleans, Julius Caesar, Napoleon Bonaparte, and Oliver Cromwell.[61] Notwithstanding the despair he felt regarding Mexico's political situation, on a more personal front he was content. In marked contrast, his great friend Bocanegra had not recovered from the impact that the war with the United States had had on his life. Unlike Tornel, who still found the energy to stage a comeback in the political stage of the capital, Bocanegra abandoned politics. Although he briefly returned to Mexico City in 1848 to serve as deputy for San Luis Potosí, he did not stay for long and retired from politics altogether, dedicating the rest of his years to writing his *Memorias*, which were not published until 1892, thirty years after he died.

Nevertheless, between 1850 and 1853, Tornel was not as active or prominent in Congress as he had been when he had served as deputy in 1826–1828. His most memorable intervention as senator revolved around the part he played in presiding over the committee that was set up in 1851, and was in active deliberation well into 1852, to explore the possibility of creating a canal that could unite the Atlantic with the Pacific at the Isthmus of Tehuantepec.[62] Tornel, in line with the balancing act Ignacio Trigueros had carried out as minister of the exchequer in the 1841–1844 administration, proposed the protectionist measure that two Mexican companies should be responsible for the canal work (Compañía de Guanajuato and Compañía de Payno, Pesado and Olarte) while allowing foreign and, in particular, U.S. investment to finance the project.[63]

The reason that Tornel's role as senator was relatively minor can be accounted for only by the fact that he decided, following Alamán's example, to write his own history of independent Mexico, of which the first (and only, because of his subsequent death) unfinished volume was published by Ignacio Cumplido, first in serialized form in *La Ilustración Mexicana* in 1852 and subsequently as a book in its own right in 1853:[64] the *Breve reseña histórica de los acontecimientos más notables de la nación mexicana, desde el año de 1821 hasta nuestros días*. Rather than dedicate his time and energy to making himself heard in Congress, Tornel decided that it was more important to project his evolved *santanista* ideology in a historical account of the first three decades that would, by the slow and careful indoctrination of others, ensure the perpetuation of his own new ideology.

TORNEL, THE HISTORIAN

The *Breve reseña histórica* is first and foremost a documented account of the first national decade (1821–1829). Although its narrative centers mainly, albeit somewhat erratically, on the years between the Plan of Iguala (1821) and the rise of Vicente Guerrero to the presidency in January 1829, numerous allusions are made to subsequent events, such as the 1836 Texan campaign and the Mexican-American War (1846–1848). The passages of the book dedicated to the Arenas conspiracy (1827) and the Revolt of Montaño (1827–1828), with their corresponding inserted documents, remain the most detailed account of this period, providing a particularly useful historiographical source of information for any study of these years.

As Lucas Alamán went on to acknowledge in the last volume of his *Historia de Méjico*, he used the noted pages of Tornel's "Reseña histórica" (as published in *La Ilustración Mexicana*) when writing about Arenas and the Montaño Revolt since Tornel offered the most informed account, having been in a position of power at the time these events occurred.[65] Nevertheless, a study of the *Breve reseña histórica* clearly illustrates how Tornel had come to view the nation's politics by 1852. At one level, it tells us more about Tornel's late *santanismo* than what he actually thought as a young *yorkino* in the mid-1820s. His reiterated praise of Santa Anna, coupled with his representation of the political class's failures (regarding issues such as the economy, the chosen constitution, the adoption of a federalist charter, the political participation of the masses, the abused freedom of the press, the importance of the Catholic church, and the need for a strong executive), offer insight into the ideas the *santanistas* had come to embrace in the wake of the 1847 debacle.

Perhaps the most striking aspect of Tornel's historical account is its tone. From beginning to end Tornel conjures up a strong sense of pathos in his narrative. With remarkable consistency, the history of the first national decades is presented as a tragedy in which Tornel allows himself the literary luxury of lamenting with particularly emotive language, using forceful images and numerous allusions to ancient Roman history, the fall of a country that appeared to have so much in its favor when it became independent. As is expressed in the quote from Virgil with which the book begins, "Thus in you do I understand such a great desire / To listen to the brief account of our grief, / Even though memory may want to hold back its tears, I will proceed with our mournful history [*Sed si tantus amor casus cognoscere nostros / Et breviter Trojae supremum audire laborem, / Quanquam animus meminisse, luctuque refugit / Incipiam*].'" Tornel's *Breve reseña histórica* is thus a "mournful history" in which, time and again, he reminds his readers of how many of his countrymen's hopes of the early 1820s vanished over time: "Why have we abandoned a path that could have led us to a state of indisputable prosperity? Why have evil political passions become prevalent over generous sentiments, sentiments which are proper and genuine in the Mexican people? Ah! The times of hope pass in nations with the speed of lightning, and those of despair and misfortunes last for too long in the cycles of time."[66] It is a text that epitomizes the stage of despair the Mexican political class found itself in after the war and is very much in line with other pieces Tornel was writing at the time. His 1850 speech during the annual celebrations of independence expressed with parallel lyricism that very sense of lost hope and despair that shrouds the narrative of the *Breve reseña histórica*:

The dawn of another 27 of September lights with golden sunrises the faces of happy men, whose chests are full of joy, whose souls are in ecstasy, contemplating the greatest of fortunes [that lie ahead]. When the sun poured torrents of light on one of the most beautiful valleys in the universe, the streets and squares of this proud city, this very garden where we stand congregated today, sad as it is at present, threatened by autumn, were full of a vast crowd who had gathered to celebrate the arrival of the Liberator, the hands up in the sky to bless him. . . . The people who walked with him raised arcs of triumph . . . and no ominous fears were felt at all; their hopes were so great as the very event they were celebrating. And yet . . . these hopes have escaped before our eyes, like the fabulous scenes of a theater.[67]

Tornel's lament was not just an expression of the angst he felt over those three wasted decades that he came to portray as having been characterized by their civil conflicts and the loss of half the national territory. By highlighting where they had gone wrong, Tornel was projecting his evolved ideology. The way the hopes of the 1820s degenerated into the despair of the early 1850s was not the result of fate. They had made mistakes, and his focusing on these showed his clear intent to propose, albeit indirectly, a corrective political proposal. By blaming federalism, Congress, certain economic policies, the behavior of the parties, the excesses of the press, the involvement of the masses, and a long list of incompetent or self-interested politicians, Tornel was arguing that in order to avoid the destruction of Mexico, these ideals and individuals should be replaced by others that defended centralism, a strong executive, different economic policies, a nationalist antiparties *santanista* movement, censorship, a dictatorship, and a small council of *santanistas* with the great Santa Anna at the head of the nation. The need for this change of direction was also presented as being extremely urgent. Echoing Alamán's own conviction that it was probably only a matter of years before the United States annexed the rest of Mexico,[68] Tornel argued that "there is a threat of new misfortunes, and even of a definitive and tragic cataclysm that may end with our political existence, the glory of our race, of our language and of the religion of our forebears." For this reason it was important that they studied their own history, so that when all was lost, at least the memory would remain "of everything that we are, everything that we have, everything that we are worth, . . . [and of] the great injustice that led the Mexican nation to become a tragic victim."[69] Tornel's tragic vision of Mexico was not in any way unique. As had been noted in an 1849 calendar: "For war? We aren't [any good]. For governing? We don't know how. Thus why do we exist?"[70]

Representative of the *santanistas'* military belief in antipolitics, the parties were mainly to blame. It was the parties that perverted the army by inviting it to use its force to intervene in national politics. They instigated divisions and factionalism by pursuing party interests, sacrificing in the process what was best for the nation. They tampered with the nation's legal system, its constitutions, and its authorities to please their own damaging ends, thus contributing to the chaos and a generalized propensity toward disregarding the laws of the land that came to form part of everyday life in the republic. They consciously misinterpreted the political systems that were established, thinking only about their members and supporters, and consequently corrupted every aspect of Mexico's political life. Their extreme and belligerent behavior also led to inhuman condemnations and recriminations that resulted in plunging the country into a state of civil conflict. Intent on destroying their opposition, they turned insignificant events into major catastrophes by deliberately exaggerating their importance, finding conspiracies and enemies where there were none, or where they did not deserve the attention they were given, gratuitously provoking the anger of a volatile and easily incensed people. In a country where the "imagination of the people is as ardent as the sun that shines, and its passions are as terrible as the lava of its volcanoes," the parties' behavior resulted in the inevitable decline and fall of a nation that upheld with reason so many hopes on the eve of independence. And when the parties came to power, they invariably abused it, finding jobs for their supporters, subjecting their enemies to suffer the brunt of their tyrannical dispositions. Moreover, obsessed with finding work for their supporters rather than hoping to reform the country in an honest bid to improve its condition, the parties lied time and again, hiding their real intentions behind the "hypocritical mask" or wording of one *pronunciamiento* or another. It was impossible to moderate the parties and thus of no use to attempt to create a political system in which they may surface. So long as there were parties, civil wars would feature prominently in the life of the nation.[71] Clearly Tornel was arguing for the creation of a nationalist *santanista* government in which there would be no space for different political parties. Anyone who was a *santanista* could join the nationalist movement, but there would no longer be a moderate, a radical *puro*, or a conservative party. Inevitably, this would be difficult to implement in a system where there were elections. However, Tornel had ceased to believe in the suitability of a representative government. Mexico needed a dictatorship in which parties and factions could not exist.

Each one of the constitutions had been a failure, as confirmed by three decades of instability in which every charter had been ignored, abused, and ultimately overthrown by force. Constitutions were nothing other than pieces of paper written to be later torn up. The people had been tricked by every one of them. In practice all they had been were lies, since not a single government had legally attempted to abide by them. Of course, there was a good reason for this. The people of Mexico were not yet ready to be governed by a constitutional representative system in which an elected Congress debilitated the needs of the executive. The constitutions had failed because they were either foreign imports (such as 1824 charter) or did not pay any attention to the customs and traditions of a young nation whose people were not mature enough politically to know what was best for the country and where the parties had come to the fore and done as they pleased with the law. There was no point in having a constitution when all it did was set down unrealistic and impracticable laws that eventually would be ignored or overruled by force. Again, although Tornel did not explicitly defend imposing a dictatorship in which there would be no constitution to limit or restrict its executive's decisions, it can be inferred from his condemnation of Mexico's past constitutions, Congress's tyranny during Iturbide and Victoria's terms in office, whether as emperor or president, and his depiction of the people as passive, volatile, or easily seduced, set against a backdrop in which the parties had done so much to destroy any legitimacy Mexico's political class may have had, that Tornel was defending the kind of constitutionless *santanista* dictatorship that would in fact come into existence in April 1853.[72]

Tornel was not only indirectly advocating the creation of a dictatorship in terms of his condemnation of constitutions. His virulent attack on the freedom of the press was equally forceful. The press had been shamelessly abused, and the people, so easily seduced, had allowed themselves to be contaminated by the lies the newspapers of the period had published. Mexico was not ready to be exposed to a combative press, especially when the press was invariably used by the parties to scandalize the world with the most monstruous of inventions. For Mexico to prosper, there was an urgent need for a strong government to take hold of the nation and consolidate its position without being subjected to the destabilizing accusations the press was prone to inventing. Censorship had become for Tornel a necessary prerequisite if they wanted to ensure order and stability in the republic.[73]

What was also clear from his *Breve reseña histórica* was that, in Tornel's mind, federalism had played a significant part in weakening the republic, leading to the eventual loss of Texas and, later, half of the national territory to the United States. Threatened and attacked by Spain, France, and the United States during its first national decades, Mexico desperately needed a strong centralized government, to be "a strong and compact republic." However, they had mistakenly chosen to adopt a federalist charter in 1824 (which had been reinstated in 1846), which had led to the disintegration of a nation that in 1821 had been twice the size it was now. Federalism was expensive; it weakened the country's defense, led to anarchy, and had represented the first step toward a secessionist movement that had culminated in the loss of Texas, California, and New Mexico. Consistent with the views he had sustained from as early as 1834, Tornel remained a committed centralist in 1852.[74]

The way the economy had been handled had also contributed to the degradation of a country that had become by 1852 "the laughing-stock of the universe." Their first mistake had been to dismantle the tax system that the colony had imposed in New Spain when it was clear that it worked by raising the necessary revenue on a regular basis. Thereafter they had made the further mistake of becoming deeply indebted, taking on loans from British companies in what had been particularly disadvantageous terms. To add insult to injury, a propensity to throw money away, creating a proliferation of bureaucratic jobs when there was no need for them, had gradually led to an ongoing economic crisis in which the treasury was empty and there was little hope of recovery. The expulsion laws of 1827 had also had a disastrous impact on the Mexican economy, one from which they had not yet recovered. Indirectly defending the policies that had been pursued by Ignacio Trigueros in 1841–1844, Tornel was once more proposing the need for taxes rather than loans.[75] However, symptomatic of the *santanistas'* traditional ostensible defense of church privileges, Tornel was, at least on paper, strongly opposed to the nationalization of church property.

Echoing an earlier article in which he had argued that the "religious sentiment" was the fundamental conservative principle on which any orderly society remained intact in regard to the threat of social dissolution and that they needed to nurture "the seeds of religion which were planted in Mexico by our parents . . . for the good of society and for our own benefit,"[76] Tornel argued in his *Breve reseña histórica*, in words that paralleled those of Alamán, that if there was one thing that united Mexico, it was its ardent Catholicism. In other words, to attack the church amounted to attacking one of the main pillars of Mexican identity—a fundamental one at that, since religion was the only means by which social dissolution and immoral anarchy could be kept at bay:

Whoever thinks, judges and publishes [the idea that it is important to attack the church], does not know the deep roots Roman Apostolic Catholicism has buried in our ground; does not know that the corrupting doctrines that Europe has spread around the world for two centuries have not been well-received here, even by those of us who may be deemed libertines; ignores that a government without Faith in Mexico is not popular, and that its fall is [inevitable].[77]

It is following on from this that the United States appears in the *Breve reseña histórica* as Mexico's worst and most dangerous enemy. Tornel could not help noting the irony that, having once defended Santa Anna's idea of liberating Cuba from Spain, it was now far preferable that it remained a Spanish and Catholic colony than that it was freed only to become annexed by the United States. Quoting amply from his earlier *Tejas y los Estados Unidos*, Tornel forcefully criticized the United States for its expansionism, ambition, brutality, and the unjust way it had behaved toward Mexico, especially once the Mexican-American War broke out. Since another war was almost inevitable given that the United States would not be satisfied with having acquired only half of Mexico's national territory, the need for a change of government in Mexico was all the more pressing.

The need for a strong, centralized military dictatorship that could face up to U.S. aggression was implicit in Tornel's text.[78]

Tornel, albeit indirectly, was presenting the political program he would pursue in 1853. Mexico needed a strong, centralized, military dictatorship if it wanted to retain its sovereignty, and the man who was most suited to take on the executive was his old friend Santa Anna. Considering that Santa Anna's role in politics was not that significant in the first decade of nationhood, except that he led the *pronunciamientos* of 2 December 1822, 5 June 1823, and 12 September 1828, it is indicative of Tornel's political, rather than his strictly historical, intentions that the *caudillo* features so prominently in the book. Tornel provides detailed accounts of Santa Anna's involvement in the three *pronunciamientos* he staged during these years, together with a favorable narrative of his plans to liberate Cuba, his pacification of Veracruz in the wake of the Montaño revolt, and his campaign against Generals Manuel Rincón and Calderón in 1828.

Santa Anna is thus depicted as having been "a soldier of valor, genius and good fortune," an "ardent *caudillo*, whose valor has been confirmed so often in the battle field," "an eminent citizen, whose only ambition has been to feature as a philosopher and a friend of men," a man "whose inspiration always leads him towards the great and the heroic," "keener to obtain the glory of the soldier than to ambition that of the general," a man feared because of "his gigantic importance as a warrior," and yet who has always been "prudent and impartial" when in power, who has avoided becoming sullied by the factionalism of party politics, and has merited the nation's admiration for having been "eminently active," "ready to take risk," "a soldier moved by enthusiasm," "a revolutionary," a man "who possesses an unbreakable sense of civil rights," and one who has invariably "followed the voice of public opinion."[79] It is clear that Tornel was campaigning for Santa Anna's return. Further evidence of this is that when the time came for organizing his friend's return from exile, Tornel abandoned the writing of his *Breve reseña histórica* to put into practice what he had been advocating in writing since 1849.

Many of Tornel's conclusions at the end of his political life bore a great resemblance to the views Simon Bolívar had come to uphold, regarding Spanish America as a whole, over two decades earlier. The nature of the countries' population, their lack of political experience, and the propensity of their congresses to tie "the hands and even the heads of its men of state" meant that "no form of government is so weak as the democratic." They were "far from emulating the happy times of Athens and Rome"; they could not compare themselves "in any way to anything European." Given that their race was "of the most unwholesome sort," they were not in a position to "place laws above heroes and principles above men." If they attempted to do so, they would witness again "the beautiful ideal of a Haiti and see a breed of new Robespierres become the worthy magistrates of this fearful liberty." In brief, "our America can only be ruled through a well-managed, shrewd despotism."[80] To attempt to impose democracy in Spanish America was futile. Spanish America was "ungovernable. Those who worked for her independence have ploughed the sea."[81]

THE RETURN OF SANTA ANNA

Although there is no evidence of Tornel's having been in touch with Santa Anna, it would be difficult to believe that they were not in correspondence considering the events of 1853. In July 1852, Colonel José María Blancarte deposed the governor of Jalisco, Jesús López Portillo, in Guadalajara and demanded the return of Santa Anna. Although initially it was not clear whether the call for Santa Anna's return had widespread support, by the end of 1852 it had, especially given that the conservatives came to accept the idea that they could support the *santanistas* as long as Alamán could control the administration that would come about as a result of their alliance. Faced with the inevitable, Mariano Arista resigned on 6 January 1853. It was only a matter of months, with both Juan Bautista Ceballos (6 January–8 February) and General Manuel María Lombardini (8 February–20 April) temporarily taking the presidency, before Santa Anna returned from his exile in Colombia to assume the presidency for one final time.

As the *santanista* revolt started to gather momentum in the summer and fall of 1852, Alamán put aside his constitutionalist considerations, monarchical sympathies, and defense of a gradual process of evolution and led his party into an alliance with the *santanistas*. This alliance resulted in the establishment of a republican centralist dictatorship in which censorship was brutally applied to the press and in which Congress was replaced by a reduced council of ministers and intellectuals who, acting as the precursors of Porfirio Díaz's *científicos*, ensured during the first six months of the dictatorship that General Santa Anna did not allow his own personal extravagance to get the upper hand. In the often-cited letter Alamán addressed to Santa Anna on 23 March 1853, he argued that by 1853, the Conservative party, made up of "property-owning citizens [*gente propietaria*], the clergy and all those who desire what is best for their nation," believed in the following principles: (1) that the church and its privileges should be respected and protected, for the Catholic faith was the only tie left that united the Mexican people; (2) that any anticlerical and anti-Catholic publications should be censored; (3) that the government needed to be strong, even though he stressed that it was important that it was subjected to certain "principles and responsibilities" in order that it did not abuse its power; (4) that the federation should be dismantled and replaced by a centralist system; (5) that any form of representative system based on elections should be eradicated for the time being; (6) that the army needed to be large, albeit proportionate to times of peace; (7) that the army could be supplemented by militias made up of property-owning citizens like those that had been formed under the colony; and (8) that Santa Anna, because of his energy, was the ideal person to lead this political proposal.[82] Clearly by 1853, the proposals of the conservatives and the *santanistas* had finally converged.

Tornel asked permission to go to Xalapa on 18 March 1853.[83] As Fernando Díaz Díaz points out the *santanistas* "were apparently led by José María Tornel."[84] It is not surprising that he took an active part in restoring Santa Anna to power. Coinciding with Santa Anna's arrival in Veracruz on 1 April 1853, Tornel proclaimed Santa Anna president from Xalapa.[85] Faced with no significant opposition, Santa Anna became president for the last time on 20 April. Tornel was rewarded with the Ministry of War on the same day, in spite of the fact that Alamán tried to prevent Santa Anna from including him in the cabinet. Santa Anna was not prepared to negotiate over the inclusion of his old friend, Tornel, in the government.[86] As John Lynch argues, "This was a dictatorship but one which took pride in its ideals of modernisation, an early model of 'order and progress,' hallmarks of Alamán's conservatism,"[87] and equally of Tornel's *santanismo*.

From April to September the dictatorship demonstrated through its legislation that *santanistas* and conservatives alike were serious about their intention to impose the "principle of order" throughout the republic. On 22 April all federal authorities were abolished. On 25 April the *Ley Lares* ended all freedom of the press. On 11 and 14 May two decrees were issued formalizing the centralization of political power and the organization of a new direct taxation system. On 20 May it was agreed that henceforth the regular army would be made up of a record number of 90,000 troops. In August the so-called Law of Conspirators was passed, decreeing that anybody found guilty of conspiring against the regime would be court-marshaled and executed immediately. In September the Jesuits were allowed to return to Mexico, almost a century after their expulsion from New Spain.

Although a dictatorship that attacked all civil and political liberties was established in April 1853, Santa Anna's despotic tendencies during the first six months were in fact controlled by his small council of enlightened ministers, and there was an equally committed attempt on their behalf to motivate industry, promote education, and solve the problem of the lack of resources. Alamán (minister of relations), Tornel (minister of war), and Antonio Haro y Tamariz (minister of the exchequer) were distinguished intellectuals whose careers had been characterized by their great liberal expectations, patriotism, and ability to write eloquent historical and political studies. They were hoping to use Santa Anna's authority to reform the nation gradually and peacefully, establishing the kind of order and stability that had been so elusive until then.

The first months of the dictatorship were in many ways an early version of the dictatorship Porfirio Díaz would succeed in imposing from 1876 to 1910. The *santanista* nationalist antiparties movement claimed to be apolitical, not unlike the *porfirista* slogan that argued at the end of the century that with General Díaz there was "little politics, plenty of administration." Instead of a Congress, enlightened state builders, again not unlike General Díaz's *científicos*, surrounded Santa Anna and worked on ways in which progress and modernity could be achieved, advising and controlling the dictator. As Enrique Krauze has noted recently: "Díaz represented, quite accurately in effect, Alamán's program . . . yet *from* a liberal legitimacy, *from* a liberal order." It was a "monarchic life with republican forms."[88]

As is evident from the circulars Tornel issued as minister of war, if there was one aspect of his political ideology that had not changed, it was his belief in having a strong and large regular army. As far as his beliefs regarding the army were concerned, the reforms he put forward were completely consistent with his ideals of 1835. He demanded the expansion of the armed forces; restoring the Regiment of Grenadiers, the battalions of Mestitlán and Tuxpán, the squadrons of lancers of Tulancingo, Córdoba, and Toluca, creating the battalion and the squadron of lancers of Monterrey. He also demanded "an increase in the provisions of the infantry and the cavalry as well as clothes for all the corps." He ensured that the lottery system he had devised to make the military service fairer and to see that it incorporated honorable citizens was reinstated. He issued orders guaranteeing the promotion of education among the rank and file of the army, that the hospitals were well served; and that the widows and orphans of the heroes who had died in Jalisco in 1852 received their rightly deserved pensions. He enforced severe punishments on deserters. He legislated reducing the number of generals and reformed the circumstances in which the Cross of Honor could be awarded.[89]

Tornel and Santa Anna's friendship was rekindled. The two men based themselves in Tacubaya issuing decrees daily. It would appear that finally the dream of *santanistas* like Tornel had been accomplished. Enjoying the laurels of victory, in what Jan Bazant describes as a mood of "expansion," it is alleged that Tornel, while chatting with Santa Anna and Antonio Haro y Tamariz, laughed and said, "Our system of government consists basically of Señor Haro, minister of the exchequer, looking for money, so that I can throw it away as minister of war."[90] Nevertheless, Tornel, as he had always done, worked hard to ensure that power rested with them. He created a secret police whose main aim was to purge the army of any undesirable individuals, and he kept a tight control of Benito Juárez's movements in Oaxaca.[91]

Tornel and Alamán's optimism soon proved to be unfounded. When Alamán died on 2 June, the administration lost any control it might have had over Santa Anna. Haro y Tamariz resigned on 5 August, depriving the government of its leading economist. On 11 September at ten o'clock in the morning, Tornel suffered from a severe attack of apoplexy and died, leaving Santa Anna on his own to decide the future of the country. To quote Bazant, Haro y Tamariz's resignation "together with Alamán and Tornel's deaths . . . had a profound impact on Santa Anna's behavior. The president lost his moral sense and became an autocrat."[92] After September 1853, the dictatorship ceased to formulate a political project and became a personalist tyranny whose sole purpose appeared to be to keep Santa Anna in power. After Alamán, Haro y Tamariz, and Tornel were gone, Santa Anna created the extravagant Distinguished Mexican Order of Guadalupe in November and went on to proclaim himself *Su Alteza Serenísima* (His Serene Highness) in December.

It was the beginning of the end. A regime that became increasingly tyrannical, coinciding with the rise of a new generation of liberals as represented by Benito Juárez, signaled the end of an era. By 1854 the dictatorship had succeeded in infuriating just about everybody. The conservatives felt betrayed by the fact that Santa Anna was doing little to pacify the increasing popular discontent, which was threatening to destroy their property. The moderates and the radicals despised everything about the regime and what it represented: its constitutional illegality, its repressive measures, and so on. On 1 March 1854 the Plan of Ayutla was proclaimed, and what would become one of Mexico's bloodiest civil wars before that of the *Reforma* (1858–1861) began. By the summer of 1855 the Revolution of Ayutla succeeded in overthrowing the regime, and on 16 August 1855, Santa Anna was forced into exile. Without Tornel to work for him in the capital and having been overtaken by a new period in Mexican history, Santa Anna was not able to return to Mexico until 27 February 1874, a sad octogenarian whose death on 20 June 1876 passed unnoticed.

11 SEPTEMBER 1853

Tornel died without seeing how the last *santanista* experiment, like all the others, went wrong. Quite fittingly it was precisely on 11 September, the anniversary of the glorious *santanista* victory of Tampico, which Tornel had done so much to commemorate in his capacity as Santa Anna's leading propagandist, that he died at the age of fifty-eight. Although María del Carmen Vázquez Mantecón explores the hypothesies that he committed suicide and that he was even assassinated, poisoned in the same way that Nicolás Bravo was a few months later, both of these conjectures remain unlikely and impossible to prove.[93]

On 12 September, Luis de Ormachea sent out letters asking the various corps to present themselves at the Colegio de Minería on 13 September at eight o'clock in the morning, for Tornel's funeral.[94] Santa Anna "ordered that magnificent funeral rites were performed for Sr. Tornel, and that all the military and civilian authorities of the Republic dressed in mourning for three days in homage to the memory of the minister who had been so influential in the triumph of the *santanista* party."[95] All schools were asked to be in mourning for nine days, and the Compañía Lancasteriana organized eight masses in Tornel's honor.[96] The president's grief was not disguised, although he surprisingly did not attend the funeral. He had lost the one friend who had helped him rise to power throughout his political career. Whether Santa Anna was prepared to acknowledge it or not (he did not mention Tornel once in his autobiographical *Historia militar y polítcia*), Tornel, acting as his loyal informer in the capital, his master manipulator and conspirator, his most talented propagandist, a key player in the all-important ministry of war, and even as the key ideologue of his political movement, had become his most outstanding and influential supporter. Without him, coincidentally or not, Santa Anna was never able to return to the presidential seat again. Juan Suárez y Navarro, on 11 September, wrote the following letter to all high officials in the Mexican army:

Dear Sir—

Today at ten o'clock in the morning the *General de División*, Minister of War and Marine, Don José María Tornel died as a result of a sudden attack of apoplexy. This sad and deplorable event has filled the Excellent President and the whole cabinet with grief and consternation, because if at any time and in any circumstances the loss of a general and politician of such eminent virtues, talents and patriotism would be lamentable, today, as a worthy member of the government, as he has been on previous occasions, his loss is irreparable. His endeavors and hard work to achieve the high mission he had accepted to contribute to the regeneration and progress of our mother country, giving her a responsible direction, will be sorely missed.

The entire nation knows and appreciates the merits and distinguished services that His Excellency *Señor* Tornel will present to posterity as one of her favorite sons. His Excellency the President, possessed by the deepest and most just grief, has given me the order of informing your Excellency of such a tragic event, and there is no doubt that you will share the profound sentiments of pain which have gripped the Supreme Head of State and his ministers. These sentiments affect the author of these lines with equal vigor, as an honest friendship accompanies the memory of our great obligations to the illustrious deceased.

God and Liberty. Mexico 11 September 1853,

Juan Suárez y Navarro.[97]

NOTES

1. Regarding Santa Anna's trial in 1845 see Carlos María de Bustamante, *El nuevo Bernal Díaz del Castillo o sea Historia de la Invasión de los angloamericanos en México* (Mexico City: SEP, 1949), pp. 15–24.

2. *El Siglo XIX*, 8 June 1845.

3. María del Carmen Vázquez Mantecón, *La palabra del poder. Vida pública de José María Tornel (1795–1853)* (Mexico City: UNAM, 1997), pp. 146–147.

4. See Mariano Paredes y Arrillaga Archive, Nettie Lee Benson Latin American Collection, University of Texas at Austin, 140/1–47.

5. See their correspondence in *El Siglo XIX*, March–May 1843.

6. Manuel María Giménez, *Memorias del coronel Manuel María Giménez, ayudante del campo del General Santa Anna, 1798–1878* (Mexico City: Lib. Vda. De Ch. Bouret, 1911), pp. 262–264.

7. Francisco de Paula Arrangoiz, *México desde 1808 hasta 1867* (Mexico City: Porrúa, 1968), p. 389.

8. Mariano Riva Palacio Archive (henceforth referred to as MRP), Nettie Lee Benson Latin American Collection, University of Texas at Austin, Nos. 140/143, Paredes y Arrillaga to José María Tornel, 10 May 1842.

9. Michael P. Costeloe, "Los generales Santa Anna y Paredes y Arrillaga en México, 1841–1843: Rivales por el poder o una copa más," *Historia Mexicana* 34: 2 (1989): 421.

10. Paredes y Arrillaga to Santa Anna, 29 April 1842, in Genaro García (ed.), *Documentos inéditos o muy raros para la historia de México*, vol. 56 (Mexico City: Porrúa, 1974), pp. 20–21.

11. Two of these letters were printed in *El Republicano*, 9 April 1846. Noted in Vázquez Mantecón, *La palabra del poder*, p. 149.

12. José Fernando Ramírez, *México durante su guerra con los Estados Unidos*, in Genaro García (ed.), *Documentos inéditos o muy raros para la historia de México*, vol. 59 (Mexico City: Porrúa, 1974), pp. 459–466.

13. *El Tiempo*, 12 February 1846.

14. See Miguel Soto, *La Conspiración monárquica en México, 1845–1846* (Mexico City: Editorial Offset, 1988).

15. Pedro Santoni, *Mexicans at Arms. Puro Federalists and the Politics of War, 1845–1848* (Fort Worth: Texas Christian University Press, 1996), pp. 103–104.

16. Ibid., p. 105.

17. It is worth noting that from the beginning, Tornel attempted to publicize the fact that he did not belong to Paredes y Arrillaga's traditionalist faction. On taking the post of minister of war, he declared that it was his intention to serve the government, not a particular party, and that he hoped it would be the members of Congress who decided what form of government would be eventually adopted. See Vázquez Mantecón, *La palabra del poder*, p. 148.

18. VGF: No. 2180, José Eduardo Salas to Gómez Farías, 29 October 1846.

19. VGF: No. 2408, Ventura de Mora to Gómez Farías, 20 January 1847.

20. Vázquez Mantecón, *La palabra del poder*, pp. 149–151.

21. AHM: Exp. XI/III/I-93, letters by Mariano Aguilar and Tornel, 16, 23 October 1846, 26 January, 25 February 1847.

22. AHM: Exp. XI/III/I-93, letter by Tornel, 26 January 1847.

23. AHM: Exp. XI/III/I-93, letter by Tornel, 25 February 1847.

24. Ramírez, *México durante su guerra con los Estados Unidos*, p. 534.

25. Ibid., p. 535.

26. AHM: Exp. XI/481.3/2640, letter by Tornel, 19 August 1847.

27. Ibid.

28. Ibid., letter by Tornel, 22 August 1847.

29. Ibid., letter by Tornel, 19 August 1847.

30. AHM: Exp. XI/481.3/2651, letter by Tornel, 24 August 1847.

31. Ibid., letter by Tornel, 26 August 1847 (includes account by *Alcalde 1ero Constitucional* of Tacuba).

32. AHM: Exp. XI/481.3/2640, letter by Tornel, 26 August 1847.

33. AHM: Exp. XI/481.3/2647, letter entitled "Carros del enemigo" by Tornel, 27 August 1847.

34. AHM: Exp. XI/481.3/2651, letter by Tornel, 27 August 1847.

35. Ramírez, *México durante su guerra con los Estados Unidos*, p. 544.

36. AHM: Exp. XI/481.3/2656, letter by Tornel, 12 September 1847.

37. For the Mexican-American War, see Josefina Zoraida Vázquez, *La intervención norteamericana 1846–1848* (Mexico City: SRE, 1997).

38. AHM: Exp. XI/III/I-93, letter by Antonio Haro y Tamariz, 25 May 1853.

39. Vázquez, *Don Antonio*, p. 31.

40. AHM: Exp. XI/III/I-93, letter by Tornel, 26 February 1848.

41. *El Monitor Republicano*, 19 November 1847.

42. AHM: Exp. XI/III/I-93, letter by Tornel, 1 July 1848.

43. For regional indigenous and agrarian revolts and conflicts for this period, see Moisés González Navarro, *Raza y tierra: la guerra de casta y el henequén* (Mexico City: El Colegio de México, 1970); Leticia Reina, *Las rebeliones campesinas en México, 1819–1906* (Mexico City: Siglo XXI, 1980); Evelyn Hu-Dehart, *Yaqui Resistance and Survival: The Struggle for Land and Autonomy, 1821–1910* (Madison: University of Wisconsin Press, 1984); Marie Lapointe, *Los mayas rebeldes de Yucatán* (Mexico City: El Colegio de Michoacán, 1983); Cecile Gou-Gilbert, *Una resistencia india. Los yaquis* (Mexico City: INI/Centro de Estudios Mexicanos y Centroamericanos, 1985); John Tutino, *From Insurrection to Revolution in Mexico: Social Bases of Agrarian Violence, 1750–1940* (Princeton, NJ: Princeton University Press, 1986); Friedrich Katz (ed.), *Revuelta, rebelión y revolución: la lucha rural en México del siglo xvi al siglo xx*, 2 vols. (Mexico City: Era, 1990); Carmen Vázquez Mantecón, "Espacio social y crisis politica: La Sierra Gorda 1850–1855," *Mexican Studies/Estudios Mexicanos* 9:1 (1993): 47–70; and Michael P. Costeloe, "Mariano Arizcorreta and Peasant Unrest in the State of Mexico, 1849," *Bulletin of Latin American Research* 15:1 (1996): 63–79. For the years 1848–1853, see Moisés González Navarro, *Anatomia del poder en México (1848–1853)* (Mexico City: El Colegio de México, 1977).

44. Lucas Alamán to Santa Anna, 23 March 1853, in Gastón García Cantú (ed.), *El pensamiento de la reacción mexicana. Historia documental*, vol. 1 (1810–1859) (Mexico City: UNAM, 1994), p. 315.

45. Ibid., p. 314.

46. José María Tornel, *Discurso pronunciado en la alameda de la ciudad de México en el dia 27 de septiembre de 1850* (Mexico City: Imp. de I. Cumplido, 1850), p. 12.

47. *La Palanca*, 19 June 1849.

48. Tornel, *Discurso[. . .] 1850*, p. 5.

49. *La Palanca*, 3 May 1849.

50. Ibid., 14 June 1849.

51. Ibid., 3 May 1849.

52. Tornel, *Discurso . . . 1850*, p. 13.

53. José María Bocanegra, *Memorias para la historia de México independiente, 1822–1846* (Mexico City: Fondo de Cultura Económica, 1987), vol. 3, pp. 39, 330–331.

54. *La Palanca*, 19 June 1849.

55. Ibid., 5 June 1849.

56. Ibid., 26 May 1849.

57. Ibid., 10 May 1849.

58. The complete run of *La Palanca* (1 September 1848–16 November 1850) can be found in the British Library, Colindale [F.Misc.181].

59. Váquez Mantecón, *La Palabra del poder*, pp. 89, 102.

60. See Michael P. Costeloe, "La Historia de México de Lucas Alamán: Publicación y recepción en México, 1849–1850,"*Memorias de la Academia Mexicana de la Historia* 38 (1995): 121–123. Also *El Siglo XIX*, 20, 24, 26, 27 November 1849.

61. Vázquez Mantecón, *La palabra del poder*, p. 161.

62. See *Dictamen de la comisión especial de Tehuantepec del senado, encargada de ecsaminar las varias resoluciones dictadas con motivo del privilegio exclusivo concedido a D. José Garay, y de proponer la que deba adoptarse, atendido el estado que guarda actualmente este negocio* (Mexico City: Imp. O'Sullivan y Nolan, 1851); and José María Tornel, *Voto particular del señor senador D. José María Tornel, individuo de la comisión especial que entiende en los negocios relativos al Istmo de Tehuantepec, sobre privilegio de abrir la via de comunicación* (Mexico City: Imp. de Vicente García Torres, 1852).

63. Tornel, *Voto particular*, pp. 26–27.

64. María del Carmen Vázquez Mantecón, "José María Tornel y Mendívil," in Virginia Guedea (ed.), *Historiografía mexicana, Vol. 3: El surgimiento de la historiografía nacional* (Mexico City: UNAM, 1997), pp. 360–361.

65. Lucas Alamán, *Historia de Méjico*, vol. 5 (Mexico City: Editorial Jus, 1969), p. 8.

66. Tornel, *Breve reseña histórica*, pp. 3, 30.

67. Tornel, *Discurso . . . 1850*, p. 11.

68. *El Universal*, 24 November 1848.

69. Tornel, *Breve reseña histórica*, p. 135.

70. *Undécimo calendario de Abraham López; arreglado al meridiano de México y antes publicado en Toluca para el año de 1849* (Mexico City: Imp. de A. López, 1849), p. 23.

71. Tornel, *Breve reseña histórica*, pp. 21, 42, 78, 81, 90, 91, 109, 130, 132, 134, 180, 181, 235.

72. Ibid., pp. 6, 7, 12, 21, 107, 296.

73. Ibid., pp. 80, 163, 236, 259, 260, 323, 382.

74. Ibid., pp. 13, 20, 39, 50, 148, 149.

75. Ibid., pp. 9, 10, 12, 20, 53, 54, 116–129, 171, 176, 177.

76. José María Tornel, "El sentimiento religioso. Principio conservador de las sociedades," *El Siglo XIX*, 17 April 1843, pp. 2–3.

77. Tornel, *Breve reseña histórica*, p. 64.

78. Ibid., pp. 50, 51, 78, 85, 134–160, 181.

79. Ibid., pp. 10, 11, 39, 41, 73, 77, 332, 333, 349.

80. Vicente Lecuna and Harold A. Bierck, Jr. (eds.), *Selected Writings of Bolívar*, 2 vols. (New York: Colonial Press, 1951), pp. 188, 189, 624.

81. Quoted in Joseph Conrad, *Nostromo* (London: J. M. Dents & Sons, 1923), p. 186.

82. García Cantú (ed.), *El pensamiento de la reacción mexicana*, pp. 313–316.

83. AHM: Exp. XI/III/I-93, letter by Tornel, 18 March 1853.

84. Fernando Díaz Díaz, *Caudillos y caciques. Antonio López de Santa Anna y Juan Álvarez* (Mexico City: El Colegio de México, 1972), p. 237.

85. Ibid., p. 242.

86. Vázquez Mantecón, *La palabra del poder*, p. 168.

87. John Lynch, *Caudillos in Spanish America, 1800–1850* (Oxford: Clarendon Press, 1992), p. 353.

88. Enrique Krauze, *Siglo de Caudillos* (Barcelona: Editorial Tusquets, 1994), p. 311.

89. See the *Circulares del ministerio de guerra y marina* held in the Colección Lafragua, Biblioteca Nacional, for the following dates: 25 April; 12, 30 May; 9, 11, 16, 22 June; 1, 2, 5, 16, 20 July; 13, 30 August 1853.

90. Jan Bazant, *Antonio Haro y Tamariz y sus aventuras políticas 1811–1869* (Mexico City: Colegio de México, 1985), p. 68.

91. Díaz Díaz, *Caudillos y caciques*, p. 246.

92. Bazant, *Antonio Haro y Tamariz*, p. 72.

93. Vázquez Mantecón, *La palabra del poder*, pp. 24–26.

94. AHM: Exp. XI/III/I-93, letter by Luis de Ormachea, 12 September 1853.

95. Manuel Rivera Cambas, *Antonio López de Santa Anna* (Mexico City: Editorial Citlaltépetl, 1958), pp. 200–201.

96. Vázquez Mantecón, *La palabra del poder*, p. 22.

97. AHM: Exp. XI/III/I-93, letter by Juan Suárez y Navarro, 11 September 1853.

6

Conclusion

A study of José María Tornel y Mendívil's life, and, in particular, his relationship with Antonio López de Santa Anna, offers two important insights into the politics of Independent Mexico. At one level it proves the extent to which Tornel's politics, and those of the political class at large, evolved as the hopes of the 1820s degenerated into the despair of the 1840s. The numerous accusations that were directed at Tornel by a significant number of his contemporaries, in which he was portrayed as a turncoat, an opportunist, and a cynical politician who repeatedly changed sides in order to secure a position in government, can no longer be taken at face value. As I have already shown in *Mexico in the Age of Proposals, 1821–1853*, these accusations were remarkably common at the time, affecting politicians and factions that encompassed the entire political spectrum of Independent Mexico. Evidently the pursuit of power was never absent in Tornel's writings, actions, and machinations. It would be naive to suggest that all that he wanted was what was best for Mexico. Nevertheless, it remains the case that he tried consistently to improve the political and social situation of the republic, accepting that his national projects belonged to a changing ideology that represented the interests of the *hombres de bien* and a reformist *santanista* army. Whether it was by reforming the army, pursuing a hard-line policy on law and order, or promoting education, it becomes evident that Tornel sought a political solution to Mexico's ongoing crises. His gift with words gave him a prominence in the cultural life of the country that was shared by only a small minority of politicians. He was unique in the army as a man who besides playing a major role in the political life of the republic, was also among the nation's emerging elite of writers. Although his most eloquent adversaries (Lorenzo de Zavala, Carlos María de Bustamante, and José María Luis Mora) were persistent in portraying him as a Machiavellian wheeler-dealer who could be a federalist as well as a centralist, depending on the circumstances, they were nevertheless prepared to recognize his merits, albeit grudgingly, as one of Mexico's most inspired writers. It is not surprising, in this sense, that when the Spanish poet and dramatist José Zorrilla wrote one of the first critical essays on Mexican literature since independence, included in his volume of poetry *La flor de los recuerdos* (1855), Tornel appeared, with Francisco Sánchez de Tagle, as one of Mexico's *literati* "deserving of an honorable mention."[1]

A study of his political career, paying close attention to the context in which he moved, shows how misleading and, essentially, inaccurate was Zavala's dictum that Tornel was a man whose political opinions could not be known, since "he never adopts a permanent color."[2] As this book has illustrated in its narrative of the first national decades, Tornel proposed a number of influential political projects that changed in response to the different crises that affected the newly formed nation. His changes from insurgent to *iturbidista* (1821) and from *iturbidista* to federalist republican *yorkino* (1823–1825) arose as responses to the inability of the insurgents to bring about independence on their own, and to the failure of the First Mexican Empire. His conversion from a radical federalist republican *yorkino* to a moderate one in 1828 was the result of the polarization of politics that characterized the end of Guadalupe Victoria's presidency, with the imposition of the expulsion laws of 1827, the advent of an increasingly extremist agenda on the part of the *yorkinos* in the wake of the battle of Tulancingo, and the violent eruption the political participation of the masses brought with it as represented in the traumatic Parián riot of 1828. His subsequent change from moderate federalist republican to moderate centralist republican (1834–1835) was also a case of Tornel's trying to come to grips with a changing reality. The perceived failure of the 1824 Constitution paired with Tornel's own experience of the Texan question led him to abandon his federalist beliefs in the quest for a system that could strengthen the republic to meet the threat of U.S. expansionism and the unpatriotic and divisive behavior of the American colonizers in Texas. In similar fashion, his repudiation of the 1836 Constitution came about as it became obvious that the Supreme Conservative Power was ineffective in dealing with the problems the country was undergoing: the federalist revolts of 1838, 1839, and 1840 and the French Pastry War (1838–1839). It was only after the additional failure of the *santanista* experiment of 1841–1844, with its centralist republican 1843 Constitution, that Tornel finally became a reactionary centralist republican who believed in the need for a dictatorship (1849–1853). His political transformations, although opportune in some cases, were nevertheless consistent in the way that his views clearly changed in response to the specific political contexts with which he was faced.

As one political experiment after another failed to provide Mexico with the order, stability, and prosperity its political class had dreamed of achieving in 1821, Tornel, with the benefit of experience, renounced certain ideas in order to adopt new ones, in the hope that the day would come when they would succeed in finding a proposal that, in marrying tradition with modernity, and idealism with pragmatism, would consolidate a long-lasting and stable political system. It was only once Iturbide's pseudo-monarchist proposal (1822–1823), the federalist proposals of 1824–1835 and 1846–1853, and the centralist proposals of 1835–1841, 1841–1843, and 1843–1846 had all failed to save Mexico from an increasingly unstable and violent situation, that Tornel finally abandoned his faith in constitutionalism and embraced the proposal that imposed the dictatorship of 1853–1855. The despair of his last years was more than understandable. Not only had the dreams of 1821 proved unattainable. Tornel had witnessed a series of foreign military interventions (1829, 1838–1839, and 1846–1848), the loss of Texas (1836), the emergence of the brutal Caste War in Yucatán (1847–1852), a long list of *pronunciamientos*, all of which had been further tarnished by an economy that was beginning to appear beyond salvage in the 1850s. As Josefina Zoraida Vázquez rightly noted regarding the changes most of the politicians of the period underwent, these "should not strike us as anything extraordinary; these were times of change, in which people had to respond to a changing reality. They did not observe the events like us; they lived them, suffered them, and, above all, they did not understand them."[3] A study of Tornel's life exemplifies only too well how this was the case. In the same way that R. J. Salvucci came to the conclusion, in reviewing Jan Bazant's biography of Antonio Haro y Tamariz, that "[Haro's] life is a metaphor for mid-nineteenth century Mexican politics,"[4] Tornel's adventures and misadventures would appear to be equally representative of the ups and downs that characterized Mexican politics in the aftermath of independence.

A study of Tornel's life goes a long way to accounting for Santa Anna's own changes and political behavior. It also proves the extent to which Santa Anna's repeated rise to power relied on Tornel,[5] who went on to become his informer in the capital, his leading propagandist, and his master intriguer. Would Santa Anna have been as well informed as he was about events in the capital on all those occasions he retired to his hacienda or was away in exile had it not been for Tornel? Would Santa Anna have acquired such notoriety and prestige, eventually being compared to Napoleon, recovering in the process from such major disasters as the 1836 Texan campaign and the 1847 debacle, had it not been for Tornel's eulogies to the *caudillo*? Would Santa Anna, from Veracruz, have been in a position to organize the concerted *pronunciamientos* of 1834, 1841, and 1842, without the invaluable help of Tornel? The answer to each one of these questions is probably not. Tornel was in many ways what, at the end of the twentieth century, has come to be known as a spin doctor. He was Santa Anna's exceptionally industrious spin doctor. And yet he was much more than a wizard of propaganda. In the end, Tornel provided Santa Anna and the *santanistas* with their antiparties, antipolitics, nationalist ideology. It was Tornel who ensured that the regular army became a predominately *santanista* institution and was equally instrumental in giving *santanismo* a strong populist slant through his exertions in the field of education. While Santa Anna appeared to be mainly preoccupied with ensuring that he was in control of his home province of Veracruz, it was Tornel who gave the *caudillo* a voice in national politics by consistently representing the *caudillo*'s interests in the capital (with the noted exception of their years of estrangement, 1844–1847) and placing his verbal dexterity at Santa Anna's disposal. Without Tornel, Santa Anna was not able to return to power after his fall of 1855.

This study offers new insight into the intellectual process by which one of the most prominent politicians and writers of the early national period evolved in constant response to the many crises Mexico underwent between 1810 and 1853. Although the evolution of the different factions and their leading exponents followed different courses and involved the seeking of different solutions to those Tornel pursued, they were nevertheless inspired by the same crises and turning points of the first national decades. In the same way that a study of the political evolution of Lucas Alamán or José María Luis Mora may assist us in understanding the different stances their particular factions came to hold at different times, a study of Tornel's life serves to help us appreciate with greater clarity the beliefs the *santanistas* sustained between 1821 and 1853. Tornel emerges as a key figure in the way that his own particular ideas and actions offer a fundamental insight into how and why the *santanistas* at large, together with Santa Anna, went from advocating a radical liberal agenda in the 1820s to defending a diametrically opposed reactionary one in the 1850s. Furthermore, by appraising Tornel's own essential contribution to Santa Anna's success during these years, this study offers a new insight into the *caudillo*'s own ideological maneuvers, as well as an explanation for his repeated rise to power.

There is still much work to be done before we arrive at a truly satisfactory interpretation of Independent Mexico and the role Santa Anna played in it. Further research needs to be undertaken regarding Santa Anna's activities in Veracruz before we can know for certain whether his reluctance to assume the presidency stemmed from his own personal preference for life in the hacienda or whether it was more a case of his believing that it was more important for him to control the politics of Veracruz, as long as he had Tornel representing his interests in the capital. Tornel himself deserves to be researched more fully. It is already clear from the two books about him (María del Carmen Vázquez Mantecón's *La palabra del poder* and this one) that Tornel does not necessarily inspire entirely identical interpretations of his role in politics. Vázquez Mantecón's study views Tornel as a writer who gave as much importance to Agustín de Iturbide, Guadalupe Victoria, Vicente Guerrero, and Anastasio Bustamante as he did to Santa Anna; this study offers an interpretation of his political career that links him to Santa Anna. Moreover, his merits as a writer have not been given the attention they deserve. An entirely new study is waiting to be written that focuses primarily on his literary output and the contribution he made to Mexican and, for that matter, Latin American literature in the nineteenth century. Nevertheless, Tornel's importance is beginning to be taken into account, something that can be evidenced by the recent publication of two books dedicated to his career. Tornel emerges as a key player in early republican politics, as one of Mexico's most interesting and controversial nineteenth-century politicians and as the man who did so much to enable Santa Anna to become one of the most notorious and influential generals of Independent Mexico.

NOTES

1. José Zorrilla, *La flor de los recuerdos. Ofrenda que hace a los pueblos hispano-americanos don José Zorrilla, Tomo 1* (Mexico City: Imp. del Correo de España, 1855), p. 418.

2. Lorenzo de Zavala, *Albores de la república* (Mexico City: Empresas Editoriales, 1949), p. 187.

3. Josefina Zoraida Vázquez, *Don Antonio López de Santa Anna. Mito y enigma* (Mexico City: CONDUMEX, 1987), p. 13.

4. R. J. Salvucci, "La parte más difícil'. Recent Works on Nineteenth-Century Mexican History," *Latin American Research Review* 28:1 (1993): 108.

5. Also see Will Fowler, "The Repeated Rise of General Antonio López de Santa Anna in the So-Called Age of Chaos (Mexico, 1821–1855)," in Fowler (ed.), *Authoritarianism in Latin America since Independence* (Westport, CT: Greenwood Press, 1996), pp. 1–30.

Glossary

agiotista	moneylender
aguardiente	liquor
alameda	central park
alcabala	tax
alcalde	mayor, town hall councillor, seniority of which was denoted by the added numbers (i.e. 1°, 2°, 3° etc.)
Alteza Serenísima	Serene Highness (title first adopted by Father Miguel Hidalgo in 1810)
ayudante	aide, assistant
ayuntamiento	town hall, municipality
Bases de Tacubaya	1841 political charter
Bases Orgánicas	1843 Constitution
campesino	peasant
capitalino	native, inhabitant of the capital
capitular	town hall administrator, bureaucrat
caudillo	national rather than regional chieftain, leader
científicos	positivist intellectuals who assisted General Porfirio Díaz during the latter half of his dictatorship (1876–1910)
cívicos	civilian militias
Comisionado Regio	Royal Agent (refers to Spanish agent sent to Mexico in 1827 by Ferdinand VII)

cura	priest
diezmo	church tax
ejército de vanguardia	frontline army
escocés/es	member/s of the Scottish Rite of Masons, consolidated in Mexico after 1816 during War of Independence
estanco de tobaco	tobacco monopoly
exaltado/s	radical/s
fuero	corporate privilege or exemption, inherited from the colony, applied to the army and the church
gachupín/es	Spaniard/s
Generalísimo	Supreme General (title first adopted by Father Miguel Hidalgo in 1810)
gente decente	the middle and upper middle classes, "proper/decent" people
gómezpedracista/s	supporter/s of General Manuel Gómez Pedraza
grito de Dolores	call to arms with which War of Independence started (16 September 1810)
guadalupe/s	clandestine Creole movement that supported the insurgents from Mexico City during the War of Independence
hacienda	a rural private estate
hacienda de caña	sugar cane *hacienda* / mill
hombres de bien	the more affluent members of Mexico's emergent political class
hombres de privilegio	see *hombres de bien*
hombres de progreso	liberals in favor of progress, freedom of the press, and so forth
imparciales	faction created in 1828 by Valentín Gómez Farías and Francisco García to counter the influence of the *yorkinos*
indigenismo	historical philosophy that grants greater importance to the influence Mexico's ancient civilizations have had on the present (of the 1820s) than that represented by the Spanish colonial administration
indigenista	a defender of *indigenismo*
indultado	insurgent who handed himself in to the Spanish authorities during the War of Independence accepting the granted viceregal pardon
indulto	official pardon offered to the insurgents who surrendered
Informe del Gobierno Supremo de Coahuila	Report of the Supreme Government of Coahuila
iniciativa	proposal (within context of annual ministerial reports)

intendencia	province, state as organized under the colony
itubidista/s	supporter/s of Agustín de Iturbide
jarocho	from the province of Veracruz
jefe político	district administrator appointed by state governors
Junta de Notables	1843 constituent Junta of Worthies, handpicked by the *santanista* administration after the closure of the 1842 Constituent Congress to draft the *Bases Orgánicas*
Junta Instituyente	1822–1823 council with which Iturbide replaced the closed-down Congress
lépero/s	member/s of the urban lower classes
letrado	lawyer
leva	arbitrary method of military recruitment in which force was used
licenciado	university graduate
maleante	criminal
memoria de guerra	annual report of the Ministry of War
mestizo	of mixed race (Indian and Hispanic), within a Hispani-sized social context
mulato	of mixed race (Indian and Afro-Caribbean)
negocios pendientes	unfinished business
novenario	nine day cycle of religious festivities
novenario/s	faction created by ex-*escoceses* and moderates; included José María Luis Mora among its members
oficio	formal letter
partido del orden	party of order
patronato	the right to nominate priests and bishops
peninsular/es	Spaniards
plaza mayor	main square
poblano	from the province of Puebla
polkos	pro-clerical supporters of February 1847 revolt against Gómez Farías vice presidency; called *polkos* because (1) they belonged to affluent classes who danced the polka and (2) because the revolt was accused of favoring the United States, whose president at the time was James Polk
pronunciamiento	proposed political plan, at times resulting in or from an armed rebellion
pulque	alcoholic drink
pulquería	saloon where *pulque* is sold

puro/s	radical/s
regidor	see *capitular*
santanismo	philosophy of the *santanistas*
santanistas	faction named after Santa Anna
secretaría	secretariat
Siete Leyes	1836 Constitution
tlaco	currency made up of pieces of wood or soap used by shopkeepers when there was a shortage of real currency
vagos	idle members of the rabble
veracruzano	from the province of Veracruz
xalapeño	from the town of Xalapa
yorkino/s	members of the Masonic Rite of York, consolidated in Mexico in 1825
yucateco	from the province of Yucatán
zócalo	main square

Selected Bibliography

LIBRARIES, ARCHIVES, AND COLLECTIONS

Great Britain

British Library
Public Record Office (London), Foreign Office Papers, FO50/82–198

Mexico

Archivo de la Parroquia de San Miguel, Orizaba
Archivo General de la Nación
Archivo General de Notarías de la Ciudad de México
Archivo Histórico del Ex. Ayuntamiento de México
Archivo Histórico Militar de la Secretaría de la Defensa de la Nación
Colección Lafragua, Biblioteca Nacional (BN)
Fondo Antiguo del Colegio de San Ildefonso (BN)
Fondo Reservado (BN)
Hemeroteca Nacional (BN)

United States

Edmundo O'Gorman Collection, Nettie Lee Benson Library (NLB)
Latin American Collection (NLB)
Lucas Alamán Papers (NLB)
Mariano Paredes y Arrillaga Papers (NLB)

Mariano Riva Palacio Archive (NLB)
Valentín Gómez Farías Papers (NLB)

NEWSPAPERS AND PERIODICALS

El Aguila Mexicana, Mexico City, 1824–1826
El Amigo del Pueblo, Mexico City, 1827–1828
El Archivo Militar, Madrid, 1841
El Cardillo, Mexico City, 1828
La Columna, Mexico City, 1832–1834
El Correo de la Federación Mexicana, Mexico City, 1826–1829
El Cosmopolita, Mexico City, 1835–1843
Diario del Gobierno, Mexico City, 1835–1839
El Fénix de la Libertad, Mexico City, 1832–1833
Gaceta del Gobierno Imperial de México, Mexico City, 1822
La Ilustración Mexicana, Mexico City, 1852
El Mexicano, Mexico City, 1839
El Monitor Republicano, Mexico City, 1847
El Mosaico Mexicano, Mexico City, 1840–1842
El Mosquito Mexicano, Mexico City, 1843
El Museo Mexicano, Mexico City, 1845
La Palanca, Mexico City, 1848–1850
Registro Oficial, Mexico City, 1830–1833
El Republicano, Mexico City, 1846
El Siglo XIX, Mexico City, 1841–1853
El Sol, Mexico City, 1823–1835
El Telégrafo, Mexico City, 1834
El Tiempo, Mexico City, 1846
El Universal, Mexico City, 1848–1850
La Voz del Pueblo, 1845

BOOKS, PAMPHLETS, AND ARTICLES

Alamán, Lucas. *Historia de Méjico*. 5 vols. Mexico City: Editorial Jus, 1969.
————. *Historia de México*. 5 vols. Mexico City: Fondo de Cultura Económica, 1985.
Al Público. Mexico City: Imp. de Tomás Uribe, 1835.
Altamirano, Ignacio M. *El Zarco. La Navidad en las montañas*. Mexico City: Porrúa, 1984.
El Amigo de la Libertad, *Ultimo golpe de paz al ciudadano Tornel*. Mexico City: n.p., 1826.
Anna, Timothy E. *El imperio de Iturbide*. Mexico City: Alianza Editorial, 1991.
————. "Inventing Mexico: Provincehood and Nationhood after Independence." *Bulletin of Latin American Research* 15:1 (1996): pp. 7–17.
————. *Forging Mexico, 1821–1835*. Lincoln: University of Nebraska Press, 1998.
Anuario del Colegio de Minería Año de 1845. Mexico City: Imp. de I. Cumplido, 1846.

Anuario del Colegio de Minería Año de 1848. Mexico City: Imp. de I. Cumplido, 1849.

Archer, Christon I. "The Young Antonio López de Santa Anna: Veracruz Counter-insurgent and Incipient Caudillo." In Judith Ewell and William H. Beezley (eds.), *The Human Tradition in Latin America. The Nineteenth Century.* Wilmington, DE: Scholarly Resources, 1992, pp. 3–16.

———. "Politicization of the Army of New Spain during the War of Independence, 1810–1821." In Jaime E. Rodríguez O. (ed.), *The Origins of Mexican National Politics, 1808–1847.* Wilmington, DE: Scholarly Resources, 1997, pp. 11–38.

Arnold, Linda. *Burocracia y burócratas en México, 1742–1835.* Mexico City: Grijalbo, 1991.

———. *Política y justicia. La suprema corte mexicana (1824–1855).* Mexico City: UNAM, 1996.

Arrangoiz, Francisco de Paula. *México desde 1808 hasta 1867.* Mexico City: Porrúa, 1968.

Arrom, Silvia. "Popular Politics in Mexico City. The Parián Riot, 1828." *Hispanic American Historical Review* 68:2 (May 1988): 245–268.

Arróniz, Marcos. *Manuel del viajero en México.* Mexico City: Instituto Mora, 1991.

Bacon, Francis. *Pensamientos filosóficos, del canciller Bacon. Traducidos por el coronel José María Tornel.* Mexico City: Imp. de Alejandro Valdés, 1832.

Bakewell, Peter. *History of Latin America. Empires and Sequels 1450–1930.* Malden and Oxford: Blackwell Publishers, 1997.

Bancroft, Hubert Howe. *History of Mexico.* 5 vols. San Francisco: A. L. Bancroft & Co., 1885.

Barker, Nancy Nicholas. *The French Experience in Mexico, 1821–1861. A History of Constant Misunderstanding.* Chapel Hill: University of North Carolina Press, 1979.

Bazant, Jan. *Antonio Haro y Tamariz y sus aventuras políticas 1811–1869.* Mexico City: El Colegio de México, 1985.

———. "José María Tornel, Mariano Riva Palacio, Manuel Escandón y la compraventa de una hacienda." In Alicia Hernández Chávez and Manuel Miño Grijalva (eds.), *Cincuenta años de historia de México.* Vol. 1. Mexico City: El Colegio de México, 1991, pp. 389–400.

———. "From Independence to the Liberal Republic, 1821–1867." In Leslie Bethell (ed.), *Mexico since Independence.* Cambridge: Cambridge University Press, 1992, pp. 1–48.

Benson, Nettie Lee. *La diputación provincial y el federalismo mexicano.* Mexico City: El Colegio de México/UNAM, 1994.

Blázquez Domínguez, Carmen. *Políticos y comerciantes en Veracruz y Jalapa, 1827–1829.* Veracruz: Gobierno del Estado de Veracruz, 1992.

Bocanegra, José María. *Memorias para la historia de México independiente. 1822–1846.* 3 vols. Mexico City: Fondo de Cultura Económica, 1987.

Boletín de la Secretaría de Gobernación. *Leyes fundamentales de los Estados Unidos Mexicanos y planes revolucionarios que han influido en la organización política de la república.* Mexico City: Imp. de la Sec. de Gobernación, 1923.

Bosch García, Carlos. *Documentos de la relación de México con los Estados Unidos.* 3 vols. Mexico City: UNAM, 1983.

Brading, David. *Prophecy and Myth in Mexican History.* Cambridge: CLAS, 1984.
———. *The Origins of Mexican Nationalism.* Cambridge: CLAS, 1985.
———. *Church and State in Bourbon Mexico. The Diocese of Michoacán, 1749–1810.* Cambridge: Cambridge University Press, 1994.
Briseño Senosiain, Lillian, Solares Robles, Laura, and Suárez de la Torre, Laura. *Guadalupe Victoria primer presidente de México (1786–1843).* Mexico City: Instituto Mora/SEP, 1986.
Bustamante, Carlos María de. *Galería de antiguos príncipes mexicanos.* Puebla: Oficina del Gobierno Imperial, 1821.
———. *Juguetillo Nono. Antiguedades mexicanas. Historia del primer monarca conocido en el reyno Tulteco.* Veracruz: Imp. Constitucional, 1821.
———. *Manifiesto histórico a las naciones y pueblos del Anáhuac.* Mexico City: Imp. de Valdés, 1823.
———. *Para inmortalizar el valor heroico de los indios cascanes por causa de su libertad de la tiranía española.* Mexico City: Imp. del Águila, 1827.
———. *El nuevo Bernal Díaz del Castillo o sea Historia de la Invasión de los anglo-americanos en México.* Mexico City: SEP, 1949.
———. *Diario Histórico de México.* 3 vols. Mexico City: SEP/INAH, 1980–1982.
———. *Cuadro histórico de la revolución mexicana.* 4 vols. Mexico City: Fondo de Cultura Económica, 1985.
———. *Apuntes para la historia del gobierno del general don Antonio López de Santa Anna.* Mexico City: Fondo de Cultura Económica, 1986.
Calderón de la Barca, Madame Fanny. *Life in Mexico.* London: Century, 1987.
Callcott, Wilfrid Hardy. *Santa Anna. The Story of an Enigma Who Once Was Mexico.* Hamden, CT: Archon Books, 1964.
———. *Church and State in Mexico, 1822–1857.* New York: Octagon Books, 1965.
Castillo León, Luis. *Hidalgo, la vida del héroe.* 2 vols. Mexico City: INEHRM, 1985.
Conducta que ha observado el Ayuntamiento de Jalapa desde el 6 al 12 de enero de 1828. Xalapa: Imp. del Gobierno, 1828.
Conrad, Joseph. *Nostromo. A Tale of the Seaboard.* London and Toronto: J. M. Dent & Sons Ltd., 1923.
Costeloe, Michael P. *La primera república federal de Mexico (1824–1835).* Mexico City: Fondo de Cultura Económica, 1983.
———. "Federalism to Centralism in Mexico: The Conservative Case for Change, 1834–1835." *Americas* 45 (1988): 173–185.
———. "The Triangular Revolt in Mexico and the Fall of Anastasio Bustamante, August–October 1841." *Journal of Latin American Studies* 20 (1988): 337–360.
———. "Generals versus Politicians: Santa Anna and the 1842 Congressional Elections in Mexico." *Bulletin of Latin American Research* 8:2 (1989): 257–274.
———. "Los generales Santa Anna y Paredes y Arrillaga en Mexico, 1841–1843. Rivales por el poder o una copa más." *Historia Mexicana* 34:2 (1989): 417–440.
———. *The Central Republic in Mexico, 1835–1846. Hombres de Bien in the Age of Santa Anna.* Cambridge: Cambridge University Press, 1993.

————. "La Historia de México de Lucas Alamán: Publicación y recepción en México, 1849–1850." *Memorias de la Academia Mexicana de la Historia* 38 (1995): 105–127.

————. "Mariano Arizcorreta and Peasant Unrest in the State of Mexico, 1849." *Bulletin of Latin American Research* 15:1 (1996): 63–79.

————. "Mariano Arista y la élite de la ciudad de México, 1851–1852." In Will Fowler and Humberto Morales Moreno (eds.), *El conservadurismo mexicano en el siglo xix (1810–1910)*. Puebla: BUAP/University of St. Andrews, 1999, pp. 187–212.

Delgado, Ana Laura (ed.). *Cien viajeros en Veracruz. Crónicas y relatos.* 11 vols. Veracruz: Gobierno del Estado de Veracruz, 1992.

DePalo, Jr., William A. *The Mexican National Army, 1822–1852.* College Station: Texas A&M University Press, 1997.

Desahogo de D. J. M. Tornel bajo la firma de J. López de Santa Anna. Mérida: n.p., 1843.

DeVolder, Arthur L. *Guadalupe Victoria: His Role in Mexican Independence.* Albuquerque, NM: Artcraft, 1978.

Díaz Díaz, Fernando. *Caudillos y caciques: Antonio López de Santa Anna y Juan Alvarez.* Mexico City: El Colegio de México, 1972.

Dictamen de la comisión especial de Tehuantepec del senado, encargada de escaminar las varias resoluciones dictadas con motivo del privilegio exclusivo concedido a D. José Garay, y de proponer la que deba adoptarse, atendido el estado que guarda actualmente este negocio. Mexico City: Imp. O'Sullivan y Nolan, 1851.

Discurso sobre la influencia de la filosofía en las costumbres y en la legislación de los pueblos: o sea Manifestación de los beneficios de que le es deudor el género humano. Tradujo del francés el coronel José María Tornel. Mexico City: Imp. de Galván, 1832.

Di Tella, Torcuato S. *National Popular Politics in Early Independent Mexico, 1820–1847.* Albuquerque, NM: University of New Mexico Press, 1996.

Dublán, Manuel, and Lozano, José María (eds.). *Legislación Mexicana. Colección completa de las disposiciones legislativas expedidas desde la independencia de la república ordenada por los licenciados Manuel Dublán y José María Lozano.* 5 vols. Mexico City: Imp. del Comercio, 1876.

Ejército Mexicano. Memoria sobre la organización que se dió al ejército mexicano, y que se dedica al Excmo. Sr. Benemérito de la Patria, General de División, Presidente de la República Mexicana, D. Antonio López de Santa Anna, constante defensor de sus compañeros de armas. Mexico City: n.p., 1853.

Ferrer Muñoz, Manuel. *La formación de un Estado nacional en México. El Imperio y la República federal: 1821–1835.* Mexico City: UNAM, 1995.

Filisola, Vicente. *Representación dirigida al Supremo Gobierno por el general Vicente Filisola, en defensa de su honor y aclaración de sus operaciones como general en jefe del ejército sobre Tejas.* Mexico City: Imp. de I. Cumplido, 1836.

————. *Memorias para la historia de la guerra de Texas.* 2 vols. Mexico City: Editora Nacional, 1968.

Flaccus, Elmer W. "Guadelupe Victoria: His Personality as a Cause of His Failure." *Americas* 23:3 (1967): 297–311.

Florescano, Enrique. *Precios del maíz y crisis agrícolas en México, 1708–1810.* Mexico City: El Colegio de Mexico, 1969.

Fossey, Mathieu de. *Le Mexique.* Paris: Plon, 1857.

Fowler, Will. "José María Tornel y Mendívil, Mexican General/Politician (1794–1853)." Ph.D. dissertation, University of Bristol, 1994.

———. "Valentín Gómez Farías: Perceptions of Radicalism in Independent Mexico, 1821–1847." *Bulletin of Latin American Research* 15:1 (1996): 39–62.

———. "The Repeated Rise of General Antonio López de Santa Anna in the So-Called Age of Chaos (Mexico, 1821–1855)." In Will Fowler (ed.), *Authoritarianism in Latin America since Independence.* Westport, CT: Greenwood Press, 1996, pp. 1–30.

———. *The Mexican Press and the Collapse of Representative Government during the Presidential Elections of 1828.* Liverpool: ILAS, 1996.

———. "The Compañía Lancasteriana and the Elite in Independent Mexico, 1822–1845." *TESSERAE Journal of Iberian and Latin American Studies* 2:1 (1996): 81–110.

———. *Military Political Identity and Reformism in Independent Mexico. An Analysis of the Memorias de Guerra (1821–1855).* London: ILAS, 1996.

———. "El pensamiento político de los santanistas, 1821–1855." In Luis Jauregui and José Antonio Serrano Ortega (eds.), *Historia y nación, vol. 2. Política y diplomacia en el siglo XIX mexicano.* Mexico City: El Colegio de México, 1998, pp. 183–226.

———. *Mexico in the Age of Proposals, 1821–1853.* Westport, CT: Greenwood Press, 1998.

———. "Civil Conflict in Independent Mexico, 1821–1857. An Overview." In Rebecca Earle (ed.), *Civil War in Nineteenth-Century Latin America.* London: Macmillan/ILAS, in press.

———. and Morales Moreno, Humberto (eds.). *El conservadurismo mexicano en el siglo xix (1810–1910).* Puebla: BUAP/University of St. Andrews, 1999.

Fuentes Mares, José. *Santa Anna, aurora y ocaso de un comediante.* Mexico City: Editorial Jus, 1956.

Gadow, Hans. *Through Southern Mexico.* London: Witherby & Co., 1908.

García, Genaro (ed.). *Documentos inéditos o muy raros para la historia de México.* Vol. 56. Mexico City: Porrúa, 1974.

———. (ed.). *Documentos inéditos o muy raros para la historia de México.* Vol. 59. Mexico City: Porrúa, 1974.

García Cantú, Gastón (ed.). *El pensamiento de la reacción mexicana. Historia documental.* Vol. 1: *(1810–1859).* Mexico City: UNAM, 1994.

Gilliam, A. M. *Travels in Mexico during the Years 1843 and 44.* Aberdeen: George Clark & Son, 1847.

Giménez, Manuel María. *Memorias del coronel Manuel María Giménez, ayudante de campo del General Santa Anna, 1798–1878.* Mexico City: Lib. Vda. De Ch. Bouret, 1911.

Gómez Pedraza, Manuel. *Manifiesto que Manuel Gómez Pedraza, ciudadano de la república de Méjico, dedica a sus compatriotas; o sea, una reseña de su vida pública.* Guadalajara: Imp. de Brambila, 1831.

González Navarro, Moisés. *Raza y tierra: la guerra de casta y el henequén.* Mexico City: El Colegio de México, 1970.

———. *Anatomía del poder en México (1848–1853)*. Mexico City: El Colegio de México, 1977.

González Pedrero, Enrique. *País de un solo hombre: el México de Santa Anna*. Vol. 1. Mexico City: Fondo de Cultura Económica, 1993.

Gou-Gilbert, Cecile. *Una resistencia india. Los yaquis*. Mexico City: INI/Centro de Estudios Mexicanos y Centroamericanos, 1985.

Green, Stanley C. *The Mexican Republic: The First Decade, 1823–1832*. Pittsburgh: University of Pittsburgh Press, 1987.

Guedea, Virginia. "El golpe de estado de 1808." *Universidad de México* 48 (1991): 21–24.

———. *En busca de un gobierno alterno: Los Guadalupes de México*. Mexico City: UNAM, 1992.

———. (ed.). *La revolución de independencia*. Mexico City: El Colegio de México, 1995.

Guerra, François-Xavier. *Modernidad e independencias. Ensayos sobre las revoluciones hispánicas*. Mexico City: Fondo de Cultura Económica, 1993.

Gutiérrez Estrada, José María. *Carta dirigida al Escmo. Sr. Presidente de la República, sobre la necesidad de buscar en una convención el posible remedio de los males que aquejan a la República y opiniones del autor acerca del mismo asunto*. Mexico City: Imp. de I. Cumplido, 1840.

Hale, Charles A. *El liberalismo mexicano en la época de Mora, 1821–1853*. Mexico City: Siglo XXI, 1987.

Hamill, Jr., Hugh M. *The Hidalgo Revolt. Prelude to Mexican Independence*. Westport, CT: Greenwood Press, 1970.

Hamnett, Brian R. *Raíces de la insurgencia en México. Historia regional, 1750–1824*. Mexico City: Fondo de Cultura Económica, 1990.

Hu-Dehart, Evelyn. *Yaqui Resistance and Survival. The Struggle for Land and Autonomy, 1821–1910*. Madison: University of Wisconsin Press, 1984.

Humboldt, Alexandre de. *Essai politique sur le Royaume de la Nouvelle-Espagne*. 2 vols. Paris: Imp. de J. H. Stone, 1811.

Hutchinson, Charles A. "The Asiatic Cholera Epidemic of 1833 in Mexico." *Bulletin of the History of Medicine* 32 (1958): 160–173.

Joutel, T. *Diario histórico del último viaje que hizo M. de la Sale para descubrir el desembocadero y curso del Missicipi*. Trans. José María Tornel y Mendívil. New York: Imp. José Desnoues, 1831.

Katz, Friedrich (ed.). *Revuelta, rebelión, revolución: la lucha rural en México del siglo xvi al siglo xx*. 2 vols. Mexico City: Era, 1990.

Krauze, Enrique. *Siglo de caudillos*. Barcelona: Tusquets Editores, 1994.

Lapointe, Marie. *Los mayas rebeldes de Yucatán*. Mexico City: El Colegio de Michoacán, 1983.

Lecuna, Vicente, and Bierck, Jr., Harold A. (eds.). *Selected Writings of Bolívar*. 2 vols. New York: Colonial Press, 1951.

Loveman, Brian, and Davies, Thomas (eds.). *The Politics of Antipolitics: The Military in Latin America*. Lincoln: University of Nebraska Press, 1978.

L. R. *Victoriosa defensa del esclarecido patriota gobernador del distrito, ciudadano José María Tornel*. Mexico City: Imp. de Ontíveros, 1828.

Lynch, John. *The Spanish American Revolutions, 1808–1826*. New York: Norton, 1973.

———. *Caudillos in Spanish America, 1800–1850*. Oxford: Clarendon Press, 1992.

——— (ed.). *Latin American Revolutions, 1808–1826. Old and New World Origins*. Norman: University of Oklahoma Press, 1994.

Malagón Barceló, J. de (ed.). *Relaciones diplomáticas hispano-mexicanas: Documentos procedentes del Archivo de la Embajada de España en México*. 3 vols. Mexico City: Editorial Jus, 1949–66.

Manifestación que el Escmo. Ayuntamiento hace al público de esta capital de las últimas ocurrencias sobre las contratas de limpia de ciudad. Mexico City: Imp. de Tomás Uribe y Alcalde, 1834.

Méndez Reyes, Salvador. *Eugenio de Aviraneta y México*. Mexico City: UNAM, 1992.

Mora, José María Luis. *Obras sueltas*. Mexico City: Porrúa, 1963.

Moya Palencia, Manuel. *El México de Egerton 1831–1842*. Mexico City: Porrúa, 1991.

Muñoz, Rafael F. *Santa Anna. El dictador resplandeciente*. Mexico City: Fondo de Cultura Económica, 1983.

Noriega Elío, Cecilia. *El constituyente de 1842*. Mexico City: UNAM, 1986.

O'Gorman, Edmundo. *México. El trauma de su historia*. Mexico City: UNAM, 1977.

Olavarría y Ferrari, Enrique de. *Episodios históricos mexicanos*. 4 vols. Mexico City: Fondo de Cultura Económica, 1987.

Olivera, Ruth R., and Crété, Liliane. *Life in Mexico under Santa Anna, 1822–1855*. Norman: University of Oklahoma Press, 1991.

Ortiz Escamilla, Juan. "Las élites de la capitales novohispanas ante la guerra civil de 1810."*Historia Mexicana* 46:2 (1996): pp. 325–357.

El Patriota Observador, *Gracias singulares del C. Coronel José María Tornel, gobernador del distrito federal que se le recuerdan para que evite su caída y no le suceda lo que a la ilustre víctima de Padilla*. Mexico City: Imp. de José María Gallegos, 1828.

Payno, Manuel. *Los bandidos de Río Frío*. Mexico City: Porrúa, 1996.

El Pega Recio. *Las tenazas de San Dimas agarran pero no sueltan*. Mexico City: Imp. de Ontíveros, 1828.

Peña y Peña, Manuel de la. *Dictamen de la comisión del Supremo Poder Conservador, aprobado por éste, contestando a la protesta de Tornel, que se publica por acuerdo del mismo Supremo Poder*. Mexico City: Imp. de I. Cumplido, 1839.

Piña, Juan. *Pascuas al Gobernador*. Mexico City: Imp. de Manuel Fernández Redondas, 1834.

Poniatowska, Elena. *Fuerte es el silencio*. Mexico City: Ediciones Era, 1989.

Quien todo lo huele, *Luego que Gómez Farías se informe de este papel, le da el cholera morbus al gobernador Tornel*. Mexico City: n.p., 1834.

Quinlan, David M. "Issues and Factions in the Constituent Congress, 1823–1824." In Jaime E. Rodríguez O. (ed.), *Mexico in the Age of Democratic Revolutions, 1750–1850*. Boulder, CO: Lynne Rienner Publishers, 1994, pp. 177–207.

Reina, Leticia. *Las rebeliones campesinas en México, 1819–1906*. Mexico City: Siglo XXI, 1980.

Réplica de varios españoles al señor Tornel en su contestación a las cuatro palabras. Mexico City: Imp. de J. M. Lara, 1841.

Rivera Cambas, Manuel. *Antonio López de Santa Anna.* Mexico City: Editorial Citlaltépetl, 1958.

———. *Los gobernantes de México (1822–1843).* Vol. 4. Mexico City: Editorial Citlaltépetl, 1964.

Rodríguez O., Jaime E. *El nacimiento de Hispanoamérica. Vicente Rocafuerte y el hispanoamericanismo, 1808–1832.* Mexico City: Fondo de Cultura Económica, 1980.

——— (ed.). *Patterns of Contention in Mexican History.* Wilmington, DE: Scholarly Resources, 1992.

———. "Intellectuals and the Mexican Constitution of 1824." In Roderic A. Camp, Charles A. Hale, and Josefina Zoraida Vázquez (eds.), *Los intelectuales y el poder en México.* Mexico City: El Colegio de México/UCLA Latin American Center Publications, 1991, pp. 63–74.

Romero Avilez, Cayetano. *Cuando hay modo de tener, nada detiene a Tornel.* Mexico City: Imp. de Antonio Alcalde, 1833.

Salado Alvarez, Victoriano. *La vida azarosa y romántica de Carlos María de Bustamante.* Mexico City: Editorial Jus, 1968.

Salvucci, R. J. " 'La parte más difícil.' Recent Works on Nineteenth-Century Mexican history." *Latin American Research Review* 28:1 (1993): 102–110.

Samponaro, Frank. "La alianza de Santa Anna y los federalistas, 1832–1834. Su formación y desintegración." *Historia Mexicana* 30:3 (1981): 359–380.

Santa Anna, Antonio López de. *Manifiesto que hace público el teniente coronel D. A. López de Santa Anna, comandante general de la provincia de Veracruz, sobre lo ocurrido con la persona del coronel D. Manuel de la Concha, asesinado al amanecer del día 5 del corriente en los extramuros de la villa de Jalapa, camino de Veracruz.* Puebla: Imp. de Pedro de la Rosa, 1821.

———. *Proclama del sr. coronel D. Antonio López de Santa Anna a los habitantes de Veracruz en la ocupación de aquella plaza.* Mexico City: Imp. de Mariano Ontíveros, 1821.

Santoni, Pedro. *Mexicans at Arms. Puro Federalists and the Politics of War, 1845–1848.* Forth Worth: Texas Christian University Press, 1996.

Simplicio el Tapado, Justo. *Preguntas al Payo del Rosario, sobre la escandalosa y criminal conducta del señor gobernador.* Mexico City: Imp. de José María Gallagos, 1828.

Sims, Harold D. *La expulsión de los españoles de México (1821–1828).* Mexico City: Fondo de Cultura Económica, 1984.

———. *The Expulsion of Mexico's Spaniards, 1821–1836.* Pittsburgh: University of Pittsburgh Press, 1990.

Solares Robles, Laura. *Una revolución pacífica. Biografía política de Manuel Gómez Pedraza, 1789–1851.* Mexico City: Instituto Mora, 1996.

Solís Vicarte, Ruth. *Las sociedades secretas en el primer gobierno republicano (1824–1828).* Mexico City: Editorial ASBE, 1997.

Sordo Cedeño, Reynaldo. *El congreso en la primera república centralista.* Mexico City: El Colegio de México/ITAM, 1993.

———. "El general Tornel y la guerra de Texas." *Historia Mexicana* 42:4 (1993): 919–953.

———. "El pensamiento conservador del partido centralista en los años treinta del siglo xix mexicano." In Will Fowler and Humberto Morales Moreno (eds.) *El conservadurismo mexicano en el siglo xix (1810–1910)*. Puebla: BUAP/ University of St. Andrews, 1999, pp. 135–168.

Soto, Miguel. *La conspiración monárquica en México, 1845–1846*. Mexico City: Editorial Offset, 1988.

Staples, Anne. *La iglesia en la primera república federal (1824–1835)*. Mexico City: SepSetentas, 1976.

———. *Leona Vicario*. Mexico City: SEP, 1976.

——— (ed.). *Educar: Panacea del México Independiente*. Mexico City: SEP, 1985.

———. "El rechazo a la revolución francesa." In Solange Alberro, Alicia Hernández Chávez, and Elías Trabulse (eds.), *La revolución francesa en México*. Mexico City: El Colegio de México, 1992, pp. 161–167.

———. "Clerics as Politicians: Church, State, and Political Power in Independent Mexico." In Jaime E. Rodríguez O. (ed.), *Mexico in the Age of Democratic Revolutions, 1750–1850*. Boulder, CO: Lynne Rienner, 1994, pp. 223–241.

———. "Leer y escribir en los estados del México independiente." In Angel San Román Vázquez and Carmen Christlieb Ibarrola (eds.), *Historia de la alfabetización y de la educación de adultos en México. Del México prehispánico a la Reforma liberal*. Vol. 1. Mexico City: SEP/El Colegio de México, 1994, pp. 137–187.

———. "Una falsa promesa: la educación indigena después de la independencia." In Pilar Gonzalbo Aizpuru and Gabriela Ossenbach (eds.), *Educación rural e indígena en Iberoamérica*. Mexico City: El Colegio de México/Universidad Nacional de Educación a Distancia, 1996, pp. 53–63.

———. "El impulso al conocimiento académico, 1823–1846." In *La evolución de la educación militar en México*. Mexico City: Secretaría de la Defensa Nacional, 1997, pp. 113–134.

———. "Los poderes locales y las primeras letras." In Pilar Gonzalbo Aizpuru (ed.), *Historia y Nación*. Vol. 1: *Historia de la educación y enseñanza de la historia*. Mexico City: El Colegio de México, 1998, pp. 47–61.

———. "La educación como instrumento ideológico del estado. El conservadurismo educativo en el México decimonónico." In Will Fowler and Humberto Morales Moreno (eds.), *El conservadurismo mexicano en el siglo xix (1810–1910)*. Puebla: BUAP/University of St. Andrews, 1999, pp. 103–114.

———. *Letras y libros. La educación mexicana de Iturbide a Juárez*. Mexico City: El Colegio de México, in press.

Stevens, Donald F. *Origins of Instability in Early Republican Mexico*. Durham, NC: Duke University Press, 1991.

———. "Temerse la ira del cielo: los conservadores y la religiosidad popular en los tiempos del cólera." In Will Fowler and Humberto Morales Moreno (eds.), *El conservadurismo mexicano en el siglo xix (1810–1910)*. Puebla: BUAP/ University of St. Andrews, 1999, pp. 87–101.

Swett Henson, Margaret. *Lorenzo de Zavala. The Pragmatic Idealist*. Forth Worth: Texas Christian University Press, 1996.

Tanck de Estrada, Dorothy. "Las escuelas lancasterianas en la ciudad de México, 1822–1842." *Historia Mexicana* 23 (1972–1973), pp. 494–513.

———. *La educación ilustrada, 1786–1836.* Mexico City: El Colegio de México, 1984.

Taylor, William B. *Magistrates of the Sacred. Priests and Parishioners in Eighteenth-Century Mexico.* Stanford: Stanford University Press, 1996.

Tenenbaum, Barbara A. *México en la época de los agiotistas, 1821–1857.* Mexico City: Fondo de Cultura Económica, 1985.

Thompson, Waddy. *Recollections of Mexico.* New York: Wiley, 1847.

Tornel y Mendívil, José María, *Valor y constancia es nuestra divisa.* Puebla: Imp. de Pedro de la Rosa, 1821.

———. *El grito de la patria.* Puebla: Imp. de Pedro de la Rosa, 1821.

———. *La aurora de México.* Mexico City: Imp. de Celestino de la Torre, 1821.

———. *Manifiesto del origen, causas, progreso y estado de la revolución del imperio mexicano, con relación a la antigua España.* Puebla and Mexico City: Imp. de Ontíveros, 1821.

———. *Derechos de Fernando VII al trono del imperio mexicano.* Mexico City: n.p., 1822.

———. "Contestación al articulo comunicado del ciudadano Dr. Joaquín Infante inserto en los números 148 y 149 de este periódico." *El Sol* (23, 24 November 1823), pp. 647–648, 651–652.

———. "Palabra y escritura." *El Sol* (10 December 1823), pp. 715–716.

———. "Esplicación de los documentos con que se quiere manchar el honor del Coronel José María Tornel y se prueban con otros sus servicios y padecimientos en obsequio de la Patria." *El Aguila Mexicana*, Supplement, 2 September 1826, pp. 1–4.

———. "Federación." *El Correo de la Federación Mexicana*, 13, 24 August 1827, pp. 1–4, 2–3, respectively.

———. *Oración pronunciada por el Coronel José María Tornel, diputado al congreso de la unión, vice-presidente de la compañía lancasteriana de México, socio de número de la academia de legislación y economía de la misma ciudad, y corresponsal de la de amigos del país de Zacatecas, en la plaza mayor de la capital de la federación, el día 16 de septiembre de 1827, por acuerdo de la junta de ciudadanos que promovió la mayor solemnidad del aniversario de nuestra gloriosa independencia.* Mexico City: Imp. del Águila, 1827.

———. *Carta del Sr. Tornel sobre el manifiesto de señor Pedraza.* Mexico City: Imp. del Aguila, 1831.

———. *Manifestación del C. José María Tornel.* Mexico City: n.p., 1833.

———. *Memoria del secretario de estado y del despacho de guerra y marina, leída en la cámara de representantes en la sesión del día veinte y tres de marzo, y en la de senadores en la del veinte y cuatro del mismo mes y año de 1835.* Mexico City: Imp. de I. Cumpildo, 1835.

———. *Tejas y los Estados Unidos de América en sus relaciones con la república mexicana.* Mexico City: Imp. de Ignacio Cumplido, 1837.

———. "Máximas de Napoleón sobre el arte de la guerra, con notas muy interesantes apoyadas en las campañas de Tirena, Conde, Montecuculli, Gustavo Adolfo, Federico, Napoleón y otros grandes capitanes, traducidas por el general J. M. Tornel." *Diario del Gobierno*, 24, 26, 28, 30 April; 2, 4, 6, 8, 10, 12, 14, 18, 20, 22, 24, 26, 28, 30 May 1838.

————. "Instrucción secreta que dió el gran Federico a sus oficiales, particularmante de caballería, para su gloriosa campaña de Baviera, traducido por el general José María Tornel." *Diario del Gobierno*, 22, 26, 28 August; 1, 11 September; 16, 19, 21, 26, 29 October 1838.

————. *Memoria de la secretaría de estado y del despacho de la guerra y marina, leída por el Escmo. Sr. General D. José María Tornel, en la cámara de diputados el día 7 de enero de 1839, y en la de senadores el 8 del mismo.* Mexico City: Imp. de I. Cumplido, 1839.

————. *El general José María Tornel a sus amigos.* Mexico City: Imp. de I. Cumplido, 1839.

————. *Carta del general José María Tornel a sus amigos, sobre un articulo inserto en el Cosmopolita del día 17 de agosto del presente año.* Mexico City: Imp. de I. Cumplido, 1839.

————. *Protesta del general José María Tornel y Mendívil, individuo propietario del Supremo Poder Conservador, contra el decreto espedido por éste en 9 del presente mes sobre reformas de la constitución.* Mexico City: Imp. de I. Cumplido, 1839.

————. *Respuesta del general José María Tornel y Mendívil al escrito que formó el Escmo. Sr. Lic. D. Manuel de la Peña y Peña, que acogió el Supremo Poder Conservador, e imprimó y circuló el gobierno como suplemento de su diario, contra la protesta que el espresado publicó en 30 de noviembre del año anterior, sobre el decreto espedido en 9 del mismo mes, acerca de las reformas de la constitución.* Mexico City: Imp. de I. Cumplido, 1840.

————. *Manifestación de la validez del decreto de 13 de mayo de 1840, espedido por el Supremo Poder Conservador, y satisfacción a los reparos hechos por el Supremo Gobierno en el 5 del corriente.* Mexico City: Imp. de I. Cumplido, 1840.

————. *Discurso que pronunció el Escmo. Sr. General D. José María Tornel y Mendívil, individuo del Supremo Poder Conservador, en la Alameda de la Ciudad de México, en el día del aniversario del la independencia.* Mexico City: Imp. de. I. Cumplido, 1840.

————. "A. D. José María Gutiérrez Estrada. O sean Algunas observaciones al folleto en que ha proclamado la destrucción de la república, y el llamamiento al trono mexicano de un príncipe estrangero." *El Cosmopolita*, 31 October 1840, pp. 1–8.

————. "La ciudad de Baltimore en 1831 (Sacado de los apuntes del Escmo. Sr. General D. José María Tornel, sobre los Estados Unidos)." *El Mosaico Mexicano* 3 (1840): 330–334.

————. *La muerte de Cicerón.* In *El Mosaico Mexicano* 5 (1841): 7–22.

————. "Noticias sobre las poesías aztecas." *El Mosaico Mexicano* 5 (1841): 143–144.

————. "Consideraciones sobre la elocuencia de Mr. Courtin." *El Mosaico Mexicano* 5 (1841): 361–376.

————. "La Providencia en el Nuevo Mundo." *El Mosaico Mexicano* 5 (1841): 529–534.

————. "Beneficiencia para con los animales." *El Mosaico Mexicano* 6 (1841): 57–66.

———. "El Lord Byon a los napolitanos. Estancias." *El Mosaico Mexicano* 6 (1841): 73–75.

———. "Historia. Bosquejo de la administración de los Incas en el Perú." *El Mosaico Mexicano* 6 (1841): 97–104.

———. *Manifestación presentada a la cámara de senadores por el General José María Tornel, apoderado de las diputaciones de cosecheros de tabaco de las ciudades de Jalapa y Orizaba, pidiendo la reprobación del acuerdo sobre amortización de la moneda de cobre, por medio del estanco de aquel ramo.* Mexico City: Imp. de I. Cumplido, 1841.

———. *Vindicación del General José María Tornel, administrador de la renta del tabaco del departamento de Veracruz, por la ligereza con que se le ha acusado de omisión en el cumplimiento de sus deberes, ante la dirección general de la renta.* Orizaba: Imp. de Mendarte, 1842.

———. *Discurso pronunciado por el Exmo. Sr. General Ministro de Guerra y Marina, Don José María Tornel, en la sesión del 12 de octubre de 1842 del Congreso Constituyente, en apoyo del dictamen de la mayoría de la comisión de constitución del mismo.* Mexico City: Imp. de I. Cumplido, 1842.

———. *Reglamento de la Compañía Lancasteriana de México.* Mexico City: Imp. de Vicente García Torres, 1842.

———. "El sentimiento religioso. Principio conservador de las sociedades." *El Siglo*, 17 April 1843, pp. 2–3.

———. *Fastos militares de iniquidad, barbarie y despotismo del gobierno español, ejecutados en las villas de Orizaba y Córdoba en la guerra de once años, por causa de la independencia y libertad de la nación mexicana, hasta que se consumió la primera por los Tratados de Córdoba, celebrados por d. Agustin de Iturbide y d. Juan O'Donojú. Dálos a luz como documentos que apoyan las relaciones del cuadro histórico de la revolución y a sus espensas D. José María Tornel.* Mexico City: Imp. de I. Cumplido, 1843.

———. *Memoria del secretario de estado y del despacho de guerra y marina, leída a las cámaras del congreso nacional de la república mexicana, en enero de 1844.* Mexico City: Imp. de I. Cumplido, 1844.

———. "Discurso pronunciado por el Exmo. Sr. General José María Tornel y Mendívil, director del colegio de minería, en la solemne distribución de premios de sus alumnos, que se verificó el día 16 de noviembre de 1845." *El Museo Mexicano* 1 (1845): 179–184.

———. *Discurso pronunciado en la alameda de la ciudad de México en el día 27 de septiembre de 1850.* Mexico City: Imp. de Ignacio Cumplido, 1850.

———. *Voto particular del señor senador D. José María Tornel, individuo de la comisión especial que entiende en los negocios relativos al Istmo de Tehuantepec, sobre privilegio de abrir la vía de comunicación.* Mexico City: Imp. de Vicente García Torres, 1852.

———. *Breve reseña histórica de los acontecimientos más notables de la nación mexicana desde el año de 1821 hasta nuestros días.* Mexico City: INEHRM, 1985.

Torre Villar, Ernesto de la (ed.). *Los Guadalupes y la independencia.* Mexico City: Porrú, 1985.

———. *La independencia de México.* Madrid: Editorial Mapfre, 1992.

Tutino, John. *From Insurrection to Revolution in Mexico: Social Bases of Agrarian Violence, 1750–1940*. Princeton, NJ: Princeton University Press, 1986.

Undécimo calendario de Abraham López; arreglado al meridiano de México y antes publicado en Toluca para el año de 1849. Mexico City: Imp. de A. López, 1849.

Vagts, Alfred. *A History of Militarism: Civilian and Military*. London: Blackwell, 1959.

Varios españoles al señor Tornel. Última respuesta. Mexico City: Imp. de J. M. Lara, 1841.

Vaughan, Mary Kay. "Primary Schooling in the City of Puebla, 1821–60." *Hispanic American Historical Review* 67:1 (1987): 39–62.

Vázquez, Josefina Zoraida. "Los primeros tropiezos." In Daniel Cosío Villegas (ed.), *Historia general de México*, vol. 3. Mexico City: El Colegio de México, 1977, pp. 1–84.

———. *Don Antonio López de Santa Anna. Mito y enigma*. Mexico City: CONDUMEX, 1987.

———. "Iglesia, ejército y centralismo." *Historia Mexicana* 39:1 (1989): 205–234.

———. "Los pronciamientos de 1832: aspirantismo politico e ideología." In Jaime E. Rodríguez O. (ed.), *Patterns of Contention in Mexican History*. Wilmington, DE: Scholarly Resources, 1992, pp. 163–186.

———. *La intervención norte-americana 1846–1848*. Mexico City: Secretaría de Relaciones Exteriores, 1997.

——— (ed.). *México al tiempo de su guerra con Estados Unidos (1846–1848)*. Mexico City: Fondo de Cultura Económica/El Colegio de México, 1997.

———, and Meyer, Lorenzo. *México frente a Estados Unidos (Un ensayo histórico 1776–1988)*. Mexico City: Fondo de Cultura Económica, 1989.

Vázquez Mantecón, Carmen. *Santa Anna y la encrucijada del estado. La dictadura (1853–1855)*. Mexico City: Fondo de Cultura Económica, 1986.

———. "Espacio social y crisis política: La Sierra Gorda 1850–1855." *Mexican Studies/Estudios Mexicanos* 9:1 (1993): 47–70.

———. *La palabra del poder. Vida pública de José María Tornel (1795–1853)*. Mexico City: UNAM, 1997.

———. "La patria y la nación en el discurso de José María Tornel, 1821–1852." *Tiempos de América* 1 (1997): 131–140.

———. "José María Tornel y Mendívil." In Virginia Guedea (ed.), *Historiografia mexicana*. Vol. 3. *El surgimiento de la historiografia nacional*. Mexico City: UNAM, 1997, pp. 357–389.

Verdadera segunda parte de las gracias singulares del ciudadano coronel José María Tornel, gobernador del distrito federal. Mexico City: Imp. de José María Gallegos, 1828.

Villoro, Luis. *El proceso ideológico de la revolución de la independencia*. Mexico City: UNAM, 1967.

Ward, Henry George. *México en 1827*. Mexico City: Fondo de Cultura Económica, 1995.

Zamacois, Niceto de. *Historia de Méjico, desde sus tiempos más remotos hasta nuestros días*. 12 vols. Barcelona: J. F. Parres y Cía, 1879–1880.

Zavala, Lorenzo de. *Albores de la república*. Mexico City: Empresas Editioriales, 1949.

————. *Obras. El historiador y el representante popular.* Mexico City: Porrúa, 1969.

————. *Obras.* Mexico City: Porrúa, 1976.

Zorrilla, José. *La flor de los recuerdos. Ofrenda que hace a los pueblos hispano-americanos don José Zorrilla, Tomo I.* Mexico City: Imp. del Correo de España, 1855.

Index

About the Author

WILL FOWLER lectures in Latin American and Spanish History literature at the University of St. Andrews in Scotland. As well as having edited four volumes of Mexican and Latin American political history, he is the author of *Military Political Identity and Reformism in Independent Mexico, An Analysis of the Memorias de Guerra, 1821–1855* (1996), and *Mexico in the Age of Proposals, 1821–1853* (Greenwood, 1998).

ISBN 0-313-30914-0

90000>